PLURAL AND CONFLICTING VALUES

Plural and Conflicting Values

MICHAEL STOCKER

CLARENDON PRESS · OXFORD

Oxford University Press, Walton Street, Oxford OX2 6DP

Oxford New York Toronto
Delhi Bombay Calcutta Madras Karachi
Petaling Jaya Singapore Hong Kong Tokyo
Nairobi Dar es Salaam Cape Town
Melbourne Auckland

and associated companies in
Berlin Ibadan

Oxford is a trade mark of Oxford University Press

Published in the United States
by Oxford University Press, New York

First published 1990
Reprinted 1990
First issued in paperback 1992

British Library Cataloguing in Publication Data
Stocker, Michael
Plural and conflicting values.
1. Ethics
I. Title
170
ISBN 0–19–824055–4

Library of Congress Cataloging in Publication Data
Stocker, Michael
Plural and conflicting values   Michael Stocker.
Bibliography: p.   Includes index.
1. Ethics. 2. Values. I. Title.
BJ1012.S83   1989   170—dc20   89–9275
ISBN 0–19–824055–4

Printed in Great Britain by
Biddles Ltd, Guildford and King's Lynn

I dedicate this book to
Beatrice and Jule Stocker
and to Eve Stocker

ACKNOWLEDGEMENTS

I AM deeply indebted to the many people who have discussed these issues with me during the last several years. I have tried to acknowledge my indebtedness for particular help, but my gratitude and apologies now to those I have failed to thank. For their very generous help in reading drafts of the manuscript, I am indebted to Jonathan Bennett, Pauline Chazan, Charles Larmore, Michael P. Levine, Lynne McFall, John Robertson, Michael Slote, and students in my graduate seminar at Syracuse University, Spring 1988, Cheryl Barbour, Jeff Borrowdale, Frances Howard, Christopher Knight, Alastair Norcross, and Michael F. Patton, jun. My thanks are owed to Frances Howard for help with copy-editing and indexing.

For his sustaining discussions during a year spent at Oberlin College in 1985, my deepest thanks and appreciation to Norman Care. And for a decade of shared philosophical life in Melbourne, Australia, my very warmest thanks are given with pleasure to Graeme Marshall.

I would also like to acknowledge my lasting debt to Roderick Firth. I started graduate work in philosophy in 1961 with an enthusiastic, knowing, and easy dismissal of ethics—perhaps not uncommon in those days. Through his kindness, his strengths as a teacher and philosopher, his depths as a person, and through the way he brought these together, he helped lead me to my present fascination with ethics, its importance, and its complexities. He is remembered with affection and respect, and is sorely missed.

Versions of several of the chapters have been published in whole or part. I hereby thank the publishers for their permission to reprint.

'Dirty Hands and Conflicts of Values and of Desires in Aristotle's Ethics' appears under the same title in *Pacific Philosophical Quarterly*, 67 (1986), 36–61.

Part of 'Akrasia: The Unity of the Good, Commensurability, and Comparability' appears in an earlier form as 'Akrasia and the Object of Desire,' in Joel Marks (ed.), *The Ways of Desire* (Chicago: Precedent Books, 1986). The first part of it appears as 'Some Structures for Akrasia', *History of Philosophy Quarterly*, 1 (1984), 267–80.

Part of 'Moral Conflicts: What They Are and What They Show' appears under the same title in *Pacific Philosophical Quarterly*, 68 (1987), 104–23.

M.S.

SUMMARY TABLE OF CONTENTS

CONTENTS

INTRODUCTION

NEITHER plural values nor conflicting values can be understood without understanding the other. And to understand ethics, we must understand both. They raise obvious and pressing problems in social and political theory. They also raise important problems within one person or one ethical theory—the locus of this work. Not surprisingly, then, they have received a considerable amount of attention recently—an amount of attention they fully deserve.

So, I welcome the fact that they are now being studied. But I do not welcome many of the things claimed of them. Here are three representative assertions made about them recently:

Plurality and conflict depend on and show a fragmentation of value and the disparate traditions that help make up our evaluative world and sensibility.

A choice between plural values involves a conflict of values.

Conflict requires plurality.

Sometimes concluded from those three and sometimes offered on their own, we find these four other recent and representative claims:

Plural values are incommensurable and thus incomparable.

There is no rational way to compare and choose between plural values, nor therefore to resolve conflicts.

Plurality and conflict preclude sound judgement and decision, allowing only vacillation and indecision, or simply plumping for one option or another.

A rational ethics requires an evaluative and conflict-free monism.

As I will argue, to understand plurality and conflict, these and similar claims must be rejected. And this is what I will do.

There are, of course, problematic areas that involve plural values and conflicting values. And plurality and conflict can, of course, create problems. Moreover I see no theory, much less an algorithmic one, which solves all these problems. But plurality and conflict are absolutely commonplace and generally unproblematic features of our everyday choice and action. They had thus better not be a bar to sound judgement, resolute and informed action, and a sound and rational ethics.

Throughout, I will attempt to locate and correct those aspects of our ethical thought which have led—misled—us to think otherwise. These include an overconcern with action-guiding act evaluations, such as 'ought' and 'duty' and a concomitant unconcern with other evaluations of acts, with evaluations that are not of acts, and quite generally with moral psychology. They also involve thinking of ethics, and especially of action-guiding act evaluations, in terms of abstract rather than concrete value, i.e. asking only whether an act is the best act, rather than how and why it is good or best. They further involve an overdependence on maximizing theories of evaluation and rationality.

I have divided the work into four Parts, each of which considers one central topic. Part I—Chapters 1–4—focuses on the nature and problems of conflict. Part II—Chapters 5 and 6—focuses on the question of whether plural values preclude sound judgement. Part III—Chapters 7 and 8—discusses whether conflict requires plurality. Part IV—Chapters 9 and 10—discusses maximization, with special emphasis on plurality.

There is another way to divide these chapters—in terms of two emphases. One emphasis is on a particular issue. In Chapter 1, 'Dirty Hands and Ordinary Life', the issue is dirty hands—whether what is justified can be, none the less, immoral. Chapter 2, 'Moral Immorality', considers a cognate issue, whether what is immoral can none the less be admirable. Three other chapters take up particular issues about conflict and plurality in Aristotle's ethics and moral psychology: Chapter 3, 'Dirty Hands and Conflicts of Values and of Desires in Aristotle's Ethics', Chapter 5, 'Courage, the Doctrine of the Mean, and the Possibility of Evaluative and Emotional Coherence', and Chapter 7, 'Akrasia: The Unity of the Good, Commensurability, and Comparability'.

The other emphasis is a more general and abstract consideration of a topic. Chapter 4, 'Moral Conflicts: What They Are and What They Show', takes up some general issues about conflict, which are raised particularly about dirty hands in Chapters 1 and 3. Chapter 6, 'Plurality and Choice', takes up the general issue of whether plurality is an impediment to sound choice. That issue is discussed in Chapter 5 in regard to Aristotle's account of courage. Chapter 8, 'Monism, Pluralism, and Conflict', discusses whether conflict, and especially whether rational conflict, requires plurality. This is discussed in regard to weakness of will in Chapter 7. Chapters 9 and 10, 'Maximization: Some Conceptual Problems' and 'Maximization: Some Evaluative Problems' take up some general issues about maximization which are raised in earlier chapters.

The same topics are taken up more than once and in more than one way. Also each chapter is intended to stand on its own. Thus there is some repetition. But as suggested in the *Philebus* (24e) it may be necessary, or at least useful, to say some things more than once to secure agreement and understanding.

I rely frequently on Aristotle. As noted, three chapters are devoted to discussions of his ethics and moral psychology, as are various sections of other chapters. My reasons for this have to do, in large part, with how I came to these problems. Although, early in my studies, I was convinced by G. E. Moore and W. D. Ross of the plurality and incommensurability of moral considerations, I did not consider plurality and incommensurability problematic. Two works on Aristotle's ethics, and an examination of a charge frequently made against his ethics, changed this.

The first work, taken up in Chapter 5, argues that because courage involves plural and incommensurable values, victory and danger, and the proper emotions towards these, confidence and fear, there are severe problems in seeing how courage can involve a mean—either in one's concern with these values or in one's emotions. Since they do not shade into each other, how can too much of the one be too little of the other, and how, then, can there be a mean of, or between, them? As I will be concerned to argue, this problem can be solved by seeing how incommensurable values and emotions can fuse into complex wholes of disparate and incommensurable values and emotions, and can thus be assessed as lying or not lying in a mean.

This has direct application to the more recent and quite general worry that where we have incommensurable values, sound comparisons and sound judgement will be impossible—that there is no sound way to compare unlikes with unlikes. This general worry is taken up in Chapter 6, which shows that virtually all our choices concern plural and incommensurable considerations and that we are, none the less, able to make sound judgements—by fusing these considerations into complex wholes of disparate and incommensurable elements.

The second work on Aristotle, discussed in Chapter 7, argues that coherent akrasia, weakness of will, requires plural values. This work was concerned to show how Aristotle's pluralism could thus easily allow for akrasia, whereas the monism found in the *Protagoras* makes akrasia conceptually impossible. This easily generalizes to the view many now have, taken up in Chapter 8, that conflict quite generally requires plurality. As the leading idea can be put, 'There could be no conflict between two options if, as one sees, they have the very same attractive features. Thus, conflict requires difference.'

As I will be concerned to show, both in regard to Aristotle and more generally, this linking of conflict and plurality depends on a seriously mistaken understanding of reason and reasons for acting and of the role of affectivity and emotion in action. I will, however, argue that there are very close connections between plurality and conflict, and especially rational conflict—and that we may have to characterize each in terms of the other.

The charge made against Aristotle's ethics is that he leaves no room for moral conflicts in general or dirty hands in particular— i.e. cases where no matter what one does, one will do something wrong. We are told that this is so because he thought his good people could resolve all issues and act resolutely, no matter how difficult the situation. Some contemporary philosophers see this as a simple implication of his and Plato's somewhat different doctrine of the unity of virtues. But conflicts—because they involve doing what is wrong, no matter what one does—show that such a person is at best an unrealizable ideal.

As I will be concerned to argue in Chapter 3, this is a mistaken account of Aristotle's ethics and moral psychology. His good people may well be able to resolve issues and act resolutely in virtually any situation. None the less, as shown by what he says about mixed acts—those acts that somehow are both voluntary and not— he recognizes that it is possible even for a good person to have no choice but to do what is wrong. As he says at the beginning of *Nicomachean Ethics* 3, a person may be able to save his family from a tyrant only by doing a base or shameful act.

This, however, allows that such a person can see clearly what is to be done and will act resolutely. In the case at hand, the person should save his family and he should do this resolutely—despite the fact that he will have to do what is base. Thus, there is conflict. It is not a conflict of indecision and vacillation, but a conflict within a single moral appreciation of what is to be done. The conflict is within the one complex whole composed of disparate and incommensurable elements. Such conflict is best understood in moral psychological terms and as having to do with the conflicting elements of a situation that are seen and felt as conflicting, even where the agent also sees clearly what is to be done and resolutely takes that course of action.

This line of thought is also pursued in Chapter 1 in regard to dirty hands, and in Chapters 2 and 4 in regard to conflicts more generally. Here I argue that to understand conflicts—and not to see them as posing serious, even catastrophic, problems for ethics and ethical theory—we cannot approach them as our contemporary ethical theories more or less force us to do. That is, we cannot see them simply as involving incompossible action-guiding act evaluations, telling us at once to do and not do a given act. Rather, we must recognize that there are other important evaluations of acts than action-guiding ones. And we must also see that there is more to evaluate than acts. One way to get at these other areas is, as already suggested, via a study of the moral psychology of conflict. For this will help us see that there are properly conflicting ways to appreciate the complex wholes that we are faced with when we decide and act, especially where there are conflicts.

My approach to plurality and conflict—both my past approach and also as I now think of the issues—is thus directed by my concern with Aristotle's ethics and moral psychology. I find this entirely natural, since, as I see matters, plurality and conflict are at the heart of his ethics and moral psychology. And, also as I see matters, if we keep our problems with plurality and conflict in mind while examining his treatment of them, we will come to a better understanding of both our problems and our ethics and moral psychology, as well as his. (Much the same applies to Plato, to whom I also turn.)

However, I know that many do not share my appreciation of Aristotle—especially on these topics. I would be pleased if my chapters on Aristotle move them towards my view. But there are some who find it distracting to discuss a contemporary or abstract issue by means of a historical text or philosopher. It is partly for this reason that, despite the repetition involved, I have tried to make each of the chapters self-contained. Those who want to pursue the contemporary and abstract issues about plurality and conflict without recourse to Aristotle can simply omit Chapters 3, 5, and 7. Those who want to concentrate on Aristotle can omit the others. For my own part, I still find it best to think about these topics together.

PART I

Conflict

I

Dirty Hands and Ordinary Life

CAN there be acts of dirty hands—acts that are justified, even obligatory, but none the less wrong and shameful? To borrow an example from Michael Walzer, can it be justified, even obligatory, for an official to torture someone to force him to tell where his fellows have hidden a time bomb among the innocent populace? And if, as Walzer suggests, it can be justified, even obligatory, to do this, can it also be wrong and shameful? This question has recently attracted much attention, but little agreement.[1]

I am indebted to Norman Care for our discussions of these issues. Along with those mentioned below, my thanks are owed to John Campbell, C. A. J. Coady, Michael P. Levine, Graeme Marshall, Robert Pargetter, Laurence Thomas, and the Philosophy Departments of the University of Wisconsin at Madison, Oberlin College, Ohio State University, Columbia University, the University of Melbourne, the University of Adelaide, Georgetown University, the University of California at Riverside, and Syracuse University.

[1] Here is a partial, chronological list: M. Merleau-Ponty, *Humanism and Terror* (Boston: Beacon Press, 1971); T. Nagel, 'War and Massacre', *Philosophy and Public Affairs*, 1 (1972) 123–44; M. Walzer, 'Political Action: The Problem of Dirty Hands', *Philosophy and Public Affairs* 2 (1973) 160–80; R. Brandt, 'Utilitarianism and the Rules of War', *Philosophy and Public Affairs* 1 (1972) 145–65; R. M. Hare, 'Rules of War and Moral Reasoning', *Philosophy and Public Affairs* 1 (1972), 166–81; B. Williams, 'Ethical Consistency' and 'Consistency and Realism', *Problems of the Self* (Cambridge: Cambridge University Press, 1973), and 'Conflicts of Values', *Moral Luck* (Cambridge: Cambridge University Press, 1981); B. Williams and J. J. C. Smart, *Utilitarianism, For and Against* (Cambridge: Cambridge University Press, 1973); T. McConnell, 'Moral Dilemmas and Consistency in Ethics', *Canadian Journal of Philosophy*, 8 (1978), 269–87; R. Marcus, 'Moral Dilemmas and Ethical Consistency', *Journal of Philosophy*, 77 (1980), 121–36; P. Greenspan, 'Moral Dilemmas and Guilt', *Philosophical Studies*, 43 (1983), 117–25; P. Foot, 'Moral Realism and Moral Dilemmas', *Journal of Philosophy*, 80 (1983), 379–98; T. Hill, 'Moral Purity and the Lesser Evil', *The Monist*, 66 (1983), 213–32; S. I. Benn, 'Private and Public Morality: Clean Living and Dirty Hands', in S. I. Benn and G. F. Gaus (eds.), *Public and Private in Social Life* (London: Croom Helm, 1983); B. Barry, 'Tragic Choices', *Ethics*, 94 (1984), 303–18; A. Donagan, 'Consistency in Rationalist Moral Systems', *Journal of Philosophy*, 81 (1984), 291–309; M. Slote, 'Utilitarianism, Moral Dilemmas, and Moral Cost', *American Philosophical Quarterly*, 22 (1985), 161–8; C. Korsgaard, 'The Right to Lie: Kant on Dealing with Evil', *Philosophy and Public Affairs*, 15 (1986), 325–49; I. Levi, *Hard Choices* (Cambridge: Cambridge University Press, 1986); M. C. Nussbaum, *The Fragility of Goodness* (Cambridge: Cambridge University Press,

More accurately, there has been little agreement over the question of whether there can be cases of dirty hands. But there has been widespread agreement that dirty hands cases are conceptually problematic even to the point of being contradictory. I will argue that they are conceptually unproblematic and are, indeed, instances of ordinary, everyday, evaluative phenomena. I will also argue that they have been thought problematic only because our ethical theories have over-concentrated on act evaluations and have misunderstood even them.

My goal, then, is at once to correct our ethical theories and also to show dirty hands conceptually unproblematic. I will use each to accomplish the other. Thus, at times I will be concerned with general structures of action, choice, and evaluation, and at times with particularities of dirty hands.

The dirty hands cases I am concerned with are (1) justified, even obligatory, but (2) none the less somehow wrong. Some call such acts dilemmas. But I reserve 'dilemma' for cases where there is no right act open to the agent and where every option is simply wrong. Others call acts that satisfy (1) and (2) conflicts. They are, indeed, conflicts. But they are a special sort of conflict—special even beyond what is given by (1) and (2). For they involve dirty acts, and not every wrong act is also a dirty act, nor does every conflict involving wrong acts involve dirty hands. These distinctions will come out below.

1. SOME STRUCTURES OF OVERALL, ACTION-GUIDING EVALUATIONS

Many think it impossible that an act be at once (1) justified, even obligatory, but also (2) none the less somehow wrong. I will argue that this seems problematic only because of serious errors made by our ethical theories. They over-concentrate on overall, action-guiding act evaluations, e.g. 'ought', 'right', and 'duty'.[2] Further,

1986); and S. Bishop, 'Connections and Guilt', *Hypatia*, 2 (1987), 7–23. References will be to these works. Other works are listed in C. Gowans (ed.), *Moral Dilemmas* (Oxford: Oxford University Press, 1987).

[2] On the excessiveness of the concern, see my 'Act and Agent Evaluations', *The Review of Metaphysics*, 27 (1973), 42–61, 'Rightness and Goodness: Is There a Difference?', *American Philosophical Quarterly*, 10 (1973), 87–98, and 'The Schizophrenia of Modern Ethical Theories', *Journal of Philosophy*, 73 (1976), 453–66. See

they misunderstand both what they over-concentrate on and other large portions of our evaluative world.

Much recent work in ethics has been on how to characterize action-guiding evaluations. We can ignore the controversies over these characterizations. What is of importance for us are two interrelated points of general agreement about such evaluations: that they are action-guiding and that they are overall evaluations.

Let us turn first to action-guidingness. These evaluations say of acts whether they are or are not to be done. So, Isaac Levi says that ' "ought" statements represent advice as to what is to be done rather than fragments of moral epiphenomenology . . .' (27–8). It is thus natural to restrict these evaluations to acts we can do and to hold that 'ought' implies 'can'.[3]

Usually, the 'can' is understood causally. However, as is especially important for conflicts in general and dirty hands in particular, it must also be understood morally. This is to understand it in terms of what is morally possible—i.e. what is morally permissible.

The causal and the moral here, as so often, part company. There is no causal difficulty in sticking a pin in a baby for one's sadistic amusement. Further, some argue that a doing or non-doing that is causally necessitated is not a fully-fledged human act. Indeed, the person may not even seem an agent of such a doing or non-doing. But where the impossibility is only moral, there is no such trouble. For here, it is not the act but only the choice that is forced, and forced by moral considerations. It is only in the sense of having no moral choice that here the agent has no choice. And this could hardly tell against the possibility of action even in the very fullest sense.

Whether 'can' is taken causally or morally, if 'ought' implies 'can' and if evaluations are action-guiding, what one cannot do cannot be what one ought to do. Turning now from act evaluations to agent evaluations, many take the doctrine that 'ought' implies 'can' as showing that an agent cannot be criticized for not doing what cannot be done. Thus, in these ways, to hold that 'ought'

also S. Wolf, 'Moral Saints', *Journal of Philosophy*, 79 (1982), 410–39, and 'Above and Below the Line of Duty', *Philosophical Topics*, 14 (1986), 131–48; and B. Williams, *Ethics and the Limits of Philosophy* (Cambridge, Mass.: Harvard University Press, 1985).

[3] See my ' "Ought" and "Can" ', *Australasian Journal of Philosophy*, 49 (1971), 303–16.

implies 'can' is to hold that doing exactly what is to be done—
which some see as perfect practice—makes for a perfect act or at
least one such that neither it nor its agent can be faulted.

These understandings of the 'ought' implies 'can' doctrine thus
deny moral relevance to impossible oughts—oughts we are unable
to obey. Dirty hands, however, involve impossible oughts. What is
morally unavoidable is said to tell against act and agent. In Walzer's
example, even if the torture is justified, perhaps obligatory, it none
the less stains both the act and the agent.

It is, of course, controversial whether torture in such a case, or
ever, can be justified, much less obligatory. But the same points
can be made about not torturing the prisoner. Even if not torturing
is justified, perhaps obligatory, what this involves can still tell
against both the act and agent. Even if morality requires that the
injuries and deaths of the innocents must be endured, they are
matters of moral moment and matters for extreme regret. (To
simplify matters, I will not take up three interrelated questions we
now see posed by dirty hands: Is the non-doing of an act of dirty
hands the doing of another act of dirty hands? What are the
relations between dirty hands and the doctrine of double effect?
What are the relations between dirty hands and the distinction
between doing and not doing?)

Let us now turn to the second point of general agreement: that
the act evaluations we are interested in are overall evaluations.
This allows that these evaluations are reached on the basis of
partial considerations which may point in different directions. After
all, it is a commonplace that there are reasons for and against
doing almost any act. But, it is held, the evaluations we are
concerned with are reached by taking these various considerations
into account and resolving them into one overall evaluation. So,
we no longer have partial, conflicting considerations, but rather
one overall evaluation—that we ought to do a given act or that
we ought not to do it.

Dirty hands cases, however, involve more than an overall,
action-guiding evaluation. The partial, constituting values retain
their moral relevance. So, in Walzer's example, the disvalue of the
torture is not taken into account only in determining the overall
value of authorizing it. (Nor is the disvalue of the deaths and
injuries of the innocents taken into account only in determining
the overall value of refusing to authorize it.) The dirty feature does

not merely make a negative contribution to the dirty act. It remains as a disvalue even within that justified, perhaps obligatory, whole—a disvalue which is still there to be noted and regretted. As Bernard Williams says in 'Ethical Consistency', the dirty feature is a remainder within the act (179).

The dirty feature is taken into account once in determining the overall value of the act and again on its own. It is thus double-counted. Further, when it is taken up again on its own, it is taken up in an evaluation that is not action-guiding. Despite the dirty feature, the act is to be done. None the less, because of the feature, the act is regrettable.

Dirty hands, thus, involve double-counted impossible oughts and non-action-guiding act evaluations. For these reasons, it is charged that dirty hands are impossible or at the very least involve severe conceptual problems.

Thomas Nagel, Walzer, Williams, and others hold that despite these conceptual problems, we must recognize that there are dirty hands. Richard Brandt, R. M. Hare, and others, in large measure because of these problems, hold that claims about dirty hands must be explained away—e.g. as a bad mixture of heuristics and ethics. They hold that people must be alive to moral costs, but that if an act is right overall and if the agent is justified in thinking it right overall, then this is all there is to think about it morally. The act is wholly unexceptionable and the agent has nothing to regret or feel shame or guilt about.

I will present a third option. Even though dirty hands are morally problematic, they are conceptually unproblematic. Double-counted impossible oughts and non-action-guiding act evaluations are perfectly general and conceptually unproblematic features of our acts. Further, the reasons advanced to show their incoherence, instead of embodying good moral or conceptual sense, depend on radically implausible views of value and action. Thus, to be adequate, ethical theories must allow for dirty hands, for impossible oughts, and for non-action-guiding act evaluations.

2. SOME FOUNDATIONAL FEATURES OF CHOICE AND ACTION

We can begin to show why adequate theories must allow for these by examining two features of dirty hands: they are cases of moral conflict and they are cases where one is morally compromised in doing what is morally justified, perhaps required. Now, some think that dirty hands are conceptually problematic, even to the point of impossibility, because they think this of moral conflicts. So too, some think it impossible to be compromised in doing what is justified, much less in doing what is required.

Consider, then, this current account of conflict given in terms of incompossibility:[4] there is a conflict of value where (1) x has value, (2) y has value, and (3) it is possible for either x or y, but not both, to be actualized. Correlatively, there is a conflict of desire where (1) x is desired, (2) y is desired, and (3) it is possible to get either x or y but not both. (For simplicity, throughout this work I write as if there are only two incompossible items.)

However, a foundational point about choice, and thus about action, is that a choice is a choice of which values and desires to satisfy and which not to satisfy. For, except in the rarest of cases, there are evaluative and desiderative considerations for doing each of the jointly impossible acts. Thus, in the sense given by the incompossibility account, virtually every choice and act involves conflict. But unless one's life is unfortunate beyond description, it is false that almost every choice and act is conflicting. And it is also false that almost every choice and act is problematic.

Similarly, nearly every choice and act requires a compromise between values, even moral values. But again, unless one's life is unfortunate beyond description, not all such compromises are compromising.

Thus, the incompossibility account does not show what is problematic, or even that there is anything problematic, about conflicts. Similarly for dirty hands and being compromised in doing what is justified. None the less, that account helps us see a foundational point about choice and action: acts have costs. Acts typically involve, and some acts simply are, means which are not also ends. These means are not sought or even welcomed for themselves. We do them only because in the circumstances they help us achieve our goals. Further, acts typically involve opportunity costs. We forgo certain goals we would like to achieve because in the circumstances forgoing them helps us achieve other goals.

⁴ See e.g. F. Jackson, 'Internal Conflicts in Desires and Morals', *American Philosophical Quarterly*, 22 (1985), 105–14. See also Williams, 'Ethical Consistency', pp. 167 ff.

A cost considered *qua* cost, and not *qua* what it is a cost for, is better not endured than endured. But what it is a cost for can, despite its having a cost, be better had than not had. Thus, the general structure of choice involves having to forgo what is valued and in this way suffering losses. At the least, it requires omnipotence to avoid having to pay costs and suffer losses. And if Leibniz is right, not even omnipotence may be sufficient. For even the best world can contain parts that, on their own, are bad, and are costs for achieving what is best.

My claim so far is that it is perfectly general and conceptually unproblematic that almost every act has costs and that these can be seen at once as costs and also as justified. This, of course, is to say that it is perfectly general and conceptually unproblematic to double-count those costs: once in taking them as costs and once in holding that despite their being costs, what they are costs for is justified. It is also to make a non-action-guiding act evaluation. That the cost is to be borne is an action-guiding act evaluation. That the act none the less has a cost is, or grounds, a non-action-guiding act evaluation.

Thus, double-counted unavoidable costs and non-action-guiding act evaluations are perfectly general and conceptually unproblematic. Why, then, think dirty hands problematic, much less incoherent?

3. HOW ARE THESE COSTS TAKEN UP?

Even if my claims about the generality of costs are accepted, the parallel between ordinary acts and dirty hands might not be. First, dirty hands have double-counted impossible oughts, not merely double-counted unavoidable costs. Second, dirty hands do not merely have double-counted impossible oughts, those oughts are regretted. Thus, dirty hands cases cannot be explained simply in terms of a negative contribution the dirty part makes to the act. And in any case not all negative contributions involve dirty hands.

I agree entirely with these points. It would be wrong to see the dirty feature as simply a cost and as simply making a negative contribution to the act. The whole act does not simply have a somewhat lesser value than it would but for the dirty part. Nor is the dirty part just one cost among many. None the less, these common and non-dirty features can play many of the structural roles which lead philosophers to hold that dirty hands are conceptually problematic, if not incoherent.

To see this, we can start by noting that many justified costs are also regretted. Sometimes regretting them is justified, even required, as will be taken up below. But sometimes it is not justified. Some people regret what should not bother any reasonable person: e.g. having to pay a completely reasonable charge for a dinner in a restaurant, rather than being given it as a present by the proprietor. To turn to opportunity costs, some people regret having to choose between one ordinary nice dessert and another.

This speaks about being bothered by costs. The issue might seem different in regard to simply noting them. How, it might be asked, could noting what is true be objectionable? My reply is to consider what we might call a taxi-meter sensibility of accurately noting the cost of everything. For someone with such a sensibility, there would be intertwined with the pleasure of giving a present to a child a full awareness of its cost; and with the appreciation of a drive in the countryside, the cost per mile. (Perhaps these problems hold only for finite beings, like us, and not for infinite ones.)

Clearly, we must go beyond the empirical issue of which conflicts and double-counted costs and oughts are noted. We must confront the issues of which should be taken up and how they should be taken up. We must, that is, turn to an ethics and a moral psychology of attention and involvement—as found in Aristotle, Weil, and Murdoch.

As these theorists show, some conflicts and some double-counted costs and oughts should not be taken up at all, and certainly not with regret. But some others, despite its being permissible or even obligatory to bear them, are quite properly taken up, and with regret. Here we might consider the following cases: (1) jettisoning goods in a storm to save the ship and crew (as in the *Nicomachean Ethics* 3. 1), (2) paying taxes, (3) the pain caused by filling a cavity, (4) giving up one's education to take a job in order to support one's family, (5) choosing between a job and a family.

4. THE SPECIAL MORAL NATURE OF DIRTY FEATURES

Let us now leave the general structures of action and evaluation and take up some particularities of dirty hands. There is an obvious reply to my argument that both dirty hands and more ordinary acts share the structural features of double-counting and non-action-guiding act evaluations. It will be said that they differ in their particularities and it is these differences that show dirty hands to be problematic. So, we will be reminded that in dirty hands cases, what is double-counted. has a particular moral character. The dirtying features of dirty hands—the double-counted impossible oughts, the remainders—are in important ways moral costs. But so is the loss of an education, as in (4) above.

As a second attempt, we might thus qualify the claim about the dirty features and say that these are absolutely wrong in the sense of being always wrong. Some ethicists will see this as incompatible with holding that acts of dirty hands are justified, even obligatory. Using W. D. Ross's terms, they hold that if the dirty act and part are justified, even obligatory, then any wrongness must be overridden and thus that here there is nothing wrong; and if there is nothing wrong, then there is nothing absolutely wrong.

This reply, however, conflates action-guidingness and wrongness. What is here overridden and merely prima facie is the action-guidingness of those features. Their wrongness is not overridden. This distinction between action-guidingness and wrongness underlies Ross's own claim in *The Right and the Good* that the overriding of some, but not all, prima facie duties properly involves compunction.[5] That ethicists have conflated these two sorts of overridingness and prima facieness—and more importantly, that they have focused so exclusively on what is action-guiding—is central to my explanation of why they have been unable to allow for or understand dirty hands.

This distinction between sorts of overridingness is important. But giving up one's education to support one's family may also always be wrong in a way that grounds compunction. Second, we need a way to characterize, not simply to isolate, the dirty parts of dirty hands. We also need a way to characterize those other wrong acts that remain wrong even when justified.

Let us start by noting that among the dirty features of dirty hands are people being wronged, they and their trust, integrity, and status as ends are violated, dishonoured, and betrayed: innocents are killed, tortured, lied to, deceived. Dirty hands can

[5] Oxford: Oxford University Press, 1963, 28.

also involve other sorts of harms and wrongs—e.g. the destruction
of a holy place or a great work of art. They sometimes involve the
violation of a principle rather than a person: e.g. agreeing not to
prosecute terrorists in order to end a hijacking.

I think we can get at the special nature of these dirty moral
costs—and show that they are not simply costs, nor even simply
moral costs—by examining what sort of moral conflicts they
involve.[6] So for example, not benefiting someone and more clearly
harming someone—perhaps most clearly harming a friend or loved
one—may always be ground for conflict and regret. But the wrong
that is the ground of the conflict of dirty hands goes beyond not
benefiting or harming. As said already, it is a violation and a
betrayal of a person, value, or principle.

In paradigm cases of dirty hands, the costs are important moral
costs: e.g. to save one's country in a desperate war, one betrays
an innocent person, perhaps even an innocent friend, to those
trying to kill him. But, dirty hands, or at least slightly soiled fingers,
can involve less important wrongs—e.g. to deceive the enemy into
thinking that his loyalties have changed, a secret agent publicly
insults his old teacher.

These, it might be remarked, all involve political or at least
institutional and public immoralities. This might suggest that dirty
hands are morally peculiar because they involve politics and indeed
that they are morally peculiar in just the ways that politics are.
After all, we always knew that politics is a particularly dirty
business. As Walzer reminds us (164), Machiavelli argued that
rulers must learn not to be good, and Horderer, in Sartre's play
Dirty Hands, holds that it is not possible to govern both well and
innocently. Thus, politics is not a home for ethics and shows little
about ethics—except its limits.

However, the non-political, including the personal, also allows
for dirty hands. Suppose that the marriage of relatives has been
seriously troubled, but is now on the mend. Pleased for them, I
offer to do whatever I can. Drawing me aside, my cousin says there
is something I can do. As her husband suspects, she had been
having an affair. Unless his suspicions are allayed, there will be no
chance of a reconciliation. For both her sake and his, she asks me
to help convince him that she had not been having the affair. She

---

[6] My thanks are owed to Kimon Lycos for help here. See Williams, 'Ethical
Consistency'.

asks me to help her keep the truth from him, perhaps even to deceive or lie to him. This, I suggest, can involve dirty hands.

5. SOME FEATURES OF DIRTY HANDS AND SIMILAR ACTS

If dirty hands involve a violation of a person, principle, or value, two related issues must be addressed. It must be shown how, given that it is a violation, it can be justified, and also how, given that it is justified, even necessary, it can be a violation.

We can make some headway on both questions by starting with the fact that in at least many cases, the circumstances which justify the dirty hands are, themselves, immoral. In Aristotle's case of having to do what is base to save one's family, there are the tyrant's immoral threats.[7] In Walzer's torture case and in Nagel's case of bombing enemy civilians to break their country's will, there are the immoralities of war. And in another of Walzer's cases, that of acceding to a corrupt ward boss's demands for a bribe, there are the immoral demands and implied threats.

I think it difficult to overestimate the importance of the role of immorality in creating situations which necessitate and justify acting with dirty hands. In at least many cases, including those just mentioned, were it not for the immorality, there would be no need or room for dirty hands. The issue is important enough to stop and show that the immorality of the circumstances can provide the specific difference between cases of dirty hands and other cases.

Consider two cases presented by Patricia Greenspan. The first is that of a doctor who through no one's fault has to choose between saving one patient or the other or, what is unthinkable for the doctor, letting them both die. The choice clearly can involve regrets, perhaps even anguish. But it does not seem to involve dirty hands. Contrast this with the case of Sophie from Styron's *Sophie's Choice*. Upon entering a Nazi concentration camp with her two children, she is told by an officer that only one of the children will be allowed to live, that she must choose which of them this will be, and that if she does not choose, both will be killed. She picks one. And does so with dirty hands.

The contrast with the doctor case is not that only Sophie has

---

[7] *Nicomachean Ethics* 3. 1, 1110a6 ff. I discuss this in ch. 3.

strong, special obligations. Doctors have such obligations to their patients. Nor is the contrast due to the fact that she is the child's mother. For, if simply through natural calamity, people have to choose which of their desperately undernourished children will get the required food and which will not—i.e. which will live and which will die—the death can be double-counted and a source of continuing anguish. But this does not seem to involve dirty hands.

For the final pair of cases, you are in charge of the rescue of passengers from a sinking ship. In both cases, you take all that your lifeboats can hold, leaving some to die. In the first case, you use a fair procedure to choose those to be saved and those to be left. In the second, you are ordered to choose the ones who are to live and those who are to die on the basis of their religion or race, with the threat that otherwise your boats will be smashed, preventing anyone from being saved. You accede to the threat. Both cases allow for, perhaps demand, regret. But only the second case seems to me to involve dirty hands.

If these cases are representative, it is too little to say simply that the justifying and necessitating circumstances of these cases of dirty hands are themselves immoral. They are immoral in a particular way. They are violations of moral autonomy and selfhood—and this in a particularly vicious way. The agent is immorally coerced to take part in, perhaps even to help implement, an immoral project.

Many of the clearest cases of dirty hands involve such immoral coercion. And as just seen, immoral coercion is the specific difference between at least some acts of dirty hands and other similar acts which do not involve dirty hands even though they too are justified but none the less somehow wrong. Some further comments and examples would be useful here.

As argued in ' "Ought" and "Can" ', if I culpably make myself unable to do what I ought to do, it can still be true that I ought to do it. For example, if I am unable to repay my debts because I deliberately or negligently wasted the borrowed money, my inability does not relieve me of the obligation to repay the money. Thus, when the time comes to repay the debts, whatever I do will be wrong. For even if I then do what, from among those acts I can do, I should do, I will still fail to do one thing I ought then to do—repay the debts.

At least in the simple and usual case of being culpably unable to repay the debts, I do not act with dirty hands. Perhaps the most important reason is that the agent is also the creator of the situation that necessitates the choice.

So, let us change the case so that someone else has embezzled from my account, leaving me enough to pay only some of my creditors. Repaying those to whom I have the strongest obligation and not repaying the others would, once again, be justified, even obligatory. But this act, too, does not seem a case of dirty hands. One way to put this is that the relevant ought-judgement here is more clearly of the situation than of my act: 'It ought to be that I be able to repay them' or 'I ought to be able to repay them', rather than 'I ought to repay them'. Yet this act is importantly similar to the paradigm of dirty hands—the case where one agent is morally forced by someone else's immorality to do what is, or otherwise would be, wrong.

One possible explanation of why this does not involve dirty hands is that even though I was forced by another's immorality to choose not to repay some creditors, I was not forced to choose to help implement that person's evil project. For, as the case is naturally taken, the embezzler wants my money simply to have it to spend. Had the embezzler instead been intent on immorally harming those I would thus be unable to repay—and more clearly, intent on forcing me to help implement this immoral project—my non-repayment would then be, or come very close to being, an act of dirty hands.

It seems important here that it is another's immoral plan that is to be implemented. For suppose that with malice aforethought and in order to prevent pangs of conscience from stilling my immoral hand, I had intentionally put myself in a position where I could repay only some of my creditors: here my non-payment would not seem to involve dirty hands.

One thing to note here is that the circumstances of dirty hands at once necessitate and also justify the wrongful act. But, given my culpability for those circumstances, although they necessitate, they also condemn my act. So, if this is not a case of dirty hands, we are once again given strong reason to connect dirty hands and being immorally coerced to help another's immoral project.

Perhaps there could be a case of dirty hands where I now repent of an immoral project that I set in train, but am coerced by the circumstances to further that project—backing out would be too terrible for innocent people, even though continuing will also be terrible. But because of the moral distance between me now and me at the inception of the project, allowing that this might involve dirty hands would, I think, more help than hurt my suggestion.

These, then, are some considerations in favour of the suggestion that what is special about dirty hands, setting them apart from other conflicts where one is unable to avoid doing what is wrong, is that they involve being coerced to help implement another's evil project. Even if this claim is right about only some important cases of dirty hands, it is important in at least the following five ways.

First, it helps show why dirty hands, despite being morally very problematic, are not conceptually problematic. For whatever can be said about being immorally coerced to help another's immoral project, it cannot be said that it is conceptually incoherent or even problematic.

Second, we can see in what way Nagel is right to hold that in dirty hands cases we are prevented from engaging in the proper reaction to evil—fight it—and are, rather, forced to help implement it. It is not that we have, even temporarily, adopted an evil end, much less adopted evil as our end. Rather, even if we do the dirty act in order to minimize evil, in the doing of that act, we are helping implement an evil project. In doing that act of dirty hands, our action, in its very detail, is following the dictates of evil.

Third, we see why politics is so naturally a home for dirty hands—if, as many hold, it is also the natural home of immorality and immoral coercion. We also see why dirty hands are also found outside politics.

Fourth, in so far as immoral circumstances are important for dirty hands, it is only to be expected that dirty hands are morally so difficult. As we know, one of the most intractable moral problems is how to act morally in immoral situations. (On this see e.g. John Rawls's *A Theory of Justice* on non-ideal theories. See also Korsgaard, 341 ff.)

Fifth, dirty hands remind us of the perhaps archaic view that the immorality of the world can irredeemably stain our acts and lives. They show that not only one's own immoralities, but also another's immoralities, can make it impossible to avoid doing what is immoral. They show, contrary to a Kantian theme, that our acts are not fresh moral starts. Their moral nature depends sometimes not only on us and what we can do at the time of the act, but also on what we have done previously. It can also depend on others and what they do. We thus see that the moral nature of our acts is in the same mixed category as meaningfulness and Aristotelian eudaimonia: importantly within our control but also importantly outside our control.

These five points clearly show the importance of the connection between dirty hands and being coerced to implement another person's evil plans. But for a fuller understanding of dirty hands, some other points should be made—some supporting and some taking away from that connection.

First, some have a problem in seeing how even a paradigm case of dirty hands such as Walzer's torture case involves being morally coerced to help implement an immoral project. They object that there is no reason to think that the person who may be tortured, or those he acted with, intended that he be tortured. However, for this to serve as an objection, it must follow from an act's not being intended that it is not part of a project.

I am unsure whether that does follow. For torture and similar abominations are hardly mere parts of civil war. Nor do they stand to civil war simply as expectable consequences, as an inability to repay debts stands to being robbed. Rather, they are better thought of as constituents of such a war.

Second, I earlier said that 'the wrong and the ground of conflict of acts of dirty hands goes beyond not benefiting or harming . . . it is a violation and a betrayal of a person, value, or principle'. However it is clear that there can be violations and betrayals which are justified, but not because they involve being morally coerced into helping implement another's evil project.

To modify a case already mentioned, if people stupidly—only stupidly, not immorally—waste their money, they may have no moral choice but to let down, even betray, others and the trust others have placed in them and thus to violate important principles. We might here consider parents who have been stupid with their money and who are thus unable to help pay for a child's education, but must instead spend their remaining money on necessities and on repaying serious and pressing debts.

As already claimed, however, this is not a case of dirty hands, despite the fact that what is done is, although justified or even obligatory, regrettable, shameful, and perhaps even morally humiliating. Thus, instead of showing that immoral coercion is not necessary for dirty hands by showing that justified betrayals and violations do not require immoral coercion, this case rather shows that not all justified betrayals and violations involve dirty hands.

Perhaps, however, some justified betrayals and violations which do not involve immoral coercion are cases of dirty hands. In particular, perhaps circumstances which are only very difficult, but which do not involve immoral coercion, can justify betrayals and violations which are cases of dirty hands.

Consider these six candidates: first, terminating an intimate relationship—e.g. a marriage or close friendship—where through no one's fault it no longer has significance for one of the people but still does for the other, who also depends greatly on the relationship and strongly wants it to continue. Second, a 'needed organ case', where killing one innocent person and transplanting that person's organs would save many other innocent people.[8] Third, the sacrifice of Isaac, almost performed by Abraham. Fourth, the act of a military commander who, through stupidity or simple bad luck, orders his men into an untenable situation and then, to avoid still greater damage to the pursuit of the battle, has to abandon them to their fate. Fifth, a case where to get the best candidate appointed, one allows immoral, e.g. racist or sexist, jokes about other candidates to go unchallenged.[9] Sixth, to do useful research, one accepts dirty money.[10]

It is clear that these acts involve harms, perhaps wrongs, and also betrayals and violations. It is also clear that they involve, perhaps require, regrets and even compunction. Many think it clear that leaving the relationship can be justified. It is unclear whether taking the needed organs could be justified. Few things are clear about the sacrifice case. I have found little agreement over the question of whether any of these three are cases of dirty hands. But I have found considerable agreement that the fourth, fifth, and sixth cases do involve dirty hands.

If immoral coercion is not necessary in all cases of dirty hands, we might wonder why it is so important, perhaps even necessary, in others. And if it is not always necessary, we might wonder why it is so difficult to construct very serious—i.e. very immoral—cases

---

[8] Myrna Frances Kamm suggested this use of the needed organ case.

[9] My thanks are owed to John Robertson for these fourth and fifth cases, and to him and Emily Robertson for discussion of them and the general importance of immoral coercion.

[10] My thanks are owed to Patricia Greenspan for this case.

of dirty hands which do not involve immoral coercion, and so easy to construct very serious cases of dirty hands which do involve immoral coercion.

At least the beginnings of a general answer has, in effect, already been given. Dirty hands cases do not simply involve mere bads and harms. Nor, therefore, are they wrong simply because they involve these. Rather, they involve betrayals and violations of people, principles, or values.

Here I want simply to suggest some reasons why being coerced into helping implement an evil project is so important for—even if not always necessary for—such violations. First, an evil person can make it near enough impossible for others who are moved by moral considerations to avoid moral violations. For example, in the boat rescue case, your precise order is to choose those to live and those to die by a procedure which is immoral, and this is backed by the further immorality that unless the order is carried out all the passengers will die. It is this complex of immorality that gives you no moral option but to act with dirty hands.

Where there is no such immoral threat, you could instead choose those to be saved by a fair procedure, thus avoiding dirty hands. I do not think it mere hopefulness to believe that natural difficulties are rarely so 'intelligent' and so 'exacting' that they force our hand at every turn.

Second, that an act will help implement an evil plan is, itself, a strong moral reason not to do it. Morality requires us not to co-operate with evil and often to help fight it. It is, itself, a violation to do what one is immorally coerced into doing.

These two reasons can combine in a particularly vicious way— to have to do what is a violation because one has been immorally coerced to do it seems an evil which goes beyond the 'mere combination' of these two evils. What I mean is suggested by a related sort of case. It can be painful to do what, on its own, we do not want to do simply because we do not want to do it. So too, it can be painful to do what someone we hate tells, or simply wants, us to do simply because we hate that person. But the pain of these combined can exceed by far the 'sum' of these pains. I mean the pain of doing what, on its own, we do not want to do when, further, we have been made to do it by someone we hate.

To the extent that these last suggestions are well taken, we can see why immoral coercion may well not be necessary for dirty hands. But we can also see why it is so important for dirty hands, especially for serious cases of dirty hands.

6. STRANGE THEORIES OF VALUE AND THE DENIAL OF DIRTY HANDS

As I hope has been made clear, the features that are double-counted and that figure in the non-action-guiding evaluations of dirty hands are the normal and unproblematic moral features. They are exactly those taken into account in reaching action-guiding act evaluations. Only their circumstances are special.

After all, being dirty is not peculiar to cases of dirty hands. Many other acts are dirty in just the ways that dirty hands cases are dirty. What is special about cases of dirty hands then is not that they are dirty, but that they are none the less justified or even obligatory. And the reasons they are justified or even obligatory are the usual sorts of reasons that other acts are justified. Nor are dirty hands cases special because they involve costs, remainders, or conflicts. Many other acts involve these, too.

Put generally, then, it is unclear why non-action-guiding act evaluations of double-counted impossible oughts should be thought conceptually problematic. Put more particularly, it is unclear why dirty hands cases should be thought conceptually problematic. Indeed, it is unclear what values and evaluations would have to be like to make these problematic.

Perhaps one of these five pictures—three about value and two about evaluation—is held: (1) Value is seen as a metaphysical point, lacking all morally distinguishable features. (2) Value is seen as so organic that after constituting the constituted value, the constituting values disappear as values. (3) Values are seen as so interdependent that it is held that whatever is incompatible with what is to be done, thus cannot be good in any way, and that whatever is necessary for what is to be done, thus cannot be bad in any way. (4) Evaluations are understood as simply and completely comparative: e.g. we are concerned simply to find the top-ranked act. Or finally, (5) evaluations are understood in terms of preferences, where all we are concerned with is finding what is most preferred. So understood, evaluating is seen on the model of using a beam balance—and indeed, a beam balance hidden from view. For the weighing is seen as being concerned only with which pan is heavier and thus we have no interest in, or are unable to examine, the contents of the pans. Rather, on this view as well as the others, we are interested only in which act is to be done and neither why it is to be done nor in its other moral features.

These pictures might appear hyperbolic, but they seem accurate to the views that find dirty hands conceptually incoherent. For those views must hold either that, if justified, there could be nothing wrong in, say, a betrayal. Or alternatively, that there could be no betrayal because whatever is justified cannot involve a betrayal. Apart from some such picture as those just given, why would one even entertain either of these suggestions?

There is little reason to accept these pictures. To be sure, some ethicists at least seem to accept them. But their ethical views do not appear to commit them to do so. Thus, although many utilitarians espouse such a view, I see nothing in utilitarianism requiring this. It can allow for regret at any bad that must be endured and at the fact that what is required is not better than in fact it is. Here we might note Michael Slote's point that utilitarianism need not be concerned only with the happiness of all *in sensu composito*, but can also be concerned with the happiness of each *in sensu diviso*. After all, utilitarianism does not construct the good of each from the good of all, nor does it construct the good from the best or the right.

To say that utilitarianism can, thus, allow for remainders is one thing. It still remains to be seen whether it can allow for dirty hands. For it still remains to be seen whether it can allow for violations which go beyond simply wrongs or harms, or whether it can accord immoral coercion its special role, or whether it can allow for the moral emotions which I will shortly argue are central to dirty hands.

Before continuing, it must also be said—in what may be a back-handed defence of utilitarianism—that just as utilitarianism may be unable to account for the special dirty features of dirty hands, it may also be unable to account for having to act with dirty hands. It is often thought that utilitarianism all too easily requires doing what is dirty because what so often justifies that has to do with many people, great needs, catastrophes, and the like—which seem to involve well-being, the natural home of utilitarianism.

But even when dirty hands are justified by such considerations, utilitarianism may still be unable to account for that. The reason is simply that many-person, public action is often not correctly understood in utilitarian terms. (I suspect that it is because they distrust, perhaps despise, the realms of governmental or business action that many anti-utilitarians think that these realms are open to a utilitarian account. This is guilt by association—in each direction.) Often, governmental, business, and other large-scale action is concerned with such deontological considerations as duties of office, national or professional honour, prestige, and esteem, contractual arrangements, and the like—and not just well-being. And of course, when political leaders, those in business and so on, are concerned with well-being, it is usually only the well-being of those they think they have a duty to serve.

To return to the central argument, let us put aside the question of what utilitarianism and other contemporary theories can or cannot recognize. Those not caught up in these theories will find it hard not to recognize that such important objects of evaluation as a world do not fit those strange pictures of values and evaluations given above. So, Leibniz held that even the best of all possible worlds can none the less contain various miseries and disasters. So too, we can hold with Aristotle that a life can be a life of eudaimonia, perhaps even marvellous beyond all hopes and expectations, despite its containing some costs and misfortunes.

As with worlds and lives, so with acts: there is no need to confuse what is here and now best or right with what is perfectly good or wholly right. Even what is best or right can have features that are and remain bad or wrong. One can be justified in doing an act that ineliminably has a part it would be wrong to do on its own—and more importantly for us, which remains a wrong, albeit a justified wrong, when done in doing what is right.

7. MORAL EMOTIONS AND DIRTY HANDS

Moral remainders do not give the whole story of dirty hands. Double-counted impossible oughts are not only had by acts of dirty hands, they are also taken up and noted e.g. with regret. Further, acting with dirty hands is said to rob us of our innocence and to require shame and guilt. Some comments on how this is possible and, again, unproblematic will be useful. This will advance our understanding of dirty hands, and more generally of non-action-guiding act evaluations.

Once we abandon those strange pictures of value and valuation, we can see how acts which are justified or even obligatory can provide the ground of regret, shame, or guilt. (For our purposes, we need not distinguish shame and guilt.) Those acts can contain the objects of those emotions—namely the double-counted remainders. These, of course, are also the grounds of the non-action-guiding act evaluations. And here it must be remembered that those who act with dirty hands do not merely cause what is terrible. They have chosen, even if coerced, to bring about what is terrible.

Even if it is agreed that there are objects for those emotions, two reasons might be advanced to show that it is pernicious to think that those emotions could be warranted. First, it might seem that if an act merits regret, shame, or guilt, it should not be done wholeheartedly, if done at all. It would thus seem that dirty hands could be done only with vacillation and uncertainty. But if such acts are to be done, it may well be better that they be done well—i.e. resolutely and wholeheartedly.

This worry is not pointless. Some people faced with mixed considerations do vacillate. To act resolutely, they need to see an act as being of only one clear moral sort. The above strange views of value and evaluation might thus be useful for them. But other people are able to act resolutely, and in this sense wholeheartedly, even where they see moral mixtures, and in this sense are not wholehearted. They are able to form a unified view of a whole even though they still see the parts of the whole as parts.

The second charge of moral perniciousness starts from the fact that shame and guilt involve retributive negative feelings, which the agent and others can take to be deserved. These can involve the desire for atonement and cleansing, e.g. by punishment. The charge continues that just as it would be immoral to exact judicial punishment on agents of dirty acts—after all, they are doing what is right, even obligatory—so it is a moral error for anyone including the agents themselves, to think they deserve blame and other punishment. (This, of course, is not to talk about cases where the agent is culpable for having to act immorally. But, as noted above, it is unclear that these would even be cases of dirty hands.)

The reason guilt or shame would be mistaken, we are told, is that they require a connection between agents and the grounds of the guilt or shame: I cannot be ashamed of or feel guilty about something unless, as I take things, I am connected with it in such a way that it reflects poorly on me. But, as just noted, the agents we are concerned with are not culpable for the dirty part of the dirty act. Therefore, it does not reflect poorly on them. And therefore, both morally and conceptually, they cannot be ashamed of or guilty about it.

To be sure, there are forms of shame and guilt that are appropriate only if one is responsible in a full moral and causal sense for the object of shame or guilt—and thus require that one could and should have avoided doing it. And, of course, if they take note of shame and guilt at all, it is natural for those ethicists who hold that 'ought' implies 'can' and think that the main concern of ethics is duty and other action-guiding notions to focus on such shame and guilt.

None the less, there are other forms of shame and guilt which do not require culpability. So, for example, there is shame and guilt in regard to one's ancestors and in regard to one's fellow citizens, colleagues, and others with whom one identifies. So too, there is shame and guilt over what one merely brings about—e.g. the shame and guilt even a careful driver might feel over the death of a child who suddenly darts in front of the car.[11]

That people experience these other forms of shame and guilt is undeniable. Some think they are unjustifiable, however. To show this mistaken I would, following Hume, argue that one's self is at least one of the central objects of shame and guilt and that these other objects both do and must play a role in our constitution of our self, especially the self we evaluate morally. I would also argue against the contrary view of the self by showing how untenable it is to hold that the self—or more particularly, the self that is evaluated by shame and guilt—is simply a product of the person's own actions.[12]

There are, then, different sorts of guilt and shame. From the agent's own point of view, some involve feeling that one has a

[11] See H. Morris, *On Guilt and Innocence* (Berkeley: University of California Press, 1976); R. M. Adams, 'Involuntary Sins', *Philosophical Review*, 94 (1985), 3–31; and Bishop, 'Connections and Guilt'.

[12] On this, see Merleau-Ponty, *Humanism and Terror*, and J.-P. Sartre, *Being and Nothingness* (New York: Philosophical Library, 1956) and *Anti-Semite and Jew* (New York: Schoken Books, 1965).

defect and some involve feeling oneself defective. Some, that is, involve hating the sin and some hating the sinner. Still others involve feeling that one has been violated, compromised, dirtied. We need hardly wonder how and with what justification people feel violated, compromised, and dirtied if they have been coerced into helping implement another's immoral project. We might well wonder how else they should feel. Should they be indifferent? Or should they simply be pleased because they did what was morally required?

Let us now turn to third person judgements. There are various ways we regard other people who have done what merits shame or guilt. Some, of course, we blame in a fully retributive way, thinking they deserve condemnation and punishment. Some we only pity and some we admire for how they bear their moral burdens, such as being immorally coerced to help implement another's evil project. Even, indeed especially, in this last case we can feel fortunate to have been spared their moral burden of guilt and shame and also, at least as importantly, their moral burden of having done what occasions and justifies their guilt and shame.

Thus, there need be no conceptual or moral error in thinking that even though agents of dirty hands are morally unable to avoid the dirty act, they can and should feel guilty and ashamed for doing it. Nor need there be any error in thinking that they can or should feel the need for atonement and cleansing, e.g. by punishment. Not all sorts of guilt and shame require culpability, and one and the same thing can be a punishment or a cure. Thus, we must reject those views which find shame and guilt over dirty hands conceptually or morally incoherent.

But even if recognized as coherent, it is asked why these emotions should be had. The issues here are complex. But a brief reply should be useful. These emotions are important, and indeed morally important, for the reasons it is important for people to have the correct emotions: because they are central and essential constituents of human life.

As Aristotle stressed, a good life requires one to act well and also to have the right emotions. We can reinforce this by noting what so many ethicists now seem to have forgotten: a life without emotions would be at best a pathologically deficient life—perhaps

the life of a severe schizophrenic, psychopath, or sociopath.[13]
Emotions are not simply part of the phenomenology of morality,
much less its epiphenomenology. They are at the heart of it.

We must, then, reject the charge that guilt and shame over dirty
hands are incoherent or morally unimportant. But we should also
question the contrary claim that dirty hands must evoke guilt and
shame. For example, Walzer (section v) and others hold that those
who act with dirty hands should suffer from guilt and shame,
because their suffering shows that they are good people who know
the gravity of what they do. It is said that those who do not regret
their acts of dirty hands either do not see or do not care that they
are bad.

We must, however, at the least take into account different forms
of moral and emotional character. We should contrast the emotional
warmth Aristotle requires for good people with Stoic and Buddhist
coolness.[14] So too, we should note that some good people are
emotionally hotter and others cooler. Sometimes a strong emotion
shows care for the forgone value, and coolness shows a lack of
care. But sometimes heat is shallow and synthetic, show and
bluster, while coolness goes along with a quiet, deep appreciation
of the value. Thus, even though it is clear that some good people
show their goodness by shame and guilt over dirty hands, it is
unclear that all good people do.[15]

8. DIRTY HANDS AND ACCEPTABLE MORAL THEORIES

At the outset I claimed that double-counting and giving moral
weight to impossible oughts and allowing for non-action-guiding
act evaluations are what make dirty hands seem conceptually
problematic. I have been concerned to argue that these are not
restricted to the extreme and disquieting cases of dirty hands in
particular and conflicts more generally. They are found across the
board—in important and unimportant cases, in the centre and at
the extremes, in political and private cases. They cannot, therefore,

[13] See e.g. my 'The Schizophrenia of Modern Ethical Theories', 'Psychic Feelings:
Their Importance and Irreducibility', *Australasian Journal of Philosophy*, 61 (1983),
5–26, and 'Affectivity and Self-Concern: The Assumed Psychology in Aristotle's
Ethics', *Pacific Philosophical Quarterly*, 64 (1983), 211–29.

[14] See my 'Affectivity and Self-Concern'.

[15] My thanks are owed to David Armstrong here.

be passed off as aberrations found at the outer limits of ethical theory. Instead of being mysterious or objectionable, they are commonplace and unproblematic.

My point is not that we can show prima facie objectionable features to be unobjectionable by showing that they occur all over the place. The world can be generally objectionable. Rather it is first, that those features are clearly not objectionable where they are not conflicting; second, that I cannot see any relevant differences between those cases and those where they are conflicting.

My argument to show that dirty hands are conceptually un-problematic has focused on the similarities between them and other cases which present no conceptual problems. It will be useful to see that the same conclusion follows from focusing on three differences.

First, the loss of some values is not even regrettable. Suffering those losses is not regrettable in the circumstances or perhaps at all; and we should not spend any time regretting them. But matters are importantly different for some other losses, including those involved in dirty hands.

Second, the non-regrettable conflicts are often shown to be non-regrettable by showing that they really do not matter. From a moral perspective, they are really not important. Thus, we have an outside and a higher standpoint from which to see that they are unimportant. But we cannot have this for the conflicts of dirty hands. They are important and they are moral.

Third, it does not seem possible for finite beings to live and act without having to choose between values and thus without having to suffer losses. But it does seem possible, even if humanly very unlikely, to live and act without having to suffer the losses of dirty hands. At the least, it does seem possible, even if humanly very unlikely, that we do not create immoral situations which necessitate dirty hands.

These three differences, however, do not seem to me to show a conceptual incoherence. The first merely attests to the fact that dirty hands involve moral conflicts. The second fails to understand that no matter what level the *moral* judgement, it is none the less a moral *judgement*.

The third difference points, not to conceptual incoherence, but to the grounds for moral sadness or even outrage. It points to the fact that even good people may be unable to remain innocent and

avoid shame and guilt, and that even good people may not be able
to avoid emotional devastation—here caused by doing what is
immoral.

We must not confuse this with the possibility that even good
people, acting morally, may be unable to avoid acting evilly, in
ways meriting full retributive shame, guilt, and punishment. Having
avoided that confusion, we can recognize that even without any
shame and guilt, much less dirty hands, good people can and do
lose their innocence and wholeness and indeed suffer emotional
devastation—e.g. by their family being killed by evil people or by
a natural disaster.

The demand that it must be possible for us to be good and also
innocent, and also to retain emotional wholeness, is not a demand
for a conceptually or even a morally coherent morality. It is, rather,
a demand for something else—a morally good world or at least not
an evil or bad world.

Perhaps a moral theory which denies the possibility of dirty
hands could none the less be right about the sort of culpability that
merits retributive punishment and to this extent be right about
what is to be done. Perhaps such a moral theory could also tell us
how to live in a good world. As Ruth Marcus suggests, 'ought'
might well imply 'can' in the sort of world there ought to be.
(Putting the issue in terms of the iterability of 'ought' suggests—
correctly, I think—that dirty hands cases involve many of the issues
important to the Good Samaritan paradox.)

To be right about these matters would be to be right about much
of importance. But our moral world is not a good world. We
therefore need to know more than simply what is to be done and
how to avoid culpability. We need a moral theory that allows for and
indeed gives prominence to dirty hands and thus double-counting,
impossible oughts, and non-action-guiding act evaluations.

I will conclude with a brief comment on some aspects of the sort
of moral theory we need. One of these can be usefully presented
by taking up an objection that has been levelled against my
argument. To show the need for non-action-guiding evaluations,
I argued that in dirty hands and many other cases, it is morally
insufficient simply to do the act that is to be done—e.g. the act of
dirty hands. Rather, one should at once do it and also take it up
in certain moral-emotional ways, e.g. with regret. It has been
replied that this does not show the need for non-action-guiding

evaluations, but only that 'is to be done' is here not the action-guiding evaluation and that, e.g. 'is to be done and regretted' is.[16]

Two replies must be made here. First, if this is an action-guiding act evaluation, it shows as mistaken an important claim about such evaluations: namely that an agent's best is good enough, and that if the agent does what is to be done, there can be no criticism of the act or agent. For in the case of dirty hands, even after the regret, all is not well.

The value of the regret and the disvalue of what is regretted do not join together to make matters completely all right and beyond question. Nor do they join together in one simple whole, with one simple value. Even while seeing the value of that whole, we can see and regret the disvalue of its parts. Even if the act is justified, perhaps obligatory, and even if the violation is properly regretted, the moral violation remains a moral violation. Perfect practice can be defective.[17]

Second, 'is to be done and regretted' is not an action-guiding act evaluation. Thus, if I am right, an adequate ethical theory cannot be a theory only about action-guiding act evaluations. This is obvious if we count as such evaluations only those evaluations put forward as such by our ethical theories. For 'is to be regretted' is not one of these.

The important point here is not the historical one that 'is to be regretted' would be a new action-guiding evaluation. It is that for conceptual reasons, it is not an action-guiding evaluation. It is an evaluation of an agent, telling how a good person will appreciate the act, and an evaluation of a situation, telling us that it is regrettable. This connects with the traditional point that regret is not an activity, but a passivity or a state.[18]

Some might think this is to quibble or to give undue respect to the way our theories have understood action-guiding evaluations and that we should allow 'is to be regretted' as an act evaluation. This, however, is precisely to transcend act evaluations and theories of act evaluations. For it rejects as unimportant for ethics the foundational metaphysical distinctions among doing, being, and

---

[16] Isaac Levi, for one, raised this in discussion. See his *Hard Choices*, ch. 2, especially sect. 3.

[17] My thanks are owed to Graham Nerlich here.

[18] See e.g. R. M. Gordon, 'The Passivity of Emotions', *Philosophical Review*, 95 (1986), 371–92. See too, J. L. A. Garcia, 'The *Tunsollen*, the *Seinsollen*, and the *Soseinsollen*', *American Philosophical Quarterly*, 23 (1986), 267–76.

having, and the foundational ethical distinctions among evaluations of acts, agents, and states.

It thus rejects the very distinctions and categories that are needed to give content to the claim that an evaluation is an act evaluation or is action-guiding. Without these distinctions and categories, the terms 'act evaluation' and 'action-guiding' may be used, but only as empty honorifics.

My point here is not to endorse the use made of these distinctions and categories by our ethical theories—e.g. that there are no, or no important, conceptual connections between act and agent evaluations. On the contrary. I have argued elsewhere that if we endorse those uses, then for both conceptual and moral reasons, our ethical theories will be inadequate.[19] I of course welcome allies. But it must be recognized that in rejecting these uses, we are not on the way to a different and better account of act evaluations. We are on the way to a different and better sort of moral theory.

Our new and better theory will deny that 'ought' implies 'can' and that doing exactly what is to be done, perfect practice, must be unexceptionable. It will also give prominence to double-counting, impossible oughts, and non-action-guiding act evaluations.

[19] ' "Ought" and "Can" ' and 'Act and Agent Evaluations'.

2

Moral Immorality

IN 'Dirty Hands and Ordinary Life', and also in 'Dirty Hands and Aristotle's Ethics', and in other chapters, it is argued that immorality by either the agent or others, as well as other defects, can make conflict unavoidable. In this chapter, I want to show other ways in which a different sort of defect can also necessitate conflict. The conflict here is a conflict of virtues.

I. ADMIRABLE IMMORALITY, AN INTRODUCTION

Dirty hands show one important sort of conflict, that between an act's being right and its being, none the less, somehow wrong. Dirty hands thus show us the possibility that what is morally required may be regrettable. We might naturally wonder whether what is immoral can be welcomed. In *Goods and Virtues*,[1] Michael Slote argues that this is possible—that there can be cases of admirable immorality.

He does not argue for what he calls the strong thesis that 'immoral behaviour as such may (sometimes) be admirable' (*GV*, 79). Nor does he argue for the weak thesis that trades on the fact

that we may sometimes admire certain aspects of immoral actions or find people admirable for traits whose possession makes them more likely to act wrongly. According to this weaker thesis, we may admire a robber for his daring while deploring his criminal tendencies. But this is not something we would want to call 'admirable immorality'. For what we admire in the robber's act, the daring, can be conceptually prised apart from its

My thanks are owed to Marcia Baron, Norman Care, C. A. J. Coady, Raimond Gaita, Frank Jackson, Graeme Marshall, Justin Oakley, Michael Slote, and Robert Young, and to those commenting on versions of this work read at La Trobe University and the Australian National University.

[1] Oxford: Clarendon Press, 1983, referred to below as *GV*.

immorality . . . we can easily understand what it would be like for a
daring individual to have no tendency to exhibit that quality except in
good causes (GV, 79).

Rather, he argues that in various cases the immorality cannot
be prised apart from what is admired: the immorality here is
internal or essential to what is admired. In this chapter, I will
consider only two of his cases—that of a perhaps fictionalized
Gauguin whose admirable passion for his art was internally
connected with his immorally abandoning his family, and that of
a perhaps fictionalized Churchill, whose admirable single-minded
commitment to victory over the Nazis was internally connected
with his ordering the immoral bombing of civilian targets in German
cities.

If as Slote holds, and I agree, inseparability does figure in the
account of admirable immorality, it must be understood correctly.
After all, we can easily change the stories so that in straightforward
ways, the robbers' daring is inseparable from their immoral actions:
only when excited by illegalities and immoralities are they able
to face danger with aplomb. But this would hardly show them
admirable for their coolness and courage in their robberies.

2. OVERRIDINGNESS AND ADMIRABLE IMMORALITY

I shall argue that the inseparability found in admirable immorality
is a special sort of moral inseparability, importantly similar to the
connection between the goods and bads in dirty hands. It is in this
that I find the importance of admirable immorality.

Slote, on the other hand, thinks admirable immorality important
for another reason: it shows that '. . . we should reject the
metaethical thesis that moral considerations are always overriding'
(GV, 77). As with dirty hands, conflicts are once again taken as
showing the need to overthrow or severely limit morality. And as
with dirty hands, once again, I disagree. Such cases of admirable
immorality are ordinary moral phenomena and do not have those
severe implications for ethical theories. I will first argue that
admirable immorality does not bear against the overridingness of
moral considerations, and then show that, and how, it is an
ordinary moral phenomenon.

I do see one way that the admirable immorality of Gauguin shows that moral considerations are not always overriding. This way is a complex of holding that Gauguin had a duty to support his family; that he did not have a duty to paint, much less to abandon his family in order to paint; and that what he did was, none the less, admirable. If we hold these three views, we must also hold that violation of duty does not preclude admirability.

But there are two main sets of problems here. First, at least the usual understanding of the claim that morality is overriding is that moral considerations are decisive, e.g. over inclination, in determining what is to be done. However, admirability here concerns the agent and is an agent evaluation: Gauguin or his passion for painting is admirable. And even though there are important connections between such agent evaluations and act evaluations, they are distinct enough that what is decisive for the one need not be for the other.[2]

The second main problem is that what is here shown not decisive is morality narrowly understood—i.e. morality understood as having to do mainly, if not only, with duty. This, of course, continues the assumption that Gauguin did not have a duty to paint.

Some, of course, may dispute that assumption—holding him to have had a duty to paint, a duty owed to posterity, the world, or art itself. On this view, we would not have a case of duty clashing with other considerations, but of one duty clashing with another. And indeed, this is what we seem to have in the Churchill case: his duty not to harm innocent civilians clashing with his duty to save his country. Thus, it is difficult to see how at least the Churchill case could be taken as showing considerations of duty being over-ridden by other sorts of considerations.

However, if we do not think Gauguin had a duty to paint, we could see his case as involving a clash between duty and other considerations. And if we think his passion for painting admirable, we can see this as a case where violating a duty is admirable. But, even apart from the mixture of act and agent evaluations, the import of this is unclear. For what we seem to have is a case showing that there are other moral considerations than those of duty and that these other moral considerations are not always overridden by duty.

---

[2] See my 'Act and Agent Evaluations', *Review of Metaphysics*, 27 (1973), 42–61.

But we hardly need cases of admirable immorality to show this, even if they do show it. Almost any sort of painting comes at least close to doing this—if we accept the understandings of 'duty' offered by many of our contemporary ethical theories. According to them, it is difficult to see how painting could be justified. After all, one could instead be helping those in need. In such circumstances either painting would have to be unjustified or duty can be overridden by other moral considerations.

That considerations of duty do not always take precedence over other moral considerations is also shown by supererogation, self-regard, and friendship.[3] It is not my duty to act supererogatorily. But I may do so. If the supererogatory act includes the duty—as in going the second mile, where the first is required—I have an option either simply to do my duty or to do it and also the supererogatory (part of the) act. This is a simple option. But some supererogatory acts also create a contrary-to-duty option—a moral option not to do one's duty. For example, my running into a burning building to rescue someone can be supererogatory, even if it makes me unable to do my duty, e.g. attend a department meeting.

Self-regard also generates moral options. There are simple options where I would not violate a duty by allowing someone to take my share of some goods, even though I would be completely justified in taking my share. There are also contrary-to-duty options. It does seem a duty not to cause—perhaps not even to allow—harm to innocent others. None the less, I may have the option of saving myself from being harmed even if in saving myself I allow, or cause, harm to innocent others.

Friendship also creates options. I may well not violate a duty either by seeing or not seeing a friend. This is a simple option. But friendship also creates contrary-to-duty options (and not simply because of their self-regarding or supererogatory aspects).

Consider a case where an old friend is about to leave town for several years. It may well not be my overall duty to visit the friend.

[3] See e.g. my *Supererogation*, doctoral dissertation, Harvard University, 1966, especially ch. 6, 'Duty Precluding Supererogatory Acts', and 'Agent and Other: Against Ethical Universalism', *Australasian Journal of Philosophy*, 54 (1976), 206–20; M. Slote, 'Morality and Self–Other Asymmetry', *Journal of Philosophy*, 81 (1984), 179–92; F. M. Kamm, 'Supererogation and Obligation', *Journal of Philosophy*, 82 (1985), 118–38; and S. Wolf, 'Above and Below the Line of Duty', *Philosophical Topics*, 14 (1986), 131–48.

Speaking on the phone might be sufficient. Or if I really should make the visit, I may do nothing wrong by staying for only a short while. None the less, I do not think it excessively lax to hold that it can be all right to stay the entire afternoon, even if this involves not doing what is my duty, e.g. attending the department meeting.

Some who agree that it is all right to do these other acts deny that they involve contrary-to-duty options. They deny that in these circumstances we may justifiably not do our duty, holding rather that these are cases where it is all right not to do what, but for those other considerations, would be our duty. However, this disagreement is far less important than what we agree about: that considerations of duty are not always decisive.

My conclusion, then, is that for reasons independent of admirable immorality we must reject the view that considerations of duty are the only moral considerations or are always decisive. Suppose then that we give up those views and recognize that painting has immense value—both aesthetic value and the more general value of good human activity. The question now would be which values are here more important—those connected with Gauguin's painting, or those connected with his family.

Even if we think that overall he did the right thing, we could still think of his course of action as immoral in the way that acts of dirty hands are at once immoral and justified: the immoral part of the justified whole is a remainder which is properly taken up in certain moral-emotional ways.

Perhaps, however, abandoning his family was unjustified even on the broader understanding of morality. Even so, we might admire his not giving up his painting. This would be to admire what is immoral. We could reverse the structure of dirty hands and hold that the Gauguin case involves a whole which is immoral but which contains an admirable remainder. Structurally, this is common enough. So, we can admire one part of a plan or political platform that overall is bad.

3. OVERVALUING AND ADMIRABILITY

To see the importance of the similarities between admirable immorality and dirty hands, let us start by considering over-valuing—being overcommitted to—a value or principle. To do this, it will help to assume that there is a proper or ideal range of commitment to values and principles and that anyone whose commitment falls in that range is, to that extent, a good person.

What then of someone whose valuing falls outside that range? Some overvaluings may, of course, be supererogatory or otherwise permitted. But at least some will be immoral. And some of these will be immoral because they involve undervaluing other values or principles. So, it is possible to overvalue promise-keeping, with a concomitant undervaluing of harm. Here promises which are so harmful that they really ought not be kept are kept, and people who, properly, do not keep promises to avoid such harm, are condemned as morally lax or corrupt.

Even where overvaluing involves immoral undervaluing, it can be admirable. Again, we can consider those who take certain of their duties too seriously. As I believe is clear, we can think well of such overvaluers—and think well not only of them, but of them for their moral excesses. Just as we may turn to someone who overvalues Wagner to learn what is valuable and important about his music, overvaluers in ethics may show us what is valuable about their favoured goods.

My claim, of course, is not that overvaluing is always admirable, but that it can be admirable. Whether it is, seems to be dependent on the following: (1) The reasonableness of overvaluing that value—e.g. whether the overvalued value is relatively unimportant, like etiquette, or very important, like freedom or equality. (2) The reasonableness of thinking that the overvalued value will be satisfied. So, we might distinguish between Gauguin overvaluing his art and novice artists overvaluing theirs. (3) Why the person overvalues. The person might be young and thus naturally over-enthusiastic, as Aristotle suggests concerning young men who overvalue honour. Or the person might be neurotically frightened of a contrary value—as a person might be of sexual intimacy and thus overvalue purity. Or the person might be a true believer or enthusiast who simply overvalues now one and now another value.

4. THE UNAVOIDABLE EVILS IN ADMIRABLE IMMORALITY

Perhaps, then, the Gauguin and Churchill cases do involve over-valuing certain values and a correlative undervaluing of others.

But this is hardly sufficient for understanding these cases of admirable immorality. To show this, it will be necessary to take up some other topics. I will focus on the Churchill case since, as noted earlier, the values it involves are uncontentiously moral ones.

Churchill's single-mindedness is said to be immoral because it was inseparably connected with the immorality of bombing civilians. Two distinguishable things are here said to be immoral: Churchill's bombing the civilians and his trait of single-mindedness. They are also said to be admirable because they are part of, even necessary to, the best Churchill could do or be.

Even those who deny that 'ought' implies 'can' may have trouble with allowing that his bombing the civilians and his trait of single-mindedness were necessary for the best he could do but are none the less also immoral. For this holds not only that a person's best may not be good enough, but that it may be immoral. I will here be concerned to dispel that worry.

In the discussions of dirty hands, I showed how acts which are immoral can be permitted or even obligatory. One of the most important explanations of this possibility is that acting in immoral circumstances can make the immorality necessary. But Churchill was clearly acting in immoral circumstances—circumstances so immoral as to warrant even the strongest action.

However, that is a description of the conditions for dirty hands. And in acting with dirty hands, one need not have a discreditable character or trait. To be sure, we often have serious moral worries about those who commit acts of dirty hands. But rather than think poorly of such people, we may pity or admire them.[4]

So, the fact that Churchill did such terrible acts in such a situation cannot give us the entire account of why or how his character is flawed. Whether it is even part of that account is a difficult issue. Perhaps acting in such a situation is relevant only to his single-mindedness being admirable despite its immoral flaw. Perhaps such a character with such a flaw could not even be tolerated, much less found admirable, except in a fight against monstrous immorality.

We need not pursue this issue. For we have independent, even if related, reasons for holding that Churchill's character was flawed,

[4] My thanks are owed to Raimond Gaita for urging in discussion and in unpublished material the importance of such pity. See his ' "Better One than Ten" ', *Philosophical Investigations*, 5 (1982), 87–105.

despite the fact that the flaw was an essential part of the character he needed in order to achieve the great and admirable good he did achieve. This account focuses on the fact that another person or at least an ideal agent could have saved England but without doing those immoral acts.

By not having to focus just on Churchill, we are spared from investigating the very difficult relations between acts and traits. In particular we do not have to reconcile two claims which are each plausible but in severe tension. The first is that traits are neither necessary nor sufficient for acts which express them—and thus that on at least many occasions, even if only by fighting against his single-mindedness, Churchill could have acted with a wider-ranging concern without impairing his effectiveness in prosecuting the war.[5] The second is that traits are not mere summaries of how a person acts, thinks, and so on, but rather have some sort of explanatory force—and thus that we have no reason to think realistic a claim that Churchill could have acted more morally without acting less effectively.

To see that in evaluating an agent we do not rest with an examination of what just that agent could have done, let us start with a technique closely allied to morality. In judging whether a doctor performed an operation poorly, we do not ask only whether that particular doctor could have done better. We also ask whether good, or perhaps ideal, doctors would perform it that way. The comparison class is composed, albeit in unclear ways, of good doctors as they are at the time of operation and good doctors as we imagine they could and should be.

It may well be that no doctors will ever be as we imagine they could and should be. None the less, in forming our comparison class, we are not free to ignore all reality constraints. So, we do not consider the Perfect Doctor who can cure, or better yet prevent, any and all ailments simply by wishing or by the laying on of hands. One conservative suggestion is that we judge our present medical practice and practitioners in the light of realistically

---

[5] This seems the gravamen of one part of Owen Flanagan's claim that there are no admirable but immoral traits, in his 'Admirable Immorality and Admirable Imperfection', *Journal of Philosophy*, 83 (1986), 41–60. As I trust has been shown in this and other chapters, there is little reason to accept another of his claims about admirable immorality—that it shows and depends on irresoluble conflicts of values, much less of incommensurable values.

envisaged progress—e.g. in the light of our reasonable expectations about the next generation of medicine and doctors.

This, I think, is borne out by the fact that it is now a matter of keen regret if our loved ones recently suffered or died from diseases for which there are now cures. And no matter how good the medical practice and practitioners were then, that they lacked the cure for those diseases limits how well we do and can think of them. But diseases we think medical science will, despite its best efforts, still be unable to deal with for generations to come are, I suggest, more likely to be seen as merely unfortunate natural facts.

Let us now turn from medical to moral judgements. Here too, we use the test of what a better person could have done. Suppose I am concerned about the pain I caused when I ended a friendship. If I think that even a far more sensitive person would have ended the relationship and in much the same way, then I can think well, or at least not poorly, of how I acted. But if I think that someone with only a bit more sense than I then had could have handled matters far better than I did, then I can think poorly of what I did and of myself. This is so even if I was then doing the best I could and I was in no way culpable for being unable to do better.

As in the medical case, we must have a reasonable ideal in the light of which to make judgements. It is one thing to base the criticism on an attainable, or at least an approachable, ideal or exemplar. It is another to base it on e.g. an all-loving, all-powerful, and all-knowing God.

The reality constraints relevant to the Churchill case force us to consider what was possible, including importantly what was politically possible. Had it been possible for nearly anyone who could there and then have attained political power to achieve the good Churchill did while avoiding his wrongs, Churchill and his trait might well have been seen as primitive and simply deplorable. To this extent, Churchill's being, for all practical purposes, the only person who could have achieved what he did achieve is important for his being admirable.

None the less, even if he was, or was reasonably believed to be, the best then and there available, we can readily imagine a significantly better political leader—an exemplary political leader, who could have achieved the proper goals in a proper way. Of course, instead of being able to imagine these things, we may only be able to imagine that we can imagine them. We may be so unable to fill out the details of the cases, that it may well be only in a manner of speaking that we can imagine someone being as effective as Churchill without his defects.

This manner of speaking might be understood as a reflection, perhaps also an unarticulated justification, of the transformation of a harm into a wrong. As Sartre puts the point, only what can be seen as eliminable can be seen as wrong. What is seen as unalterable is seen as natural and at worst lamentable. Thus, our ability to see something as a defect, as wrong or immoral, is intimately connected with our ability to imagine someone sufficiently like the person with the defect not doing the harm or not having the trait.

These points can be illustrated in a familiar and unfraught area: judging philosophers. We criticize even the best and most illuminating historians of philosophy for not being better critical, inventive, and original philosophers. Similarly, we criticize powerfully original philosophers for their mistakes about history. We criticize them even if, as we believe, their philosophy is excellent and any change would involve a net loss: any gain on their weak side would involve a greater loss from their strong side. We criticize them and their work even though, as we believe, they are then and there doing the best they could do.

Indeed, we might also think that they are doing the best that anyone could do. For we might think that no one will have enough time or a combination of talents to be able to develop both of these excellences. This would be to think that these philosophical excellences are humanly incompatible. Or, we might think that creativity requires transforming, not interpreting, what others have thought. This would be to think that the incompatibility is more of a conceptual one.

If there is either sort of incompatibility, then these intellectual virtues of philosophy are not unifiable within one person. But it is unclear whether there really is such an incompatibility. We do know that at least most of us must choose whether to favour one or the other of these virtues. We know that our imperfect realizations of these virtues are not unifiable within at least most of us. But I think we know too little about human possibilities and even about the nature of philosophy to declare on whether perfect realizations of these virtues, either severally or jointly, are possible.

We are in a similar position, I suggest, in regard to Churchill's single-mindedness and his being sensitive to the interests of those caught up in his single-minded pursuit. We have good reason to believe that at least most of us must choose between single-mindedness and sensitivity. We also have good reason to believe that Churchill, too, could not realize both of these virtues to the full. But we know too little to know whether their perfect realizations are severally or jointly possible.

So far I have argued, first, that even if no one could have had a better character than Churchill, we can none the less recognize that his character was morally flawed, and second, that even though it was morally flawed, it was none the less admirable. We should now see that admirable immorality may be possible even without the strong requirement that no one could have had a better character.

Let us, first, consider the parallel in philosophy. As is obvious, many we count as admirable philosophers do not reach the highest level of perfection. Strong and original philosophers with a good eye for significant problems can be admirable even without being as strong, original, and clear-sighted as possible. So too they can be admirable even if other philosophers are still more admirable. Being good enough may well be enough. So too one can be an admirable philosopher even if one could have done or been better. Trying hard enough may well be enough.

In making these claims I recognize that it is not easy, and perhaps not even possible, to give a general characterization of how short one can fall and still be admirable. I also recognize that the parallel with the Churchill case might be disputed. For here we are concerned with immorality, not just lack of philosophical perfection. So, it might be held that necessary immorality is tolerable, perhaps even justified, but that unnecessary immorality is not. And in the relevant sense, Churchill's immoralities would not have been necessary if it had been easy to find a better leader or if he himself could have been better.

However, I think it false that only necessary immorality is tolerable. If it were, then anyone unable to do a given activity without acting immorally would be morally constrained to leave that activity to others who could do it in a morally better way. Correlatively, a person who could do it in a morally better way would be under great moral pressure to do it in place of the morally less able person. And a third party charged with choosing who is to do that activity would be under similar pressure not to choose the latter. This, however, would impose very great and ultimately unfair responsibilities on 'better agents'.

Suppose that I am less skilled than you in giving directions to subordinates, and thus that I sometimes give unjustifiable offence where you would not. On the view in question, I should leave the job to you. But you may have your own work to do, and my job may include giving those orders. Further, I might do my job well enough, notwithstanding my inabilities, for it to be justifiably my job, rather than yours or some third person's.

Allowing only the morally most able to act can, thus, impose unfairly on them. It can also unfairly deprive others—the vast majority of us—of important responsibilities and indeed of important possibilities for acting and living well. For it is almost certainly true that much of what we do could be done in morally better ways by someone else. In near enough any domain of action and living—one's job, family life, pastimes, and so on—one may well be unable to avoid certain defects that other people could avoid.

For example, a loving parent might none the less sometimes get unjustifiably, and immorally, angry at a child—where an equally loving, but somewhat calmer parent would not. But until these sorts of immoralities become very great, few conclude that the sometimes irascible parent should not have had the child or should now turn it over to someone who would be calmer.

Of course, immorality is to be deplored. And of course, sometimes one should quit, or be made to quit, the field in favour of a better person. But, in some cases where another would avoid your mistakes and immoralities, you are still entitled to pursue that activity. Further, in some cases, it would be wrong for others, or perhaps even you, to turn the activity over to someone else. This is just as well. Otherwise, we would be morally forbidden to do, or at least counselled not to do, much of what is so morally important that we do.

In this way, then, it is morally important and perhaps even morally for the best that we be allowed to do what is not morally best or perhaps not even morally good. This, if correct, shows only that even unnecessary immorality may be tolerable, or may have to be tolerated. It does not show that it, or its agents, can be admirable. But I think it clear that in some cases of unnecessary immorality, people may still be admirable. Otherwise, few if any people would be admirable parents—and so too for other tasks, statuses, and jobs.

Finally, I think it clear that the grounds of the admirability and of the immoralities can be inseparable. There is no reason to think that we can separate the character traits of the parent into those that ground admirability and those that give rise to the immoralities. Each, for example, may be the true expression of the parent's love for the child. This may therefore not be a perfect love. But it can none the less be admirable love. We might of course wish that it were better. But we might also realize that any attempt to make it better would run too great a risk of making it worse. And we might also realize that, even when judged against the better forms of love as found in better parents, this love is very good indeed.

Even if I am right about these cases, Churchill might not have been admirable if someone else, or if he, could have been better. Perhaps such grave immoralities as his can be excused as being inseparable parts of what is none the less admirable only if in the strongest of terms, they were truly unavoidable.

But then, evaluating Churchill is very difficult. There are, first of all, the difficulties in appreciating exactly what the war situation was like. Secondly, there are great difficulties in trying to formulate useful general rules about how to compare different goods and bads. We can talk easily enough—but with a corresponding lack of usefulness—about grave immoralities which could be easily avoided. But in real situations our evaluations must be pitched at a far more realistic level. We must realize that with many people, their strengths are also their weaknesses. Aristotle may be arguing for a similar claim when he writes that

he who aims at the intermediate must first depart from what is the more contrary to it . . . For of the extremes one is more erroneous, one less so; therefore, since to hit the mean is hard in the extreme, we must as a second best, as people say, take the least of the evils . . . (*NE* 2. 9, 1109a30 ff., tr. Ross).

5. CONCLUSION

We have seen that there can be various forms of admirable immorality. We have also seen that admirable immorality poses few, if any, special demands on moral theory. About all that a theory must do to allow for it is to recognize that even if we do our best, that may not be good enough. Even when we are admirable, we can be flawed even to the point of immorality. For our strengths can also be, or involve, our weaknesses.

This is to talk about us—and not about moral exemplars, e.g. Aristotelian good people or moral saints and heroes. Perhaps they could not be admirably immoral. Perhaps the possibility of admirable immorality depends on human weakness and defect. If it does, then in even more ways than discussed here, it is the agent-oriented analogue of dirty hands.

In any case, admirable immorality, like dirty hands, turns out not to be paradoxical, nor even to pose problems for ethical theory. Rather, they both show how immorality and defect can and must be allowed for in ethical theory. They show that with people, as with acts, what is good may be joined with what is bad and that even when joined with each other they each can retain their separate identities as good and bad.

3

Dirty Hands and Conflicts of Values and of Desires in Aristotle's Ethics

I WILL here argue that Aristotle explicitly allows for dirty hands and also conflicts of values and of desires—even in good people. This goes against the received view. But I will argue for my views rather than against those of others. I will take up dirty hands first, and then conflicts of values and of desires. In each case, I will start by giving a brief characterization of these issues as they arise in contemporary philosophical work and then Aristotle's treatment of them. This will involve discussing some issues in Aristotle's accounts of voluntariness, mixed acts, eudaimonia, and pleasure, and their bearing on dirty hands and conflicts of values and of desires. (I use 'eudaimonia' to avoid the difficulties with e.g. 'happiness' or 'flourishing'.)

The topics of dirty hands and conflicts of values and of desires form a natural unity at the heart of value and moral psychology, and also—or better, thus—at the heart of Aristotle's ethics. By taking dirty hands and those conflicts as serious problems for Aristotle, we will discover—not of course for the first time, but from different perspectives—some of his more penetrating ethical thoughts. We will understand those issues better by seeing what Aristotle has to say about them.

I. DIRTY HANDS: A BRIEF CHARACTERIZATION

In this section, I summarize some points made in 'Dirty Hands and Ordinary Life'. An act is one of dirty hands if (1) it is right, even

With some changes, this chapter appeared under the same title in *Pacific Philosophical Quarterly*, 67 (1986), 36–61. Versions were read at the University of Wisconsin, Madison, Oberlin College, the University of South Carolina, Columbia, and Charleston College. I am grateful to them and to Nancy Sherman for their help.

obligatory, (2) but is none the less somehow wrong, shameful, and the like.[1] So, in Walzer's case of torturing someone to compel him to reveal where his group has planted a bomb among innocent civilians, the torture can be justified, even obligatory, but none the less wrong and shameful. Dirty hands, especially because of the evaluations in (2), are said to be problematic for ethical theories.

These evaluations are not overall, action-guiding evaluations like the ones in (1), nor are they merely prima facie considerations or considerations that usually apply but in this case do not. They hold even though avoiding them would be morally worse and indeed would involve failing to do one's overall obligation. In other ways, too, dirty hands involve cases where one ought to do what morally, one cannot do. They thus give weight to impossible oughts, violating the doctrine that 'ought' implies 'can'.[2]

Further, the dirty features—the impossible oughts—are double-counted. In determining that the act is to be done, they are taken into account. They tell against that act, but not with enough force to make it overall wrong. However, by focusing on these features as dirty, they are given moral weight all over again, now on their

---

[1] See e.g. M. Merleau-Ponty, *Humanism and Terror* (Boston: Beacon Press, 1971); T. Nagel, 'War and Massacre', *Philosophy and Public Affairs*, 1 (1972), 123–44; M. Walzer, 'Political Action: The Problem of Dirty Hands', *Philosophy and Public Affairs*, 2 (1973), 160–80; R. Brandt, 'Utilitarianism and the Rules of War', *Philosophy and Public Affairs*, 1 (1972), 145–65; R. M. Hare, 'Rules of War and Moral Reasoning', *Philosophy and Public Affairs*, 1 (1972), 166–81; B. Williams, 'Ethical Consistency', and 'Consistency and Realism', *Problems of the Self* (Cambridge: Cambridge University Press, 1973); B. Williams and J. J. C. Smart, *Utilitarianism, For and Against* (Cambridge: Cambridge University Press, 1973); T. McConnell, 'Moral Dilemmas and Consistency in Ethics', *Canadian Journal of Philosophy*, 8 (1978), 269–87; R. Marcus, 'Moral Dilemmas and Ethical Consistency', *Journal of Philosophy*, 77 (1980), 121–36; P. Greenspan, 'Moral Dilemmas and Guilt', *Philosophical Studies*, 43 (1983), 117–25; P. Foot, 'Moral Realism and Moral Dilemmas', *Journal of Philosophy*, 80 (1983), 379–98; T. Hill, 'Moral Purity and the Lesser Evil', *The Monist*, 66 (1983), 213–32; S. I. Benn, 'Private and Public Morality: Clean Living and Dirty Hands', in S. I. Benn and G. F. Gaus (eds.), *Public and Private in Social Life* (London: Croom Helm, 1983); B. Barry, 'Tragic Choices', *Ethics*, 94 (1984), 303–18; A. Donagan, 'Consistency in Rationalist Moral Systems', *Journal of Philosophy*, 81 (1984), 291–309; M. Slote, 'Utilitarianism, Moral Dilemmas, and Moral Cost', *American Philosophical Quarterly*, 22 (1985), 161–8; C. Korsgaard, 'The Right to Lie: Kant on Dealing With Evil', *Philosophy and Public Affairs*, 15 (1986), 325–49; I. Levi, *Hard Choices* (Cambridge: Cambridge University Press, 1986); M. C. Nussbaum, *The Fragility of Goodness* (Cambridge: Cambridge University Press, 1986); S. Bishop, 'Connections and Guilt', *Hypatia*, 2 (1987), 7–23; and other works listed in C. Gowans (ed.), *Moral Dilemmas* (Oxford: Oxford University Press, 1987).

[2] The following discussion of these issues compresses points developed in my ' "Ought" and "Can" ', *Australasian Journal of Philosophy*, 49 (1971), 303–16.

own, and are taken as reasons against doing that act and reasons for regretting doing it. They remain dirty even though justified. For good reason, then, Bernard Williams in 'Ethical Consistency' calls them remainders (179).

Williams, Nagel, Walzer, and others hold that despite these and other problematic features, an adequate moral theory must take account of dirty hands. In large measure because of these problematic features, Brandt, Hare, and others hold that what are seen as dirty hands must be explained away—e.g. as a bad mixture of heuristics and ethics.

2. THAT ARISTOTLE ALLOWS FOR DIRTY HANDS

I will here present a third position, Aristotle's: double-counting and impossible oughts are not incoherent or conceptually problematic. Moreover, there are dirty hands and they do not show ethics to be conceptually incoherent or even problematic. Rather, they show that our lives can be morally difficult.

It has been said that Socrates, Plato, and Aristotle—as subtle and impressive as their ethical works are—see the moral world as being too simple. Perhaps as an implication of their claims of the unity of virtues, they think that there can be no cases of dirty hands and no conflicts of values. In any case, the good person will always do what is to be done and do it without anguish, trouble, doubt, and bother. 'Excellence with ease' might be thought their epigram.

Some say that our life is morally more difficult than theirs. At the least, we are less guided by our social stations than the Greeks were. It is also said that we have so many more possibilities for good or ill. If right, this might explain why they, unlike us, neither experienced nor discussed dirty hands.

But perhaps these are illusions of perspective—perhaps the past, by being past, loses its detail of complexity. After all, tragedy is the Greeks', not our, art form. Nor were they innocents about conflicting demands and loyalties—as shown by Alcibiades.

No matter—we are told that Socrates, Plato, and Aristotle did not discuss these issues. It is true that dilemmas and dirty hands do not figure in the headings of their ethical topics. But Aristotle does discuss these issues under the heading of *mixed acts* in *Nicomachean Ethics* 3. 1.

The main topic under discussion there is voluntariness, *to hekousion*. To help present his views on this, Aristotle offers three cases. The second—and nowadays, the most discussed—case is that of jettisoning cargo in a storm to save the ship. Aristotle says that 'apart from circumstances no one voluntarily throws away his property, but to save his own life and that of his shipmates any sane man would do so' (1110a9 ff.).[3] Here we have a completely justified act—an act it requires insanity not to do.

But even though it is entirely justified, there are still things to be said against it, and it is still to be regretted. So here, we have a case that is not one of dirty hands but which is like dirty hands in being overall justified, even morally obligatory, but which none the less has constituting disvalues which are double-counted. They remain as disvalues and as objects of negative emotions.

But of course, this is not a case of dirty hands. For it is not a case where what is right to do is also, somehow, immoral. And it might seem that Aristotle denies the possibility of dirty hands several lines after discussing the jettisoning, when he says

there seem to be some acts which a man cannot be compelled to do, and rather than do them he ought to submit to the most terrible death: for instance, we think it ridiculous that Alcmaeon in Euripides' play is compelled by certain threats to murder his mother! (1110a26 ff.)

If the reason this act must not be done is simply that it is immoral, Aristotle would preclude the possibility of dirty hands. Indeed, contrary to his usual sensibility, he would be making the hyper-moralistic claim that rather than do any immoral act, we must submit to anything, even the most terrible death.

But to take his claim as applying to every immoral act is to misunderstand it. To see this we must take note of why Aristotle made this claim about matricide. The matricide case follows that of jettisoning the cargo. Between the presentation of the two cases, Aristotle gives three patterns of circumstances in which acts can be done. These patterns show the sort of voluntariness of acts. And those two cases illustrate two of those patterns.

There is, first, the pattern in which it is justified to suffer 'some

---

[3] Unless otherwise noted, all references are to the *Nicomachean Ethics* and all translations are by Rackham.

disgrace [*aischron*] or pain as the price of some great and noble object'. This is the category of jettisoning the cargo. Normally—i.e. in general or in the abstract—suffering such disgrace or pain would not be justified and thus one should not do such acts. But in those circumstances—'at the actual time when they are done' (1110a13)—it can be right, indeed praiseworthy, to do particular instances of acts of those kinds (1110a20 ff.). Since they are praiseworthy, they are also voluntary (1109b31). Thus, as we see, what is important for voluntariness is not what holds normally, but what holds at 'the time of action', i.e. in regard to the particular act (1110a14).

This might suggest that Aristotle holds that there can be justifying reasons, perhaps having to do with disgrace and pain, for every sort of immoral act. But—and this is the point of his comments about Alcmaeon—some acts do not admit of justifying reasons, at least not of that sort. This is the second pattern: here the goal is not worth the disgrace or pain, or at least not the greatest disgraces, *aischista* (a22 ff.). Here suffering the disgrace or pain is also voluntary, but now blameworthy—or better, blameworthy and thus voluntary.

We could subdivide the second pattern of circumstances by focusing independently on the sort of act that is not to be done or alternatively on the 'reasons' which do not justify doing it. Focusing on the act, we could take Aristotle as making the general claim that there are no justifying reasons at all for matricide. Focusing on the reasons, we could take him as making a limited claim that the agent's pain and disgrace cannot justify matricide. The latter could allow that if, for example, one's mother were about to open the city gates to the enemy, killing her is justified, even obligatory.[4]

Now to the third pattern: '. . . in some cases again, such submission though not praised is condoned, when a man does something through fear of penalties that impose too great a strain on human nature, and that no one could endure' (a23 ff.). If this speaks only about penalties, and not what they are penalties for, there might well be penalties which could compel some instances of matricide and other acts taken up in the second pattern. (Here as throughout, I use 'compel', not where Aristotle would use '*baion*', standardly translated as 'force' or 'cause', but where he would use '*anangke*'.)

---

[4] My thanks are owed to Brian Mooney for help here.

But perhaps Aristotle holds that a person can endure just any penalty—or at least a lot more than usual—rather than do such acts. If so, he would hold that whether a person can endure a given penalty depends not only on what it is in itself but also on an evaluation of what enduring the penalty will gain. None the less, he differs from Sartre, who does hold that, since he believes that considerations can be powerful enough to compel a person to act. This is the compelling of the third pattern.

However, even if matricide can be compelled by unendurable penalties, this shows only that it can be compelled, not that it can be justified. This is the internal point of the matricide case: some acts cannot be justified. Either they cannot be justified at all or at least they cannot be justified by self-regarding reasons.

Its external point, i.e. its role in the argument, is a common Aristotelian one—refining earlier points. The jettisoning case shows that there can be reasons concerning pain and disgrace for doing what normally there is no reason for doing. The matricide case blocks what some might take the jettisoning case to suggest: that there can be such justifying reasons for every act, no matter how bad it normally is.

The jettisoning case also has internal and external points. Its internal point is to show that even though jettisoning the goods might seem not to be voluntary because normally no one would do such an act, it is voluntary since it is here and now done for justifying reasons. And this—to turn to its external point—is used to show something about an earlier 'somewhat similar' act (1110a8).

This act is the one where 'a tyrant having a man's parents and children in his power commands him to do something base [*aischron*], when if he complies their lives will be spared but if he refuses they will be put to death' (1110a6 ff.). Both because it is base and also because it is compelled by those threats, doing what the tyrant wants might naturally be thought not to be voluntarily done. (We might note that these threats are importantly self-regarding: they are directed against the agent's family, not against just something he values.)

But as the jettisoning case shows, voluntariness has to do with the particular act and its reasons. Thus, to see whether doing that base act and complying with the threats is voluntary, we have to look at it and the considerations for doing it in their full particularity.

If these considerations are reasons, the act can be voluntary. If they are good reasons, the act can be right to do.

So, we have three cases—the hostage case, the jettisoning, and Alcmaeon's matricide—which form an explanatory series. In the next section, I will discuss what sets these cases apart from each other and from other and more ordinary acts. (A topic for another work would be why so many commentators focus on the jettisoning case, neglecting the hostage and also the matricide cases.)

What is important for us here is that Aristotle's presentation and development of this explanatory series make it clear that he holds that the man in the hostage case can act, not only voluntarily, but also rightly in complying with the tyrant's threat—and indeed, I think it is suggested, only by complying.

But then, Aristotle holds that there can be good, even conclusive, reasons to do what is base. There can be acts which are right, but which none the less are base. There can be dirty hands.

It might seem that my argument for this important conclusion puts too much weight on the one sentence mentioning the hostage case. Even when we add the one sentence setting out that first pattern of circumstances—those that justify, indeed require, suffering 'some disgrace [*aischron*] or pain as the price of some great and noble object'—the case might seem too slight. Perhaps Aristotle is not saying that what the person is compelled to do is base but only what would normally be base. Here, because of the circumstances which justify or require doing it, it is not base.

My reason for taking Aristotle as saying that the act here is base and not simply that normally such acts are base has to do with features of his claims both in 3. 1 and elsewhere in the *Nicomachean Ethics*. My case also finds support in the *Eudemian Ethics* (e.g. 2. 8—see the comments on the agent's pain at 1225a17 and 24–5, in connection with a5).[5] But to avoid issues about the relations between these two works, I will consider only the *Nicomachean Ethics*.

My claim about the case discussed in 3. 1 is that the act is base. The contrary view holds that such an act would normally be base but, because of the exact nature of this act, it is not base. The issue concerns the status of the conjoint claim that such acts are base and that base acts are not to be done.

---

[5] My thanks are owed to Steven Strange for this reference and for other help.

The view opposed to mine must understand the claim in some such way as the following: (1) it is merely a rule of thumb, or (2) it has moral relevance only if the act is not special the way this one is, or (3) it has moral relevance only if there are no stronger contrary considerations. Some would add, or (4) it gives only prima facie considerations. My reason for not adding (4) is that the notion of being prima facie is indeterminate between (3), perhaps joined by (2), and an understanding that allows an overridden prima facie consideration to have some moral weight and relevance—e.g. the relevance, as Ross puts it, of compunction.[6]

Now Aristotle clearly holds that in this case baseness is not decisive. The act is right and it, or the agent for doing it, can be wholly praiseworthy—i.e. praiseworthy and in no way blame-worthy. We should expect this. For the agent in the hostage case may well be acting from a wholly good character—one that is in no way bad. The badness of the act stems from the circumstances, not the agent's character. In so far as Aristotle's is an ethics of character primarily and of acts secondarily, this has primary importance.

But our issue does not concern the decisiveness of baseness in this case. It concerns its relevance. Aristotle does not say that it is irrelevant for this act. In fact, what he says tells strongly for its relevance.

He says that mixed acts 'approximate rather to the voluntary class' (1110a12) and not that they simply are voluntary. If there were reasons only for doing the act and none against doing it, it would presumably be simply voluntary. To be mixed, there must be reasons both for and also against doing it. The mixture is a mixture of reasons—for and against.

Further, the reasons against doing it must be non-decisive. The major reason against doing the act is that what is to be done is base. (I will here ignore what would only aid my case—the baseness of complying or having to comply with threats.) But to hold that baseness here provides such a reason is to hold that what is normally the case—this sort of act is base and base acts ought not be done—is morally relevant even for this non-normal act.

The difference between the normal case and this one, then, is not that baseness has moral relevance only in the normal case but

[6] *The Right and the Good* (Oxford: Oxford University Press, 1963), 28.

not in this case. On the contrary, it has to do with the different sorts of moral relevance of baseness in the two cases. In both cases it is relevant. Normally it is decisive. Here it is not.

In what follows, I will develop the sort of relevance it has for this act. This will show how, although the act is justified and perhaps required, it is also base and a ground for regret.

3. EUDAIMONIA: THE IMPLICATIONS OF MIXED ACTIONS

It is important to see how Aristotle allows for dirty hands and the implications of this. This is important in itself and also for the way it helps us see that he allows for dirty hands.

In 3. 1 Aristotle gives two clear cases of mixed acts: the base act and jettisoning the goods. Below, I will explain why Alcmaeon's matricide is, at the least, not clearly a mixed act. The clear cases raise two important questions about their distinguishing features. What distinguishes each from the other? What distinguishes them from non-mixed acts? To answer these questions—and thus to understand Aristotle on dirty hands—we must take up some issues concerning eudaimonia and action.

Let us start with the second question: what distinguishes mixed acts from other sorts? The answer to what makes those two cases mixed acts seems simple: as Aristotle says, apart from the circumstances no one would do them.

But rather than solving our problem, it seems instead to pose another one. This other one arises from Aristotle's division of acts that are worth doing into those that are worth doing for their own sake, those that are worth doing both for their own sake and for the sake of something else, and those that are worth doing only for the sake of something else. Acts of the second sort are at once means and ends. Those of the last sort are what I shall call mere means. (Sometimes this division is better put in terms of different acts and sometimes in terms of aspects of one and the same act.)

Our problem concerns mere means—and perhaps also acts that are both means and ends. The problem comes from the conjunction of what is true by definition of mere means and two obvious facts. By definition, if mere means are worth doing, this is due to their ends. One obvious fact is that at least most of our worthwhile goals cannot be achieved except by the use of mere means. The other is that at least most of our goals are achieved by means, and thus at least most of our acts involve means.

But then, at least many of our ordinary and worthwhile acts are mixed acts. For they involve mere means—doing what, apart from the circumstances, no one would do.

I think we must accept this or show a difference between these ordinary cases involving mere means and Aristotle's mixed acts. Showing this difference will also help us understand Aristotle's view of dirty hands, and of conflicts both of values and of desires.

To give the discussion a focus, let us take as an example of mere means the ship's captain paying the crew. I think we can assume that this is not something the captain enjoys or sees good in itself. In straightforward economic terms, it is a loss. It goes on the debit side of the ledger. This is not to require that the captain is insensible to the welfare of the crew, taken as good in itself, but only that this act involves aspects which are losses, and thus are, in this sense, mere means.

My question is why Aristotle did not seem even to notice this cost, much less put it forward as a case of mixed action, whereas he did mention throwing the goods overboard. Before answering for Aristotle, let us briefly mention some ways we might explain why jettisoning the cargo, but not paying the crew, is seen as raising issues about voluntariness.

One reason is that crew costs are normal parts of trading. So, we might expect them to be noted as problematic at a time of changing from using slave labour to hired hands, and jettisoning the goods not to be noted as problematic if that is an everyday occurrence. But the unusual is not usually thought of as an important moral category.

Further its role as an explanatory category is unclear. Some usual costs do get noted and are thought of as raising serious questions of voluntariness—e.g. some taxes that we have always had, especially if they are seen as unfair or immoral. (This, of course, has special relevance to the base act.) But only some immoralities are noted. Someone who for years has had to pay off the local politician to keep in business may now not notice this at all, or see it simply as a normal operating cost.

Even where the cost of something is seen as fair, having to pay it might still stand out as a remainder. So, you might be willing to pay a crew member for painting the boat. But if your child paints it and then asks for the wages, that may rankle.

Perhaps we would differentiate between paying the crew and jettisoning the cargo on the grounds that the former does not go against the point of the enterprise, whereas jettisoning the goods does. As T. H. Irwin puts it, mixed acts involve someone being 'compelled to choose rationally actions that are against his rational plan'.[7] He goes on to say

The contradiction here is only apparent. The captain's rational plans include delivering his cargo, not abandoning it; but if he is to be a rational planner at all, he must survive, and to do that he must violate part of his rational plan and do what is needed to stay alive. . . . staying alive is necessary for any rational plans at all (136–7).

This suggests, however, contrary to what the second pattern shows, that Aristotle holds that saving one's life is always justified. Further, even were Irwin correct, his account of mixed acts would, rather than answer our question about their nature, seem to raise a new question about the nature of acts in general: what is the proper size, and what are the identity conditions, of acts and rational plans?[8]

What I mean is this: looked at on a small scale, the rational plan of the captain on pay-day is to pay the crew. Considered in regard to the goal and the attendant rational plan the captain can then be imagined to have—namely, to be wealthy, to keep his money—this is irrational. Considered simply as a paying of the crew or as a diminution of funds, no one would choose to pay the crew. But, of course, it is chosen in the circumstances— circumstances apart from which no one would choose to do it: a crew is needed for a trading voyage, one cannot get a crew except by paying them. So, obviously, it is rational to pay the crew from the larger perspective of conducting a successful trading voyage.

But jettisoning the goods also can be seen in regard to different perspectives—different sized rational plans. From the point of view delimited by the time of the storm, throwing the goods overboard

---

[7] 'Reason and Responsibility in Aristotle', in A. O. Rorty (ed.), *Essays on Aristotle's Ethics*, (Berkeley: University of California Press, 1980), 136–71, 136.

[8] See e.g. D. Charles, *Aristotle's Philosophy of Action* (London: Duckworth, 1984) and 'Aristotle: Ontology and Moral Reasoning', *Oxford Studies in Ancient Philosophy* (Oxford: Oxford University Press, 1986); and C. Freeland, 'Aristotelian Actions', *Nous*, 19 (1985), 397–414.

is not economically rational. Even expanding the point of view to the whole of the trading voyage, it is not economically rational. But, to go beyond Aristotle's description, from the point of view of conducting a successful trading enterprise, extending over several voyages, it is economically rational. Jettisoning the cargo then and there saves the ship and crew, making it possible to recoup those losses in later voyages and come out ahead.

Some would use these points to suggest that we should see mixed acts as showing that there are many ways to describe acts. Given one description, an act has certain goals, which in turn determine whether and how that act is rational. But given another description, that act must be seen as having other goals and it must therefore be rational or irrational for different reasons.

However, this is distinctly non-Aristotelian, indeed anti-Aristotelian, in one vital way. It fails to accord to eudaimonia its paramount architectonic role: eudaimonia is the ultimate goal of every act. No matter how rational an act may be in regard to some other goal, if it is not rational in regard to eudaimonia, it is not rational. And no matter how irrational an act is in regard to another goal, if it is rational in regard to eudaimonia, it is rational. In regard to the way it determines rationality, then, eudaimonia is not simply one goal among many, it is *the* goal.

I will use this to explain how complying with the tyrant's threats and jettisoning the goods are mixed. Again, I will be concerned to show both what distinguishes them from each other and what distinguishes them from other acts which also involve means, even mere means. To do this, some brief comments on eudaimonia are needed.

Eudaimonia is a human good. Better put, it is *the* human good. Here I will focus on its being good for humans. We can leave aside the frequently discussed—and notorious or at least difficult—claim that what is good for humans must have to do with what is peculiar to humans. For what is now important for us is another—infrequently discussed but still difficult—point intended by calling eudaimonia good for humans. This is that eudaimonia 'is a good within human reach' (1. 6, 1097a34).

To recast what was said earlier, it is an obvious fact that it is not within human reach to achieve goals without means, nor without means which are merely means. Neither is it within human reach to achieve eudaimonia without these means. Of course, on

Aristotle's view some means—e.g. some ways of gaining one's livelihood—do preclude eudaimonia. But this is because of the particular nature of those means, not their simply being means. Using means, even mere means, is as such no bar to eudaimonia and does not raise issues about voluntariness.

Were this not so, then because of the need for means including mere means, eudaimonia would be outside the realm of the humanly attainable. Perhaps it would be in the realm of the divine, where wishing or willing makes it so. This is the realm that Sartre, as so often making an Aristotelian point, calls the magical.

This issue is important enough to put in a related way. Aristotle requires that eudaimonia be good both unconditionally and finally. In 'Aristotle and Kant on the Source of Value', Christine M. Korsgaard argues from this that the practical virtues and their exercise are not constitutive of eudaimonia. Their goodness is not, as required, unconditional. It is, instead, conditional—and on defects. For example, courageously saving one's city is not so much, itself, a good as a prevention of what is bad. Nor is their goodness final. So, a courageous act is done to secure something else that is good, e.g. peace and safety. Thus, it cannot have final goodness. Other practical virtues also help us deal with defects and are aimed at the elimination of those and the creation of something else of value. Thus, the practical virtues cannot be constitutive of eudaimonia, nor can a practical life, as such, be eudaimon. Only a contemplative life could be eudaimon.[9]

This argument goes wrong in much the same way as it is mistaken to think that mere means must preclude eudaimonia. The 'defects' dealt with by the practical virtues are essential to human, especially social and political, life. Like mere means, which may also be seen as defects, they are necessary for human life. Our life is not found or perfected in a condition where those defects have been eliminated. Our life is found and perfected in dealing well with those defects. Dealing well with them is what we do: i.e. it is an activity, *energeia*, not a process, *kinesis*. Indeed, it is one of the most important human activities. To engage in those activities is to be human—and to engage in them well is to be a good human. This is to say that these defects help constitute the human condition—

---

[9] *Ethics*, 96 (1986), 486–505. See also *Principia Ethica*, sect. 132; and J. M. Cooper, 'Contemplation and Happiness: A Reconsideration', *Synthese*, 72 (1987), 187–216.

where 'the human condition' is definitive of what it is to be a good person and thus what it is to be a person. Beings who do not suffer those defects are not political beings needing political life to achieve their true being. They are not humans, but perhaps gods.

The practical virtues are thus not conditionally good in a way which rules them out as constitutive of human eudaimonia—e.g. in the way that Aristotle in the *Politics* (7. 13, 1332a12 ff.) says justified punishments are only conditionally good. Indeed, he immediately goes on to contrast such conditional goods with practical virtuous acts, which Korsgaard says are only conditionally good, holding that 'actions which aim at honour and advantage are absolutely [*not conditionally*] the best' (tr. Jowett) and can help constitute eudaimonia.

Let us now focus more directly on mixed acts. My account of mixed acts—both what distinguishes the two from each other and what distinguishes them from acts which involve ordinary mere means—can be put as follows: what makes mixed acts mixed has to do with how they stand to eudaimonia. They tell against eudaimonia, even though morally they must be done. What distinguishes them from each other is how they tell against eudaimonia.

We can start by noting that eudaimonia constitutively involves certain things. Some it constitutively includes, such as 'wisdom, sight, and certain pleasures and honours' (1. 6, 1096b17 ff.). Others, it constitutively excludes, such as a loss, or even a mere lack, of honour. As well, eudaimonia includes and excludes certain things externally.[10] These are importantly the possession or the lack of material goods, peace, friends, and family.

The differential bearing of these on mixed acts can be found in Aristotle's claim that a person who has eudaimonia

will not be dislodged from his eudaimonia easily, nor by ordinary misfortunes, but only by severe and frequent disasters, nor will he recover from such disasters and become eudaimon again quickly, but only, if at all, after a long term of years, in which he has had time to compass high distinctions and achievements. (1. 10, 1101a10 ff.)

This gives us the material for making the distinction between our mixed acts and the ordinary sorts of acts which involve mere

[10] See e.g. J. M. Cooper, 'Aristotle on the Goods of Fortune', *Philosophical Review*, 94 (1985), 173–96.

means. For if even misfortunes, provided they are ordinary ones, do not preclude eudaimonia, the costs of usual mere means could hardly preclude it.

But, as noted, severe and frequent disasters—those that cause or constitute 'misery and misfortune' (1. 5, 1096a2)—can make it difficult, if not impossible, to get or maintain eudaimonia. Priam is naturally mentioned here (1. 9–10). He lost all material goods. Far more importantly, his family was destroyed and, worse, dishonoured. Further, he had to abase himself to Achilles to get Hector's body for burial.

Base deeds are among those severe disasters that can make eudaimonia difficult if not impossible. This is obvious in the case where there is no good reason for doing what is base. For only an evil or bad person could act that way, and such a person cannot have eudaimonia.

But it also holds, I suggest, where a good person is morally compelled to do what is base. We can be helped in seeing why this is so by noting these points. Aristotle's ethics is importantly one of achievement. On his view, to be a eudaimon person, and in this sense a good person, one must have honour, pride, and self-esteem, which, in turn, require doing well at good and important activities (e.g. 4. 2–4, and *Rhetoric* 2. 2). Thus, again on his view, one cannot have eudaimonia, if one does what is base—even if one does it for the best.

In the *Politics*, Aristotle writes that '. . . he who violates the law can never recover by any success, however great, what he has already lost in departing from excellence' (7. 3, 1325b6 ff., tr. Jowett). But he here seems to be talking about a person who violates the law for no good reason. If so, Aristotle can consistently also hold that doing what is base, at least when that is for the best, is not an absolute bar to eudaimonia. One swallow does not make a summer. Perhaps, as with other disasters, even after the disaster of doing what is base, it is possible to 'recover after a long term of years . . . compass[ing] high distinctions and achievements'. None the less, doing what is base can still tell constitutively, severely, and often decisively, against eudaimonia.

Loss of material goods does not, as such, preclude eudaimonia. But, eudaimonia does require an adequate supply of external goods (1. 8, 4. 1, and *Politics* 1, *passim*). Having too few of them, and thus losing too many of them, endangers and may preclude eudaimonia.

In summary, then, our two mixed acts differ from each other in the way they tell against eudaimonia. One does so constitutively, the other externally. They differ from ordinary justified, even required, acts involving mere means because only they tell against eudaimonia. The distinction can be put this way: Mere means are such that, apart from the circumstances, one could not infer that they would be in a eudaimon life. But what make mixed acts mixed are such that, apart from the circumstances, one could infer that they would not be in a eudaimon life.[11]

It must be emphasized that my concern with mixed acts has not been with them, as such, but with them—and especially the tyrant case—as a way of showing that Aristotle allows for dirty hands. Our two mixed acts are both justified even though they tell against eudaimonia and this is what is important about them. But I have not been concerned to argue that those conditions are necessary or sufficient for being a mixed act. I will conclude this section with some considerations that would have to be examined to see whether they are necessary or sufficient.

In regard to their being necessary: they preclude any eudaimonic act from being mixed, even if it includes a bad feature; and they preclude all unjustified acts from being mixed.

The latter, however, was not why I said that Alcmaeon's matricide is not a mixed act. Nor was my reason that there were reasons only against the matricide. After all, his act, like almost every act that should not be done, has something to be said for doing it. My reason is that his reasons were ridiculous. They are thus like mere costs in not making the act mixed.

In regard to their being sufficient: we will have to accept as mixed a whole range of *faute de mieux* acts and lives. For example, the acts and lives of those who voluntarily or out of necessity gain their livelihood in ways which are demeaning enough to preclude eudaimonia, but not so demeaning as to be unjustifiable, making death preferable. (If these are mixed, Aristotle's understanding of voluntariness opens the way for a powerful social critique.)

Whether necessary or sufficient, however, that characterization of mixed acts in terms of being justified despite telling against eudaimonia shows that Aristotle allows for dirty hands.

[11] So Eugene Garver suggested putting the distinction.

4. ACTING *FOR* EUDAIMONIA AND FOR *EUDAIMONIA*

My claim that mixed acts tell against eudaimonia might seem to run into difficulties with the very argument used to establish it. For I held both that mixed acts tell against eudaimonia and also that an act is rational if done for eudaimonia and irrational if done against eudaimonia. I might thus seem committed to holding that mixed acts are irrational or done in ignorance. Irrational, because they tell against eudaimonia. Or if that is not seen, then done in ignorance. But Aristotle clearly allows that mixed acts can be rational and done in full knowledge.

To save my claim, some comments are needed on what it is to act for eudaimonia. This will involve comments both on what it is to act *for* eudaimonia and also on what it is to act for *eudaimonia*. As we will see, these involve important and difficult issues. For our purposes, however, it need only be shown that these are general issues for Aristotle, not ones arising just from mixed acts or my account of them, and also that these issues are neutral to my account.

FOR eudaimonia. This is the question of in what ways, or even whether, Aristotle is a teleologist. I have discussed some of the complexities of this elsewhere, so I can be brief here.[12] In doing a mixed act the agent, unless ignorant, should believe that doing it will harm, perhaps preclude, the chances of getting eudaimonia. But it is a principle of teleological rationality that one acts rationally in doing a given act to achieve a given goal only if one believes something like 'my doing that act will improve, or at least not lessen, the chances of getting that goal'.

Now, it certainly seems that Aristotle holds that rational action must be teleologically rational. From the opening lines of the *Nicomachean Ethics*, we read that action is for the sake of a good, and we are soon told that, to be rational, our acts must be done for eudaimonia. This, of course, reports how the standard English translations put Aristotle. The connectives translated by 'for the sake of' or simply 'for' are, at least typically, '*dia*' and '*heneka*'. According to Aristotle, agents act *dia* or *heneka* eudaimonia and this is necessary for rational action. So it might seem that to deny

---

[12] 'Values and Purposes: The Limits of Teleology and the Ends of Friendship', *Journal of Philosophy*, 78 (1981), 747–65.

that Aristotle espouses teleological rationality, I must contest that translation.

The Greek would allow it to be contested. Both '*dia*' and '*heneka*' can be translated by 'on account of' or 'because of', as well as by 'for' and 'for the sake of'. Thus, where Aristotle writes that action is *dia/heneka* eudaimonia, the Greek allows him to be taken as holding that action is for eudaimonia or as holding that action is done on account of or because of eudaimonia.[13] What the difference is can be brought out in a way that also shows that the problem is not how to translate, but how to interpret, '*dia*' and '*heneka*'.

We can see this by seeing that 'for' and 'for the sake of' need not be understood teleologically. So, parents may plead with a young child, 'Do this for our sake.' They can be taken as inviting the child to obey them, simply as such, rather than as presenting a goal to be achieved. But, perhaps such a goal may be presented—namely, pleasing the parents.

Since that use of 'for the sake of' is ambiguous, we would do better to consider believers' claims that they are acting for God's sake, e.g. because God is so good, deserves our obedience and respect, and the like. Here, there is an ideal to be respected or served, rather than a goal to be achieved. Of course, we could say that there is a goal to be achieved, e.g. obeying God or showing respect. But instead of rescuing teleology, this shows that even talk of goals need not be teleological.[14]

My suggestion is that eudaimonia need not serve as a teleological goal, but can serve as an ideal to be respected even by acts which, as the agent sees, will not help achieve it. Correlatively, its absence can serve as a proper object of disrespect. (What these are like is indicated in my comments on acting *dia/heneka* courage, below.)

This suggestion is not motivated simply, or even importantly, by an attempt to accommodate my account of mixed acts. We will see an easier way to do that. Rather, for quite general reasons, it often seems better to translate Aristotle's uses of '*dia*' and '*heneka*' non-teleologically. This can be brought out by looking at his claim

[13] See T. Penner, 'Verbs and the Identity of Actions: A Philosophical Exercise in the Interpretation of Aristotle', in O. P. Wood and G. Pitcher (eds.), *Ryle: A Collection of Critical Essays* (London: Macmillan, 1970), with special attention to his comments on goals, e.g. nn. 7, 29, and 38.

[14] A strictly similar issue is discussed in my 'Rightness and Goodness: Is There a Difference?', *American Philosophical Quarterly*, 10 (1973), 87–98. My thanks are owed to Peter Herbst for discussions of these issues in regard to Aristotle.

that acting virtuously involves acting *dia/heneka* the relevant virtue or even *dia/heneka* virtue in general, i.e. nobility, or *dia/heneka* eudaimonia.

Let us consider acting courageously in defence of and for the sake of one's city. In so far as this is understood teleologically—as being done for the sake of courage, virtue, or eudaimonia—it too easily seems an instance of posturing, self-indulgence, preciousness, self-servingness, or something else of similar unattractiveness. (I pass over the not unattractive, but also constitutively unimportant, activity of getting and keeping the virtue.)

But we can understand it non-teleologically: the courageous act is done for the city and from and with courage. Courageous action here would not be for courage, but would be guided by its canons and criteria. It would be done from an appreciation of what courage involves, why one should act courageously, why courage is here and now called for, and so on.

Eudaimonia is not left out of this account. For on Aristotle's view, eudaimonia is what is good for a person and a person's conception of what is good and proper is importantly that person's conception of eudaimonia.

This does not deny the important Aristotelian connections between acting for and acting from. Nor does it deny that in some cases Aristotle clearly holds that we do seek to get eudaimonia and that this is essential for rational action. Rather, it denies only that he holds that this is always necessary for rational action.

Further, in denying that he is a thoroughgoing teleologist, especially because he does not always require teleological rationality, I am denying only that he is a teleologist in the way we understand teleology. Our understanding of it, but not his, is in terms of an agent's intentions, purposes, and goals—where these are understood in the light of our, not his, psychological theories. For us, but not him, a purpose requires a purposer. He of course allows that goals, as understood by our psychological theories, can be had and sought by agents. But he also allows that goals do not require this.[15]

For EUDAIMONIA. So far I have argued that my account of mixed acts is consistent with Aristotle's claim that rational action is for eudaimonia, provided that this is taken non-teleologically. I now

---

[15] This distinction between teleologies is discussed in my 'Values and Purposes', especially sect. I, which relies on R. Sorabji, *Necessity, Cause, and Blame* (Ithaca: Cornell University Press, 1980), especially ch. 10.

want to show that my account can be shown consistent with taking him to be, even in our sense, a teleologist. This will require modifying the claim that rational action is for eudaimonia. But this is needed in any case, not simply for my account of mixed acts.

The need arises as follows. Eudaimonia constitutively includes such good things as 'wisdom, sight, and certain pleasures and honours' which are good 'even without accessory advantage' (1. 6, 1096b17 ff.). Further, '. . . honour, pleasure, intelligence, and excellence in its various forms, we choose indeed for their own sakes (since we should be glad to have each although no extraneous advantage resulted from it) . . .' (1. 7, 1097b2 ff.). That is, even if seeking or obtaining those goals will not conduce to eudaimonia, it would still be rational to seek and obtain them. But then an act can be rational even if it does not conduce to eudaimonia.

Thus, we must take Aristotle here as holding that to be rational, an act need not be done for eudaimonia and thus that there are extra-eudaimonic values and goals.[16] Alternatively, we must show that even where seeking these goals will not conduce to eudaimonia, there is none the less a eudaimonist reason and motive for seeking them. In what follows, I will put some points in favour of the latter. My goal, however, is not to defend that option but rather to show how my account of mixed acts can be shown consistent with an interpretation of Aristotle as espousing teleological rationality.

There is, however, a simple eudaimonist reason for seeking and getting those goals even where that will not conduce to eudaimonia: to the extent one does not have them, one's life is less human and less good, where these notions are understood in terms of eudaimonia. As might have been said, those people's lives will be less eudaimonic.

To be sure, some goods and goals are such that there is no intrinsic difference between missing them by a little or a lot. They would be like the goal of winning a three-candidate election contest: only one wins and both the others simply lose. That the second did better than the third is true but irrelevant. (This can have extrinsic relevance, e.g. for getting nominated next time.)

But eudaimonia is not such a goal. The absence of eudaimonia can be treated concretely, as having determinate and evaluable content. Being further away from eudaimonia is, in itself, worse

---

[16] My thanks are owed to Terry Penner for raising this issue and for other help with this section.

than being closer to it. (Here we would do well to examine Aristotle's claims about the justifiability, indeed the necessity, of choosing the lesser of evils e.g. the *Politics*, 7. 13, 1332a10 ff.) It is worse not only abstractly—by being further away from eudaimonia; it is worse concretely, in terms of what being at that distance from eudaimonia is like.

Talk about what is worse concretely might be thought to concede the point that there are values other than eudaimonia—namely those in terms of which we describe the concrete condition. But that does not require values other than eudaimonia. For there are also ways—the very same ways—of describing what eudaimonia, itself, is concretely like and, to this extent, why it is the human good.

Two bad reasons might suggest the contrary. First, it might be thought that eudaimonia is simple—like Moore's goodness, like a metaphysical point or a glassy sphere, with no distinguishable features. But that is false to Aristotle's conception of eudaimonia.

Second, it might be thought that if one says why or how something is good, one thereby shows that one does not think that it has ultimate value. For it might be thought that something can be shown good only by showing it to be an instance of what is good in a more fundamental sense. (See *Principia Ethica*, sect. 39.) This, however, makes serious, and non-Aristotelian, errors about the nature of evaluation and justification.

My suggestion, then, is that we may well have a way to put in thoroughly eudaimonist terms both the claim that the constituent and external goods of eudaimonia are good whether or not they are conducive to eudaimonia and also the claim that the constituent and external bads of the absence of eudaimonia are bad whether or not they conduce to its absence. As noted above, I am not concerned to argue that this is the correct way to read Aristotle but only to show that my comments on mixed acts are neutral to whether we do read him this way or rather take him to be, even in part, a non-eudaimonist.

If Aristotle is not a thoroughgoing eudaimonist, then my account of mixed acts may have to be modified. Perhaps all mixed acts will tell simply against eudaimonia, and not also against those other principles. Or perhaps, they will tell sometimes against it, sometimes against others, and sometimes against both. In any case, they will not be done, at least not simply, for eudaimonia.

5. CONFLICTS OF VALUES AND OF DESIRES, AND ARISTOTLE

To complete our study of Aristotle on dirty hands, let us now turn to Aristotle on conflicts of values and of desires. I will here be more concerned with conflicts, not between values and desires, but within values and within desires. The conflicts important for us come in different varieties. At the outset, it will be adequate to put them in terms of merely incompossible values or objects of desire. Later it will be important to put them in moral psychological terms.

Put in terms of incompossibility, a conflict of values involves three elements:[17] the agent (1) values x, (2) values y, and (3) takes it that it is possible to get either but not both. Another sort does not require an agent, at least not one doing the valuing: (1) x is valuable, (2) y is valuable, and (3) it is not possible, or not possible for a given agent, to get both. Both we and Aristotle have a clear analogue to the first triad in regard to desires. We seem to lack an analogue for desire to the second triad. But with his understanding of what a normal or healthy being would desire—which gives a paradigm form of desire—Aristotle does have an analogue to the second triad (e.g. 3. 11).

The issues I am concerned with are not whether there can be any of these various conflicts, but whether Aristotle held there can be. As I think can be quickly seen, the discussion of dirty hands has already shown that he holds that there can be both sorts of conflicts of values. This is the topic of this section. The following sections take up conflicts of desires.

If we are concerned simply with conflicts of values understood in terms of incompossibility as given above, then it is clear—but not interesting—that Aristotle allows for such conflicts. For every case of mere means, and even of means which are also ends, is a case of such a conflict. For in such cases, there is a cost which is an unavoidable means to one's goal. I take this not to show that Aristotle recognizes conflicts of values, but rather to show that the characterization of such conflicts in terms of mere incompossibility does not single out the conflicts of values we are concerned with, namely the interesting and controversial conflicts of value. These, however, are given by the characterization of mixed acts, to which we must briefly return.

[17] See e.g. Williams, 'Ethical Consistency', and F. Jackson, 'Internal Conflicts in Desires and Morals', *American Philosophical Quarterly*, 22 (1985), 105–14.

Aristotle discusses mixed acts in order to illuminate voluntariness. Put briefly, he holds that an act is voluntary if it is an expression of the person's character and that it is such an expression if it is in accord with, and flows from, the person's values and desires. Some have taken him as holding that an act is fully voluntary if it is the act that, on balance, values or desires point to. Others have taken him as holding that an act is voluntary in its proportion of satisfied to unsatisfied values and desires.[18] We can be neutral on this issue and hold that values are such central constituents of one's character that to act in a way expressive of one's values is thereby to act from character, and that this is to act voluntarily.

The converse does not hold. For one acts voluntarily in acting from desire, not simply with desire. One acts with desire where one's desire is informed by and 'listens' to reason. One acts from desire where the desire is 'on its own' and does not listen to reason, where it, not reason, supplies the goal of action. Those agents who lack reason, such as children and animals, can act only from desire. Adults can act with desire, i.e. from reason and with desire. But often they act from desire.

To act either from or with desire is to act voluntarily. So too, to act from emotion, not simply with emotion—e.g. from anger, not merely with anger—is to act voluntarily. But it may well not be to express one's values.

For our purposes, the one-way relation—if one expresses one's values in action, one acts voluntarily—is sufficient. But the other direction is also important. As seen, some people in acting voluntarily do not express their values. But good people in acting well do express their values in acting voluntarily. To put this in terms of choice, *prohairesis* (not characterized until 3. 2), good people, acting well, act from choice, and to act from choice is to express one's values in action. To act from choice is, of course, to act voluntarily. Further, eudaimonia is what good people value and want—indeed all people value and want it, but in various ways only good people do this correctly.

As even these brief remarks show, cases of mixed acts are cases of conflicts of values. For in those cases, even good people can be compelled by the moral circumstances to act in a way which tells

---

[18] My thanks are owed to David Charles for discussing this and much else in this chapter with me.

importantly against eudaimonia, i.e. against what the agent values and what is valuable.

Thus, Aristotle holds that there are conflicts of values. More importantly, he holds that there are not just conflicts of mere incompossibility, but also important conflicts.

6. CONFLICTS OF DESIRE IN ARISTOTLE

Let us start with some comments on various sorts of desire. One important divide is between occurrent desires and underlying or dispositional ones. For an account of character, especially as understood by Aristotle, we need to examine both. But for our present purposes, we can focus on occurrent ones.

Here, too, there are different sorts. There is a decision-related sense of desire. This is desire that is acted on. It is the sort of desire found in belief–desire psychologies: what, in conjunction with belief, is said to be necessary and sufficient for explaining action.

In regard to such desire, acting on the desire—perhaps simply making an effective decision—ends the conflict. And indeed, in some cases, once an act is done or a decision made, no more thought and no more desire is given to the non-favoured desire.

But there are other sorts of desire. In some cases, the non-favoured desire remains as a nagging and unanswered demand. It can remind us of what might have been, with the various modalities such announcements can have. It can also lead to resentment, ambivalence, half-hearted action, vacillation, turmoil, and so on. These are only a very few of the possible outcomes of such conflicts. Exploring these varieties helps us see that in regard to desires, too, we need to go beyond characterizations of conflicts in terms of mere incompossibility.

To show that Aristotle allows for serious conflicts, we can start with people who are not good. We can begin by noting that at least most of the conflicts and ways of resolving them mentioned above are discussed by Aristotle, especially in his discussion of these four defective character sorts: the self-controlled (*enkrates*), the weak-willed (*akrates*), the licentious or self-indulgent (*akolastos*), and the bad (*kakos*).

The last two are defective in desiring, and indeed valuing, the wrong sorts of things. The first two are defective even though they value—and at least in that sense desire—the right sorts of things. For they also desire the wrong sorts of things and these desires are in conflict with what they recognize they should do. They vacillate and are ambivalent.

These various people, in their different ways, desire the wrong sorts of things, at the wrong times, in the wrong ways, and so on through the ways of going wrong. One central sort of desire involved in going wrong concerns those especially potent and unruly sources of conflict—the epithumetic, bodily desires, the ones we share with animals. Not surprisingly, Aristotle argues that, at least in their most unruly forms, they must be absent from, be silenced in, good people. So they will not even be around to create a conflict of desire in such people.

But in his discussion of bodily pleasures, he allows that temperate people can and should enjoy some of these pleasures. A standard way of taking him is as holding that good people will see and feel the pleasurableness of only those pleasures that they should or may seek. But I am unsure of this interpretation. He writes

The temperate man . . . takes no pleasure at all in the things that the profligate enjoys most . . . nor in general does he find pleasure in wrong things . . . nor does he feel pain or desire when they are lacking, or only in a moderate degree, not more than is right, nor at the wrong time, etc. (3. 11, 1119a12 ff.)

The first part, 'The temperate man . . . lacking', supports that interpretation. But the modification, starting with 'or only', strongly suggests that even in a temperate person there can be some pain— 'a moderate degree, not more than is right'—in forgoing some pleasures that should be forgone. This, if right, sustains my worry. Those pains are the pains of unfulfilled desire. They could be avoided, and pleasure had, by getting what here is, and should be, forgone.

Further, even where Aristotle holds that temperate people will not be pained by forgoing some pleasures, the context suggests that he is saying more than that they do not enjoy such things because they do not desire them. He is also saying that they here and now see a pleasure—i.e. one which, if they partook of it, would be pleasant. And he is also saying that without pain and without desire, without ambivalence, they forgo these pleasures (e.g. 3. 11, 1118b34). Such pleasures call into question the near-necessary connection some see Aristotle as making between pleasure and desire.

The explanation of why Aristotle would have different categories of pleasures that a good person should forgo is that some pleasures are in themselves bad, but others are bad only in the circumstances. His explanation of this is that the activities or objects of the former sort are bad as such. They are the sorts of things that are bad as such, e.g. adultery. But those of the latter are bad only in the circumstances. It is not bad as such to enjoy a piece of cake, but if this interferes with important affairs or is one piece too many, in those circumstances it is bad.

Pleasures that are licit in themselves, but in the circumstances bad, are importantly like ordinary costs: good people can see these costs as costs, pay them without hesitation or regret, and without compromising eudaimonia. So too, good people can see these pleasures as pleasures, as having to be forgone, forgo some without even having desired them, and forgo others without—too much, anyway—hesitation or regret and without compromising eudaimonia. Indeed, in both cases, paying those costs and forgoing those pleasures are necessary for eudaimonia. This, of course, is to speak about the ordinary way these costs and pleasures confront people. For it is possible to go wrong in regard to, and be ruined by, either.

It might be thought that, if correct, I have exposed an outright contradiction in Aristotle's thought, showing that good people both desire and do not desire the forgone epithumetic pleasures. But, as I will be concerned to argue, this fails to note an important distinction between sorts of desire.

7. SOME COMMENTS ON ARISTOTELIAN PLEASURES AND CONFLICTS

To explain this, it will help to raise a foundational issue in Aristotle: the relation between pleasure and value. There are many controversies about Aristotle's final understanding of pleasure, e.g. the relations between the accounts in *Nicomachean Ethics* 7 and 10. But it is not controversial that on Aristotle's view there are intimate connections between pleasure and *energeia*—often translated as 'activity'. The basic and correlative ideas I want here to suggest are, first, that an *energeia* involves or is the actualization of what is valuable, valued, or desired and that *energeia* thus involves or is a pleasure, and second, that pleasure is or involves the actualization of what is valuable, valued, or desired and thus it is or involves an *energeia*.[19]

I will mention two ways these very rich ideas are important for our concerns. The first has to do with the issues concerning teleology and eudaimonia taken up in section 4 in the discussion what it is to act *for* eudaimonia.

Pleasure is characterized in terms of being or involving an *energeia* which is perfect or unimpeded. So, suppose then that we set off to reach the top of the mountain, but fail. Since the goal is not achieved, it would seem that the activity must be impeded or imperfect. But then it should not be pleasurable. Yet, we may have found intense pleasure in what we did—e.g. in making a valiant effort.

Perhaps it will be said that making the effort is the activity and that it was unimpeded and perfect. To do this is to do something I welcome. It is to understand *energeia* non-teleologically, i.e. not in terms of intentions and goals. We did not set out to make a valiant effort, but to reach the top. It might be replied that making that effort was intended—namely, as a means. Even if this is right, that act is intended as a means. And as such, it is impeded and imperfect. Its end is not achieved. Yet it was pleasurable.

Our intentions were not realized. But our values were actualized in making the effort—e.g. those involved in pushing ourselves to the limit, using our skills, and the like. It is their actualization that is pleasurable and this actualization is also unimpeded and perfect.

This is not presented as an objection to Aristotle, but rather as his view. For, his claim is not that an *energeia* requires satisfying one's intentions. It need only actualize one's values. (Aristotle would add, 'and thus oneself'.) That is sufficient for *energeia* to be teleological on his, but not on our, understanding of the notion.

We can put the issue as a point of translation. The Greek allows us, and we would do better, to translate *energeia* by 'actualization' than 'activity'. For, 'activity' can be understood in terms of an

---

[19] I am indebted here, and on the two points below, to Penner, 'Verbs and the Identity of Actions', and L. A. Kosman, 'Aristotle's Definition of Motion', *Phronesis*, 14 (1969), 40–62 and 'Substance, Being, and *Energeia*', *Oxford Studies in Ancient Philosophy*, 2 (1984), 121–49. On *energeia* as actualization, see also A. Grant, *The Ethics of Aristotle* (London: Longmans, Green and Co., 1874), vol. i, Essay IV (2).

intention, where this in turn is understood in terms of a goal which we set out to achieve by doing the act. But as pleasure shows, *energeia* cannot require that. (We are thus helped to see how people can make a mistake about what is pleasing without making the different mistake of not knowing what they intend.)

The second way Aristotle's understanding of pleasure is important for us is the way it helps us to understand the emotional condition of the agent of an act of dirty hands in particular and of mixed acts in general. Aristotle characterizes emotions as 'those states of consciousness which are accompanied by pleasure or pain' (2. 5, 1105b23 ff.). His discussions throughout the *Nicomachean Ethics* and the *Rhetoric* make it clear that this is importantly a conceptual accompaniment.

It is not merely that emotions conceptually involve pleasure and pain. It is that emotions conceptually involve values and these conceptually involve pleasure and pain. Emotions are 'registerings' of how one's values and disvalues are faring in the world. If what one values is going well, one is pleased. That is, one experiences one of the emotional modalities of pleasure, e.g. pride. Similarly for pain.

Of particular importance for us, this conceptual connection gives us an internal explanation of why being compelled to do something is painful. (See e.g. 3. 1, 1110b12 ff.) It is not as if such pain must show wilfulness and a questionable concern for getting our own way. Rather, the pain includes, and may simply be, the pain of having to frustrate our values or actualize what we disvalue.

More generally for our concerns, this conceptual connection gives us the means of showing why Aristotle and we can hold that it is ridiculous to regret mere means as such, but that it is entirely proper to be ashamed of, or otherwise regret, the dirty part of justified, even obligatory, acts. What is worth regretting is what is bad. To regret having to use means to get our goals would thus be to think such use is bad. But that invokes a non-human, perhaps a divine, standard for goodness and badness. And this is ridiculous.

Acts of dirty hands, however, involve their agents in frustrating some of their serious values and in actualizing some of their serious disvalues. It is entirely proper, and not to be wondered at, that one regrets the realization of what one seriously disvalues or the frustration of what one seriously values, and all the more so if one is the agent. This is so even if one also properly has a stronger contrary moral emotion in response to the very same act.

Earlier I said that simply doing what is base, as distinguished from acting with a base character, tells against eudaimonia. This can now be put in terms of moral emotions. The regret proper to dirty hands—e.g. in the tyrant case—does not require shame about oneself. At the least, it does not require shame about having a bad character, but only at having done what is base. I here will follow Aristotle in not discussing the possibility that one might lose one's virtue, perhaps even become base, as a result of doing or simply having to do morally required base acts.[20]

Although this discussion of conflict and moral emotions is important for understanding dirty hands, it may seem to be getting away from the issue, conflicts of desires. But for two important reasons, it is not. First, in good people there is a coincidence of what is valued and what is desired, and necessarily so. Thus, where we find a conflict of desires in such people, we also find a conflict of values. And since they experience conflicts of values, e.g. in the dirty hands cases, at least there they also experience conflicts of desires.

This may seem somewhat quick. So let me take up the second point. Aristotle writes

For the feeling of pleasure is an experience of the soul, and a thing gives a man pleasure in regard to which he is described as 'fond of' so-and-so: for instance a horse gives pleasure to one fond of horses, a play to one fond of the theatre, and similarly just actions are pleasant to the lover of justice . . . (1. 8, 1099a7 ff.)

Does this last mean that if I am a lover of justice and my child is justly executed, I must take pleasure in that?[21]

In the *Rhetoric*, we read that Amasis found his son's execution terrible and fearful (2. 8, 1386a19 ff.). While there is no indication whether Amasis was a lover of justice, there is little reason to think that his reaction shows him not to be. He can see the execution as at once just and also terrible and fearful. The execution actualizes

[20] As Martha Nussbaum points out in *The Fragility of Goodness*, 338, the possibility of being corrupted by the circumstances is discussed in the *Rhetoric* at 2. 14.

[21] It was this question by Christopher Joyce that brought home to me that the sorts of conflict of values and of desires found in courage, taken up in the next section, are a general feature of Aristotle's ethics.

one of his values, justice, and destroys for ever another of his values (or the bearer of that other value), his son.

The notion of double-counting is important here: even those who agree that the execution is overall justified need not evaluate the action simply by discounting the positive value of justice being done by the disvalue of the death. This, presumably, would give a situation of positive, even if not very great, value. As such, it should be a source of, even if not very great, pleasure.

As I think is clear, the correct way to understand how Amasis and others close to his son saw the situation requires allowing that the disvalue stands out as a moral remainder and is double-counted. This explains why, despite being acknowledged as justified, the execution is no pleasure at all for them. It also helps explain Aristotle's account of conflict of desires in good people.

A correlative way to put the matter is in terms of a difference found within goods internal to eudaimonia—namely, being good conditionally or absolutely. As put in the *Politics*:

> . . . just punishments and chastisements do indeed spring from a good principle, but they are good only because we cannot do without them—it would be better that neither individuals nor states should need anything of the sort—but actions which aim at honour and advantage are absolutely the best. The conditional action is only the choice of a lesser evil; whereas these are the foundation and creation of good. (7. 13, 1332a12 ff., tr. Jowett.)

Once again, this helps explain why, despite being acknowledged as justified, the execution is no pleasure at all for Amasis. And once again, it also helps explain Aristotle's account of conflict of desires in good people.

8. COURAGE AND PLEASURE

These last and correlative points can be expanded by taking up what many see as another problem area for Aristotle on desire—courage. Aristotle requires that courageous people face battle without cowardice, without deserting their comrades, throwing down their arms, turning tail, and the like. However, he also allows—indeed requires—courageous people to appreciate the dangers and have appropriate fear. But, fear involves a desire to avoid danger. So courage, it would seem, must involve both a desire not to do and also a desire to do those prohibited things and, thus, must be contradictory.

But to think this contradictory is to conflate importantly different, even if importantly connected, forms of desire. The desire proper to courage, and to the fear proper to courage, is the desire constituted by seeing, appreciating, and feeling the danger and the value of life and safety. This desire does not involve being moved to escape. More exactly it does not include—and courage precludes—a desire that is constitutive of emotional fragmentation, vacillation, ambivalence, uncertainty about what to do, indecision, emotional turmoil, and conflict. Similarly, good people do not desire forgone epithumetic objects in ways that involve vacillation, turmoil, and the like. Indeed, it seems that they will not desire, but only see as pleasurable, some forgone epithumetic pleasures.

Rather, these forms of desire are characteristic of enkratics and akratics. They are at war with themselves. They vacillate. They are ambivalent. Their desires fight against their judgement. They are riven.

This, we might note, shows that Aristotelian akrasia is not depicted accurately as knowingly not doing what one believes best. For, it is possible to know what is best and knowingly not do that without any conflict and without akrasia. This is shown, e.g. by the young and others who are similarly controlled by passion (1. 3). They have not yet reached the level of moral development and integration from which they can fall into akrasia.[22]

The lack of moral and emotional integration shown by enkratic and akratic people thus differs from those of immature and bad

---

[22] See my 'Affectivity and Self-Concern: The Assumed Psychology in Aristotle's Ethics', *Pacific Philosophical Quarterly*, 64 (1983), 211–29; and N. O. Dahl, *Practical Reason, Aristotle, and Weakness of the Will* (Minneapolis: University of Minnesota Press, 1984).

For similar reason, if weakness of will as understood by us involves conflict, it cannot be characterized in terms of knowingly not doing what is best. But even without requiring conflict, that characterization fails. For one need not act weakly in knowingly not doing the best—if e.g. doing that would be supererogatory or would benefit oneself. See my *Supererogation* (doctoral dissertation, Harvard University, 1966), 'Rightness and Goodness: Is There a Difference?', 'Agent and Other: Against Ethical Universalism', *Australasian Journal of Philosophy*, 54 (1976), 206–20; S. Wolf, 'Moral Saints', *Journal of Philosophy*, 79 (1982), 410–39 and 'Above and Below the Line of Duty', *Philosophical Topics*, 14 (1986), 131–48; M. Slote, 'Morality and Self–Other Asymmetry', *Journal of Philosophy*, 81 (1984), 179–92; and F. M. Kamm, 'Supererogation and Obligation', *Journal of Philosophy*, 82 (1985), 118–38.

people. And these, of course, stand in sharp contrast with the harmonious integration found in good people. Some care is needed in detailing this harmony, as shown by the case of courage. One sort of harmony—but not the relevant sort—would be formed by having the disvalues involved in the dangers simply discount the overall value of the courageous act, and having done this evaluative work, disappear from both the evaluative and the emotional scenes.

But in Aristotelian courage, it is essential that its constitutive dangers are double-counted: they both discount the overall value of the battle and also remain as recognizable bads. Courage involves having the proper fear and also the proper confidence towards what is dangerous, with these fused together in a harmonious whole. It does not involve having some single homogeneous emotion toward a homogeneous complex, which is merely reduced in value by what is dangerous.

Nor, for similar reasons, does courage involve now seeing the act under one description and now under another—now as involving what is worth getting and now as involving what is worth avoiding. Both descriptions, both aspects, must be kept in mind, but conjoined in a whole—a whole that none the less allows the dangers to retain their own separate existence, to be double-counted.

Allowing that the danger remains a distinct bad even when part of what is morally required is important for the general concerns of this work. This can be brought out in a way that explains what is, even if often not recognized as, Aristotle's very puzzling claim about courage: that attaining victory is pleasurable, but that acting courageously need not be pleasurable and indeed can be painful (3. 9).

This needs explaining for two reasons. First, by saying that only victory is pleasurable, it seems that we are here treating acting courageously as a process, *kinesis*, not an actualization, *energeia*. But even though some pleasures are 'incidental to a process' (7. 12, 1153a10), acting courageously is—since it is acting virtuously—an *energeia*. Second, this *energeia* expresses the character, and the values, of a truly virtuous person, acting in the best circumstances— i.e. the best circumstances for acting with that virtue. It should thus be unimpeded or perfect—to give the characterizing terms of pleasure offered in 7 and 10.

Now, it might be said that the external circumstances of

courageous action impede it and prevent it from being perfect. As Aristotle says, 'the happy man requires the goods of the body, external goods and the gifts of fortune, in order that his activity may not be impeded by lack of them'.[23]

However, the loss or risk of loss of these goods is internal to courageous acts. Thus, if they were impeded by that, they would all be impeded. But then, either they could not be virtuous or alternatively virtuous action would not have to be, and here could not be, perfect and unimpeded.

It is thus fortunate that we have a way internal to courageous action to explain why such action is not pleasurable even when it is unimpeded: the danger of death and injury are internal to courageous action and they remain as bads. It is not that they are simply bad 'on their own' but good in the circumstances. Nor are they parts of a whole which is good in a way that should make it an object of pleasure. Rather, they remain as values and objects of desire which conflict with those that are and should be enacted.

In this way courageous acts are, or are very close to being, mixed acts. Precisely because—as they must—they involve danger, courageous acts risk making eudaimonia difficult, if not impossible. And indeed, if courageous, the young risk not getting eudaimonia at all because they risk dying before they have had time to attain it (1. 7, 1098a18 and 9. 8, 1169a29 ff.).

What is here important, however, is the sort of conflict good people have when acting courageously. It does not involve vacillation, ambivalence, turmoil and indecision. Rather, it involves a certain sort of pain and lack of pleasure—because important goods are threatened and there is the risk of suffering important bads. In contrast, forgoing epithumetic pleasures need not involve pain for good people. Here, good people will see and feel that no very important good is forgone.

But of course, those who value epithumetic pleasures highly— the self-indulgent or soft, *malakos*—may well find it painful to forgo such a pleasure, even for a greater one. Moreover, forgoing the lesser one can diminish, even eliminate, the pleasure of the greater one. This is not only consistent with Aristotle's account of pleasure and pain, it is part and parcel of it: as our values and disvalues differ, so do our pleasures and pains.

---

[23] 7. 1153b17 ff. See also 1. 8, 1099a32 ff. The passage from 7 is more significant for us since its topic is clearly pleasure and impeded acts, and not just happiness.

9. CONCLUSION

Thus, Aristotle does not hold that all choices among values or resolutions of desires are easy or can be made and executed with a light heart or pleasure. Even good people can experience sadness, lack of eudaimonia, disgrace, perhaps even anguish—because even for such people, there are dirty hands and conflicts of values and of desires.

4

Moral Conflicts: What They Are and What They Show

THE main focus of this chapter is conflict—in particular, value conflict, but also conflicts of desire. There is widespread agreement that if there are value conflicts, they pose serious problems for ethics.[1] Ethics would then be impractical—telling us to achieve all

My thanks are owed to the Monash University philosophy department for their help with this chapter. A portion of this chapter appears under the same title in the *Pacific Philosophical Quarterly*, 68 (1987), 104–23.

[1] See e.g. M. Merleau-Ponty, *Humanism and Terror* (Boston: Beacon Press, 1971); T. Nagel, 'War and Massacre', *Philosophy and Public Affairs*, 1 (1972), 123–44; M. Walzer, 'Political Action: The Problem of Dirty Hands', *Philosophy and Public Affairs*, 2 (1973), 160–80; R. Brandt, 'Utilitarianism and the Rules of War' *Philosophy and Public Affairs*, 1 (1972), 145–65; R. M. Hare, 'Rules of War and Moral Reasoning', *Philosophy and Public Affairs*, 1 (1972), 166–81; B. Williams, 'Ethical Consistency', and 'Consistency and Realism', *Problems of the Self* (Cambridge: Cambridge University Press, 1973), and 'Conflicts of Values', *Moral Luck* (Cambridge: Cambridge University Press, 1981); B. Williams and J. J. C. Smart, *Utilitarianism, For and Against* (Cambridge: Cambridge University Press, 1973); T. McConnell, 'Moral Dilemmas and Consistency in Ethics', *Canadian Journal of Philosophy*, 8 (1978), 269–87; R. Marcus, 'Moral Dilemmas and Ethical Consistency', *Journal of Philosophy*, 77 (1980), 121–36; P. S. Greenspan, 'Moral Dilemmas and Guilt', *Philosophical Studies*, 43 (1983), 117–25; P. Foot, 'Moral Realism and Moral Dilemmas', *Journal of Philosophy*, 80 (1983), 379–98; T. Hill, 'Moral Purity and the Lesser Evil', *The Monist*, 66 (1983), 213–32; S. I. Benn, 'Private and Public Morality: Clean Living and Dirty Hands', in S. I. Benn and G. F. Gaus (eds.), *Public and Private in Social Life* (London: Croom Helm, 1983); B. Barry, 'Tragic Choices', *Ethics*, 94 (1984), 303–18; A. Donagan, 'Consistency in Rationalist Moral Systems', *Journal of Philosophy*, 81 (1984), 291–309; M. Slote, 'Utilitarianism, Moral Dilemmas, and Moral Cost', *American Philosophical Quarterly*, 22 (1985), 161–8; W. Sinnott-Armstrong, 'Moral Dilemmas and Incomparability', *American Philosophical Quarterly*, 20 (1985), 321–9, 'Moral Dilemmas and Moral Realism', *Journal of Philosophy*, 84 (1987), 263–76, and *Moral Dilemmas* (Oxford: Basil Blackwell, 1988); C. Korsgaard, 'The Right to Lie: Kant on Dealing with Evil', *Philosophy and Public Affairs*, 15 (1986), 325–49; I. Levi, *Hard Choices* (Cambridge: Cambridge University Press, 1986); M. C. Nussbaum, *The Fragility of Goodness* (Cambridge: Cambridge University Press, 1986); and S. Bishop, 'Connections and Guilt', *Hypatia*, 2 (1987), 7–23. References below are to these works. For further reference, see C. Gowans (ed.), *Moral Dilemmas* (Oxford: Oxford University Press, 1987).

the conflicting values. Or it would be incomplete—not telling us which value to achieve. Or it would be non-realistic—denying that here there is a fact of the matter.

But there is disagreement over what this shows. Some conclude that, since there are conflicts, ethics must be impractical, incomplete, or non-realistic. Others conclude that there are, or had better be, no conflicts. For impractical theories block action and encourage romanticism and escapism. Incomplete ones encourage indecision, uncertainty, vacillation, irresolution, and the like. And non-realistic ones that allow for conflicts give us these same two options.

One important source of this disagreement lies in what is agreed to—that if there are value conflicts, they pose serious problems for ethics—and more importantly in the fact that this may well be correct about our ethical theories. For they are so exclusively concerned with action-guiding evaluations—e.g. this act is obligatory—that they have no way of understanding conflict except in terms of conflicting action-guiding evaluations. They thus see only two alternatives: reject conflicts or accept impracticality, incompleteness, or non-realism.

There is another alternative, which I shall here pursue: a better ethics. This better ethics does not limit its concerns to act evaluations. It also recognizes that not even all act evaluations are action-guiding. Further, it holds that at least many conflicts are conflicts between action-guiding and non-action-guiding act evaluations and that they do not force our theories into impracticality, incompleteness, or non-realism.

I. THE INCOMPOSSIBILITY ACCOUNT AND MODIFICATIONS

Let us start with an account of value conflict in terms of incompossibility: there is a conflict wherever (1) act *b* has value, (2) act *c* has value, (3) it is possible to do *b* and *c* severally but not jointly. Correlatively for conflicts of desire.[2] Perhaps this account is useful for some understandings of 'conflict'—which, after all, can

---

[2] See e.g. F. Jackson, 'Internal Conflicts in Desires and Morals', *American Philosophical Quarterly*, 22 (1985), 105–14. See also Williams, 'Ethical Consistency', 167 ff. As will be seen, I agree almost entirely with how Williams describes conflicts and how he argues against those who deny that there are conflicts. We disagree, however, over the theoretical implications of conflicts—e.g. over their bearing on the question of whether ethics can be practical, complete, and realistic.

be a philosopher's term of art. But it is clearly inadequate for at least many important understandings of 'conflict'.

Of most importance for us now is that nearly every choice involves what this account labels a conflict. But not every such choice involves a conflict—not every such choice is conflicting, at least not rationally conflicting. Indeed, one of the more natural explanations of why someone finds choice in general conflicting is extreme and generalized ambivalence or some other neurotic debility centring on choice.

Let us, then, try to restrict ourselves to rational conflict. This may rule out conflict over unimportant matters. For if what one must give up in order to resolve a conflict is unimportant, it might be rational simply to give it up rather than be conflicted. At the least, this seems true in some cases where only one option is important—e.g. choosing between spending a few minutes filling out a form in order to get a life-saving vaccination or reading a newspaper for those few minutes. It also seems true in some cases where both options are unimportant—e.g. choosing between vanilla and chocolate ice-cream for dessert.

What then of choices involving serious options, e.g. whether to get married or not, or to this person or that one, or whether to pursue an academic or public service career? Even such choices are not always conflicting. Sometimes it can be perfectly easy to decide between such options. And it does seem that lack of conflict here can be rational. We do, after all, admire some for seeing their way easily through such decisions. But on the other hand, we also admire some people for the way they are taken up with, and even conflicted by, these decisions. We may praise them for their sensitivity.

Perhaps, then, we should relativize our inquiry to the sort of people involved. So perhaps if in the past I have had difficulty in seeing the different sides of a question, it may show progress that I now can agonize over a decision, and if you have had difficulty in making decisions it may show progress that now you can act without second thoughts. But in any case, we would still need to know what sort of conflict it would be admirable for a given sort of person to be conflicted by.

Some would answer this question by holding that truly conflicting options must be moral options. If morality is understood broadly, e.g. in terms of whatever has value for a good human life, non-conflicts again count as conflicts. For in that broad sense of morality, at least most serious options are moral options. And as we have seen, not all serious options are conflicting.

If we understand this restriction in terms of morality narrowly construed—in terms of duty, rightness, and the like—much the same problem arises. In some cases where the options are moral in the narrow sense, there is no conflict at all. Indeed, this is the typical relation between incompossible prima facie duties, as will be discussed in the next section. But, as discussed in 'Dirty Hands and Ordinary Life', 'Dirty Hands and Aristotle's Ethics', and 'Courage', many important moral conflicts, including those of dirty hands, do involve conflicting duties.

We thus need to differentiate between those duties which are and those which are not conflicting when jointly impossible. Correlatively, we need to differentiate between those broadly moral options which are and those which are not conflicting when jointly impossible. As will be seen, there is no one way and certainly no simple way to make these differentiations. We should thus not be surprised that conflicts do not admit of one or any simple characterization.

2. CONFLICTS OF PRIMA FACIE DUTIES AND OF OVERALL DUTIES

The recent discussion of conflicts has been, largely if not entirely, in terms of morality construed narrowly—i.e. in terms of duties and conflicts of duties. The question has been whether there can be conflicts of actual and overall, not merely prima facie, duties.

The conflicts in question are usually presented as external or circumstantial conflicts of duties: i.e. conflicts because of and only in the circumstances. For example, in Kant's case in his *On a Supposed Right to Lie from Altruistic Motives*, it is only because of the circumstances that the duties of saving the life of an innocent person and of telling the truth conflict. Perhaps, however, there can also be internal conflicts: i.e. cases where the options are, as such, opposed to each other.[3]

---

[3] For some examples of internal conflict, we can turn to the *Republic* 4. 437 ff. which shows Leontius's *thumos* standing in an internal conflict to his desire to see the corpses; and to the *Nicomachean Ethics* 7. 3, 1147a34 ff. which shows reason in internal conflict with akratic desire. As these examples show, internal conflict can be asymmetrical. For *thumos* is concerned with honour and is thus internally

It may be difficult to think of internally conflicting duties, but virtues, ideals, and ways of life do present plausible candidates. At the least, it often seems impossible to meet the demands of, say, both moral sensitivity and resoluteness, or the demands of both a practical life and a contemplative one. For what the one seems to require, the other seems to discourage or even forbid. (If this is right, we may not be able to join Plato and Aristotle in holding that the virtues are unifiable.) Thus, a complete study of moral conflicts would go beyond conflicts of duties or of values of acts.

But to make the present inquiry manageable, I too will ask whether there can be conflicts of actual, and not merely prima facie, duties. The issues can be put in terms of an outline of a theory of duties borrowed from W. D. Ross. On this view, there are plural, *sui generis* sorts of consideration—e.g. keeping a promise and pleasure—each of which on its own is a reason for acting. Instances of these considerations have different strengths, both in regard to other instances of the same consideration and in regard to instances of other considerations.

So, because of their exact natures as promises, there can be a stronger reason to keep this promise than that one; and because of their exact natures as acts of promise-keeping and as acts of producing pleasure, there can be a stronger reason to keep this promise than to produce that lot of pleasure, but a stronger reason to produce this lot of pleasure than to keep that promise.

As this is meant to make clear, and for reasons discussed in 'Plurality and Conflict', I am here concerned with the differing strengths of instances of these considerations, rather than the differing strengths of sorts of considerations: this act of promise-keeping versus this act of producing pleasure, rather than promise-keeping versus producing pleasure. What is important for us is how our ethical theory makes use of these comparative strengths.

The outline theory recognizes that in the way given by the incompossibility account of conflicts—(1) act *b* has value, (2) act *c* has value, (3) it is possible to do *b* and *c* severally but not jointly— there can be conflicts between the various considerations. For example, it can be possible to keep this promise or produce that pleasure but not do both. The theory—or the higher level justification

opposed to the desire to see the corpses because that would be dishonourable. But the desire to see them does not find *thumos* as aiming at dissatisfaction but only as getting in the way of satisfaction. Desire is thus only externally opposed to *thumos*.

of the theory—claims that it is a complete and a practical theory of act evaluation. To be complete, it must tell us in every situation what may or must be done. To be practical, it must never tell us to do what is impossible.

The reasons for wanting a theory to satisfy these ideals of completeness and practicality are obvious. Of particular importance to us are these: if a theory is incomplete, it can encourage or even force indecision, uncertainty, vacillation, irresoluteness, and the like; if it is impractical, it can encourage romanticism and escapism—e.g. thoughts about what acts it would be nice to do, if only they could be done—instead of action. These, not surprisingly, are just the defects or features many see engendered by conflicts.

For our outline theory to be complete and practical, it must resolve conflicts. It cannot simply hold that there is a reason to do one act and also a reason to do the other—e.g. to keep the promise and to produce the pleasure. Nor can it hold that we should do both acts. Our theory claims to be able to resolve these conflicts. The resolution works by taking into account not simply the reason for action created by each consideration, but the strength of these considerations.

One version of the theory tells us that we are to act upon the strongest reason. (A better theory would not require maximization, but for present purposes, this is unimportant.) It can allow that there still are reasons for doing the other acts, but it is no longer interested in what there is simply a reason to do. It is now interested in what is to be done and it understands this in terms of what there is the strongest reason to do. An obvious way to try to satisfy that interest is by understanding each reason, so far as it tells us what is to be done, as a reason in the first sense with the rider 'on the condition that there is no stronger reason to do something else'.

It is claimed that restricting attention to only such conditionalized reasons eliminates conflicts of incompossibility—or all serious ones, anyway. For if promise-keeping or producing pleasure is here weaker than the other, or indeed weaker than any other reason, it does not show what is to be done. If the reasons are equal first in strength, the theory can hold that any top-ranked act may be done and that one of them—i.e. any one of them—is to be done.

3. THE SHARED ASSUMPTION THAT ETHICS IS ACTION-GUIDING

In this way, then, various theories claim to eliminate conflicts. Recently this claim has come under intense discussion. Many hold that conflicts have not thus been eliminated. Here we might consider Ruth Marcus's argument about what is surely possible: in good faith and with due caution, one makes two solemn and important promises which, as things turn out, conflict. To keep the one precludes keeping the other. Or we might consider a case Bernard Williams presents to make a closely related point. This is the case of Jim, who has either to take part in the killing of one innocent person or to allow many innocent people to be killed.

Many hold that in these cases whichever act is done, something wrong is done. Jim's taking part in killing the one innocent person would be wrong, even though it saves the others. His not taking part in the killing would also be wrong, because of what this allows. Similarly in Marcus's case: to keep one promise precludes keeping the other. At least part of the reason for saying that whichever act is done, something wrong is done is that whichever act is done, the agent can clearly regret not doing the other act.

Cases and arguments like these are central to many arguments that ethics cannot be complete and practical. Some conclude that ethics must be silent in such cases, others that it requires us to do both of the jointly impossible acts.

Alan Donagan, on the other hand, argues that there appear to be conflicts in such cases because only rough and imprecise formulations of duties have been considered. He claims that a full and correct understanding of the duties—one which takes account of how they incorporate so-called exceptions and qualifications and how they take account of circumstances—would show that they cannot conflict.

Now, I do agree that only the broad outlines and leading details of the supposedly conflicting duties and the circumstances of conflict have been discussed. This is so, despite the fact that far more detail has been given than is usual in ethical discussion. We are thus confronted with two important questions: would a fuller discussion of these conflicts lead to a clear, or clear enough, resolution of them? Second, is ethics complete and practical? But there is a prior question that is also important: why has it been thought by both sides that these cases of conflict even bear on, much less settle, the issue of completeness and practicality?

The answer to this last question lies in an assumption both sides make. The assumption is that conflict is between action-guiding evaluations. Thus, it is held that to resolve a conflict is to find out what is to be done, and that rational conflict is not possible if it is clear what should be done. There is the correlative assumption that doing what it is clear one should do cannot be regrettable.

Marcus and others argue from their claims that there are cases where it is impossible to avoid conflict to their conclusion that ethics is not complete and practical. They also argue correlatively from their claims that there are cases where regret is unavoidable to their conclusion that ethics is not complete and practical. Donagan argues from his claim that ethics is, or can be, complete and practical to his conclusion that there need be no cases of unavoidable rational conflict—and correlatively no cases of unavoidable regret.

Contrary to these views, my own view is that to understand conflicts and to understand their bearing on ethical theory, we must question and ultimately reject the assumption that conflict is between action-guiding evaluations. It is to this that I now turn. I shall put my arguments largely in terms of whether conflict—especially rational conflict—is unavoidable. Strictly similar arguments hold about whether regret is unavoidable.

It is entirely natural—and virtually inevitable—for contemporary ethical theorists to take it that rational conflict is not possible if it is clear what should be done. To see this, some brief comments on the history of recent ethics will help.

As it is usually understood, the history of our normative ethical theories starting at least with Kant and reaching full pitch with the utilitarians and their opponents is importantly a history of controversies over act evaluations and in particular over the moral characterization of what is to be done.[4] These controversies have been conducted in terms of morality narrowly construed—i.e. over how to understand 'ought', 'duty', 'obligatory', 'right', and the like.

These disputes are important. But for our purposes, it is even more important that they share the basic assumption that a study of those notions is the study of ethics or at least the important and central part of ethics. On their view, ethics is at least largely

---

[4] I put this forward as the current understanding of our history, not as the correct history. For arguments that it is not right about Kant, see O. O'Neill, 'Consistency in Action', in *Morality and Universality*, N. T. Potter and M. Timmons (eds.), (Dordrecht: Reidel, 1985); S. D. Hudson, *Human Character and Morality* (Boston: Routledge & Kegan Paul, 1986); and J. B. Schneewind, 'Natural Law, Skepticism, and Methods of Ethics', *Journal of the History of Ideas*, 52 (1991), 289–308.

concerned with action-guidingness, and action-guidingness is to be understood in terms of duty, rightness, and the like.

This limited understanding of ethics has recently been under serious, and I think successful, attack. It is now coming to be seen—with Plato, Aristotle, Hume, Kant, and indeed nearly all the important classical ethicists—that ethics is concerned with more than acts. Thus, ethics is not concerned exclusively with action-guiding evaluations. Nor will it deal with other ethical concerns simply in terms of their importance for acts—e.g. see motivation and character as ethically important but only because proper motivation and good character are important for proper action. Rather, it will give independent prominence to agents and situations and it will focus on the virtues, character structures, emotions, and intimate relations such as love and friendship—to name only some areas of important moral concern taken up in this work.[5]

This is to speak of matters of ethical concern that a concentration on the ethics of acts might naturally be expected to ignore or slight. But further, it is now coming to be widely recognized that our ethical theories which concentrate so much on action-guiding evaluations get even these evaluations wrong. For example, their accounts of duty, rightness, and the like leave no space for the important moral options created by supererogation, self-regard, and friendship.[6]

Acknowledging these serious moral options forces more than a recharacterization of duty, rightness, and the like. It also forces a reconsideration of the view that action-guiding evaluations tell us virtually everything of moral importance about acts.

We can see this by seeing how theories concerned with action-guiding evaluations might handle these options. They can hold that

---

[5] Because of the size of the literature on this, it becomes difficult to single out particular works. Good bibliographies are found, however, in G. E. Pence, 'Recent Work on Virtues', *American Philosophical Quarterly*, 21 (1984), 281–97, and S. D. Hudson, *Human Character and Morality*.

[6] On conflicts between duty and supererogation see my *Supererogation* (doctoral dissertation, Harvard University, 1966), especially ch. 6, 'Duty Precluding Supererogatory Acts', and F. M. Kamm, 'Supererogation and Obligation', *Journal of Philosophy*, 82 (1985), 118–38. On the relevance for duty of differences between self- and other-regarding values, see e.g. my 'Agent and Other: Against Ethical Universalism,' *Australasian Journal of Philosophy*, 54 (1976), 206–20, and M. Slote, 'Morality and Self–Other Asymmetry', *Journal of Philosophy*, 81 (1984), 179–92. On conflicts between duty and friendship see my 'The Schizophrenia of Modern Ethical Theories', *Journal of Philosophy*, 73 (1976), 453–66 and 'Friendship and Duty: Toward a Synthesis of Gilligan's Contrastive Ethical Concepts', in E. Kittay and

what is to be done is a disjunction of either what they originally said is to be done or one of these options. That is, what is to be done is found in the disjunction of either what is overall obligatory or what is supererogatory, self-regarding, or friendly.

But there is no reason to think that those three options are the only options that can justify not doing what is one's duty—or what, but for the option, would be one's duty. Thus, it is unclear how the latter disjunct is to be completed, or even if it can be completed. If it cannot, the theory is indeterminate.

To escape indeterminateness, the theory might claim to be giving us only the minimum needed in order to do what is to be done, or act in a morally proper way. But if a theory, especially by its own understanding of itself, gives us only such a minimum, it cannot claim to tell us everything of moral importance about acts. And indeed, by allowing for the disjunction of duty or those three options, the theory shows that it acknowledges that there are important moral facts about acts which go beyond whether or not they are to be done.

Another way these theories might try to handle this problem is by expanding the notion of action-guidingness beyond that of morality narrowly construed and simply include these options as action-guiding. After all, these evaluations are evaluations of acts and even though they do not tell us what is to be done, they do give advice, telling us what it would be, e.g. good, prudent, nice, or friendly to do.

However, this last move is ill-conceived because of a radical misunderstanding of what it is to be action-guiding. Supererogation, self-regard, and friendship tell against the action-guidingness of ethics not only by showing that an adequate ethics of acts must go beyond duty and rightness. They also show that an adequate ethics must go beyond acts and act evaluations.

A supererogatory act may well be good and also non-obligatory. But so is my having a cool drink when thirsty. Yet it is hardly supererogatory. The reason here is not that this act is self-regarding. For there may well be self-regarding supererogatory acts, and not every non-obligatory act that benefits another person is

D. Meyers (eds.), *Women and Moral Theory* (Totowa, NJ: Rowman and Allanheld, 1986). See also Susan Wolf, 'Moral Saints', *Journal of Philosophy*, 79 (1982), 410–39 and 'Above and Below the Line of Duty', *Philosophical Topics*, 14 (1986), 131–48.

supererogatory. The reason, rather, is that I am not morally praiseworthy for having the drink and that to be supererogatory the agent must be praiseworthy.[7] Thus, supererogation shows in two important ways why ethics must be concerned with more than duty and other similar action-guiding notions: supererogatory acts are optional and they involve agent evaluations.

The value of friendship and acts of friendship is also bound up with motivation and character—not simply with acts. With friendship even more than with supererogation, it can be the thought that counts. I can treasure my friends thinking well and warmly about me, not simply their doing well by me. Not surprisingly, evaluations of friendship are not simply action-guiding. Among other things, they are also evaluations of agents.[8]

4. NON-ACTION-GUIDING ACT EVALUATIONS

I now want to show in yet a different, even if related, way that our moral concerns extend well beyond action-guidingness even when they are restricted to acts. I will do this by showing that there are important act evaluations which are not action-guiding. I will begin with a general discussion of non-action-guiding act evaluations and then, in later sections, apply this to conflicts. Throughout, I will be primarily concerned to show that judgements using 'ought' can be either action-guiding or non-action-guiding. To a lesser extent, I will also show this of other evaluations, such as 'wrong' and 'good to do'.

In my ' "Ought" and "Can" ' it is argued that even if I cannot

---

[7] See e.g. my 'Professor Chisholm on Supererogation and Offence', *Philosophical Studies*, 21 (1967), 87–94, and 'Agent and Other: Against Ethical Universalism'. However, not all acts that are good, non-obligatory, and also done with morally good intentions are supererogatory. In this I disagree with N. K. Badhwar's argument in 'Friendship, Justice, and Supererogation' (*American Philosophical Quarterly*, 22 (1985), 123–31) that since acts of friendship meet those conditions, they are supererogatory. I also disagree with Thomas Hill's argument in 'Kant on Imperfect Duty and Supererogation' (*Kant Studien*, 62 (1971), 55–77) that since Kant at once holds that imperfect duties are good but not obligatory and also allows for imperfect duties, he can thus allow for supererogation. In both cases, the better conclusion is that those conditions are not sufficient for supererogation. I would suggest that in addition, supererogation requires moral heroism or saintliness, or lesser forms of them.

[8] See e.g. my 'The Schizophrenia of Modern Ethical Theories', and 'Values and Purposes', *Journal of Philosophy*, 78 (1981), 747–65, and 'Friendship and Duty'.

do an act, it can still be true that I ought to do it. This is clearest if I am culpable for my inability. So, it would be at best a bad joke for me to suggest that since I have squandered my money, I no longer ought to repay my debts now. 'I ought to repay my debts now' is still true. However, if I cannot repay the money now, 'I ought to repay my debts now' cannot be action-guiding. But then, 'I ought to repay my debts now' is at once true but not action-guiding.

Some may say that it can be action-guiding in regard to some future act—e.g. repaying the debt as soon as I can. I will discuss this below. For now, it is sufficient that it be agreed that 'I ought to repay my debts now' is here and now true even though here and now it cannot be action-guiding.

Culpable inabilities, then, are a rich source of non-action-guiding act evaluations. Another source is found in an issue somewhat similar to that of whether 'ought' implies 'can'. This is the question of whether 'ought' implies, or at least depends on, 'will' or alternatively 'should'—i.e. whether what a person ought to do depends on other things that the person will do or alternatively on other things that the person should do. As currently discussed, this is the issue of actualism versus possibilism.

Consider this presentation of the issues by Frank Jackson and Robert Pargetter.[9] They ask us to consider whether Professor Procrastinate ought to accept an invitation to review a book:

He is the best person to do the review, has the time, and so on. The best thing that can happen is that he says yes, and then writes the review . . . However . . . were Procrastinate to say yes, he would not in fact get around to writing the review. Not because of incapacity or outside interference or anything like that, but because he would keep on putting the task off. . . . [Thus, his saying yes would] lead to the book not being reviewed at all, or at least to a review being seriously delayed. (235.)

Jackson and Pargetter argue that even though Procrastinate ought to do the complex of both agreeing to do the review and then writing the review, since he will never write it, he ought not to agree in the first place. Whether or not they are right, the considerations they adduce are powerful. After all, it will be far

⁹ 'Oughts, Options, and Actualism', *Philosophical Review*, 95 (1986), 233–55, esp. 233, 235. A contrary view is found in I. L. Humberstone, 'The Background of Circumstances', *Pacific Philosophical Quarterly*, 64 (1983), 19–34. Both provide useful references to other works on this subject.

worse if he does agree than if he does not; no one with proper editorial concerns—e.g. getting books reviewed—should ask Procrastinate to do the review; the author will have every right to complain if it is offered to Procrastinate or if he accepts. This is part of their argument for actualism, which is

the view that the values that should figure in determining which option . . . ought to be done . . . are the values of what would be the case were the agent to adopt or carry out the option . . . We will call the alternative view that it is only necessary to attend to what is possible for the agent, Possibilism. (233.)

Possibilists hold that Procrastinate should agree to do the review.

The issue here also attends more serious cases, such as whether to provide clean syringes to heroin addicts to help stop the spread of acquired immune deficiency syndrome, AIDS—assuming, of course, that addicts should not, but will, continue to use heroin and will, if it is the only one available, use an unclean syringe. It will, however, be easier to discuss the dispute between actualism and possibilism in terms of less tragic cases.

I here want to use the debate between actualists and possibilists, without entering into it. I think it clear that there is a sense in which it is not action-guiding to tell Procrastinate to agree to write the review or that he ought both to agree to write it and also to write it. Since he simply will not write the review, telling him to do so will not guide him to do so. The point here is not about what he ought to be told by someone else. Since he will not write the review, his agreeing will be worse for everyone than would his not agreeing. (This of course may not settle whether it would, therefore, be worse *simpliciter*.)

One way to put these points is in terms of evaluations of an incompossible option he might have. Suppose that during the coming month Procrastinate could either do the review or do some research, but not do both. Suppose further that he should do the review instead of the research. On those suppositions, he ought not do the research. But when we add the fact that he will not do the review, we might well think that he ought to do the research. He will then have done at least something of value.

To argue this way might well seem to let considerations of practicality override morality. It may seem that so long as agents can do a given act, the fact that they will freely not do it cannot bear on whether they ought to do it. As Kant says in the Introduction to *The Doctrine of Virtue*, 'We must not determine ethical duties according to our estimate of man's power to fulfil the law; on the contrary, we must estimate man's moral power by the standard of the law . . .' (XIII, Akademie, 403, tr. Mary J. Gregor). In Sartrian terms, we might say that oughts address us in our freedom, not in our facticity, especially not our culpable facticity. And, of course, Procrastinate will be engaging in blatant bad faith if he reasons that since he will not do the review, he ought not agree to do it or that he ought to do something else instead.

The conclusion of these thoughts is that one should not think or tell Procrastinate that he ought to do the research. This would be well on the way to condoning immorality—tailoring moral judgements to accommodate immoralities.

To see how severely we will have to tailor our moral judgements to immorality, suppose that Procrastinate has agreed to do the review and is sitting at home trying, as it were, to do it. Even now, actualists hold that one can think and tell him that he ought instead do the research.

To reinforce the point, consider the case of Default who has borrowed some money. Suppose that, as usual, he will simply not get around to repaying it. Many think it clear that Default ought to save the money needed to repay the debt. But according to actualists, since he will not repay the debt, he ought not do this but ought rather spend the money on a worthy cause or simply on a good time, even though this will make repayment impossible. Possibilists and others will say that this does not even reach the level of expediency, but is out-and-out immorality parading as good sense.

Actualists hold that these expressions of outraged morality seem fine in the abstract, but go much too far in letting considerations of what is ideal override considerations of what is real and practical and thus really possible. We must, they say, face the facts and be realistic. We must aim at what in the circumstances can be achieved. To base ought judgements on what people merely can do, rather than on what they will do, is to waste resources, miss opportunities, and achieve nothing. Indeed, it fails to achieve what can be achieved and instead involves posturing, rule worship, or some other form of paying obeisance to unmet ideals.

To make their point, actualists can invite us to consider the ideal of co-operation. Suppose, they tell us, you and I are rowing together, it is important to reach our destination, and it would be best if you row only on one side and I only on the other. None the less, it would be silly or worse for me to row only on one side if you do not row at all or if you row on both sides. I ought then row on both sides. Here, as generally, we must face the facts and be realistic rather than mouth or even try to implement unrealizable ideals.

(Put in terms of deontic logic, simplification does not hold. 'It ought to be that I do a given act' does not follow from 'it ought to be that both I do that act and you do another'. Put schematically, Oa does not follow from O(a & b).)

To this, possibilists can reply that invoking co-operation gives actualism an unwarranted patina of respectability. Matters are entirely different where the agent who is to act is also the agent who has acted culpably. Here one cannot argue from the fact that following an ideal would be worse than doing something else to the conclusion that the agent thus ought not follow the ideal but rather do that other act. Otherwise Procrastinate and Default not only get away with their immorality, they are rewarded for it. Immorality becomes the justification for immorality.

And indeed—to move away from problems with conjunctive oughts—it seems that by following the line of actualists, we should hold that the simple and immoral fact that one will not do an act that one should do could show that one ought not do it. For it will be better to do what is next best than it would be to do neither what is next best nor what one should do.

The argument now seems to be taking on the familiar lines of arguments over consequentialism. Actualism seems a consequentialist view and possibilism a non-consequentialist one. But this is an artefact of the fact that Jackson and Pargetter present the issue in terms of consequential values. (They do this, they say, to simplify matters.) Thus, like many consequentialists, they suggest that it is evaluatively irrelevant whether a given value is or is not brought about by a free act. So, the fact that Procrastinate freely will not do the review is treated as simply one fact among others— in principle no different from his not doing it because someone or something else makes it impossible.

But the actualism–possibilism debate cuts across the debates over consequentialism. To mention one point, the moral considerations taken into account in the debate between actualism and possibilism may be consequentialist, e.g. pleasure, or non-consequentialist, e.g. reparations.

More importantly, the central actualism–possibilism debate is over which circumstances are rightly taken into account in evaluating acts. So, deontologists who follow Ross hold that one ought to do the strongest prima facie duty. But they can disagree whether this is what is strongest in the actual world, which may include immoralities of your own and those of others, or whether it is what would be strongest if you, and perhaps others, did what you ought to do.

Some have charged that Ross's deontology is virtually a form of consequentialism. But if one of the reasons for this is that it is compatible with actualism, then even some forms of Kantianism are consequentialist. For whether or not Kant was clear on this matter, Kantians can disagree about the world in which we are to test our universalized maxim. It could be this one, with its immoralities, or it could be an ideal or at least a better one.

Sometimes it is clear which world Kantians must invoke. So, in judging whether to punish a wrongdoer, or whether to set up institutions for punishing future wrongdoers, we do not test our maxim in an ideal world where people do what they should do. Rather we turn to a world which involves immorality—e.g. the immorality that is to be punished. But it is unclear whether in judging whether to keep a promise, I should test my maxim in my actual world, which includes broken promises as well as other immoralities, or whether the maxim should be tested in a better world, e.g. one in which promises are kept. If the former, it is unclear whether the immoralities can include mine. And if they can, it is unclear whether these can include broken promises.

Consequentialism, too, is as such neutral to the disputes between actualism and possibilism. First, it is possible to be a con-sequentialist—albeit not of the usual sort—and still distinguish between values that are and those that are not brought about by free human action. Second, it is possible to be a consequentialist and also to be a possibilist. So, ideal utilitarians tell us to consider what would happen if everyone did a given sort of act even where it is known that not everyone will do such acts. Indeed, many of the debates between actualism and possibilism traverse the same grounds as those over accounts of duty in terms of possible consequences.

These two points show what independently seems right: the distinction between actualism and possibilism fails to draw a distinction unless we specify which values are involved (or perhaps unless we specify that in both cases the same values are involved). For there are pairs of ethical theories which make the same judgements even though one is actualist and the other possibilist. So, ideal utilitarians and Rossians may agree about the keeping of promises, both in particular and in general. But their accounts of this obligatoriness differ. Ideal utilitarians invoke possibilist considerations about e.g. happiness or security, while Rossians give an actualist account in terms of the intrinsic rightness of promise-keeping.

I will not enter further into the controversy between actualism and possibilism. For, as noted, I want to use it, not discuss it.

My use of it is this: we have contrary pairs of ought judgements— 'Procrastinate ought to agree to do the review' and 'Procrastinate ought not to agree to do the review', and 'Default ought to save to repay the debt' and 'Default ought not save to repay the debt'. Such contraries cannot both be action-guiding evaluations.

Perhaps one of them is action-guiding. And if it is, that would be important. But what is more important for our present purposes is that both evaluations are bona fide ought-judgements about the act. Thus, an ought-judgement about an act need not be action-guiding.

Even actualists can agree that there is something importantly right about claims by possibilists that Procrastinate ought to agree to do the review and that Default ought to save the money. They could gloss these as making ideal judgements: 'Ideally, they ought to . . .' They could also gloss these as giving grounds for thinking poorly of, even punishing, Procrastinate or Default. After all, it would be strange to think poorly of people for not doing something, or to punish them for not doing it, unless one thought that in some sense or other they ought to have done it.

Possibilists, similarly, can agree that there is something importantly right about claims by actualists that Procrastinate ought to refuse and that Default ought not to save the money. For they can agree that there is a moral need to cut our losses—even our moral losses—and make the best of a bad situation. They could gloss those judgements to make it clear that they are second best judgements—or, since they are often not even that good, *faute de mieux* judgements: 'Since they will not do what they really ought to do, they at least ought to . . .' After all, they will almost certainly agree that Procrastinate's doing neither the review nor the research would be worse than his doing the research instead of the review. And it does seem that at least *faute de mieux* one ought to avoid what is worse.

5. WHY THERE ARE NON-ACTION-GUIDING ACT EVALUATIONS

So far I have argued that not all evaluations are act evaluations and that not all act evaluations are action-guiding evaluations. I now want to suggest why the latter is so. I will do this by suggesting a theoretical framework to justify and give the conceptual location of at least some non-action-guiding act evaluations. This will help us see that even though we certainly want to know whether an act is to be done, we also and quite properly are concerned with other ways of appreciating and evaluating our acts.

I will undertake this by focusing on the role of immoralities in act evaluations and the relations between practical and ideal ethics. As will be seen, just as these reasons help justify and locate non-action-guiding act evaluations, these evaluations help give substance to those reasons. My account may thus appear circular. But I think that the better understanding is that these reasons and evaluations are intimately interrelated.

Immorality. As mentioned above, my culpable inability to repay a debt now does not make it false that I ought to repay it now. That would indeed be an easy way to be free of one's obligations. But if repaying the debt were the only thing I ought to do now, I would be in an impracticable stalemate: the only act I ought to do is impossible for me to do. Thus, ethical theories which deny that 'ought' implies 'can' and recognize that, despite my inability, I ought to repay the money now, might seem impractical. But this need not be so. They can recognize that since I cannot do that act, there is something else I ought to do.

It would be misleading to see this other act as only something I ought to do instead of repaying the debt. It is, rather, what I ought to do *faute de mieux*, since I cannot do what I really ought to do. But since I cannot do what I really ought to do, that *faute de mieux* act is, in an action-guiding sense, precisely what I ought to do. As well, it may be that because of my culpable inability, I ought to do still other things—e.g. make amends.

Thus, two different questions about oughts are generated by an inability to do what one really ought to do: 'What ought one to do now that one cannot do what one really ought to do?' and 'What ought one to do to make up for not doing what one really ought to do?' To the former, we might answer that one ought to do what *faute de mieux* ought to be done, and to the latter that one ought to make amends, apologize, and make good any loss some other time.

The reasons which make it impossible to do what one really ought to do and make it necessary, instead, to do the *faute de mieux* act are important in more ways than simply making it true that one ought to do that act. At least often they figure in the moral characterization of the act. This is to say, once again, that it can be misleading to say only that that act is what one ought to do. It is what *faute de mieux* one ought to do, e.g. because of one's immorality. My point here is that the culpable inability does not merely make a given act the act that ought to be done. It also helps constitute the moral nature of that act—as being what *faute de mieux* ought to be done. Here we might compare engaging in community service—e.g. painting the meeting hall—as part of judicial punishment. As in the *faute de mieux* case, why the act is to be done is part of the moral nature of what is to be done. It is misleading to describe the act simply as painting the hall. It is painting the hall as part of one's sentence.

Inabilities engendered by immorality thus help justify and locate non-action-guiding act evaluations. These evaluations also help us understand those inabilities. They show that an ethical theory can be practical even if it denies that 'ought' implies 'can'. For they show that even if an action-guiding 'ought' implies 'can', there are other important and non-action-guiding 'oughts', which need not imply 'can'.

To conclude these comments on the role of immoralities, I want to suggest another way they may be important in explaining why there are both action-guiding and non-action-guiding act evaluations. This will also suggest one reason why actualism and possibilism raise such tangled issues.

Moral exemplars—good people—play various interrelated roles

in ethical thinking and life. First, until we are morally competent and can find out for ourselves what is morally correct, we must rely on exemplars as guides. Second, even after we are morally competent, how such exemplars would act and feel can serve as a guide to how we should act and feel. Third, part of our justification for claims—perhaps even part of what we mean by claims—that we should act or feel in certain ways is that exemplars would do so. These suggested roles of exemplars are, of course, drawn from Aristotle. But some are also found elsewhere, such as in Roderick Firth's account of the ideal observer.

If exemplars do play these roles, we have an explanation for at least some of the tensions between actualism and possibilism, and more generally an explanation of how immoralities can generate seemingly conflicting ought-judgements. For we will, then, understand a question which asks what Procrastinate is to do as asking what a good person in his circumstances would do. But an essential feature of his circumstances is that he is morally weak and not good. Since a good person is morally strong and good, the question thus asks what a morally strong and good person who is morally weak and not good would do.

Recourse to moral exemplars also involves us in such contrary judgements when confronted with, not immorality, but weakness or incapacity. Suppose that you have once again entered into an intimate relationship in which you are dominated—the sort of relationship you seem ineluctably drawn into. Accepting and reasoning on the basis of your weakness, those who care for you might be glad that you are now no longer alone and they might hope that you will be able to make the best of the present relationship. But reasoning on the basis of how mature and healthy people should relate, they can be sad that you are now involved in yet another of those relationships and they might hope that you will soon break it off.

Such contrary-to-possibility judgements and questions do make sense of a certain kind. But they also commit us to contrary claims and answers, depending on which aspect of the impossible complex is focused on and taken as the background for evaluating. This helps explain the contrary ought-judgements about Procrastinate's freely not doing the review. When we focus on and argue from his freedom, it seems clear that he ought to accept. But when we argue from the fact that he will not do the review, it seems clear that he ought not to accept. Similarly in the relationship case.

Some might instead suggest that such contrariety shows that we should not use exemplars in our ethics. But even if this is possible, it is not clear that it is desirable. At the least, it would involve a wide-ranging change and disruption to our ethical thought and understanding. For as just suggested in connection with the relationship case, it seems a feature not only of our judgements concerning immoralities, but also of our judgements about imperfections.

Practical and ideal ethics. The second reason we should expect there to be both action-guiding and non-action-guiding evaluations is that our ethical life and thought are a mixture of both the practical and the ideal. What I mean by the practical and the ideal can be seen by looking at theorists or theories which emphasize the one or the other. So, in political theory and practice we would compare the struggles between practicality and pragmatism, on the one hand, and idealism and the demand for purity, on the other.

The practically-minded can be taken as seeing their task as making the best of a bad business, cutting moral losses, and striving only for what is humanly practicable and in that sense possible. They insist on rules and principles which we can reasonably expect people to implement and which will thus work.[10]

They hold that if a moral view will not be accepted and acted on, then it does not hold. They thus seem to be actualists about the value of accepting and acting on moral views. Quite naturally, then, both actualism and a concern with an ethics that will work attract the same charges of immorality. Once again, it may seem that an immoral unwillingness to do what one ought to do provides its own reward. But once again, there is the same sort of reply: 'These charges of immorality are expressions of dangerous and essentially immoral idealism.' So, actualists reject as silly, or even dangerous, those moralities which ask more of people than they will deliver. This might be called the wise administrator's approach to ethics.

There are of course problems over what is to be counted as practical. It is often difficult to know whether reaching for what

[10] See R. Brandt, 'Toward a Credible Form of Rule Utilitarianism', in H.-N. Casteneda and G. Nakhnikian (eds.), *Morality and the Language of Conduct* (Detroit: Wayne State University Press, 1963); and *Principia Ethica*, sect. 98.

seems unattainable will show that it was really attainable. Further, working for the unattainable often achieves something else, if only a salutary reminder or example. We might call these factual impediments to knowing what is practical.

A more theoretical impediment is provided by a systematic ambiguity or unclarity in ethical thought about practicality. The practical is sometimes understood as the practicable: i.e. what can be done or achieved. This is an evaluatively neutral and largely metaphysical understanding. Practical-mindedness here involves little, if anything, more than holding that 'ought' implies 'can'. But often the practical is understood in an evaluatively charged way, in terms of what can be done or achieved and is also worth doing or achieving.

The two senses of practicality are found in Aristotle's claim: '. . . nor are those ideas only to be regarded as practical which are pursued for the sake of practical results, but much more the thoughts and contemplations which are independent and complete in themselves . . .' (*Politics*, 7. 3, 1325b19, tr. Jowett). So too, these two senses are found in our thought about moral ideals.

The first understanding of practicality allows that if one can engage in contemplation or if one can stand up for an ideal, then doing that can be practical. This understanding of practicality allows that one can do these things in either a practical or impractical way. Some who engage in contemplation do it well, and some poorly. And some idealists are good at making their point and standing up for their ideals, while others are poor at this.

Those who are practically-minded in the second way say that those last idealists are poor at this—even at this. As this sarcasm indicates, the second understanding of practicality has it that even if one can engage in contemplation or stand up for an ideal, doing that would not be practical since it would achieve nothing. Practicability is here not in question. What is in question is the severe restriction such practical-mindedness puts on which attainable goals are worth attaining.

It might seem that I have over-specified the morally charged understanding of the practical. For I could have said simply that it excludes from the practical those attainable goals it does not find worth attaining, whatever they are, rather than saying that it excludes contemplation and standing up for ideals. But this would be to de-ethicize this morally charged understanding of practicality.

For on this understanding, practicality is to be understood in terms of hard-headed and consequentialist goals.

Hard-headedness—some would say hard-heartedness—rather than consequentialism is what is here important. After all, ideal utilitarians are consequentialists. Indeed, because of their possibilism, they are criticized for the softness shown in their concern with what ideally would be, rather than a hard-headed and tough-minded concern with what is attainable. To be practically-minded, then, is not simply to hold that 'ought' implies 'can'. Nor is it simply to be an actualist rather than a possibilist. It is to hold hard-headed views about what there ought to be.

This point is important enough—both for understanding the present issue and for understanding other issues in contemporary ethical theories—to pause to put it in a related way. As just seen, the distinction between actualism and possibilism is not usefully drawn unless we specify which values are involved. If we understand theories as agreeing to the extent they agree on act evaluations, we can get at least many actualist and possibilist theories to agree, by ensuring that they have different, but appropriately related, values.

Correlatively, for the abstract distinction between non-consequentialism and consequentialism to draw a useful distinction, we must specify which consequences are morally relevant. The historical consequentialist theories were, of course, concerned only with certain sorts of consequences, e.g. states of consciousness, rather than just whatever may be recognized as a consequence by metaphysics. We also have a strong theoretical reason for not counting as consequentialist just any consequence. For almost any feature is a consequence of something or other. Thus, both the historical and the theoretical contrasts between consequentialist and non-consequentialist theories depend on restricting the notion of consequences.

Without such a restriction, one could label consequentialist the deliberations of a legislator who decides to vote for a bill because it will protect rights. For even if rights, themselves, are understood non-consequentially, the legislator is concerned to effect their protection. To attempt to de-ethicize these central moral concepts is thus to misunderstand them.[11]

[11] On this see my 'Consequentialism and its Complexities', *American Philosophical Quarterly*, 6 (1969), 276–89 and 'Rightness and Goodness: Is There a Difference?', *American Philosophical Quarterly*, 10 (1973), 87–98.

Practical-mindedness in ethics, then, is a combination of both actualism and hard-headedness in the choice of values. Idealists see such practicality as acquiescing in immorality and defect. Idealists take ethics as requiring standing up for ideals and principles, even where, according to practical-mindedness, this does no good— even where, as Kant put it, the heavens may fall. (Contemplation seems no more important for contemporary idealists than for the practically-minded. To this extent, modern idealists are modern.)

There are problems, however, in knowing what is ideal. Of central importance to us is that there are too many ideals, some of which are too ideal. Among these are perfection itself and, more modestly, achieving all the severally possible values. As seen above in the discussion of the incompossibility account of conflict, the latter is the ideal of not having to choose among incompossible values but, instead, getting them all.

One way to see that these ideals are too ideal is that they show near enough everything lacking and conflicting. For nothing, at least among what is humanly obtainable, is perfect. And if Leibniz is right, even what is only divinely possible—the best of all possible worlds—may contain some bads and fail to include some goods. Earlier we rejected the incompossibility account of conflict because it held that virtually every choice involves a conflict. We should, similarly, reject accounts of conflict which find conflict everywhere perfection is not achieved.

What is needed is a plausible and sensible idealism—but one which, none the less, transcends mere practicality. We have a well-known, even if difficult, device for helping find such an idealism: it is to ask what it is possible for people in given circumstances to do if they act freely, rationally, and with good-will or at least without ill-will. This is central to many accounts of politics and ethics, especially social ethics. It is also central to 'the art of the possible'. So for example, in part because of its now being seen possible, we require non-discriminatory practices in the education of boys and girls that even a short while ago were, if noted at all, relegated to the merely ideal.

We have already seen that we do use this device—e.g. in the ideal judgements that people ought to do what they have culpably made themselves unable to do, that Procrastinate ought to agree to do the review, and that Default ought to save to repay the debt. This is important enough to put in another way. Many agree that 'ought' does not imply 'can' if the agent is culpable for the inability. But what is the status of culpable inability? If generally 'ought' does imply 'can', why does it not do so here? Why is there this exception or anomaly?

My answer is that it is not an exception or anomaly. Rather, it points to the vital role played in our ethical thinking by the realm of possibilities given by human freedom. What people can freely do, or what given their freedom they could have done—in the light of what they know or should have known, of course—is one of the important parameters giving the acts which are relevantly considered in questions about what ought to be or ought to be done. This has already been seen in the argument between actualism and possibilism.[12]

Having made these very brief comments about idealism, let us return to the dispute between practical and ideal ethics. It might be thought that each side of the dispute is partly right and that we really do want two sorts of ethics: an ideal ethics to express our aspirations, and a practical one to show us what in real life to do. (In political activity and terms, this often comes out as seeing the need for theoreticians and idealists on the one hand, and on the other, practical and effective leaders and politicians.)

This view is an improvement over the one which limits ethics to what is action-guiding. It at least acknowledges the existence of non-action-guiding evaluations and gives them some role.

None the less, it is seriously mistaken in the way it divides what we might call the moral work, by suggesting that practically-minded ethics is the ethics for the real, hard, and workaday world of action, and that ideal ethics is the ethics for contemplation, discussion, or religion. Were this so, then when concerned with what is here and now to be done—as opposed to what ideally should be done—we should be concerned only with what is action-guiding.

In deciding what to do, one must of course pay attention to what is action-guiding. But often, one must also give weight to what is non-action-guiding, whether one is doing what can be seen as ideal and visionary or practical and hard-headed. Even while serving an ideal, often one should be aware of what practical things one could instead be doing, e.g. what actual and pressing needs one could instead be fulfilling. And even while doing what is practicable, often

---

[12] See also Donagan, and as listed by him in n. 17, Aquinas, *Summa Theologica*, I–II, 6 *ad* 3; II–II, 62, 2; III, 64, 6 *ad* 3; *de Veritate*, 17, 4 *ad* 8.

one should be aware of what ideally one should be doing, e.g. which values one is compromising, which ideals one could instead be upholding.

Many of our ethical theories fail to see matters this way. They encourage the insensitivity of thinking that what is action-guiding is near enough everything. This is an insensitivity to ideals, and a blindness or indifference to the very real costs that even justified compromises can involve. The most that would be recognized about a justified cost is that there is a prima facie reason against incurring it which may, as here, be overridden. This is a form of crassness—many have said, a peculiarly utilitarian or pragmatic crassness—which asks only where the action is and gets its answer by looking only at the bottom line.

However, there is also the insensitivity of looking only to the ideal. This seems to forget that the world is hard and real, with urgent problems, that people are suffering and dying, that hard choices must be made and followed out resolutely, that often the best we can do is make compromises and cut our losses—and that this is necessary simply to make life tolerable, much less good. It also seems to forget that often idealism is possible only because others are leading hard-headed and practical lives.

Idealism, especially when excessively ideal, might be thought to show unworldliness. But as Hegel and Nietzsche argue, it can also show a sick or malignant cynicism, despair, or indifference—either to the way the world is or how people could make it better.

6. NON-ACTION-GUIDING ACT EVALUATIONS AND ETHICS

In this section I will continue the discussion of non-action-guiding act evaluations. Let me start by pointing out that they are in no way mysterious. They are the stuff of everyday evaluations. So, we are familiar with act evaluations which focus on how the acts came to be options: e.g. 'Because of the unjust social system, she had to choose between having a family and having a profession. Whether or not she made the right choice, she ought not to have had to make such a choice.'

So too, even where all the options are entirely acceptable, there may be negative evaluations which are read back on to them from the way they came to be options. So, I might be faced with a choice between several entirely fulfilling professions but complain that it was all laid on for me because of family connections and that I never had to worry or struggle—that I never had to make my own way. Or I might complain against the social system for giving me and others like me an easy and free choice among these professions, while restricting others to drudgery.

We are also familiar with act evaluations which give expression to ideals: e.g. 'If only the other job applicants would let their work speak for them, there would be no need for us to spend time in lobbying the selection committee.' And of course, we are familiar with evaluations of acts which are impossible because of untoward happenings: e.g. 'If only I had not squandered my money, I could repay my debts.'

It is hardly surprising that these evaluations are part and parcel of our ordinary life. They are grounded by the same considerations that ground action-guiding evaluations. The only difference is that for various circumstantial reasons these considerations here and now do not tell us what to do. Rather, they tell us how to appreciate what is to be done. In the cases considered, they tell us that what is to be done is regrettable.

So far I have focused on non-action-guiding act evaluations of bad options. Here I will simply note that there are such evaluations of good options, too. I am here not thinking of good options we have for bad reasons, where the badness is read back on to the act, as in the case of beneficiaries of unjust social systems. Rather, I am thinking of evaluations which speak of favourable features of the act that go beyond action-guidingness.

Various objections have been advanced against my claim that there are non-action-guiding act evaluations of acts—e.g. that despite the fact that an act is to be done, it is none the less regrettable. Some hold that these evaluations are, instead, action-guiding. And some hold that they are, instead, agent evaluations. To understand how I see non-action-guiding act evaluations, it will be useful to see why these objections fail. I will consider them in turn.

Various acts have been singled out as the act we are guided to do by that evaluation. Some say that the act is a future or a possible act of the same sort that now cannot be done. Some say that the act is, for example, atoning or making up for the regrettable act that here and now is to be done. And some say that the act is simply that of here and now feeling regret.

I certainly agree that if an act is regrettable, then other similar acts should be avoided. But I do not see how the fact that other acts should be avoided shows that this present act is here and now not regrettable. Indeed, it seems to show just the contrary. For it is because they possess the very same objectionable feature that this act is regrettable and the others should be avoided. Thus, 'this act is regrettable' can be a non-action-guiding act evaluation of this act, even if it is also an action-guiding act evaluation of other acts.

For similar reasons, I agree that making up for the regrettable act or atoning for it can be appropriate. But I would hold that they are appropriate precisely because of the moral nature of that act— the very same nature which also grounds the non-action-guiding act evaluation.

Let us now turn to the objection that what I call non-action-guiding act evaluations are really action-guiding act evaluations, and that the act they guide us to do is feeling regret over that regrettable act. I find this objection deeply confused. For as the notion of action figures in our understanding of action-guidingness and act evaluations, feeling or experiencing a moral emotion is not an act. Thus, however much we may be guided in regard to it, we cannot be guided to do it.

Perhaps this last claim should be modified in a way that makes it approach the first one: 'This act is regrettable' guides us to get ourselves to be able to regret, and indeed to get ourselves to regret, either this act or similar acts or both. Even if the emotion and having the emotion are not acts, such gettings are acts.

Just as this claim is similar to the first one, my reply to it is similar. I can readily accept this claim about emotional development. In no way does it show, or even suggest, that this present act is not regrettable. On the contrary. The reason we should get ourselves to be able to regret, and get ourselves to regret, doing such acts is precisely the reason this present act is regrettable.

Let us turn, then, to another set of objections—that what I call non-action-guiding act evaluations are not act evaluations at all, but are instead agent evaluations. Two different sorts of agent evaluations have been suggested: first, there are evaluations directly of agents, blaming or reproving them for their inability to avoid doing what is, for instance, regrettable. Second, there are evaluations of moral emotions that agents should have. Here, agents ought to regret not doing the impossible act. Although I will deal mainly with the second, what I say is easily extended to the first.

Many philosophers hold that act and agent evaluations are necessarily disjoint—that there are no, or no important, conceptual connections between act and agent evaluations. This claim of no conceptual connections could be used to argue that if what I said does have implications for agent evaluations, then it could hardly show anything about act evaluations.

However, this claim of no conceptual connection is seriously mistaken. I will show this here in regard to one sort of connection—a sharing of grounds.[13] In particular, I will show that some agent evaluations involved in evaluations of character defects share their grounds with some evaluations of acts. If I am right about this sharing of grounds, I can happily agree that my claims about non-action-guiding act evaluations are about agent evaluations— especially if those agent evaluations hold for the same reasons as do the act evaluations in question.

The central ideas here are straightforward. First, moral emotions can be about acts and can be grounded by what also ground evaluations of the acts. For example, that I will hurt a friend in doing what morally I must do is a reason for regretting that act, and also for the non-action-guiding act evaluation that I ought not to do it.

Second, whether or not people have a moral emotion helps show, or even helps constitute, their character. So, among the important explanations of not regretting hurting the friend is a one-eyed attention to what is to be done. To have this defect would be to fall short of even the impersonal feeling of regret that unfortunately morality can require hurting innocents. Another sort of explanation would be in terms of a general affectlessness or a general hardness of heart and lack of fellow-feeling.

I do not think we need to argue that not regretting hurting one's friend shows a defective moral character. Apart from the special

---

[13] That there are important conceptual connections between act and agent evaluations is shown more generally in my 'Act and Agent Evaluations', *Review of Metaphysics*, 27 (1973), 42–61. See also, N. O. Dahl, 'Obligation and Moral Worth: Reflections on Prichard and Kant', *Philosophical Studies*, 50 (1986), 369–99, and S. D. Hudson, *Human Character and Morality*.

considerations discussed below, I think it obvious that it does. It is constitutive of being a good person that we care about our friends and regret hurting them, even if hurting them is morally justified.

My claim, then, is that good people appreciate the moral world in ways which go beyond simply seeing what is to be done. Their moral concern extends beyond act evaluations, and their concern with act evaluations extends beyond what is action-guiding. Further, they do not merely see their moral concerns, they also feel them.[14]

So far I have talked only of feelings connected with non-action-guiding evaluations. This might suggest that only where we cannot act should we have feelings—as if feelings are a substitute for action and are irrelevant if there is action. This is mistaken. The grounds of action-guiding act evaluations are also grounds of agent evaluations. And here, too, not having the correct moral emotion towards an act—now, an act that is to be done—can involve a character defect.

Put most broadly, the defects are again those of moral-emotional coldness or of affectlessness. Having no feeling whatsoever in doing what one ought—not even a quiet feeling of rectitude, pride, or satisfaction—is a form of moral-emotional deadness. Our modern ethical theories do little to warn against this deadness. They may even encourage it—if only by their concentration on action-guidingness. Set against them, and constituting one of its signal strengths, is the Aristotelian dual emphasis on doing what is right and also having the right moral emotions in and towards what one is doing.

Indeed, once we agree that it is morally appropriate or even necessary to have certain moral emotions about acts that cannot be done, it is difficult to deny that the same holds for acts that can be done and are done. Such a denial would require something like the claim that feeling is a substitute for action.

---

[14] My claim is that such feeling is constitutive of a good and healthy person. Raimond Gaita argues that such feeling is constitutive of moral understanding, as such. (See e.g. his 'The Personal in Ethics', to appear in the Festschrift for Rush Rhees edited by P. Winch.) Thus, on his view, only what I call a good and healthy person can have correct moral understanding. My reasons for rejecting his strong claim are given in 'Psychic Feelings', *Australasian Journal of Philosophy*, 61 (1983), 5–26 and 'Emotional Thoughts', *American Philosophical Quarterly*, 24 (1987), 59–69. None the less, our agreement here is far more important than is our disagreement. For we are both, and for at least largely the same reasons, strongly opposed to dry, cognitive accounts of moral understanding. Further, if one thinks, as e.g. Aristotle did, that the primary understanding of moral phenomena is in terms of good examples or exemplars, our disagreement is shown to be even smaller.

Some might not see this, thinking that the moral emotion is directed simply at the inability to do the act, and not the act that cannot be done. To be sure, such inability can ground a moral emotion such as regret, whereas ability can ground pleasure. So too, in some cases an inability to do what one otherwise would have to do can be a source of relief. But for our purposes, two other facts are even more important. First, the very same features ground both the correlative action-guiding act evaluation and the appropriate moral emotion when a good and healthy person does what is to be done. Second, in the case where the act cannot be done, those are grounds for the correlative non-action-guiding act evaluation and the appropriate moral emotion.

One way to sustain these points would be through an investigation of the relations, especially the moral psychological relations, between emotions and actions. Such an investigation would, I suggest, show that the very same features can lead to the moral emotion and, where possible, to action. Indeed, this is an ideal of good and healthy people.

This last point about leading to action is important in the way it tells against the charge sometimes heard: that virtue ethics makes no requirements on action but rather requires or recommends only correct feeling. I will here pass over the historical illiteracy of this— e.g. that Aristotelian ethics requires both correct action and correct feeling. For I am concerned with the claim that it is possible to have feelings without acting.

This, however, seems to be simply the reverse side of the claim that one can act rightly without right feeling. And both claims are mistaken about sound and healthy people in good circumstances, even if they can be right when restricted to weak, sick, or otherwise defective people or people in bad circumstances.

To see this, let us ask what must be assumed to imagine people who have the right moral feelings about a situation they can affect but who do not even try to act in the appropriate ways. Consider a case where I see that a friend is in danger of being harmed. Suppose that I am emotionally moved—e.g. saddened—by the foreseen harm. Suppose also that I see that I could save my friend from that harm. Suppose further that I do not do what I see I can do. These suppositions seem jointly possible. But what in addition must be supposed about me to understand all these suppositions?

And once we understand them, how am I to be understood and evaluated?

Of course, I may have good reason not to go to my friend's aid. It might be too difficult or costly for me to do so. At the very least, it might not have been my responsibility. For these and other reasons, my non-action may not tell against me—at least not to the point of showing me sick, bad, or otherwise defective.

But other explanations of my non-action do show defects. For example, I retreat from being an agent to being merely a spectator. I am morally weak or lazy. I let my attention wander and fail to exercise sufficient active concern and control over what I see I should do. I suffer from any number of neurotic blocks. And so on.

To the extent these are the explanations, there are strong and important psychological, moral, and moral psychological connections among emotions, moral emotions, and action. Having thus shown the propriety of linking act and agent evaluations, we can return to the agent evaluations found in the moral emotions.

It is difficult enough simply to list, much less characterize, the moral emotions that are appropriate or needed even in regard to acts that should be done and are done. But it does seem that a sense of fitness and the proper satisfaction, pleasure, and moral ease in doing what is right are among the moral emotions one should or could appropriately have towards the doing of acts that are to be done. Often, of course, there will be pleasure in doing what is to be done, not simply because it is to be done, but because of why it is to be done, e.g. because it involves helping those in need. (We must, of course, avoid the dangers of self-satisfaction, self-righteousness, and the like.)

As difficult as it is to characterize the proper moral emotions toward simple cases of doing what is to be done, matters are far more difficult where there are conflicts. In such cases, the proper moral emotion is not a simple combination of the emotions proper to the conflicting act evaluations—say, full satisfaction and full regret. It will instead involve the one interpenetrated and informed by the other.

In the case of hurting the friend in doing what is to be done, there can be regret. But this regret can and often should be modulated by the realization that what is regrettable is morally justified or even necessary. So too, there can be satisfaction, perhaps a solemn and grave satisfaction, or a form of relief, that at least what must be done was in fact done and that the hurt was not morally gratuitous and unjustified.

This is to say that the proper moral-emotional appreciation of a conflict is a complex mixture of the moral emotions proper to each of the conflicting act evaluations. Extending an earlier claim, it is also to say that each of these act evaluations shares the same grounds as its correlative moral emotion.

It is also to say that the proper act evaluation—and at an ideal of completeness, the total act evaluation—of a conflict will be a complex of the action-guiding and also the non-action-guiding act evaluations. As said earlier, it would be crassly insensitive to hold that action-guiding act evaluations tell everything of moral importance about acts and it would also be insensitive in another, perhaps an unworldly, way to think that non-action-guiding act evaluations tell everything of moral importance about the act—as if 'it is to be done' or 'it ought to be done' tells us everything of moral importance about the morally necessary act that involves hurting one's friend.

The answer, then, to why we should be interested in moral emotions and correlative agent evaluations can now be put negatively: only a false view of ethics in general and of act evaluations in particular could think that those emotions and evaluations are unimportant.

More needs to be said about why it is important that we engage in making non-action-guiding act evaluations and why it is important that we have the correlative moral emotions. This leads to some of the most difficult and wide-ranging questions in ethics, moral psychology, and—to suggest inquiries in largely unexplored areas—moral anthropology and moral sociology.

We can see this by taking up a variant of the issue raised at the outset of the chapter: how to differentiate options which are and which are not conflicting. The question now would be how to differentiate those sets of non-action-guiding act evaluations and their correlative moral emotions which do and those which do not conflict with sets of action-guiding evaluations and their correlative moral emotions.

The simple answer is that there is conflict if these sets point in opposite directions. It is difficult to characterize such pointing, but some examples are easy enough. Conflicting with the pair of 'good to do' and satisfaction over doing what it is good to do, we have

the pair of e.g. 'good not to do' and the correlative sadness over
doing what is good not to do. However, we have already seen that
conflict cannot be understood in this simple way. For wherever the
incompossibility model is satisfied, there will be such conflicting
sets of evaluations and emotions.

We thus need a different account of conflict. We can get it, I
think, by going over some points made above. Let us start with the
view that action-guidingness is almost all that there is of importance
about act evaluations. One natural understanding of action-
guidingness is in terms of conditional reasons: reasons which show
what is to be done only if there are no stronger contrary reasons.
On such a view, there can be nothing wrong with an act that is
to be done. (An exception may have to be made for top-ranked
incompossible acts; but this is here unimportant.) In a sense, this
may be right. The act is perfect, or at least cannot be faulted, so
far as action-guidingness is concerned. More exactly—and to make
the relevant assumptions explicit—according to a practical theory
that understands wrongness simply in terms of action-guidingness,
there is nothing wrong with any act that is to be done.

Thus we see that the two claims that acts that are to be done
are perfect and that ethics is concerned only with action-guiding
act evaluations depend intimately on each other. Perhaps they are
simply different ways of putting the same claim: that the evaluations
of acts we are really concerned with are all conditional on there
being no stronger contrary evaluations. Correlatively, the claims
that acts that are to be done are not perfect and that there is more
to act evaluations than action-guidingness depend intimately on
each other. In a way, they too are simply different ways of putting
one claim: that we are concerned with evaluations of acts even if
there are stronger contrary evaluations.

The fact that acts that are to be done are imperfect allows for
rational conflict and regret, without at the same time requiring an
incomplete or impractical ethics. But imperfection as such is not
sufficient for rational conflict and regret. To hold this would be
to embrace the mistakes I earlier ascribed to the incompossibility
account of conflict and the idealism which takes perfection as the
only goal worth seeking.

We thus need a middle course between the extreme that denies
the possibility of conflict by holding that there is nothing wrong
with acts that are to be done and the extreme that finds conflict

everywhere perfection is not attained. In our present terms, we thus need an account of which groups of evaluations and emotions that point in different directions give grounds for being conflicted and which do not.

I suggest we join those who use regret as a key to conflicts. We will join them in thinking that regret can show conflict, even though we will not join them in thinking that such conflicts show ethics either incomplete or impractical. The question for us, then, is 'When is regret rational?' More exactly, 'When can it be rational to regret doing what clearly is to be done?'

It should now be obvious that we cannot expect a simple and complete account of when regret is rational. For that account will involve an account of when and, at an extreme, whether we should care about, even to the point of regretting, what could or what should have been, or whether we should instead restrict our concern to what can be and is. It is important to remember that the sort of idealism I have urged, as a counterpoise to practical-mindedness, is firmly rooted in real human possibilities. And as wrong as it may seem to regret the non-occurrence of what is merely ideal, it is also wrong simply to put up with, and not even regret, failures, harms, and evils that could easily be avoided.

This, of course, is not the end of the matter. We also need a general examination and evaluation of different sorts of moral-emotional lives and the associated forms of moral cultures and character structures. So for example, we need to adjudicate among the warmth and concern urged by Aristotle, the coolness and detachment of Stoicism and Buddhism, and the practical-mindedness of so many of our current ethical theories.

On a smaller scale, we must also examine, from both moral and moral psychological standpoints, different character types typified by different forms of conflict. Here we would examine, for instance, the important differences between (1) the conflict shown by an unwillingness to do anything that runs counter to one's desires and (2) the conflict shown by an unwillingness to do what is demeaning or what violates one's strongly held values. So too, we would examine (3) the lack of conflict shown by a ready and uncomplaining acceptance of things no matter how bad they are and how they came about. The first can easily suggest an undesirable egoism or improper self-concern. The second suggests proper pride and self-respect, while the third suggests lack of these, even to the point of abjectness and servility.

Once again, we must come to grips with Nietzsche's claims about character—e.g. that those caught up in *resentiment* will find, often because they create, conflict nearly everywhere, whereas Zarathustra-like people, those who have overcome themselves, may easily and perhaps joyously accept almost everything, even what is most conflicting. Less grandly, we must recognize that some people are possessed of a sourness, always seeing what is bad or what is simply lacking in everything no matter how good it really is. Others, of course, are possessed of a correlative uncritical, cloying oversweetness. We must also deal with the related and general issues about the nature and justifiability of optimism and pessimism, and also of general ambivalence and resoluteness.

One way to summarize these various points is by turning to a notion closely related to, if not a special sort of, conflict: that of not really wanting to do what we do. We can understand how a bank teller does not really want to hand over the money to the armed robber. But an especially complaisant teller might not mind doing this. And a teller who is glad of the harm done to the bank or the larger social or economic system by the robbery might even be pleased to do it. So too, at certain times I really do want to continue in my very good position, but at others I really want simply to laze away my days in a tropical paradise. And at still other times, I really want to be done with everything.

The possibilities, then, of really wanting or not wanting to do what we do are as various as what we do. The attitudes of desire can range from simple acceptance of just whatever one is faced with to more or less complete rejection of everything or at least everything that falls short of the totally ideal. What is needed, thus, is a schooling of desire. One must learn where to be satisfied and where to be dissatisfied, where really to want to do what one does or must do, and where not to want this. In many respects, this is to learn where not to be conflicted and where to be conflicted.

Having seen how many difficult issues must be taken up and the depth to which they must be pursued, we see that there is unlikely to be any simple and complete account of rational conflicts. But to the extent that we can see conflicts in terms of regrets and what is regrettable, in terms of what could or should have been, rather than in terms of conflicting action-guiding evaluations, some considerable progress has been made.

7. CONFLICTS AND NON-ACTION-GUIDING ACT EVALUATIONS

The application of these points about non-action-guiding act evaluations to our initial concerns with conflicts is straightforward. If, as I claim has been assumed, a conflict is a conflict between action-guiding evaluations, and if these are overall and not merely prima facie evaluations, ethics cannot be complete and practical. For where there are such conflicts, there will be no practicable answer to the question of what ought to be done.

But if a conflict is a conflict between an action-guiding and a non-action-guiding act evaluation, we need conclude nothing of the sort. We need not even conclude from them that 'ought' does not imply 'can'. Such conflicts do not prevent ethics from being complete and practical. They need not preclude, or even impede, judgement. And they show that there can be conflict—i.e. one can be conflicted—even if it is clear what is to be done and even if that act is done resolutely.

It will be useful to bring out these points through a brief consideration of several examples. Let us start with the following claim: 'Finishing the painting was the best thing I could then do and it was what I had an obligation to do. After all, I had accepted the commission. But it had no significance at all really—my country was then at war and I wanted to do something practical and useful.' Insignificance can ground an action-guiding evaluation. But it does not do so here. The agent recognizes that the painting must be done. None the less, as I think clear, the painter expresses a conflict between duty and significance, between what is here an action-guiding evaluation and a non-action-guiding evaluation.

This, however, may not seem the sort of conflict we are interested in. After all, many fail to see significance as having much to do with morality. I think they are mistaken. Either they fail to see the importance of appreciating the significance of one's acts, projects, and life or they fail to see this as part of ethics. If the former, they have a strange view of what is humanly important and valuable. If the latter, they have a strange view of ethics.

Let us, however, turn to another case of conflict which also involves a non-action-guiding act evaluation, and which is closer to what is usually seen as raising moral issues. Suppose that I have studied and taught philosophy in universities for many years and that the students I now have are unable to write well, and are largely unable to understand philosophical texts of any real complexity. Suppose further that I finally come to see that what I really must do is suspend teaching philosophy and instead give time to the essentially remedial tasks of helping them to read and write.

I may be in no doubt that this is what I must do and I may resolutely do it. But that in no way need still my regrets and sorrow for my students, anger at what has left them so unprepared, and lamenting thoughts about whether this is what I have spent my life preparing for. The regret, sorrow, anger, and laments embody and give expression to evaluations of what I see that I must do. They show my opposition to it and conflict over it. But even though they express the conflict, they need in no way involve vacillation, uncertainty, or any other form of irresoluteness. They can be simply non-action-guiding evaluations of that act.

Once again, it may be said that we are here not presented with the sort of conflict we are really concerned with—moral conflict. I think this claim is questionable. But rather than pursue that issue, let us turn to judgements which are uncontentiously moral. Even here, we will find non-action-guiding act evaluations.

Compromises are fertile grounds for our inquiry. I am here not concerned with unexceptionable compromises—e.g. our agreeing to take turns in choosing which movie to go to. Unless, for instance, you or I think that one of us should always make the choice, there should be no conflict here. Rather, the compromises I have in mind are morally compromising compromises. To do these is to be compromised.

So, some people, to keep their job, must cease criticizing the government. And, in order to vote for the better political party, we may have to endorse and thus 'give a mandate' to a political platform containing some bad, or even immoral, policies. So too, of course, for more global political choices, e.g. whether to give one's allegiance to one or another super-power or major ideology or to refuse to take sides.

Even in these cases of compromising compromises, the agent may be clear about what to do. The alternative option may be so much worse that it is not seen as a real moral option at all. And the act may be done with perfect resoluteness. None the less, there can be conflict—e.g. because of what has to be done or how it came to be what has to be done. As Ross put it in *The Right and the Good*:

When we think ourselves justified in breaking, and indeed morally obliged to break, a promise in order to relieve someone's distress, we do not for a moment cease to recognize a prima facie duty to keep our promise, and this leads us to feel, not indeed shame or repentance, but certainly compunction, for behaving as we do . . .'[15]

Such compunction involves a non-action-guiding evaluation of the act that is to be done. It shows a conflict between that act and the overridden act.

8. OTHER CONFLICTS

Although a lot of important ground has been covered, my argument has had a limited aim. It is silent on the following issues: whether there can be conflicts between overall action-guiding evaluations; whether people are conflicted by what they take to be conflicts between overall or prima facie action-guiding evaluations; whether conflicts can be generated by, or in other ways involve, uncertainty about what is to be done; and whether, if there are any such conflicts, they can be rational.

Now, there may be conflicts that involve uncertainty about what is to be done. But for that to bear on the completeness and practicality of an ethical theory, it would have to be shown that the theory itself is responsible—and indeed at fault—for the uncertainty. For any theory can be misapplied. It must also be shown that where the theory is silent on which of jointly impossible acts to do, it would not simply be all right to pick either of these acts. For a theory can be complete even if it allows that it is sometimes indifferent whether one does this act or that one.

Further, I have not been concerned with irrational conflict, e.g. that found in akrasia. Nor have I been much concerned with conflicts that involve more than one non-action-guiding act evaluation—e.g.

[15] Oxford: Oxford University Press, 1963, 28.

those between the various ideal ought-judgements noted in the discussion of actualism and possibilism.

Nor, indeed, have I tried to give conditions that determine whether an act evaluation is action-guiding or not. And it remains to be seen exactly how to distinguish these. To this extent, it thus remains to be seen whether, as I have suggested, conflicts can involve only one action-guiding act evaluation in conflict with non-action-guiding act evaluations, or whether, as Marcus, Williams, and others require, these conflicts involve conflicts between action-guiding act evaluations. The polemical position here might thus be thought of as a stand-off. I claim that the ought-judgements making up a conflict are not both action-guiding act evaluations and the others claim that they are.

Even if this were all that could be said, I think the burden of proof would have shifted to those I criticize. But more can be said. The main points are these: those I criticize have not considered whether the conflicting ought-judgements are action-guiding, for they have—with few, if any, exceptions—simply taken it that any act evaluation cast in terms of 'ought to do' is action-guiding. Thus, they have simply taken it that the form of conflicts is 'ought to do *b*' and 'ought to do *c*' where these are both action-guiding act evaluations and are severally possible but jointly impossible. One way of putting this is that they have simply assumed that the conflicts violate the doctrine that 'ought' implies 'can', that conflicts show ethics incomplete, impractical, or non-realistic.

But, as I have tried to show, it is clear that there are at least some judgements cast in terms of 'ought to do' which are non-action-guiding act evaluations. Further, I also think it clear that recourse to such evaluations shows how we account for conflict in ways that do not call into question the possibility of a complete, practical, and realistic ethics, and without having to invoke uncertainty, indecision, and vacillation.

9. THE REAL IMPORTANCE OF CONFLICTS FOR ETHICAL THEORY

I want to conclude this chapter with two points about conflicts: first about the conflicts discussed in the recent literature, and second about conflicts as understood here.

Many of the conflicts discussed in the recent literature, such as those involving dirty hands, are morally gripping, even tragic. But precisely because they involve disasters and extreme situations, they may well be less important for ethical theory than is thought. To the extent that our lives are not made up of disasters and extreme situations, there is little reason to think that an ethics that serves us well for them will serve us well generally. Correlatively, ethical theories are not shown worthless by being unable to handle tragic conflicts or by being able to handle them only in *ad hoc* ways. After all, almost every theory has some insoluble problems or makes some *ad hoc* moves. So, if conflicts are rare or at least not of central concern, ethical theories which cannot handle them well can still be accepted—even if they are seen to need some repair.

Thus, the difficulties in accommodating the conflicts discussed in the literature do not really give much incentive for a major reform of our ethical theories—e.g. away from their very great concentration on action-guidingness. But, if I am right about conflicts, the world gives us the very strongest of incentives.

The World. It is beyond argument that the world as we know it gives us grounds for regret and conflict even if we do what is to be done. Moral blindness, perhaps engendered by wilful inattention, provides one of the best explanations of not seeing this.

Hopefulness, extending well beyond mere utopianism, seems necessary for thinking that the world might be changed—or that we might change the world—so that it will no longer provide these grounds for regret and conflict. It would not include immoralities which force us to do what *faute de mieux* ought to be done. Nor would it include natural difficulties which force us to make difficult and painful choices between people or between other values.

Thus, even though we should see how to lessen or eliminate certain conflicts, I do not think we have, or even could have, any real idea of how to do this completely or in general. The present world, and those worlds we should think we could bring about, are worlds of conflict.

Us. It thus remains a question whether we take these up in conflict—and are conflicted by them. Some might think it a kindness of our ethical theories not to encourage feelings of conflict. But unless our ethics should engage in noble lies, it is difficult to see how it could even allow, much less encourage, the moral and emotional insensitivity involved in not feeling these conflicts.

Conflicts thus do pose serious problems for our ethical theories. But they do this not by showing ethics impractical, incomplete, or non-realistic. Rather, they do this by showing our ethical theories mistaken, both about what they have so over-concentrated on— acts and act evaluations—and also about the rest of the world and, above all, about ourselves.

PART II

Plurality and Judgement

5

Courage, the Doctrine of the Mean, and the Possibility of Evaluative and Emotional Coherence

VIRTUE and a good life involve a *mean* of feeling and of action. This is the claim of the Doctrine of the Mean, so central to Aristotle's ethics. Yet, despite the greatly increased respect Aristotelian ethics now enjoys, very few ethicists treat the Doctrine seriously. This is regrettable. For it illuminates many issues central to both Aristotelian and non-Aristotelian ethics.

These issues concern comparing, balancing, and choosing among plural considerations and thus concern the nature and the possibility of evaluatively and emotionally coherent acts, feelings, and lives. Indeed, what is needed to show that good sense can be made of the Doctrine is also needed to show that it is possible to compare, balance, and choose among different values and to have coherent acts, feelings, and lives.

The mean requires judgement. This immediately raises the difficult problem, which I will simply ignore, of the relations between virtue and practical wisdom. Even apart from this, it is difficult to understand or apply the needed judgement. After all, it is not an arithmetical mean, but one relative to the agent and the agent's circumstances. Further, some acts, such as adultery, do not admit of a mean. These and other considerations have led many to think that the Doctrine's talk of too little, too much, and the mean are really vacuous and that the Doctrine can give no real moral guidance and that it has at best only metaphorical or hortatory sense.

The question of whether the Doctrine is epistemologically senseless is serious and I will return to it at the end of the chapter. But

My thanks are owed to Graeme Marshall, Graham Nerlich, Charles Young, and to the Philosophy Department, Monash University, for help with this chapter.

David Pears in 'Courage as a Mean'[1] raises the prior and far more disturbing question of whether the Doctrine is conceptually senseless. In particular, he argues that there are serious difficulties in understanding what it could be for courage, especially its feelings, to be in a mean.

I will here extend his argument to show that if this is a problem, there is exactly the same problem about coherence within other Aristotelian virtues and indeed throughout an Aristotelian good life. The issue here is not simply of historical interest. For as I will show, if that is a problem for Aristotelian ethics, there is the very same problem for any ethical theory that allows for balances and mixes of plural values. I will here argue that we must, therefore, conclude either that there is no problem for Aristotle's ethics or ours, or that, contrary to all appearances, everyday and seemingly plausible and unproblematic forms of judgements are in fact unacceptable. In the appendices to the chapter, I discuss Pears's solution to the problem concerning the Doctrine.

I. COURAGE AND THE DOCTRINE

Let us turn now to a brief presentation of how Pears raises the problem about the conceptual sense or senselessness of the Doctrine's requirement that courage involves a mean of feeling: courage involves two distinct feelings, *phobos* and *tharsos*. '*Phobos*' is the easier to translate, being rendered well enough by 'fear'. '*Tharsos*' is sometimes rendered by 'confidence' and sometimes by 'boldness' or 'eagerness'. I will join Pears in using the first. Confidence has different, though importantly related, aspects or sorts. It can be taken intellectualistically—having to do with degrees of belief and certainty, as in a claim that I am confident that these calculations are right. It can also be taken as involving boldness and eagerness, as in claims about self-confidence and about facing dangers

---

[1] In A. O. Rorty (ed.), *Essays on Aristotle's Ethics* (Berkeley: University of California Press, 1980), 171–87. See also his 'Aristotle's Analysis of Courage', in P. A. French, T. E. Uehling, jun., and H. K. Wettstein (eds.), *Midwest Studies in Philosophy*, iii, Studies in Ethical Theory (Morris, Minn.: The University of Minnesota Press, 1978). My thanks are owed to Pears for our discussion of these issues, especially the problems concerning confidence taken up below.

confidently. Until Appendix 2 of this chapter, little will hang on issues of how, in this regard, we understand *tharsos*.

Pears's argument against the coherence of a mean for courage does not depend on how *tharsos* is taken on this score. It depends only on the clearly correct claim that *phobos* and *tharsos* are not species of the same sort of feeling and that they do not shade into each other. He concludes from this that *tharsos* and *phobos* are not found on the same continuum and thus cannot be in a mean.

A continuum is here thought of as, or as involving, a homogeneous scale. So understood, it is natural to think of its gradations as measuring what is shared by the things on it. As we move in one direction, we find more of that one thing, and as we move in the other, we find less. If the mean is neither too much nor too little, it should thus be somewhere on the continuum. One way, then, of putting the point that fear and confidence are not on a homogeneous continuum is that even if we combine the right amount of fear and the right amount of confidence, we would at best come up with two feelings, each of which may be correct, but not with any one feeling, much less the right or mean amount of any one feeling.

For an alternative way to put the lack of one homogeneous scale for fear and confidence, we can employ the important distinctions Pears makes about the proper objects or goals of courage. (Nothing turns on the difference between object and goal here.) Victory is what courage, or the courageous person *qua* courageous, is concerned to achieve. Danger—or more exactly, death or injury—is what must be avoided or fought against in order to achieve that. Thus, danger is the *countergoal* of courage and victory is its *external goal* (174). Victory is said to be the *external* goal in order to distinguish it from the formal or *internal* goal of all virtues and virtuous actions: nobility, *to kalon*. In what follows, we will be concerned only with victory and danger.

We can now put the problem of finding a mean of courage in terms of its constituent feelings, fear and confidence, and its countergoal and external goal. Danger is fear's proper object. Victory is confidence's proper object. (Only later will it be important to distinguish between the object of courage and that of *tharsos*.) Just as courage poses the problem of finding a mean between fear and confidence, courage also poses the problem of finding a mean between danger and victory. We must be able to find a mean between them in order to find the correct answer to whether this victory warrants this danger. (As explained in Appendix 2, Pears does not accept this account of the problem, because he does not take victory to be the goal or object of *tharsos*.)

But just as fear and confidence are not species of the same feeling and do not shade into each other, victory and danger are not species of the same thing nor do they shade into each other. Too much of the one is not too little of the other, nor does it approach, much less shade into, the other. In these two intimately related ways, Pears says, courage contrasts with *sophrosune*, temperance or moderation, which 'has a single homogeneous scale of feeling only because the feelings are always desires for the same kinds of things: food, drink, and sex' (174).

2. THE MEAN—OF COURAGE, AND MORE GENERALLY

In what follows, I will present the beginnings of a solution to Pears's worry. It is not his solution, but to discuss our differences now would be to digress. They are, however, taken up in the appendices to the chapter.

The aptness of calling victory the goal of courage and death and danger its countergoal is shown by the fact that they typically stand in antagonistic relations. To achieve victory, one must risk danger and death. To avoid danger and death, one cannot try for victory. It might thus seem only too understandable that the feelings of courage will not fall on one continuum, nor therefore admit of one mean. Thus, it would seem that courage must involve either a conflict of feelings or an absence of at least one of the mean feelings.

However, if this is right about courage, Aristotle is wrong about far more than courage. For quite generally, virtue requires taking into account a host of disparate elements. As Aristotle says about one of courage's constituents, fear, its mean involves feeling fear 'at the right time, on the right occasion, towards the right people, for the right purpose and in the right manner' (*Nicomachean Ethics* 2. 6, 1106b21 ff., tr. Rackham). Putting the point more generally, not just about fear, he says several lines later that people 'are good in but one way, but bad in many' (1106b35, tr. Ross). No argument is needed to show that time, occasion, and manner—to mention only three of these many ways—are not on a single continuum.

Perhaps, however, they do not have to be balanced against each other. In any case, Pears's argument was not cast so generally. It addressed only the problem generated by courage involving two distinct emotions, which are not on a single continuum, each with a distinct proper object, which are also not on a single continuum. But if this is a problem for courage, it is a problem for far more than courage. For clearly, different virtues are not on one continuum nor are their proper objects on one continuum. But the correct handling of many, if not most, serious practical situations requires more than one virtue.

So for example, as noted in the *Politics*, the correct use of property involves both temperance and liberality (2. 6, 1265a31 ff.). So too, fighting a battle in the correct way may require not only courage, but also being willing to spend or risk one's wealth. Getting the latter right involves liberality. Thus, acting correctly in that situation involves an interplay of two virtues, courage and liberality, and requires balancing their distinct proper objects. As Aristotle notes about a related case

some people have a law that the citizens whose land is near the frontier are not to take part in deliberation as to wars against neighbouring states, on the ground that private interest would prevent them from being able to take counsel wisely. (*Politics* 7. 10, 1330a20 ff., tr. Rackham.)

Further, to extend *Nicomachean Ethics* 3. 9, 1117b9 ff., in comparison with those having less to lose, those with more to lose in battle may have to steel themselves more, be more courageous, to do the same things. (*Politics* 2. 6, 1265a35 does hold that it is not possible to use property with courage. But this is a discussion of what pertains to property as such and not a discussion of how, as in my case, circumstances can bear on how it may be used.)

Practical situations, thus, often call for a balancing of various virtues and thus of various distinct emotions and their distinct proper objects. If such balancing is to be understood in terms of reaching a mean on a continuum with a homogeneous scale, these situations precipitate endless conflicts within the Aristotelian good person. Alternatively, if these situations do admit of a correct resolution, such resolutions cannot require a homogeneous continuum. Thus, if the Doctrine does require such a continuum, the

Doctrine can make no conceptual sense of what a good person should feel, desire, and do in these real life and multi-faceted situations.

However, these problems might not be thought central to the Doctrine. For these problems do not concern how a single virtue, on its own, is to be understood. I will postpone until the end of this chapter discussion of whether the Doctrine can apply to more than one virtue at a time.

To show in another way that if Pears is right about courage, Aristotle is wrong about other virtues on their own, we should note that other single virtues are like courage in involving distinct objects, which are not on a continuum. For example, Aristotle argues that liberality involves distinct objects—namely dispensing wealth and getting wealth. He also argues that the deficiencies and excesses of emotion and action in regard to the one are independent of, and do not shade into, those of the other (*NE* 4. 1).

Further, liberality can involve the question of which people to benefit. As this shows, even where choice is between similar items, we need judgement that goes beyond the weighing of objects on a continuum.[2]

Many of the same points can be made in terms of temperance, the virtue Pears says is unlike courage in that it involves balancing items which are on a single continuum. Let us start with some comments about the pleasures temperance is concerned with. As made clear in the *Nicomachean Ethics* (3. 10), temperance is not concerned with intellectual pleasures, say, but only with those of the body—i.e. those of food, drink, and sex. But it is not concerned with all pleasures we might think of as bodily. For example, it is not concerned with the pleasures of wine and food as these are enjoyed and practised by winetasters and cooks (3. 10). For these latter require experience and aesthetic judgement. As we might say, they of course involve taste as involving the body, in particular the tongue. But they also involve taste understood in terms of good taste.

Aristotle holds that the pleasures of concern to temperance are those given simply by and in touch. Touch, of all our senses, has the lowest sort of conceptual involvement. These pleasures do not

---

[2] My thanks are owed to Charles Young for this point about difficulties with such choices.

involve judgement and the sort of experience that informs judgement. They involve taste only by involving the taste buds, but not by involving good taste. It is in this way that 'Temperance and profligacy are . . . concerned with those pleasures which man shares with the lower animals, and which consequently appear slavish and bestial.' (1118a23 ff.) These are *epithumetic* pleasures.

Temperance is concerned only with epithumetic pleasures and not with other bodily pleasures, such as those that involve a gustatory aesthetic. Thus, the fact that pleasures of mere touch are not on the same continuum as aesthetic gustatory pleasures does not bear against Pears's claim that all the values temperance is concerned with are on one continuum. Nor does the fact that there are heterogeneous gustatory aesthetic pleasures—e.g. the ones of wine versus food, and the various ones of fine wine as well as the various ones of fine food.

But even the epithumetic pleasures present a problem for Pears. For the epithumetic pleasures of food, drink, and sex are heterogeneous and do not shade into each other.

These facts are important for us in a number of related ways. They show that in cases where we have to choose between such pleasures—e.g. between the merely epithumetic pleasure of food or of drink—there may be no continuum on which to place them. (So too, of course, for a choice between heterogeneous gustatory aesthetic pleasures.) This might be thought an embarrassment for Aristotle and perhaps also for Pears, but not an absolutely telling one. For at least primarily, the Doctrine may not be meant to choose between different pleasures, but only to assess each pleasure on its own. That is, it is not meant primarily to help us decide whether this pleasure is a more fitting and proper pleasure than that one, but rather to help us decide whether this one is fitting and proper.

Even if correct about primacy, this restriction seems inadequate as a way to save Pears. For, even if only secondarily, we do want to know how different pleasures stand to each other in regard to the mean: i.e. whether this one is further from or closer to the mean than that one, and which, if either, should be chosen here and now. But, if Pears is right, this comparison cannot be made sense of if those pleasures do not shade into each other.

It might seem that we could compare these pleasures by seeing which is closer to its own particular mean. But if there are troubles in comparing pleasures on different continua, there must also be trouble in comparing distances—lengths of continua—on different continua.

So far I have been considering what might be set aside as diversions from Pears's claim that temperance, unlike courage, involves one continuum. Let us now turn to the most serious problem posed by temperance. The problem is simply that temperance, like courage, is concerned with two different evaluatively relevant phenomena—and these are pleasure and pain. It is simply misleading to say, in this context, that temperance is concerned only with pleasure—even if, in an important way, it is concerned only with certain sorts of pleasure or pleasures. For the pleasures it is concerned with are mixtures of pleasure and pain.

The point can be made by means of the relevant desires. The natural desire for food is, or constitutively involves, hunger. But hunger is, itself, painful. So too, not satisfying that desire is painful. Temperance, then, concerns the correct balance of epithumetic pleasure and pain. If we need further argument for this, we find it in Aristotle's claim that profligates, *akolastoi*—those lacking temperance—are pained by not getting their pleasures. (Cf. *NE* 3. 11, 1119a1 ff.)

There would be a strict parallel between courage and temperance if these pleasures and pains are to be balanced against each other— if that is, we gain the one by risking the other, as we do with victory and danger. This seems to be how Aristotle thinks it typically is for profligates. Further, it may sometimes be like this for other people—e.g. when they are faced with a choice between eating a satisfyingly large meal later, putting up with present hunger, or eating a smaller meal now, with a consequent earlier return of hunger. But it does not seem it is always like this for non-profligates. Sometimes they simply sit down to their regular, temperate meal.

However even here, intermixed pains are important. While they may not be felt, they are there in a developmental-conceptual way, as given by Aristotelian habituation. For developmentally, the mechanism for acquiring the right amount of appetite for food works by experiencing and struggling with hunger. And conceptually, we learn and come to appreciate what the right amount is by this struggle.

To be sure, the pain temperance is concerned to master drives a person towards pleasure, whereas danger drives the person away from victory. But this is not enough to show a lack of parallel between temperance and courage. For that complex of pain and pleasure—as we might put it, over-stressing the point, that pain-driven pleasure—is what drives one away from the proper pleasure, which itself may include pain either as felt or in a developmental-conceptual way.

Whether or not the parallel between courage and temperance is complete, the fact that temperance involves pain is a problem for Pears. For on Aristotle's account, and in fact, even though pleasure and pain are intimately related, they are not the same, nor do they shade into each other. But then, temperance should suffer the same difficulty courage suffers from having to balance its heterogeneous objects.

There is little point in objecting that pain is the proper object of endurance, *karteria*, while only pleasure is the object of temperance. (Cf. e.g. *NE* 3. 10, 1117b24 ff. and 7. 7, *passim*.) For even if endurance is concerned with pain on its own, so to speak, temperance is concerned with pleasures that are mixed pleasures— i.e. mixtures of pleasure and pain. In this way, temperance is like courage in having heterogeneous proper objects. Indeed, were temperance concerned only with pure pleasures, it would not be an important virtue. After all, pure pleasures pose few, if any problems for us. Indeed, it seems, we cannot have too much of them (7. 14, 1154b15 ff.).

My conclusion, then, is that if there is a problem for the Doctrine engendered by the plurality and heterogeneity of the objects of moral considerations—e.g. courage's involving distinct emotions with distinct proper objects—this is a problem for far more than courage alone. It is a general and pervasive problem for a good life, and for many if not all virtues.

Although posed as a problem for the Doctrine of the Mean, lack of homogeneity is a problem for any ethics that allows for different values that need to be amalgamated. Contemporary ethical theories do not talk of a mean of different values. But they do talk of mixes and trade-offs of different and plural values. These involve balancing different goods against each other, different bads against each other, and different goods against different bads. The correct balance is hardly to be understood in terms of one continuum. But not having such a continuum is what was said to be so problematic for the Doctrine of the Mean. Thus, if the lack of such homogeneity makes the Doctrine problematic, if not incoherent, it would also do this to those contemporary theories cast in terms of mixes and trade-offs of plural values. For the problems come not from the special sort of weighing and comparing involved in determining a mean, but from weighing and comparing non-homogeneous values and elements.

3. ONE VALUE, MANY VALUES

Some may take such plurality and lack of homogeneity to show that feelings, acts, and lives must be evaluatively incoherent. Those who think that evaluative coherence is at least conceptually possible have two major alternatives: either deny that there are plural and heterogeneous values or deny that resolutions of them require a homogeneous continuum. Since my goal here is to give an account of Aristotle's Doctrine of the Mean, and since I do think that, in the requisite sense, there are different values, I shall here argue for the second alternative.

Let us start with another Aristotelian issue: How many goods does Aristotle recognize?[3] Eudaimonia is the final good among other goods. But is it simply the collection of these other goods? Is it one good among other and incommensurable goods? Are the other goods good simply because they conduce to it?

These issues force us to consider a general issue, centrally important to both Aristotelian and non-Aristotelian ethics: are all values commensurable?[4] Put intuitively, to hold that they are commensurable is to say there is, so to speak, a common coin for all goods, which not only gives their exchange rate but gives everything of value about them.

Our issues about heterogeneity and the coherence of the Doctrine

---

[3] On the number of goods recognized by Aristotle, see W. F. R. Hardie, 'The Final Good in Aristotle's Ethics', *Philosophy*, 40 (1965), 277–95; D. Wiggins, 'Weakness of Will, Commensurability, and the Objects of Deliberation and Desire', *Proceedings of the Aristotelian Society*, NS 79 (1978–9), 251–77, reprinted in Rorty (ed.), *Essays on Aristotle's Ethics*; and M. Burnyeat, 'Aristotle on Learning to be Good', ibid.

[4] See ch. 7, 'Akrasia' and ch. 8, 'Monism, Pluralism, and Conflict'. See also Wiggins, 'Weakness of Will', and 'Truth, Invention and the Meaning of Life', *Proceedings of the British Academy*, 42 (1976), 331–78; J. O. Urmson, 'A Defence of Intuitionism', *Proceedings of the Aristotelian Society*, NS 75 (1974–5), 111–19; A. Sen, 'Plural Utility', *Proceedings of the Aristotelian Society*, NS 81 (1980–1), 193–215. Wiggins and Sen give extensive references.

are part and parcel of—if not just a different way of putting—these issues about the number, the commensurability, and the comparability of goods. For, to the extent that all values, or simply those of courage, are commensurable and thus inter-substitutable, nothing about the evaluative nature of courage would be lost by holding that it is unitary in that it involves a good character trait of pursuing the good even at the risk of the bad.

Perhaps for some purposes it would still be useful to talk of harm as the proper object of fear. Such talk could be interpreted as meaning something like: the proper object of fear is a bad that comes from a certain source and that occasions certain psychological reactions. But—and this is what is here important—that a bad has a particular source or effect does not make it distinct, *qua* bad, from other bads. So, its being that particular sort of bad in no way makes comparing it with other equally distinct bads problematic.

A similar story would be told about the good, on the one hand, and the goods involved in courage, e.g. those involved in confidence and victory, on the other. And finally it would be held that the bad is wholly commensurable with the good. So in the end, confidence and fear and thus the virtue of courage are seen not really to have distinct proper objects, but exactly the same object—value. This would be generalized to all virtues. They would all be seen as having only value, taken quite generally, as their proper object.

Even if not required by this programme, it would be in its spirit to deny that distinct emotions have ultimate moral importance. For if the proper object of virtue in all situations is undifferentiated value, it would be natural to hold that the morally significant sort of feeling in a virtue would be only something like undifferentiated approval or disapproval.[5]

On this view, the facts that courage has what can be talked about as two distinct feelings and that each of these has what can be talked about as a distinct proper object do not present a real problem for the Doctrine of the Mean. The evaluative problem about courage would here be solved by giving up the claim that its constituent feelings have distinct proper objects of ultimate moral significance and perhaps also by giving up the claim that its feelings are distinct and of ultimate moral significance.

[5] See my 'Good Intentions in Greek and Modern Moral Philosophy', *Australasian Journal of Philosophy*, 57 (1979), 220–4.

4. THE MEAN OF COURAGE

However, Aristotelian courage does not require us to make the anti-Aristotelian choice between making sense of the Doctrine of the Mean and allowing for distinct, morally significant objects, values, and feelings. Similarly, we are not forced to choose between allowing for different values and the possibility of evaluatively unified acts and, ultimately, an evaluatively unified life. Both the Doctrine and the possibility of a proper mix or trade-off of different values can be saved, at least from these problems.

To see this, let us start by supposing that courageous warriors have two goals, victory and safety.[6] This would allow them, perhaps vacillatingly, to ask distinct questions focusing now on one goal, now on the other: 'Safety is attractive—so shall I run?' and 'Victory is attractive—so shall I stay?'

This plurality of goals arises in one situation, however. The soldier can ask one question about the one complex issue: 'What here and now am I to do, pursue victory or pursue safety?' As I will now argue, this obvious and commonplace circumstantial unity allows for a unity and indeed for a mean of feeling, of desire, and of action.

What Aristotle calls for in the courageous warrior is a mean of feeling. But how can there be this mean? How can we put together the distinct mean of fear and the distinct mean of confidence? My answer is that if these are understood as being independent of each other, existing on their own, then they cannot make up the courageous warrior's mean of feeling.

What I mean by such independence between feelings and their existing on their own can be brought out as follows. Dangers, obviously, differ in their dangerousness. Thus the fear appropriate to one danger may be inappropriate to another. Positive goals, such as victory, can also differ in value. The appropriate eagerness for, and boldness in pursuing, one goal may not be appropriate to another. This is to talk about dangers and positive goals—about costs and what they are costs for—independently of each other.

---

[6] For discussion of what I call safety, and why it must be understood as tending more towards self-preservation than mere safety, see C. M. Young, 'Aristotle on Courage', in Q. Howe (ed.), *Humanitas: Essays in Honor of Ralph Ross* (Claremont, Calif.: Scripps College Press, 1977), and 'Virtue and Flourishing in Aristotle's Ethics', in D. J. Depew (ed.), *The Greeks and the Good Life* (Fullerton, Calif.: California State University, 1980).

As noted, however, the goals of courageous warriors in battle are also interdependent. Warriors are faced with a complex of victory and danger. They can avoid danger only by giving up a chance for victory and they can try for victory only by risking danger.

Further, the appropriate amount of fear in any particular case is a function of the features of the complex of the danger and victory—not just of features internal to the danger. One does not show oneself to be too given to fear, too fearful, by refusing to risk life or even limb for a paltry good, especially if the good is unlikely to be achieved and the harm very likely. But by being unwilling to risk a lot, perhaps even one's life, for an important good, such as the survival of one's family, *polis*, or homeland, one does show oneself to be too fearful.

Similarly for confidence. One does not show oneself deficient in eagerness or boldness by declining to pursue a paltry good, especially if it can be obtained only at great risk. (Cf. *NE* 4. 3, 1124b7 ff.) Indeed, going for such goods in such circumstances points to an excess e.g. of boldness and eagerness. But of course, not going for important goods can indicate a deficiency of boldness and eagerness.

Before proceeding, we should note that Aristotle does not discuss a deficiency of confidence. This might suggest that he does not, or should not, hold that the correct amount of confidence is a mean of confidence. And this might suggest that he does not or should not hold that courage is a mean. I think both suggestions are to be rejected. Aristotle generally omits maladies of the spirit, such as too little desire for bodily pleasures, which involve absence or weakness of spiritedness and desire. (See e.g. *NE* 3. 11, 1119a6 ff.) None the less, this does not debar temperance from involving a mean. Nor should it debar courage.[7]

It should be clear, then, that the evaluation of what is the mean of fear or of confidence will depend on an assessment of the complex: this victory and this danger. The mean of fear is not how much fear is warranted by this danger, considered in itself. It is, rather, how much fear this complex of danger and victory warrant. In this sense at least, the complex, rather than its parts, is the

---

[7] The omitted maladies of the spirit are discussed in my 'Affectivity and Self-Concern', *Pacific Philosophical Quarterly*, 64 (1983), 211–29.

courageous warrior's object both of fear and of confidence. (Below, I will indicate what such feelings are like.)

Earlier it seemed all too natural that there should be a conflict between a courageous warrior's fear and confidence. For they were presented as being about distinct and conflicting objects, danger and victory. There does not seem the same need to find conflict within the complex feeling about the one complex object of victory and death and injury.

My point here is not that the courageous warrior's appropriate fear and appropriate confidence must be unifiable. Perhaps in at least certain cases or even in general, the requirements of fear and those of confidence about such a complex cannot be coherently satisfied. Perhaps the courageous warrior will be pulled in two directions. But just as I can see no argument to show that the feelings must be unifiable, I can see no argument to show that they cannot be.

Here we must note just how serious it is to say that there can be no coherence. If there can be no coherence simply because incommensurable items are at issue, the outcome is devastating, not merely serious. For, as argued in 'Plurality and Choice', even the most mundane, everyday, and seemingly unproblematic choices involve plural and incommensurable goods. Thus, if coherence is precluded simply by incommensurability, then for much if not all of our lives there will be no coherent, unified way to feel, desire, or act.

5. REAL UNITIES

Of course, even if I am right, all that has so far been shown is that the mean amount of fear and the mean amount of confidence may be coherently combined. Perhaps there is only a synthetic unity of mean feelings: i.e. two distinct but mutually compatible mean feelings. It has not been shown that there is any one feeling— much less a mean of feeling—that the courageous warrior can have. To show this requires showing a real unity of feelings.

To motivate this attempt, I will state a view that is importantly wrong as an interpretation of Aristotle. This view agrees that the appropriate amounts of fear and of confidence in battle are determined by the complex, which includes both their own and each other's proper object. This view continues that these feelings need have only a certain result in action, feeling, and desire: e.g. staying and fighting, and a feeling, whatever it might be, that conduces to this. So, if the person has high confidence, it is all right—perhaps even necessary to preclude rashness—to have a lot of fear. But if one has little .confidence, one had better have a correspondingly lower amount of fear. This view concludes that the person has the very same feeling no matter how those elements combine to yield that result.

Some feelings may well be like this. They may thus be thought of as additive or as resolved vector forces since their direction and their magnitude are all there is of concern to them. But fear and confidence do not come together this way—at least not in Aristotelian courage. To see what is wrong with this view, both as a general understanding of feelings and of the feelings involved in such courage, we should consider the form—or better, the forms—of determination involved in a soldier's decision to stay and fight. We should start by noting that one can be led to stay and fight by a feeling born and composed of many combinations of fear and confidence: strong fear and stronger confidence, weak confidence and weaker fear, the proper amount of both, and so on.

All of these may involve the same feeling if sameness is taken in an additive or resolved-vector-force sense. Perhaps this is as it should be. For perhaps all of them are forms of determination. But in ways important for us, they are not the same sort of determination. The very nature of one's determination to stand and fight—in particular, the feeling and desire aspects of this determination—is importantly different when born and composed, on the one hand, of strong fear and stronger confidence, and on the other, of weak confidence but weaker fear.

Descriptions of how the complex of feelings of fear and confidence stand to each other, thus, cannot be cast in terms of juxtaposition and addition. Rather, we must talk of the feelings overlaying, suffusing, interpenetrating each other: e.g. boldness shot through with fear, fear mastered by confidence, spirited but worried determination, phlegmatic determination, ambivalence.

Some further comments on such overlaying, suffusing, and interpenetrating are needed to help motivate the use of such metaphors. Let us start by asking what the courageous warriors' emotions in regard to both fear and confidence involve. One picture of what courage involves has it that once victory has been seen to be worthwhile, perhaps required—and especially once, consequent on that seeing, the victory is resolutely pursued—the fears will be dismissed. One important reason for this view is the thought that if the person still has those fears, they will provide sources of conflict and irresolution, ambivalence, vacillation, and temptation. So understood, a person with fear could not be courageous, but at best have a self-controlled, i.e. *enkratic*, approximation of courage. Such a person would do what courage requires despite the tempting and conflicting desire to flee.

But this is not Aristotle's understanding of the matter. On his view, courageous warriors maintain their fears and master them. But the sort of mastering important here does not involve a continuing struggle with the fears nor does it involve getting rid of them. It involves neither vacillation nor ambivalence. Rather, it involves integrating the dangers and the victory, the fear and confidence, into one coherent and settled emotional appreciation of the situation. Victory is sought, but not sought in the same emotional way that it would be were it thought not to involve danger.

To repeat a point made earlier: the proper emotion towards a victory that can be gained only by overcoming dangers is not the same as the proper emotion towards a less valuable but dangerless victory. This is so even if the two complexes are equally valuable— where the value of the less important victory equals the value of the more important one discounted by the greater disvalues involved in its danger.

Putting the point in terms of confidence, *tharsos*, the courageous warrior with these fears will have a different sort of eagerness. Rather than a light and easy eagerness, it will be a more solemn, studied, or regretting eagerness. This is made clear in Aristotle's claim about courage, victory, and pleasure: that attaining victory is pleasurable, but acting courageously need not be pleasurable and indeed can be painful (*NE* 3. 9).

Such solemnity, regret, and lack of pleasure need not involve indecision, vacillation, ambivalence or other lack of wholehearted-ness. The fear had by courageous warriors does not involve conflict. Rather, there is the regret or sadness that the goal involves and requires such a risk. This is what I meant when I said that the fear and the confidence have interpenetrated each other, losing their separate identities.

I can now put what I take to be the real unity in the combination of fear and confidence of a courageous person as conceived of by Aristotle. Such a person has one emotion about the complex of the external goal and the countergoal. Further, this one emotion is a correct emotion. This feeling—a complex of fear and confidence— is, itself, a mean. It is the proper, the mean, feeling towards the complex of the objects of fear and of confidence.

None the less, the death and the victory are still seen as separable. But they are seen conjointly, setting each other off, and giving each other value. Each object is given its proper value. Each object is appreciated in the light of the other. So too, the emotions forming the complex are separable, even if they suffuse and inform each other. The fear suffused with confidence is the mean amount and the confidence suffused with fear is the mean amount.

We should understand the courageous warrior's desire in a strictly parallel way. It is not a mere additive juxtaposition of those two conflicting desires—to avoid harm and to gain victory. Rather, it too is a complex formed of, and bearing the stamps of, its constituents.

Again, I am not claiming that such a real unity is possible— although I do think it is. Nor am I claiming that it is only in courageous people that fear and confidence can form a real unity. It may well do this in cowards and the rash, and in still other sorts of people, too. This latter only strengthens my claim that in order to show that such a real unity is not possible, we would have to show far more than has been shown. To deny that it is possible is, once again, either to deny that the moral universe allows enough coherence for such unity or to deny that the psyche of even good people allows for such coherence.

And also again, the generality of the problem should be noted. Large portions—both important and unimportant portions—of our lives seem possible and coherent only if we can form complex unities out of incommensurables such as goals and risks. It remains to be explained how we are able to form such unities. That is, it remains to be explained how this form of judgement is possible. But for our purposes, it is sufficient to see two things. The first is that we can form these unities and thus that there are proper objects for such judgement. The second is that such complex unities are hardly the exception, but rather the rule, throughout our acts and emotions.

6. REAL UNITIES AND THE USEFULNESS OF THE DOCTRINE

It might be suggested that I have been beguiled by the complexities of the real unities of feeling and desire. For as set out at the beginning, the problem was not simply to show how courage admits of a real unity of feeling. Rather, it was to show this while also showing that this unity can be understood in terms of the Doctrine of the Mean. And it might be suggested that my arguments for the possibility of real unities are also arguments that the Doctrine lacks useful content.

The argument against the usefulness of the Doctrine is that it in no way explains or clarifies such unities, but at best reflects their existence. So, it could well be pointed out that in arguing for the possibility of such coherence, I at no time invoked considerations of a mean but relied entirely on other sorts of general considerations. In essence, this argument is a variant of the charge that the Doctrine itself does no real work and that its talk of a mean is simply superimposed upon, if not simply window dressing for, moral views completely independent of the Doctrine.

My reply on Aristotle's behalf is that he thinks the Doctrine has moral content because he takes what are to be balanced to be those natural features of human psychology embodying our evaluative and emotional concerns.[8] My reply on my own behalf is to endorse at least the general idea behind Aristotle's claim. What I mean has already been suggested, but should be made more explicit.

The virtues are concerned with important human situations—situations which call into question important human values and concerns. At least many of these situations can usefully be seen as ones in which we have to sacrifice certain goods or objects of desire—or what appear to be such—to get others. So, it is not that the values and disvalues of danger and victory shade into each other. It is rather, that in battle we have to weigh some against others. It is, then, not as values, taken on their own, that they are

---

[8] On these issues, see S. R. L. Clark, *Aristotle's Man* (Oxford: Oxford University Press, 1975), especially ch. 3.2, and also A. O. Rorty, 'Explaining Emotions', *Journal of Philosophy*, 75 (1978).

to be balanced. Rather, they are to be balanced in our concrete situations. Given what we are and how we are situated, to give too much weight to one will force us to give too little to the other. These are facts about us and our values, not simply facts about the values on their own.

This, of course, is one-sided. For it must also be explained why the various arenas of virtue, such as battle, are important for humans—not merely why, when in those situations, we find it necessary to balance and choose among those values. Aristotle's account of the virtues helps explain this by helping explain what, at least on his view, are the central and important activities and concerns of people—and how these, in turn, involve important human values. As I mean to suggest, then, the notions of being an important human activity and of being of important human value and concern are strictly correlative—mediated in some large degree by facts about us, such as our liabilities and capacities. This is as true for courage, with its concerns about victory and danger, as it is for temperance, with its concerns about pleasure and pain.

I hope that, despite being very schematic, enough has been said to show that substance can be given to talk about balance. The substance is found in the complex wholes we make in and of our lives—e.g. a complex emotional whole of fear interpenetrated with confidence. It is also the very substance of human life and of our having to choose among our important values and concerns.

This, then, goes some way to showing that the Doctrine of the Mean, with its talk of too much and too little, and of the mean, is useful. To mention one point, it usefully modifies Aristotle's claim that the mean is a mean relative to the agent (e.g. *NE* 2. 6, 1106a31). It does this by holding not simply that the particularities of the values to be balanced are given by the particularities of the agent at that time. It further holds that agents by being agents, or better, by being special sorts of agents—human agents—have to balance considerations and, by doing this, find both for and within themselves a balance of these considerations.

In the remainder of this chapter I will make some further comments on the usefulness of the Doctrine. I will also show how what I have called the real unities of feeling and desire question various presuppositions of Pears's worries about the Doctrine of the Mean.

Complex unities of feeling, desire, and action of the sort discussed do not allow for a continuum with a homogeneous scale composed of more and less of a single good or object of desire. Further, we will no longer be able to see the balancing required by the mean on the model of what can be done by a simple hinged beam balance or a sliding beam balance—and this for two reasons. We are concerned not only with the correct ratios among opposing elements—which a beam balance would show—but also with each of these elements being in its own proper place. Further, the elements that must be balanced may well not be on a single continuum, but rather may be more orthogonally related.

So, we will need a balance which allows for many elements each of which can tip the balance pan in a different direction. Something like a pan suspended on a cord through its centre may do. Even this may be too simple. Perhaps we will need a sphere or a still higher-dimensioned object suspended at its centre. But the point can at least be illustrated in terms of the suspended pan.

Imagine the degrees of a compass inscribed on the pan. If something is put on the 40° line, the pan can be made to balance by something lighter at a point further out from the centre on the 220° line. This is to go beyond a simple, hinged balance. Even a sliding balance will not do. We need to accommodate facts like this one: the same weight at that same point can also be balanced by an array of weights in appropriate locations on the other side of the diameter at ninety degrees to that line, i.e. the 130°–310° line.

Talk of the pan so far talks only to the variety of elements that must be weighed and to the fact that differing amounts of a given element can have the same effect depending on their location. Here we should remember that fear and confidence themselves admit of degrees of excess and deficiency. And they may not be the only feelings that have to be balanced to obtain an overall balance. Where they should be located is influenced by where those others should be.

This point can be put in terms of how to picture this pan balance. It should not be thought of as a logical construction of beam balances each of which is concerned with one continuum. Thus, it is not as though each diameter is such a continuum. If it were, then the balance achieved on that diameter would be achieved by having the right gain and loss of the very same value. But, as I have been concerned to stress, the balance with which that virtue is concerned is a balance of different values—the different and opposing values which are called into question by a given sort of situation. So, the connection between items on one side of the pan and those on the other is not given by their shading into each other, but by our having to choose the proper mix of them.

On Aristotle's view the proper mix will be a balanced mix. Continuing with our metaphor, it is required that the suspended pan be balanced. But as noted above, the various weights can be out of their own proper place even if the pan is balanced. However, if there is a unity of the good, the pan can be balanced by each of the weights being in its own proper place. The proper place of each is, in this sense, a function of all the others.

Aristotle suggests that the virtues are inseparable, and in this sense unified, because of the relations between *phronesis*, practical wisdom, and the virtues (*NE* 6. 13, *passim*, especially 1144b32 ff.). The mutual determination just spoken of gives us another way to understand their inseparability and unity: wherever two or more virtues come into play, the mean of each is determined by all.

Because of the complexity of such mutual determination, we might well expect there to be no algorithm giving us the mean of each and of all—at least none that is available to us. Our pan is a device for comparing incommensurable values. And the comparability of incommensurables also seems to ensure the impossibility of an algorithm for discerning the best or even a good mix of values. Thus, we see the need for practical wisdom and why practical wisdom ineliminably involves judgement.

In various ways, then, the balancing of distinct values is complex. These complexities give us a further reason why it is not useful to think of the mean as being on a homogeneous scale. For the mean is achieved only when the pan is not simply balanced, but is balanced because each of the weights is in its proper, mean place. There need be no common units of value which are increased or decreased to reach the mean both in the overall situation and in regard to the particular virtues.

Or rather, there need be no common values unless we admit something like 'whatever tips the pan'. That would be to talk of undifferentiated value. But we will not accept this so long as we acknowledge that the morally significant features that fear involves are distinct from those that confidence involves and that both have ultimate moral significance. So too, for one virtue as compared with another.

The question for us now is whether it is useful to invoke the Doctrine of the Mean to describe what is going on with such balancing. I think it is useful. Indeed, it seems more useful in regard to such complex balancings than in regard to those that can be modelled by a beam balance. For those may give weight to the illusion that some simple mathematical calculation will show us what is appropriate. But the Doctrine comes into its own in regard to the very great complexity we now see.

It shows us that, and perhaps how, the various weights and positions mutually determine the appropriate locations of the others. Thus we see that, and perhaps how, the mean and also the excess and deficiency of the feelings taken conjointly both determine and are determined by the means, and the excesses and deficiencies, of each of the individual feelings. Perhaps it also helps us to understand what it might be to apply the Doctrine of the Mean to an entire life and thus what it might mean to say of a life, considered now as one complex, that its feelings, its desires, and its actions are properly harmonized and balanced.

To be sure, we are still left with the epistemological problems of the Doctrine of the Mean. Judgement, with all its problems, still needs to be used. In what follows I will indicate that this is not a special problem for courage. For now it is enough to note that, as shown here, the Doctrine does not have the impossible task of finding unity where there is conceptual incoherence, nor of finding commensurability where there is only comparability.

If I am right, we can see how courage can admit of a real mean of feeling and desire, even though it has—or rather is born of—multiple objects. And indeed, we can now see that courage is no embarrassment to the Doctrine of the Mean. On the contrary: precisely because of the complexity of its constituent feelings, courage is a microcosm of the Aristotelian virtuous life. For on Aristotle's view, such a life, despite its complexities, both allows for and requires a mean and a real unity of feeling, desire, and action.

To summarize: The Doctrine of the Mean holds that there is a proper, mean amount of fear to feel in regard to a given danger. If Pears is right, the Doctrine has it that this mean is determined by—and perhaps also that we can determine it by considering—a continuum of more and less of a single value. Where we have such a continuum, we could as well have a simple beam balance, to balance what is more and less. But, on Aristotle's view, the determinants of the mean of fear are heterogeneous, in-commensurable considerations such as time and amount, as well as danger and what facing the danger may gain. It is, thus, difficult, if not impossible, to understand the mean in terms of such a balance, and such a continuum. How could we weigh, e.g. time and amount against each other? How are they even to go in the pans?

And as argued, acts and emotions quite generally concern imcommensurables. Virtues, too, quite generally involve in-commensurable values. For they are concerned with important human situations, in which for systematic reasons we have to choose between incommensurable values. Its involvement with incommensurables thus shows courage to be a typical virtue, not an exception.

These considerations might be taken as arguments against the Doctrine. But I take them as arguments against trying to understand it in terms of a continuum of one value, or a beam balance. We can and should, none the less, understand it in terms of balancing and of incommensurable considerations. Its balancing is simply not limited to commensurables on a continuum, nor is it the balancing of a beam balance. Perhaps no mechanical balance models it well. But even my pan balance shows how balancing need not involve a continuum.

7. COMPLEX UNITIES

I want now to consider why these complex unities raise difficulties for Pears's worries about the Doctrine of the Mean. To bring this out, it should be useful to take note of a transition in this chapter— a transition which reflects the changes in a person who achieves Aristotelian courage. I started by talking of courage as having two distinct feelings, confidence and fear, each with its own distinct object: victory in the case of confidence, and death and injury in the case of fear. But later, I held that courage involves one complex feeling, somehow composed or born out of confidence and fear, directed at one complex object, somehow composed or born out of victory and death and injury. Only the latter is Aristotelian courage.

Thus it is false that the courageous warrior has two feelings and it is false that he is confronted with two distinct proper objects of feeling—or of desire or of action. That is true only of non-courageous people—or some of them. Perhaps it is true of the person who is becoming courageous, but it is no longer true once a person is courageous. Indeed, we might suggest that part of what it is to become courageous is for this no longer to be true.

Even if all this is accepted, it might be complained that at best only minimal progress has been made. For earlier, when we had two heterogeneous proper objects, we were confronted with the worry generated by their being incommensurable. Now we have only one proper object. But it is incommensurable within itself. There is no common coin in terms of which different states or stages, so to speak, of this object are commensurable with each other. Nor is there any common coin in terms of which different parts of the one complex feeling are commensurable.

Previously the worry was that where there is incommensurability, we cannot understand talk about the need to increase one feeling and weaken another to bring them into a balance or a mean. The worry now would be that we cannot understand talk about the need to change the one complex feeling to bring it into a balance or a mean. The point remains the same: if the two feelings are incommensurable, how can we make sense of one feeling being more or less of a mean than another, whether the latter is another feeling type or another token of the same type?

Of course, an answer has been offered—in terms of judgement. Some might think that such an appeal is thus revealed once again, or finally, as being the epistemologically vacuous rhetoric long associated with the Doctrine of the Mean. I do not think this is correct. But it is clear that a resolution of these issues can come only after a thoroughgoing study of commensurability. This will not be attempted here. What will be done to close the body of this chapter is to show just how general the issue is.

The issue is not whether there is one emotion term in regard to which we can say that one complex emotion is stronger or weaker or more in a mean. We could, if necessary, coin a new term—e.g. by hyphenation, giving us 'fear-confidence'. Nor is the issue whether emotions can be complex, with other emotions as elements. For there are many such emotions: awe, indignation, and love are three important examples. Nor is the issue whether the elements of courage go together naturally. For it is difficult to see how there is less naturalness here than there is in the complex emotion of love, or awe, or indignation. And part of what I mean by naturalness here is that these complexes help give the very substance of human life. They point to, and really are, among our central concerns.

So the issue is not one of naturalness. It is, rather, whether there is a form of judgement that we can use to evaluate these cases. Such judgement would allow for reasonable judgements about whether one instance of that complex emotion is stronger or closer to the mean than another instance. So, I may see that the love I feel today is weaker than the love I felt last week, but that it is still too strong. Similarly, a warrior might see that the demands of courage in regard to one complex unity of death and injury and victory call for more of that one complex feeling than does another complex unity of the same sorts of elements.

As easily seen, this is a very general issue. It is in no way engendered by any features peculiar to courage. Rather, all or near enough all emotions and their proper objects—and desires and their objects, and actions and lives, too—pose the very same problem. Choices between commensurables pose much the same, if not the very same, problem—as shown by the choice between whether to be liberal to this person or to that one. Since the problem is so very general, it is either very serious or not serious at all.

This has already been shown in regard to temperance. Here I will consider a strictly similar case, fear. Let us first note that as Aristotle put the Doctrine, one may well not have the mean of fear even if one has the right amount of fear, neither too much nor too little. For as noted earlier, the mean does not involve only having the right amount of fear but also feeling fear 'at the right time, on the right occasion, towards the right people, for the right purpose and in the right manner'. This shows that defenders of the Doctrine need to show how these disparate conditions can come together in one mean. It also shows that a defence of the Doctrine need not involve reducing the Doctrine simply to determining what is more and less. This is important for meeting one part of the worry about complex unities.

Another important conclusion to be drawn here is that the mean of fear involves incommensurable determinants—e.g. the right people and the right manner. This, of course, is not to show that the Doctrine is right or even coherent. But it is to show that the Doctrine, even in regard to such seemingly simple cases as fear, involves incommensurables.

Another way to see this last point is that one can fear all sorts of things—pain, harm, death, dishonour, sickness, loss of friends, and so on. Indeed, it seems that fear can be directed at almost any bad or almost any diminution of almost any good. But if these bads and goods are incommensurable, the objects of fear can be incommensurable. Thus, if courage involves incommensurability because its objects—victory, death, and injury—are incommensurable, fear also involves incommensurability.

To avoid this sort or source of incommensurability, it might be suggested that we divide up fear in terms of the kinds of objects it takes. So, we might distinguish fear of what is painful from fear of what is harmful, and these from fear of what is disgusting, and so on. This allows for incommensurability among kinds of fear. But the hope would be that within each sort of fear, there is commensurability.

This hope, however, will not be satisfied. The class of the painful, say, is itself full of incommensurabilities, both *qua* painfulness and also *qua* fearsomeness: e.g. the pain of a broken arm and the pain of a broken heart. Even within the class of physical pains, there are incommensurabilities: e.g. the pain of a burn and the pain of a stubbed toe. Neither is qualitatively the same pain, differing only, say, in quantity.

My point here is not that we cannot compare these various pains both as to their painfulness and fearsomeness. They can indeed be compared. So it can be obvious that the emotional pain of humiliatingly having one's bluff called can be less—both less painful and less fearsome—than the physical pain needed to make good the foolish boast that one can walk barefoot across the fire.

We, thus, can and do compare such incommensurable pains. That we can and do compare them is just my point. It shows that incommensurability is no bar to comparisons. It also shows that we can be more or less wise in such comparisons. This, too, is just my point. The possibility of judgement and indeed of wise, or foolish, judgement is consistent with incommensurability.

We talk, and often quite properly so, of what in such cases is more or less painful. This talk must not mislead us into thinking that here there must be commensurability—a common pain which the more painful has to a greater extent than does the less painful. For we talk, again properly, of what is more or less lovable, or awesome, or worthy of indignation, and we also talk properly of stronger or weaker love, awe, and indignation. And here at least it is obvious that these are complex in ways that involve incommensurability.

The original worry about courage was that it contains distinct and incommensurable feelings, fear and confidence, each with distinct and incommensurable proper objects, death and injury and victory. This was supposed to distinguish courage from other virtues said by Pears to allow for homogeneous continua, and to distinguish its emotions, taken together, from other emotions. But as just seen, there is incommensurability in fear taken generally and also within at least many of the different sorts of fears. In so far as incommensurability involves complexity, fear and its objects are complex. They may well be unities, but they are complex and incommensurable unities.

This argument, put so far in terms of fear and its objects, is easily generalized to other topics of concern for us. Similar arguments hold, I suggest, for every or almost every important feeling. And this, I suggest further, is true whether 'feeling' is understood as a sensuous episode, as in feeling the pain of a stubbed toe, or as a complex emotion composed of complexes of cognitive, desiderative, and affective components, as in feeling broken-hearted.

I do not take myself to have proven that incommensurability is non-problematic. But we have seen that incommensurability is a perfectly general feature of feelings, desires, actions, and indeed of much else. Thus, we have seen that, so far as commensurability and homogeneity are concerned, courage poses no special problem for the Doctrine of the Mean or for evaluative and emotional coherence in either Aristotelian or non-Aristotelian ethics. We have also seen that if talk of balancing the elements of courage involves incoherence because of commensurability and homogeneity, then in quite general ways, both important and unimportant parts of our lives are also incoherent, contrary to all appearances. And if, as I think, these are not incoherent, then—at least so far as commensurability and homogeneity are concerned—neither is talk of balancing the elements of courage.

APPENDIX I. PEARS'S SOLUTION

Pears thinks that the Doctrine can be saved. He writes

> The man whose confidence is medial will assess the chances of safety
> correctly, neither exaggerating them nor minimizing them. He will then
> have in one pan of the balance a countergoal with a certain disvalue
> and a certain probability. In the other pan he will have the external
> goal, and it too will have a certain probability and a certain value
> ('Courage as a Mean', 183).

That these contents of the pans must be balanced seems unexceptionable.
But Pears's claim that they can be balanced is problematic, especially if
put in terms of the Doctrine of the Mean. If, as he previously claimed,
victory and danger do not shade into each other and do not fall on a
continuum, how can such balancing be accomplished? Or is the balancing
they require not the balancing of the Doctrine?

Pears wants to understand their balancing in terms of the Doctrine. He
says there is a 'homogeneous scale' (182), a single continuum for
confidence where its object is evaluated in terms of the discounted value
of fear's object. Immediately after the passage just quoted, he writes that
use of this scale makes it possible that if the person of medial confidence

> decides to go for the external goal, he will do so with a correct and
> steadfast assessment of the chances of safety and a conviction that the
> external goal is worth it. If this is right, there is a graduated scale on
> which both fear and confidence are placed. It is the scale on which
> the agent's estimates of the probability of the countergoal are marked
> (183–4).

Similarly, Pears says that there is a distinct homogeneous scale for fear in
light of the discounted value of courage's object. 'On this scale fear and
confidence are related to the same factor of probability but in opposite
ways' (184).

Since he presents us with two such scales, we cannot ask how he can
find one homogeneous continuum for courage's distinct values. But we
must ask how he finds any homogeneous continuum. Further, as stressed
above, it is essential that the courageous person be able to see the situation
as a unity. So, it is unsatisfactory not to be told how or even whether
these two continua go together to give the agent one answer.

But even if these two continua can go together, they—jointly and
severally—cannot play the role required by the Doctrine. They give us
only correlations between the fear and the confidence. They give us only
hypothetical and general information, allowing us to make sense of claims
which we might frame as follows:

> The more likely the danger, the less terrible the danger needs to be

to balance or overbalance a given victory in the light of its likelihood. The more terrible the danger, the less likely the danger needs to be to balance or overbalance a given victory in the light of its likelihood.

These claims are not mistaken; but they are radically insufficient. Courageous warriors need to know whether here and now this fear and that confidence are warranted. This is importantly different from knowing what sorts of change in one of these would be required to maintain a balance between them if the other were to change. Warriors need to know how to compare the values of the danger and the victory—taken, of course, in the light of their probabilities. They need actual and particular, not general and hypothetical, comparisons. They need, in short, to know how to balance this victory and this danger.

In trying to find a mean between fear and confidence, or between danger and victory, probabilities are, of course, important. But they do not determine the answer. Probabilities without values do not provide an answer to 'What am I to do or feel?' Probabilistically discounted distinct values may be discounted, but they are still distinct. Even with probabilities, we still need a way to compare the values, probabilistically discounted or not.

APPENDIX 2. THE OBJECT OF *THARSOS*

In the body of this chapter, I have argued as though victory were the proper object of *tharsos*. But Pears denies this. He thus cuts himself off from the natural, albeit problematic, account of the mean of courage, given in terms of a mean of the objects of fear and confidence, danger and victory, and their values. In this appendix, I will argue against Pears's understanding of *tharsos*.

It might be wondered whether pursuing this, even in an appendix, is not simply to digress, but to digress over a mere matter of interpretation. There is some point to this worry: the argument given above that the Doctrine is coherent would need only slight, and mainly verbal, changes if Pears is right about *tharsos*. But this worry is also, and in more important ways, wrong. As will be seen, a correct understanding of *tharsos* is important for understanding Aristotle's account of courage, and is useful for presenting various strands of my argument about the mean.

Pears argues that for Aristotle, victory is a goal of courage, but not of *tharsos*. Fear is understood and evaluated in terms of the value of its proper goal, danger, and an estimate of its likelihood. But *tharsos* is characterized only in terms of an intellectual estimate of success. It is not said also to have victory as a goal, nor therefore to involve an evaluation of the victory. Pears writes confidence . . . certainly does not involve a desire for the external goal. Aristotle took the external goal to be victory in cases of true courage, and safety in other cases (*NE* 3. 6, 1115a33 ff.). His definition of confidence in the *Rhetoric* (1383a17–19), 'an expectation that what brings safety will be close at hand,' suggests that 'safety' or 'survival' might possibly cover all his external goals. However, confidence evidently does not involve the desire for safety in the way in which fear involves the desire to avoid harm (181).

So understood, the problem of finding a mean between fear and confidence is not finding a mean between danger and victory, but of finding one between danger and an intellectual estimate of victory. This, of course, still leaves us with any general problem there might be in finding a mean between emotions or objects that do not shade into each other.

Further, there is a real problem here. On Aristotle's view, emotions can affect and be affected by judgements. (Cf. *Rhetoric* 2. 1.) And such affecting and being affected can be correct or incorrect. None the less, finding the mean of how to be affected is not the central problem of confidence or of courage. Aristotle's comments about intellectual estimates of success do not show such estimates are the only object of *tharsos*. Nor does his silence about victory show that victory is not a goal of *tharsos*.

How, then, should *tharsos* be understood? Pears, himself, gives the materials for an answer. As he notes, Aristotle often uses '*tharsos*' in its verbal form '*tharrein*' in constructions which are translated 'to face . . . confidently' (183). Different sorts of things can be faced confidently—e.g. a person, a trial, or an enterprise. We are here concerned with the confidence of warriors in battle. Thus, if facing battle confidently requires that victory be a goal of *tharsos*, we will have shown that victory is a goal of *tharsos*.

As a start to understanding what it is to face an enterprise confidently, we might say that it involves the belief that any obstacles that may be encountered will be overcome, and thus that the enterprise will succeed. This seems partly right and partly wrong. It is right to focus on obstacles. It is wrong to require such beliefs about them. One need not believe that they will be overcome, nor that the enterprise will succeed. A more guarded judgement is sufficient—e.g. that they can almost certainly be overcome, that the enterprise has every chance of succeeding. As will be shown below, these judgements need not involve even such guarded beliefs about success.

Here we should note what is of importance about obstacles. As Sartre argues in *Being and Nothingness*, something is an obstacle only in regard to a goal. For something to be an obstacle—and thus difficult, costly, or something to be overcome—it must be this in regard to a goal. So, a collapsed bridge is an obstacle for someone wanting to cross the river. But it is an aid to someone wanting to stop that person from crossing. And it may be neither of these to someone admiring the landscape.

On Aristotle's view, courage is paradigmatically a martial virtue. Battle is what is faced confidently, and courage allows battle to be faced confidently. Pre-eminent among the obstacles in battle are the objects of fear: death and injury. Other obstacles include terrain, deficiencies in supplies, and the like. These are all obstacles to victory. Thus, if my argument is right, victory is a goal of *tharsos*.

I say a goal, not the goal, of *tharsos* since where there is no hope of victory, there can still be obstacles: e.g. to putting up a good fight. Here, putting up a good fight, not victory, would be a goal of *tharsos*. Below I argue that victory must be a primary goal of *tharsos*, and that e.g. putting up a good fight can be only a secondary goal. Here it is sufficient to note two points. First, victory is, at least often, a goal of *tharsos*. Second, Pears's argument would deny not only that victory, but also that putting up a good fight, is a goal of *tharsos*. On his view, *tharsos* is only about an intellectual estimate of success.

To be sure, intellectual estimates of the chances of success are relevant for facing things confidently. However, the relevance is more evaluative than conceptual. It is of course, constitutive of being an Aristotelian good person both that one tailor one's confidence about a task to estimates of success and also that one's estimates be reasonable.

But, it is conceptually possible for people to face a task with great confidence even if they estimate that success is very unlikely and are thus not very confident that they will succeed. Correlatively, it is conceptually possible for people to face a task with little, if any, confidence even though they estimate that success is very likely and are thus confident that they will succeed.

Those conceptual possibilities are the reason why I suggested above that believing that the obstacles will or can assuredly be overcome is not a requirement for facing a task confidently. As argued elsewhere, what rather seems needed is that one is hopeful—confidently hopeful—about overcoming the obstacles: one must have a confident cast of mind.[9]

Of course, to be a courageous and successful warrior, one might well have to believe that—be confident that—one will, or will probably, prevail. (Again, 'believe' is not exactly right.) What the successful warrior needs is to face the battle confidently and to be self-confident. These involve a belief in oneself, or more exactly in oneself as victor.

Thus, it is misleading to hold that victory is the primary goal of *tharsos*, unless such victory is understood as victory achieved by oneself. So, instead of saying that victory is the primary goal of *tharsos*, it would be better to

---

[9] See my 'Affectivity and Self-Concern', especially sect. 6. See also, 'Emotional Thoughts', *American Philosophical Quarterly*, 24 (1987), 59–69.

say that the complex of victory and the self as victor is its primary goal. And this is what I will mean in subsequent claims that victory is a goal of *tharsos*.

In order to show that victory is a goal of *tharsos*, I have so far focused on the notion of facing something confidently, and the notion of obstacles. My claim can be established in another way—by showing how courage is incomplete, perhaps even incoherent, unless victory is one of its goals, and then by showing how this requires that victory is a goal of *tharsos*.

To see how courage would be motivationally incomplete, it is essential to keep in mind that courage, *andreia*—literally, manliness—is the virtue, the excellence, of those in battle. It is in virtue of possessing and exercising this that they do well in battle. This is an important difference between our notion of courage and Aristotle's of *andreia*. For us, the general arena of courage is almost any situation involving danger and fear. At least roughly, we are courageous if we handle fear correctly. But for Aristotle, correct handling of fear is only endurance, *karteria*, the opposite of which must be something like softness, *malakia*. (Cf. e.g. *NE* 7. 7, 1150a13 ff.)

To minimize problems over the match between 'courage' and '*andreia*', in what follows I shall be concerned only with courage in battle and thus with courage where there is an external object of victory and a counter object of death and injury. To avoid other issues, I will consider only enacted courage—i.e. the courage in an act of courage—rather than the disposition or virtue of courage. Thus, when I speak of courageous people, I am speaking of those acting courageously in battle.

Even if courage does not have victory as a goal—if, for example, courage were concerned only with the correct handling of danger and fear—the intellectual estimate of the likelihood of success, e.g. victory, might play a role in courage. It could, for example, be useful in preventing fear from growing beyond its proper bounds, by stilling the false but despairing thought that victory is impossible. But if courage did not have victory as a goal, then simply standing up calmly to the enemy, perhaps calmly accepting death—with the correct estimates of success, of course—could constitute being a courageous warrior. However, death, injury, and the like are, as such, to be feared and avoided. This, we might say, is the evaluative and desiderative side of what it is to be a human. Further, especially for a warrior, death, injury, and the like are to be combatted, not simply endured.

We might, thus, require that the warrior not only stand up to, but also fight, the enemy. But this will not guarantee what we might call an all-round courageous warrior. Instead, it may give only a purely defensive warrior—a warrior who stands and fights, and fears the right things in the right amounts and the like. Not having victory as a goal, the purely defensive warrior has no reason to advance and gain victory. That offence may be the best defence is only partly to the point here. Purely defensive warriors would strive not to lose, but beyond what is needed for that, they would not strive to conquer. (Cf. *NE* 7. 7, 1150a34 ff.) One might argue that this sort of engagement would suit those intent simply on defending their city against attack. But, of course, courage is also had by more offensive warriors.

Let us now turn to the conceptual incompleteness or incoherence of courage if victory is not one of its goals. The seriousness of a danger depends both on the values intrinsically involved in the danger—the death, injury, and the like—and on the likelihood of their occurring. But what is also important for Aristotle, and us, is what course of action and what feelings are right—prudent, wise, or noble—in a given dangerous situation. Here, the value of what the act will gain, if successful, taken in the light of the chances of success must be balanced against the disvalue of the danger and its likelihood.

It is only in regard to a goal, such as victory, that one can assess how great a danger it is here and now worth risking and how much fear is here and now warranted in the light of the present danger. The need for such a comparison—the danger compared with the victory—is not simply a practical one. It is also a conceptual one. The warrior's question of whether this danger is warranted is an essentially comparative one. It asks whether the danger is warranted by the victory.

This last point is not weakened by the fact that some dangers may be too great for anyone to face, no matter what the victory. Nor is it weakened by the fact that some goals may be so important that they must be striven for, no matter what their cost to the agent.

A mere intellectual appreciation of the likelihood of success will not answer the question of whether a particular goal warrants a particular danger. That intellectual appreciation must be applied to the value of the success. Only the conjunction of these determines what it is right to do and feel about the danger.

My argument so far is that victory, not merely an intellectual assessment of its likelihood, plays essential motivational and conceptual roles in courage. As Pears says, victory is the external goal of courage. But the issue is whether victory is an object of *tharsos*, not just of courage. How, it might be asked, can victory be shown to be a goal of *tharsos* by showing that it is a goal of courage? The worry here concerns two transitions: first, from courage to *tharsos*; second, from the understanding of 'goal' as what *tharsos* is about to that of what is sought—i.e. from what *tharsos* is about to what the person with *tharsos* is about. For the claim that victory is a goal of *tharsos* is the claim that victory is an emotional object of *tharsos*. It is what *tharsos* is about. But the claim that victory is a goal of courage is the claim that victory is an end of courage. Victory is what courage, or the courageous person, is concerned to obtain.

To meet this worry, let us ask whether victory is a goal of any emotion which is a constituent of an Aristotelian virtue. Pears seems committed to answering either 'No' or 'Yes, but not of *tharsos*.' My answer is, 'Yes, of *tharsos*.'

The negative answer is implausible. It requires that victory, especially as can be gained in battle, is not the sort of thing about which one can go emotionally wrong or right, and that it is not the sort of thing admitting of too much and too little of emotion. In short, there is no mean of emotion here. It would, thus, take success out of the realm of important motives and goals in Aristotelian explanations of character and action.

This, I think, is totally implausible. It is central to Aristotle's depiction of his people that they strive for, and in other ways are concerned with, gain in general and victory in particular. So, to mention only one of many examples, in the *Politics*, he sketches the natural, if not inevitable, transitions from any increase in one's power, to an increase in one's *tharsos* or boldness, to an increase in one's courage, to an increase in one's acquisitive action—all against the background of one's desire for gain (5. 8, 1312a15 ff.). Thus, we get Jowett's nice translation, 'courage is emboldened by power' (a19). And to the question of 'Emboldened to do what?', the answer is 'Get more.'

Indeed, that the people Aristotle was concerned with were so much caught up with getting more, with victory and success, helps explain why he did not bother to mention victory as an object of *tharsos*. Everyone knew that it—it, almost above all—was a goal of confident and bold men. The practical problems were how to temper fear; so that it would be neither too great nor too small.

Thus I think we are left with the second and third answers above: victory is a goal of an emotion other than *tharsos*, or victory is a goal of *tharsos*. If the third is not the answer, then courage would be an amalgam of at least three emotions, confidence, fear, and this other emotion that does have victory as its object.

It might seem that there is a good reason for Aristotle to have allowed for three emotions. For unless he did, confidence turns out to be simply a martial virtue. But confidence—confidence in oneself and facing confidently—is also found in non-military affairs.

The following points tell against the suggestion that we take courage as involving a third emotion. First, there may be merit in the argument that since confidence can be displayed in non-martial arenas, it should not be seen as a military emotion. But in so far as the *tharsos* of courage is concerned with an estimate of success in battle, we would now have to hold that such *tharsos* is a different emotion from any non-martial self-confidence.

However, the realm of those things about whose occurrence one is confident is importantly related to the realm of those things one can face confidently and have self-confidence about. In almost every field of endeavour where confidence as estimate and confidence as self-confidence are found, they may be so tightly interrelated that they form a real unity, even if an analytically divisible one. If this is right, taking these two sorts or aspects of confidence as being really separable would hinder, perhaps even preclude, understanding each, as well as their ensemble.

Second, courage, too, has its place outside the military sphere. As with courage, so with *tharsos*, it might be held that the noblest arena for it is the military. So too, it might be held that what can be displayed there, and perhaps only there, is the noblest, the paradigm, sort of *tharsos*.

Third, silence may here be decisive. Emotions and how a good person is to stand to them are at the very centre of Aristotle's account of the virtues. Having a fixed disposition to have an emotion as one should, or this conjoined with having a fixed disposition to act as one should, is said to be what a virtue is. It would thus be very hard to explain his silence about this third emotion of courage.

We can give a more direct argument to show that *tharsos*, not some third emotion, has victory as its goal. Let us briefly canvass some features that an emotion must have if it, in conjunction with the proper handling of fear, is to play the role needed by courage. First, it has victory as its goal. Second, it must take into account the likelihood of its object, victory. So, for example, wild optimists would be very unlikely to have this emotion correctly.

To present the third feature, we should recall the earlier argument that courage is conceptually incoherent if victory is not one of its goals—because courage essentially involves balancing the value and likelihood of victory against the disvalue and likelihood of danger. A strictly similar argument applies in regard to the emotion now under consideration, whether it is *tharsos* or some third emotion. Thus, for this emotion to be correct—and for it to play the needed role in courage—it must take into account both the value and the likelihood of victory and the disvalue and the likelihood of danger.

Above it was argued that whether or not courage requires confidence that one will or may win, it requires confidence in one's winning. So, fourth, this emotion must help effect this confidence in victory and in oneself as victor. It must help effect a sort of spiritedness and derring-do, ensuring that the agent is a 'can do, will do, let me at it' sort of person. As Aristotle says, 'courage that is inspired by spirit [*thumos*] seems the most natural, and when reinforced by deliberate choice and purpose it appears to be true courage' (*NE* 3. 8, 1117a3 ff., tr. Rackham).

There is no need to continue with the question of whether it is *tharsos* or alternatively some third emotion that has these features and plays these roles. For, as should be clear, the characteristics of that supposedly third emotion are simply those I find in *tharsos*. So too, what it is to stand correctly to that emotion is simply what I have argued it is to stand correctly to *tharsos*. *Tharsos* is that emotion.

To be sure, no matter how sound these points, Aristotle might still have not taken victory to be a proper goal of *tharsos*. But I am unable to see any reason to attribute this view to him or to think that denying it on his behalf harms his account of courage.

6

Plurality and Choice

MANY hold that plural values make reasoned judgement difficult, if not impossible. So it seems to many that it is only by special pleading, not sound argument, that Socrates, Plato, and Aristotle can 'show' that the life of reason is better than that of pleasure: since proponents of each sort of life hold that their values are the highest values, in terms of which all other values are to be judged, there is no way to judge them which does not beg questions. Similarly, but now in the more explicitly political realm, many hold that where a society has plural conceptions of the social good, there is no possibility of reasoned social choice and action. So, many now hold that there is no possibility of sound choice between a liberal and an out-and-out religious conception of a good social life. At best there are compromises, unsatisfactory to all sides; at worst, there is coercion.

However, it is unclear whether the problems supposedly entrained by plural values are entrained by mere plurality or, instead, by conflicts between the various values. Even if—as discussed in 'Monism, Pluralism, and Conflict'—there can be value conflicts only where there are plural values, there seems no need for there to be conflicts wherever there are plural values. After all, there could be priority or trade-off relations that make it impossible for the different values to conflict. So it might be held that wherever the values of reason and of pleasure seem to conflict—point in opposite directions—the former are to be given pride of place, or that in certain realms the former are to hold sway and in others the latter.

There are, however, claims that plurality itself poses problems for judgement—either directly or because of conflict generated by plurality. And these are the claims I am concerned to examine in

I am indebted to Bruce Ackerman, Joshua Cohen, Tony Kronman, Charles Larmore, Henry Richardson, John Robertson, Thomas Scanlon, Amartya Sen, Judith Thomson, and Susan Wolf.

this chapter. The central claim can be put simply: if the values are really different, if there is plurality, there can be no sound way to compare them, and thus no sound way to make judgements about situations which have mixtures of the plural values. This is the negative claim. The positive claim is that only where there is one value is sound judgement possible.

The issue is whether sound judgement requires an evaluative monism. There are several very great difficulties in assessing this issue. One is the difficulty in giving identity conditions for values. Another is that, at least in the sense of monism I will develop, there have been very few evaluative monists. We, thus, have little idea—at least as presented and defended by those favourable to it—of what an evaluative monism is or what is monistic about it.

A third difficulty—which may explain the previous two—is that the worry that monism is necessary for sound judgement is not a worry that has been much developed and defended in the literature so much as it is a worry that is 'in the air'. It is a worry that I have encountered in many discussions, and which, so it seems to me, underlies many familiar moves and concerns in ethics. But it is a worry that is rarely brought out into the open and shown to be really worrisome. It is like a spectre, lurking in the philosophically shadowy background—a spectre many think we must do our best to avoid, or at least not antagonize.

Since that worry has not been clearly presented, there is that danger that I may not understand it correctly. I may thus be presenting and arguing against something at best only somewhat related to the real worry about monism, pluralism, and judgement. However, opposition to the claims and arguments presented below from monists—i.e. from those seen as monists both by themselves and by me—gives me some reason to think that I come at least close to a deeply held and deeply hidden worry about pluralism.

Let us now turn to the question of whether plural values make sound judgement and action difficult. It is given by the following line of thought:

Where we have to weigh likes against likes we can at least see which of them is greater and thus better—e.g. that this act is more pleasurable than that one, or will lead to more understanding than that one. But where there are plural values, we have to weigh unlikes against unlikes, which thus cannot be compared directly with each other. Nor do we have any trade-off schema which will allow us to compare them indirectly. It makes sense to talk of amounts of pleasure and of amounts of understanding: 'This act is more pleasurable than that', and 'Pursuing this study will increase understanding more than pursuing that one' make sense. But it makes no sense to talk about a given amount of pleasure being greater than a given amount of understanding: 'This act leads to more pleasure than that act leads to understanding' and 'The gain in pleasurableness of this act over that act is greater than the gain in understanding of that one over this' are nonsense. Thus, plural values do not allow for sound judgement and action. When faced with them, we must simply plump for one or the other.

Some have shown the need to confront these issues about sound judgement and plural values by arguments showing fragmentation among overarching sorts of values—e.g. of rights, utility, special obligation, ideals, projects, or of the personal and impersonal, the agent-centred and the agent-neutral, and so on. Others have shown this need by using arguments for plurality that may also explain this fragmentation—arguments showing that and how our moral sensibility incorporates elements from diverse backgrounds.[1] I certainly agree that to understand ethics in general and plurality in particular, we must understand these categories and facts. But as I will be concerned to argue, there is a far simpler and a far more sweeping argument for plurality, and thus also for a need to confront any problems entrained by plurality. It is that value, taken quite generally, is plural.

Quite generally, if plurality entrains difficulties for sound judgement, we are faced with those difficulties. The previous chapter, 'Courage', began my argument against those claims purporting to show that plurality does entrain such difficulties. In this chapter, I continue my argument against them. I will do this directly by showing them misleading and often false. I will also do this indirectly

[1] See e.g. T. Nagel, 'The Fragmentation of Value', in *Mortal Questions* (Cambridge: Cambridge University Press, 1979) and *The View from Nowhere* (New York: Oxford University Press, 1986); A. MacIntyre, *After Virtue* (Notre Dame, Ind.: University of Notre Dame Press, 1981); C. Taylor, 'The Diversity of Goods', in A. Sen and B. Williams (eds.), *Utilitarianism and Beyond* (Cambridge: Cambridge University Press, 1982); and B. Williams, *Ethics and the Limits of Philosophy* (Cambridge, Mass.: Harvard University Press, 1985).

by showing that plural values are the rule rather than the exception; that many, if not most, ordinary choices involve plural values; and thus that if plurality engenders those problems, then even our ordinary life at its most ordinary is problematic in these ways. If these indirect arguments are right, then either plurality allows for sound judgement and action or alternatively even at its most ordinary, and contrary to appearances, our ordinary life does not admit of sound judgement and action.

As well as arguing for pluralism, I will argue against monism. With respect to the latter, I will not be concerned to argue that monism is incoherent or otherwise impossible. It is, rather, incapable of allowing us to make sense of our moral life, and more generally our evaluative life. It requires, in effect, not only that we think that pushpin might be as good as poetry—which may well be possible; but that there is no difference in the sort of value between them. This latter is possible—in the minimal sense that it is coherent, or at least not clearly self-contradictory. But it is impossible—in a somewhat broader sense in that it is insensitive to our moral and evaluative world. Indeed, it is often insensitive to the point of being boorish. My argument against monism then is an out-and-out evaluative argument: it leads to bad ethics and evaluation, where the badness is, itself, understood in out-and-out evaluative ways.

I. THREE MARKS OF PLURALITY

Putting his own view and opposing what he presents as the Platonists' view, Aristotle writes, 'But as a matter of fact the notions of honour and wisdom and pleasure, as being good, are different and distinct. Therefore, good is not a general term corresponding to a single Idea.' (*Nicomachean Ethics* I. 6, 1096b23 ff., tr. Rackham.) In what follows, I will sketch some reasons why we might hold that these goods are distinct and different. I will not be concerned with the question of whether these are Aristotle's reasons. Rather, I will be concerned to show that if these goods are distinct and different—especially for those reasons—then plurality is absolutely commonplace and unproblematic.

Among the most important marks of plurality for our life are three that concern comparison and choice. First, only pluralism allows for qualitatively different evaluative considerations. Second, only pluralism allows us to understand how even the best act can be lacking. Third, the judgement required by pluralism is different from that required by monism.

Qualitative differences. Pluralists can hold that lying on the beach is sensually pleasant but that discussing philosophy is intellectually pleasing or is good in non-hedonic ways, e.g. by furthering understanding. Pluralists can also hold that these are different sorts of goods, not simply different sources of one sort of good. They can also hold that choice is importantly a choice among different sorts of goods, not simply of amount of good. They can recognize that choice importantly involves determining which values to pursue and which to forgo.

But according to monism, we never have to choose, nor do we ever have the opportunity to choose, between pursuing one value and pursuing another. We never have to consider whether it is worth missing out on or sacrificing one value for another. In monistic choice, the only evaluatively relevant difference between options is how they stand to one evaluative consideration—one value. And typically, difference in amount of this one value is the only relevant sort of standing.

So, for example, monists hold that the choices between lying on the beach or discussing philosophy and between playing the violin or practising judo do not turn on different evaluative considerations—differences in these activities—but rather only on differences in one common value. Monistic hedonists hold that pleasure is this one value. They tell us that these choices and all other choices are to be made simply on the basis of pleasure. So, they cannot see how people could rationally care which of these pleasures they get.

On their view, the differences between such pleasures as that of sunning oneself on the beach and of discussing philosophy are differences simply of the source of the very same thing. And since the source, *qua* source, has no importance, they attach no intrinsic importance to those differences. So, suppose I join a friend on the beach to discuss philosophy, for the pleasure from discussing philosophy, and somehow get sidetracked into simply lying on the beach and getting pleasure from that. According to monistic hedonists, I have in no way failed to get the good I was really aiming at—at least if I get as much pleasure as I was trying to get.

I have simply got it—the very same thing—from a different source. I would have no basis of rational complaint that I did not get what I wanted. Nor could I be thankful that even though I did not get what I wanted, I at least got something else of value and perhaps of at least an equal amount of value.

Of course, monistic hedonism can allow that my goal was the pleasure of philosophical discussion, not the pleasure of lying on the beach, and that I might complain if I get the one, having sought the other. But in so far as monistic hedonism is a claim about value, it could not allow that having such a goal would be sensible or rational.

One way to put this is that monists might hold that my not getting what I wanted grounds the complaint because they also hold that want satisfaction is the only value. After all, we often do see that wanting something gives, not merely registers, value. But for monists, if want satisfaction plays this role, it must be, or give, the only value. But as will be argued below, want satisfaction is a plausible value or ground of value only within a pluralism.

My claim, then, is that pluralists can, but monists cannot, see the differences grounded in evaluative differences.

Lack. The second mark of plurality is given by what it is to lack a good. To make it clear that my concern with plural values goes beyond acts and act evaluations to other matters of ethical concern, I will first put my claim about lacks in terms of a life.

Consider a life that is rich in wisdom and honour but poor in sensual pleasure. Such a life does not merely not have that good, it lacks it. There are two parts to this claim. The first is that not having sensual pleasure is a lack in the life. Some lacks are correlates of what there should be—in this case, a good or ideal life. So, a life deficient in sensual pleasure is seen as lacking by contrast with a good life: because and in so far as this life is deficient in sensual pleasure, it is not a good life.

Lacks can also be given by real possibilities: my now having to choose between understanding and sensual pleasure may help constitute what is forgone as lack. Such lacks may be seen as disappointments, as having been in one's grasp but let go. But of course, not every forgone good grounds a disappointment. Something else is needed, such as an ideal which shows, not that one should have chosen that good, but that one should have it and that having to choose between it and what was properly chosen was unfortunate. (Some structures of lacks are discussed in Chapter 4, above, under the headings of 'ideals' and 'possibilities'. Their relations with qualitative differences are discussed in Chapter 8, below.)

The second part of my claim is that having a lack is consistent with being as good as is possible in the circumstances. So, a life can be lacking in pleasure even if the only way to have additional pleasure would involve losing so much wisdom and honour that the life with greater pleasure would be overall worse. As this suggests, a life could be lacking in a particular good even if the life is as good as circumstances allow.

Monists, too, can complain about missing out on their single good. They can do this even if, as they recognize, a life is as good as it could be in the circumstances. For they can imagine that with a change of circumstances the life could have been better, and they can complain that what is here and now the best possible is not better than it in fact is. Pluralists' regrets can also be like this. But, unlike monists, they can also regret missing out on and lacking a particular sort of good.

Different forms of judgement. The third mark of different and distinct goods is given by what many find most problematic about plurality — the sort of judgement needed to compare different values, as contrasted with the sort of judgement needed to compare instances of the very same value.

The latter seems to involve only finding out which option has more of the one value. And thus, many do not see it as involving judgement at all. To be sure, seeing which option has more of one value can be difficult: e.g. it can be difficult to determine which of two beaches will offer more sensual pleasure. But the difficulties in making such a monistic comparison seem importantly different from those faced when comparing instances of plural values — e.g. the pleasures of lying on a beach and of understanding.

Indeed, many think that monists face only epistemic difficulties about the facts. As monism is often understood by monists and non-monists, it is a non-evaluative matter — a matter of ordinary 'factual' fact — which beach will offer more pleasure. Finding out what the fact is — which beach will be more pleasurable — can be difficult, and it can involve a certain sort of judgement. After all, someone with local knowledge may be in a better position than a stranger would be to judge how hot, crowded, and so on each beach will be.

However, comparisons of plural values, in addition to needing this sort of factual judgement, also need evaluative judgement. Suppose we are trying to choose between lying on a beach and discussing philosophy—or more particularly, between the pleasure of the former and the gain in understanding from the latter. To compare them we may invoke what I will call a higher-level synthesizing category. So, we may ask which will conduce to a more pleasing day, or to a day that is better spent. Once we have fixed upon the higher synthesizing category, we can often easily ask which option is better in regard to that category and judge which to choose on the basis of that. Even if it seems a mystery how we might 'directly' compare lying on the beach and discussing philosophy, it is a commonplace that we do compare them, e.g. in regard to their contribution to a pleasing day.

This involves evaluative judgement in at least three different ways. First, the higher-level synthesizing category may introduce new evaluative features, rather than being a simple collection or summary of the lower-level goods it covers. This is the way Aristotelian eudaimonia stands to its various constituting, lower-level goods, such as pleasure. At the very least, it collects them together, organizing and balancing them in regard to each other in evaluatively distinctive and proper ways. And such balance is not one of the original lower-level goods.

Second, the relation between the lower-level good and the higher-level category is evaluative. So, it is a clearly evaluative question whether this pleasure will lead to a well-spent day, or whether this pleasure would make for a day better spent than would that understanding. (As will be suggested below, and argued in 'Maximization: Some Conceptual Problems', the relation between pleasure and pleasingness is also evaluative.)

One way of summarizing these two points is that we may be unable to judge how well the higher-level category is satisfied simply by evaluating the lower-order goods on their own. We may have to evaluate those goods—how good these instances are or even whether here and now they are good at all[2]—in terms of how well they satisfy that category. (But see p. 248.)

The third reason that comparisons of plural values are evaluative has, in effect, already been seen: such comparisons need not involve just one higher-order synthesizing category, but can involve many— e.g. that of a well-spent day and that of pleasingness. Lying on the beach may be sensually more pleasing than discussing philosophy, but discussing philosophy may contribute more to a well-spent day. Thus, if we want to know what to do, all things considered, we need a way to take the various categories into account. Once again, we must judge between plural considerations. Now, however, the considerations are those of higher-level synthesizing categories.

So, we might ask which of these options is better in regard simply to a good life or in regard simply to goodness—taking these to be still higher-level synthesizing categories. If goodness itself is taken as a synthesizing category, and especially if it is taken as the highest such category, we see that the possibility of higher-level synthesizing categories is little, if anything, more than the possibility of making evaluative comparisons. The more is simply what is given by holding that comparisons are made in terms of evaluative categories.

To the extent that plural evaluative considerations do, and monistic ones do not, require us to use such higher-level synthesizing categories, the judgement needed for plural considerations will thus involve out-and-out evaluative judgement. This contrasts with the factual judgement that seems sufficient for monisms.

To take up an earlier point, some express this by saying that monistic judgements do not really involve deliberation at all, but only a form of factual judgement. Put less strongly, it might be held that monistic judgements involve deliberation only about means, but that pluralistic judgements also involve deliberation about ends. Both ways of putting the matter can be misleading. Factual judgement may involve at least some forms of deliberation. And monists can deliberate about which end is the one, ultimate end, while pluralists can come to deliberation with a predetermined and inflexible list of ends. Further, once we recognize that some means are constitutive, not merely instrumental, we can see that

---

[2] My thanks are owed to Eugene Garver for suggesting that the differences among these possibilities need to be made explicit. Some details of these possibilities are discussed in my 'Some Problems With Counter Examples in Ethics', *Synthese*, 72 (1987), 277–89.

the lower-level goods are means—albeit constitutive means—to what is given by the higher-level synthesizing categories.[3]

2. OBVIOUS PLURALITY AND ITS DENIAL

Plurality is absolutely commonplace and often enough unproblematic. Consider someone who is deciding whether to drive or to take the bus across town, or someone who has spare time and is wondering which of two long-held interests finally to take up, judo or the violin. Suppose now we ask the philosophical question of whether there are different reasons for choosing one rather than the other. I call this a philosophical question since it is obvious that there are different reasons for doing the one or the other. These are given by the obvious differences between taking the bus or car, or between judo and the violin. To mention only some, the car allows one to come and go when one wants, rather than having to follow the bus company's timetable, but the bus saves one from having to find a parking spot. And judo involves strenuous exercise and produces a fit and healthy body, increased agility, and a heightened sense of security, whereas the violin develops one's musical appreciation and ability.

Of course, people can be indifferent to these differences. Those who are looking simply for something, i.e. just anything, to pass the time, may see nothing to choose between judo and the violin—apart, that is, from how well each helps pass the time.

However, no matter what the possibility and nature of such monistic care in regard to judo and the violin, the care of many people for these is not monistic. At least for these people, they are importantly different activities, each with its own values. This is shown both in the reasons people have for choosing the one or the other, and also in the regrets about what a given choice will entrain missing out on. So, I may choose judo because I see that, on balance, I now need physical development more than musical

---

[3] Thus, we can agree with Aurel Kolnai that one, if not the, important form of deliberation is absent from instrumental calculations without agreeing that this shows Aristotle mistaken in holding that deliberation is about means. See Kolnai, 'Deliberation is of Ends', in *Ethics, Value and Reality* (Indianapolis: Hackett Publishing Company, 1978). An earlier version appeared in the *Proceedings of the Aristotelian Society*, 62 (1961–2). See also S. Morgenbesser and E. Ullmann-Margalit, 'Picking and Choosing', *Social Research*, 44 (1977), 757–85.

development. But I can none the less regret that I will miss out on the musical development.

Monism cannot allow for these evaluative differences. All questions of choice are to be answered in the same way, in terms of how the options stand to that one value. Typically, the decisive sort of standing is given by the ordering relation of which option has more of that one good, and is thus better, than the other. Apart from such issues, monists hold that there are no evaluative differences between judo and the violin. So too, there are none in other choices, e.g. between lying on a beach and discussing philosophy, between living with someone and celibacy, between a practical-political life and a scholarly-contemplative one, between a contented and an exciting life, and so on. Of course, monists can recognize that people do choose on the basis of such differences. But they cannot allow that these are, in themselves, rational bases of choice.

The differences I have pointed to—e.g. between physical and musical development or between lying on a beach and discussing philosophy—are so obvious and so obviously important and rational that we need an explanation of how any theorist could be a monist. In our tradition, there are several interrelated explanations. One starts from the thought that sound judgement and action is possible, and argues that plurality precludes such judgement. This is the topic of sections 3–4. Another explanation concerns the nature of value and evaluation, and holds that the differences I put forward as showing pluralism are not evaluative differences. This is the topic of sections 5–7.

3. A CONFUSION OF COMMENSURABILITY AND COMPARABILITY

If sound judgement requires monism, that would be a good reason to be a monist. But as large parts of this book are concerned to show, sound judgement does not require monism. In the present section, I will discuss a common misconception about commensurability and comparability that may lead some to think that sound judgement does require monism.[4]

[4] On relations among commensurability, comparability, and plurality see D. Wiggins, 'Weakness of Will, Commensurability, and the Objects of Deliberation and Desire', *Proceedings of the Aristotelian Society*, NS 79 (1978–9), 251–77, reprinted in

This misconception involves three claims: (1) sound judgement requires evaluative comparisons, (2) plural values are incommensurable, and (3) incommensurable values are incomparable. (1) and (2) may be benign, but (3) is unacceptable. So, Greek mathematics showed incommensurability between the lengths of a side of a square and its diagonal. For there are no common units, or ratios of rational numbers of these units, which express their length. None the less, what are here incommensurable admit of at least some comparisons. For example, it is mathematically provable that the diagonal is longer than its side.

However, there are problems in trying to understand the incommensurability of plural values in terms of such geometrical incommensurability. For the latter has to do with the lack of a common unit. But if a lack of a common unit shows incommensurability, it shows this even in a single value—e.g. a particular sort of pleasure. In comparing the pleasure of two sips of this wine, we no more have a common unit than we do for plural values. We may often be able to rank the pleasurableness of the sips—judge which is more pleasurable. But we cannot say by how much the one is more pleasurable than the other. We can measure neither the distance between them nor their ratio, nor—to explain those inabilities—can we say in the requisite way, how pleasurable either is. Thus, if incommensurability is a problem only for pluralism and not also for monism, it cannot be understood in terms of the absence of a common unit.

There is, however, another way to use the analogy from geometry and its talk of common units, by shifting focus from the issue of units to that of commonality. Ultimately, this is to shift attention to inter-substitutivity or fungibility. The lengths of these geometrical elements are incommensurable. But they are incommensurable amounts of one thing—length. That their lengths are inter-substitutable is shown by the fact that geometrically we can find and exchange an equal length from each and still have exactly the same figure and length.

Their difference is one of amount of length and not of what there is a different amount of—length. This, we may be told, is what allows us to compare their lengths. We may even be able to make

A. O. Rorty (ed.), *Essays on Aristotle's Ethics* (Berkeley: University of California Press, 1980); and J. Griffin, *Well-Being* (Oxford: Oxford University Press, 1986), especially ch. 5, 'Are There Incommensurable Values?' Both have aided me.

the comparisons in mechanical ways—e.g. by laying the items next to each other. Or if they are geometrical models made of a material of uniform mass, we could put them in the pans of a beam balance. We do not need units, nor therefore common units, for such ordering comparisons.

Instances of plural values càn rarely be compared in these ways. (See p. 248.) To be sure, they may fall under common higher-level synthesizing categories. And if there is an all-encompassing and highest category of value as such, they all fall under that. But their plurality has to do with differences in the nature of what differs and not simply in different amounts of a common nature. They differ *qua* value, not simply in amount of value. For this reason, many hold that we can make ordering comparisons of instances of a single value but not of instances of plural values—e.g. not between the pleasure of this sip of wine and that of the understanding to be gained by a discussion.

One way to proceed here would be to take up the various arguments which try to show that sound comparisons must be about common, inter-substitutable, and fungible features. Were I to do this, I would explore the striking similarity between that view and the view in metaphysics that instances of the same universal are instances of that universal in virtue of having a common and identical feature. I would also explore why it is thought that sound comparisons should be mechanical or algorithmic.

However, I do not propose to carry out these tasks in this work. My reason for this arises out of how I see the dynamics of the debate over pluralism, rather than the content of that debate. The order of strength and naturalness seems to be this: philosophers seem first to hold that comparisons require common features. They then seek arguments to support this thought. It is not a thought they need to be led to by arguments, and the strength of that thought seems given to those arguments, not derived from them. So I was not at all surprised when a colleague, upon hearing my claim that plural values are no impediment to sound decision, asked me to detail the miraculous decision procedure that makes such decision possible—with the clear implication that we need a decision procedure, and that it would take a miracle to give us one for plural values.

To the extent that I am right about the developmental order of the thought that comparisons require common features and the arguments for that thought, even if I could show that those arguments fail, we would probably still be faced with the original question, or a new question of how, or even whether, we can make sound comparisons except in regard to common features. I do not mean to suggest that these other philosophers would be unswayed by seeing that those arguments fail. But in my experience, they are more inclined to find new arguments than to give up that view about comparisons—so strong and natural do they find that view.

I have, however, found the indirect arguments somewhat more successful in showing that plurality is unproblematic. Thus, I will devote the majority of my time to these arguments.

4. CHOICE AND PLURALITY

As announced at the outset, my principal indirect argument involves showing that plural values are the rule rather than the exception; that many, if not most, ordinary choices involve plural values; and thus that if plurality engenders problems of judgement, then even our ordinary life at its most ordinary is, contrary to appearances, problematic. The discussion of judo and the violin above helps make this indirect argument. In the present section, I want to strengthen that argument by showing how plurality is central to choice. More exactly, I will show how those three marks of plurality—qualitative differences, lacks, and different sorts of judgement—are central to choice.

Let us return to an earlier example—that of the choice of how to get across town. Suppose that I first considered walking, taking a taxi, driving, or taking the bus. The taxi was ruled out as being too costly, and the walking as being too slow. I thus had to choose between the car and the bus. Deliberation involved weighing such different considerations as these: the car is quicker, but the bus is cheaper; taking the car requires finding a parking space, but taking the bus prevents me from returning just whenever I want; and so on. One way to see choice here is as a choice of which mix of these and other features to get and which to miss out on.

I want to make four claims about this example. First, it is an unloaded and perfectly typical case of a choice. Second, it involves plural values—e.g. pleasantness, time, money and what it can secure, freedom, ease—and the decision is reached by balancing and choosing among them. Third, it admits of a reasoned conclusion. Fourth, it may well be that both options are reasonable. It may be reasonable to take the bus or to take the car.

I will not argue for my first claim. Simple inspection will show it right or wrong. My argument for the second claim is given in my discussion of what the plurality of values consists of, as shown by those three marks. My argument for the third claim is more indirect. It is that in such typical cases of choice, often enough we seem to have no difficulties in choosing, nor in seeing—at the time or later—whether we have chosen well or poorly. Thus, if plurality presents a problem for choice, it is not one we are, at least generally, aware of. So, if plurality precludes sound judgement, then contrary to the way it seems to us, our desires, deliberations, choices, acts, and lives are cast adrift on a sea of unreason and are radically ungrounded.

My argument for the fourth claim is a variant of the third one. Suppose that here more than one option is reasonable. Some take this as the precise reason that plural values are problematic—they preclude a unique reasoned decision. But if in even such ordinary cases as this, there is no unique reasoned decision, I think the better conclusion is that such uniqueness is not a requirement of reasoned action, nor even of reason itself. (This is argued in Chapter 10.) My conclusion, then, is that such cases as this one do admit of a reasoned decision, whether unique or not. The consequence of denying this is that, once again and contrary to the way it seems to us, our lives are adrift on a sea of unreason and even our simplest and most straightforward acts and decisions involve radically ungrounded choice.

In regard to the third and fourth claims, we might wonder whether an 'existentialist' thought is at work even among our philosophers who so resolutely oppose existentialism. Put briefly, that thought is that where reason does not clearly and uniquely determine what is to be done, 'choice' involves lack of reason, arbitrariness, and the like.[5] Perhaps our philosophers reject the existentialist conclusion of this thought, rather than the thought itself—agreeing that if reason does not determine choice, then choice is arbitrary, but holding that reason does determine choice.

As noted earlier, some philosophers claim that in the absence of

---

[5] My thanks are owed to Peter van Inwagen for this suggestion.

plural considerations—in monistic evaluations—there is no room for deliberation, nor, therefore, for real choice. So, it could be held that failing such plurality, we are in the position of those about to buy a model T Ford. They had a choice of which colour to have, provided they wanted black. I do not think this is right. At the least, differences in 'mere quantity' often do seem sufficient for real choice—rather than mere picking. I might choose the larger plate of ice cream because it is larger and promises more pleasure. This is important. But it is far more important that many, if not most, of our choices simply do concern plural considerations. Even in such mundane choices as whether to take the bus or the car, we are concerned with plural considerations.

5. AGAINST THESE BEING EVALUATIVE DIFFERENCES

So far, the argument has been hypothetical: if I am right in claiming that e.g. the differences between judo and playing the violin, or between taking the car and the bus across town are evaluatively different, then plurality is obvious. I want now to consider two sorts of reasons for denying that those obvious differences between e.g. judo and the violin are evaluatively relevant differences. The first sort of reason is moral-theoretic, taken up in this section. The second, taken up in sections 6–7, is the reductive argument that these supposedly plural goods are good only as instances of one good, such as pleasure, utility, or happiness.

I want to consider two moral-theoretic claims, one that our interest in ethics must be monistic and the other that it is monistic.

The claim so far is that pluralism is obvious and that, often at least, it poses no problems for sound judgement—because, despite plurality, sound comparisons are possible. This last claim invites the following reply, which, if right, is a *reductio* of my claim about the possibility of judging plural considerations by recourse to higher-level synthesizing categories. The argument (not unlike that of *Principia Ethica*, sects. 47–8) runs as follows:

> Let us suppose that there are plural values, e.g. the sensual pleasure of lying on a beach and the understanding to be gained from discussing philosophy. Now, either we can or we cannot compare them and judge which is better. If we cannot, then

choice between them cannot involve sound judgement. Suppose, then, that we can compare them and that we do this by using a higher-level synthesizing category—e.g. being conducive to a good life. To judge that one option is, in this way, better than another is simply to judge that it is more conducive to a good life than the other. But then, we are judging these options in terms of one value, not plural values. We are no longer judging in terms of pleasure and understanding, but simply in terms of a good life. Pleasure and understanding, if now valued at all, are valued simply as means to this one good. Their entire relevance for choice is exhausted by their contribution to a good life. And thus, we are here not pluralists, but monists. Further, comparisons can be made in arithmetical or quasi-arithmetical terms. For we are simply concerned with finding out which option has more of that one good.

This argument cannot be accepted. It suggests that the relations between goods of different orders are quantitative, not evaluative. It also suggests—contrary to what is argued in Chapter 10—that we must choose the better option. Third, and here of decisive importance, it yields a thoroughly spurious monism—a monism in name only.

A good life is not a single value. There are important evaluatively relevant qualitative differences between features which conduce, equally or not, to a good life. Correlatively, there are differences between lives made good by different goods. Were this not so, and were the lower-level goods valued only as a means to a higher-level one, it would be difficult to see a life made good by understanding as, none the less, lacking another lower-level good, such as pleasure. For pleasure is now seen only as a means to a good life. But understanding has already brought that about.

It might here be replied that this can be easily seen, even on the assumption of that monism, because the life is seen as not really or ideally good. According to this reply, what is here being said is that the life would be made better—simply better—by having both understanding and pleasure.

I do not agree. I of course do agree that a life might be made better by having both. But the question is whether equally good items—acts, lives, or whatever—can have and lack different goods, and correlatively, whether equally good items can be good in different ways because they have and lack different goods.

The following example should help us answer this—in favour of pluralism. Suppose that you are trying to console me for having been unable to secure a job in philosophy by pointing out that there are other worthwhile and intellectually satisfying professions. Suppose also that I reply that I am certain that I will become interested in some other area and will find that intellectually satisfying—a source of understanding and, in turn, intellectual pleasure—perhaps as satisfying as I would have found philosophy. Even on these suppositions, I can none the less, and quite rationally, be bitterly disappointed that I will miss out on what is particular to philosophy—its particular form of understanding and its particular pleasure.

If this is right, lives, like acts, are different if what gives them value differs, not simply if they have a different amount of value. We care—and rationally so—about different values, not simply about differences in amount of one general and indifferent value. But then, we must reject the moral-theoretical argument that the very possibility of comparisons shows that ethics and judgement must be monistic—concerned only with a general and indifferent goodness and different quantities of this general and indifferent goodness.

Let us now turn to the related moral-theoretical claim that our interest in ethics as a matter of fact is monistic. This monism is found in the works of the many ethicists who hold that the main, if not the only, concern of ethics is to be action-guiding—to tell us what is to be done. To the extent that this is the only important concern, it is not of importance why acts are to be done. What is important is only whether or not they are to be done. A general and abstract sort of to-be-doneness is, thus, the only moral category of real importance.

This sort of monism is also encouraged by the maximizing view that there is one answer to the question of what we are to do: that we are to do what is best. It is part of this view that we can be concerned only with the abstract ordering relation of betterness and correlatively with the abstract notion of general goodness. But then we would have no reason to be concerned with plural sorts of goods or different ways goods are good.

This argument for monism need not be part of a theory that is seen as a monism. The materials for these arguments can be found in both avowedly monistic and avowedly pluralistic ethics. All that is required is the view that action-guidingness is the only, or the only important, concern of ethics, perhaps with a secondary concern for abstract and general goodness or betterness.

To be sure, pluralists with this moral-theoretic concern can hold that a given act is to be done or is better than another because of the particular values involved: e.g. this act is to be done because it involves understanding whereas the other is merely pleasant. Thus, pluralists can hold that plural values are important in grounding action-guiding evaluations.

But because of their concern with action-guidingness, they are centrally concerned with what these plural values ground—the action-guiding evaluation that the act is or is not to be done. Their primary concern with plural values might as well be simply a concern with different grounds of a monistic, general, and abstract to-be-doneness. And their secondary concern with plural values might as well be with a monistic, general, and abstract goodness or betterness. Thus, such pluralists might as well be taken as accepting a form of monism—albeit an abstract and degenerate form of monism concerned only with to-be-doneness, rather than the particularities of the values of acts.

Correlatively if the right act—e.g. the best act—is chosen, it will be hard for them to find any logical space for a complaint that it lacks a particular sort of good. They can, of course, join monists in complaining that what was there the best was not in fact better. But this seems to be a complaint simply that the act is not better than it in fact is, rather than that it lacks a particular sort of good. So too, they can note that the sort of feature that is often decisive is not decisive in this case. But this seems not to point to a defect in this act. As discussed in the chapters on conflict, a theorist concerned only with what is to be done will have no reason and no principled way to be concerned with remainders.

Something has gone wrong if pluralists are committed to even such an abstract and degenerate monism, if they cannot give primary importance to evaluatively relevant qualitative differences, or see how even the best act can lack a particular sort of good. What has gone wrong is traceable to the limitation of the proper ambit of moral concerns primarily to what is action-guiding and secondarily to the grounds of action-guidingness.

By showing that ethics extends far beyond the action-guiding, we will be able to save pluralism. Since the monism now under discussion is so non-threatening because it is so abstract and degenerate, talk of saving pluralism may seem hyperbolic. It would thus be better to say that pluralism comes into its own, and shows its real advantages over monism, once it is seen that our moral concern with acts goes beyond, primarily, what is to be done, and secondarily, what is better or best. For then, we will be concerned not only with the comparative ordering of various acts—which one is right, which is better than which—but at the least with why they have that order and more generally with their qualitatively distinct natures. (Some of the arguments that ethics is concerned with far more than action-guiding act evaluations are given in the chapters on conflict. Others are in the chapters on maximization.)

6. PLURALISM AND AN AESTHETIC OF PLEASURE

Let us now turn to the reductive claim for monism. The reductive claim is that the differences I pointed to as showing different goods are not themselves evaluatively relevant, but only ground or explain differences in one common value. In our tradition, the main candidates for this one value are pleasure, utility, and happiness.[6] So, we are told that what is evaluatively important about the options—e.g. judo or the violin, lying on the beach or reading philosophy, marrying this person or that one or none at all, and so on—is simply which has or promises more of the one good. It is said that what I point to are not plural goods, but only plural considerations—grounds, causes, or whatever—of one good, much as intensity and quantity are said by monistic hedonists to be different considerations which bear on overall pleasure.

My main concern here will not be to argue against this reduction—e.g. by showing that what is valuable about philosophy goes beyond the hedonic. Rather, I will be concerned to show that the 'one value' to which the various goods are supposedly reducible is, itself, not one value, but is instead a plurality. And thus, even

---

[6] Sidgwick's use of pleasure is perhaps the most instructive. On this see J. B. Schneewind, *Sidgwick's Ethics and Victorian Moral Philosophy* (Oxford: Oxford University Press, 1977), and H. S. Richardson, 'Commensurability as a Prerequisite of Rational Choice: An Examination of Sidgwick's Position', *History of Philosophy Quarterly*, 8 (1991), 181–97.

if the reduction succeeded, it would yield only a spurious monism. I will here consider pleasure. My goal will be to show that if pleasure is taken seriously as a value, it must be seen as, itself, a plurality. The arguments against utility or happiness allowing for monism are essentially the same.

Hedonism has seemed to some both an adequate and a monistic account of value and motivation. Further, it might seem that to be a monist about value or desire, one must be a hedonist. For pleasure certainly seems to be a good and it is desired.

I want now to take up the claim that hedonism is a monism. I am not concerned to argue against hedonistic monism—taken as a complete theory of either the good or of motivation. For that would suggest that it is a theory to be conjured with and taken as a live possibility. And it is too difficult to take seriously any view that holds that the choice between e.g. judo and the violin can only be a choice about one common thing, and pleasure at that. And, of course, to turn to a problem internal to the theory, taking hedonism to be a monism would require seeing pleasure and lack of pain as somehow one. This also makes it too difficult to take hedonism seriously as a monism. My goal, then, in discussing hedonism is to show, once again, just how commonplace and unproblematic plurality is—and to do this by taking seriously the claim that pleasure is a good, whether or not it is the only good.

In this section I will take up some generally neglected issues about hedonism which show why it must be seen as a pluralism if it is acceptable as even a fragment of an account of value and motivation. The next section will argue that even in regard to the more usual understanding of hedonism, pleasure must be seen as pluralistic. One of my goals here is to show that those who have taken pleasure to be a one, rather than a many, have misunderstood pleasure—and have, indeed, sold it short. Another of my goals is to use the plurality of pleasure, and our ability to compare different pleasures, as a way to show that plurality is no impediment to comparison.

Let us start by considering a case where I am trying to decide simply on the basis of gustatory pleasure which of two wines to have with dinner, a dry or a sweet white wine. Thus, I put aside questions of moral or economic value. As said, I choose simply on the basis of pleasure. And suppose that upon reflection, I see that the dry wine will go better than the sweet wine, and for that reason choose the dry wine.

To see our monism as also a hedonism and our hedonism as also a monism, we must take seriously the claim that it is simply the pleasures of the wines that are or are not valued or wanted. For to hold that we also, or instead, want or value the wines or their tastes apart from their pleasure is to reject from the outset the claim that we are concerned with monistic hedonism.

This understood, let us turn to the claim that one wine will go well here and the other will not. Some philosophers urge a comparative ordering understanding of 'not go well here'. They can agree that sweet wine and dry wine have different tastes. They can also agree that these are different pleasures—different *qua* pleasure. But if they are monistic hedonists, they would hold that 'not go well here' is to be understood e.g. simply in terms of degrees or amounts of pleasurableness. So understood, the claim is that the sweet wine is less pleasurable than the dry wine.

Perhaps this could be meant by some who take wine and its fittingness seriously. But it is a misunderstanding—again, one indicating an impoverished sense of what is evaluated—to think this is all that can be meant, or even that whatever else is meant this must also be one of the things that is meant.

To make an obvious point, the rejected wine might be more pleasurable than the dry wine—so much more pleasurable, in fact, that it is too pleasurable, overpoweringly pleasurable. A standard reply is that what this is really saying is that the whole of the dinner with that too-pleasurable wine will be less pleasurable.

This is mere hopefulness in defence of a doctrine. The more pleasurable wine can be so very pleasurable that its excess pleasurableness will make up for any loss of pleasure occasioned by an unbalanced meal. Indeed, it can be so pleasurable that those pursuing maximum pleasure will gladly forgo the pleasure of the balanced meal for that of the wine. Correlatively, those who none the less choose the balanced meal cannot be maximizing hedonists. Despite this, they might choose simply on the basis of pleasure. This is to say, of course, that gourmets and aesthetes can be concerned simply with pleasure, without also being maximizing hedonists. They are gourmets and aesthetes without those concerns being in the service of mere and general pleasure, nor of course the maximum amount of that. (The coherence of such non-maximizing hedonisms is argued for in 'Akrasia' and the chapters on maximization.)

Even were that not mere hopefulness, it is back to front. It is the greater fineness or fittingness of the wine and of its pleasure that has precedence. It is in virtue of its fineness and fittingness that it should here be favoured and chosen. Further, if this goes along with its being more pleasurable, then that is explained by the fineness and fittingness, rather than conversely.

These claims of precedence can be sustained in three, importantly different, ways. The first is to follow up suggestions from the *Philebus* that a sensible concern with pleasure is not a concern for pleasure, but rather for what is pleasing, and that pleasingness is secured by pleasures which have the correct limit, balance, and proportion. (This is discussed in 'Maximization: Some Conceptual Problems'.)

The second is given by following Plato, Aristotle, and Mill, among others, in distinguishing pleasures by their objects. Having done this, we can talk about the fineness and fittingness of pleasures by talking of the fineness and fittingness of their objects.

The third way is largely neglected by our hedonists and by other philosophers in our tradition who also claim an interest in pleasure. This involves looking at the fineness or fittingness of the pleasures in the way at least some sensualists and voluptuaries do—in terms of an aesthetic of pleasure. Such an aesthetic may talk of pleasures as feelings, but not as purely somatic feelings. Even as feelings, they must be understood as fitting together, having a proper direction and development, contrasting, growing with, and enhancing each other, and as thus occupying a complex logical space of appreciation, tone, quality, and value.[7]

I shall not try here to present even a fragment of an aesthetic of pleasure. This is done well enough in the writings of the great cooks and gourmets of France, and of course of China, Japan, and other cultures which take good food seriously. So too, of course, it is done by writers, who take erotic sensuality seriously.

Nor shall I argue that such aesthetics and the pleasures they concern are important. I shall rather simply express the hope that those who deny their existence or importance have misread and misunderstood their own lives. To modify Nietzsche, this is to hope that their pleasures are not like the product of a great clanking

---

[7] See my 'Psychic Feelings', *Australasian Journal of Philosophy*, 61 (1983), 5–26.

machine, which, however productive it may be, turns out the very same thing, differing only in size, time after time.

I want to conclude this section with several additional points. The aesthetics of pleasure are concerned, *inter alia*, with order and development. To be sure, a single sort of pleasure can have order and development—e.g. in the rhythm of its instances. But far more importantly, there is the order and development of different pleasures—pleasures which differ *qua* pleasure.

These pleasures are poorly understood, and generally not even seen, by those who urge us to understand pleasure in terms of somatic feelings. But these mistakes are also made by many who see that pleasures have conceptual content and objects, not merely causes. Aristotle may be an exception, as noted below.

Thus we must agree with Charles Taylor that hedonistic utilitarians have allowed only for shallow, and not also deep, evaluation.[8] But, it is unclear whether this is due to their utilitarianism or instead their hedonism. At the least, most of their philosophical critics have been no better at understanding pleasure and its evaluative possibilities.

Our moralists, in sum, have understood pleasure poorly. Far too many are concerned, mainly if not entirely, with quantity. The better ones are also concerned with sources and objects of pleasure. This near enough exhausts their concern with it. They thus seem like museum curators who want simply to have the most and greatest art by the greatest artists. In both cases there seems little, if any, care for the supposedly valuable items themselves.

7. PLURALISM AND PLEASURE AS MORE USUALLY CONSIDERED

We have so far touched on various sorts of pleasures: the pleasures of judo, the pleasures of playing a violin, and the sensual, voluptuary pleasures of wine. It is ludicrous to think of these as each being the same pleasure. This is so between each pleasure: the pleasures of judo are not those of wine. It is also true within each of them: the pleasures of judo include the very different pleasures of having a fit body and those of the strenuous exercise of a fit body, as well as those pleasures involved in a heightened sense of security.

---

[8] 'The Diversity of Goods', in A. Sen and B. Williams (eds.), *Utilitarianism and Beyond* (Cambridge: Cambridge University Press, 1982).

In this section, I will continue to concentrate on the plurality of sensual pleasures. For these are the sorts of pleasures most usually considered in claims favouring hedonistic monism. I will here discuss them in the way they are more often taken up, rather than in terms of an aesthetic of pleasure.

We can start by noting that, as Plato and Aristotle argue, there are importantly different sorts of sensual, bodily pleasures. There are those Aristotle says we share with animals and which are the proper concern of temperance.[9] These are the pleasures which require only the sensitivity and awareness found in touch, rather than appreciation and understanding (*NE* 3. 10).

The sensual pleasures I have been concerned with, however, do involve appreciation, discrimination, and judgement. As Aristotle says of the pleasures of the palate, these pleasures are the concerns of the artists of this area of sensuality (7. 12, 1153a26), wine-tasters and cooks (3. 10, 1118a28 ff.). These are not the concerns of animals or profligates, *akolastoi*. The former lack—and if the latter do not lack, they simply do not use and enjoy—the conceptual and aesthetic sensibility needed for these pleasures.

To help put this difference, two points should be useful. First, the difference is seen more easily if we read 3. 10, 1118a30 with Rackham as saying that profligates do not enjoy different tastes, rather than with Ross, who writes that they do not enjoy making discriminations, The latter too easily suggests that they simply do not enjoy engaging in, say, winetasting, whereas the former suggests what I find important: that they also do not enjoy what is discovered in winetasting, the tastes themselves. (The translational question is the reference of '*toutois*' in '*xairousi toutois*', 'pleased by or with them'. Does 'them' refer to discriminations or tastes?)

Second, there is a corresponding moral difference. Temperance, *sophrosune*, does not concern these discriminated sensual pleasures, i.e. the tastes and their pleasures. Excess in regard to them is softness, *malakia* (7. 1). Temperance is concerned with the pleasures of touch. Profligacy, *akolasia*, is the excess here.

As just noted, the pleasures of touch involving appreciation are also physical pleasures. Thus, there are at least two sorts of sensual pleasures: the animal or bodily ones and those that involve appreciation. We do not need to consider whether these are distinct

---

[9] See C. M. Young, 'Aristotle on Temperance', *Philosophical Review*, 97 (1988), 521–42.

or instead shade into each other nor whether there are still other pleasures. For no matter how those issues are decided, we have a plurality of pleasures. Further, even within each area of sensuality, there is plurality. The pleasure of food is different from that of drink. In either case, one could be disappointed in not getting the pleasure one sought, even if one got another equally pleasurable pleasure. Thus, there are different pleasures.

Let us briefly consider the pleasures of food. Suppose I am concerned to choose between two different meals—an omelette and a salad, say—simply on the basis of which will be more pleasurable. I may be in doubt how well either dish will be prepared and how either will suit me tonight. But suppose I am reasonably satisfied on that score. How do I choose? The answer seems simple: choose whichever I prefer, and order my preferences by the differing pleasurableness of the options.

But how am I to make this ordering? The problem is that these pleasures do not consist of some common stuff, pleasure, which the one has more of than the other. Rather, their pleasures are importantly different. One set involves the pleasures of a hot and smooth dish whereas the other involves those of a cold and crunchy one. A person looking forward to one of these pleasures, but who got the other, would have grounds for complaint: the hope was not satisfied. This is so whether or not the pleasure that is had is pleasing and satisfying, indeed whether or not it is more pleasurable, and in that way more satisfying, than the one that had been anticipated. (Again, those who hold that we value and want the tastes, not just the pleasures, disagree with hedonists, not with me.)

Even though the pleasures are different pleasures, we do compare them with each other—perhaps finding one more pleasurable than another. Some might say that we call it more pleasurable because we prefer it. But at least often, this is backwards: we prefer it because we find it more pleasurable.

This of course is to say that the satisfaction of preferences or wants cannot give us a monism. My point here is independent of the moral claim made e.g. by some liberals, that political decisions can and should be made on the basis of satisfying at least certain sorts of preferences—whether these are preferences of other people or of oneself considered as just one person among others. My point, rather, is that often enough individuals do not recur directly to their own preferences. Instead, they form their preferences and they do this on the basis of various other, and prior, considerations. And these prior, other considerations are not monistic.

This can be brought out in two ways. First, even after the preferences are formed, they do not allow for a monism. My preferences are often enough incommensurable, even if they are also comparable. Now, it is notorious that 'preference satisfaction' is taken, sometimes at once and sometimes vacillatingly, in two ways: psychologically and formally. The psychological understanding is put in terms of some state we are in because we satisfy our preferences. The formal understanding is given by the fact that one's preference is satisfied provided that one gets what one prefers—much as a logical proof satisfies certain canons of argument.

Taken in either or both ways, preference satisfaction is not a monism. The arguments that pleasure is not monistic show this about the psychological understanding. And even though I get what I prefer, understood formally, whenever I get what I prefer, it remains true that what this is, and why I prefer it, differs in different cases. I do not seek what I do because I prefer it. I prefer it because of what it is. It is not because I prefer it that it is important to me or has the value for me that it does. Rather, I prefer it because of its importance and value.

Second, as this last suggests, we must pay attention to the role of the reasoning that can ground preferences. To the extent that preferences are taken as basic or primitive, and not subject to reasoning, I generally have difficulty in seeing why I should take them as showing me what I should pursue. Again, liberalism may show others why they should let me pursue those preferences— but it does this in a way that makes my point. For liberalism can allow each of us to act foolishly and even ruin our own life, so long as we do not take others down with us. But it is difficult to see how I can—or if I can, how in good conscience I can—take such a 'liberal' view towards myself.

Here some may reply that I have failed to see that the outcome of my own deliberations will be given in a preference: 'Having weighed the considerations, I prefer this over that.' But even if my way of expressing my discovery of which preference to favour is given in terms of preferences, I can still be concerned to find a grounded preference, rather than simply a preference, which as it happens, emerges from this or that sort of consideration. The grounding and rationality are, thus, in the preference, not simply in the means of forming it.

Some might suggest that by focusing on pleasure I have chosen the wrong area of plurality to make my case, especially against a monism given by preferences or preference satisfaction. For it might be thought that since there really is no disputing taste in the realm of pleasing tastes, all we have are preferences and value constituted by them.

I disagree on the two grounds just mentioned. First, when concerned with tastes and taste, we can be concerned with the different pleasures as different pleasures, and not just as a way of gaining preference satisfaction. So, even if I want and prefer the preferred pleasure, I do not want it simply as and because it is preferred—in a way such that whichever pleasure is preferred I would, therefore, want it. Second, even if, contrary to what I think, there is no disputing taste between people, there is disputing taste within and for oneself. One can be concerned to develop a subtle, interesting, informed, and pleasing taste—i.e. good taste—and thus with the preferences-as-grounded, not simply preferences.

This is part and parcel of taking pleasure seriously. To be sure, some think that it should not be taken seriously—that we should not be concerned with how things taste much beyond their not being unpleasant. They urge us to be satisfied with satisfied preferences in food and drink, since that will allow us to get on with other and important matters. But even if right, they do not thereby hold that satisfied preferences show what is good, but only that we should be satisfied with them.

We still have not answered the question of how we can compare different pleasures and tastes in a way that allows us to form preferences and thus discover what we do or should prefer: how can we do this if the pleasures are different pleasures and different *qua* pleasure? I will not attempt to answer that question. Rather I will simply note that we do it often enough and with no problems whatsoever. Thus, despite the very real difficulties in detailing how judgement works here, the need for such judgement between plural considerations had better not entrain an impossibility of sound or reasoned choice.

We make such comparisons all the time and often with no problems whatsoever. Here we might note that the need to choose between pleasures keeps arising 'all the way down', well beyond a choice between salads and omelettes. So having chosen to have a salad, e.g. because I think it will please me more than an omelette, I may be asked to choose once again, on the basis of which will be more pleasing, whether to have a lettuce salad or an endive salad, and if a lettuce salad, whether an oil and vinegar or a lemon dressing, and if oil and vinegar then whether olive or walnut oil, and if olive oil then whether from Spain or Italy, and if from Italy then whether from Umbria or Calabria, and so on.

It is unclear how far the choices can continue. Sooner or later the restaurant will run out of options, and sooner or later I will be unwilling or unable to discriminate tastes and pleasures. Perhaps I thus show myself lacking. Or perhaps, here we have an infima species of pleasure. Using the terms from the *Philebus*, such a pleasure would be a one and not a many. As we might say, it would be a pure point of pleasure which does not contain within itself still other pleasures. But until we reach such a pleasure and ask about instances of it, comparisons of pleasures are comparisons of different pleasures.

My claim here is, of course, about how we appreciate and evaluate the pleasures. It is not that there are instances of pleasures which have only general, rather than infima, features. To hold this would be like holding that there can be an actual triangle which is neither scalene, nor equilateral, nor any other particular sort of triangle.

This said, it must be further noted that my argument for pluralism is in no way harmed by the existence of infima species of pleasures and by comparisons of instances of the very same infima species of pleasure. For my claim is not that we are asking about plural pleasures whenever we ask which of various pleasures is better or more pleasurable. My claim that there are plural pleasures is not the conceptual claim that all comparisons require or show plurality. The only conceptual claims I am here concerned to make are that there can be plural pleasures and that the pleasures with which we are familiar are plural.

Quite generally, rather than exceptionally, when we compare pleasures, we are comparing plural pleasures. So too, of course, for other more straightforwardly evaluative judgements. Quite generally, rather than exceptionally, we judge in terms of plural values and considerations rather than instances of one infima species.

8. NO SPECIAL THEORY OF JUDGEMENT FOR PLURALITY

My claim, then, is that as a rule we are confronted by plural considerations, whether the plurality is constituted by many different sub-sorts of what we might think of as one category, such as pleasure, or whether it is instead constituted by different categories such as pleasure and understanding. Moreover, even when so confronted, we often have absolutely no trouble in making decisions about what to do.

My conclusions are these: plural considerations as such are not problematic. They do not force us simply to plump for one option or another. We are often enough able to form and use higher-level synthesizing categories which allow for comparisons of plural value. This is so whether or not the categories are evaluative and whether or not the evaluations are moral. I think these are undeniable and obvious facts.

These facts must be kept in mind when we consider arguments or more inchoate worries that if we are confronted by plural considerations, we can have no sound way to judge, decide, and act. Plurality is so much the rule and is so often so unproblematic that it might well seem that philosophers who think otherwise have been as bemused by plurality as Molière's Monsieur Jourdain was by prose. This certainly holds for those who think that plurality engenders special problems of judgement. I think it also holds— although with a less harmful effect—for those who think that to explain how we come to have plural value, we must resort to overarching different sorts of value, such as agent-centred or agent-neutral, or personal or impersonal, or that we must invoke fragmentation or different ethical traditions.

Put another way, the worries that plural values make sound judgement and action impossible—unless we have some algorithmic or near-mechanical way of comparing them—seem not to come from reflection on how we actually do judge and act. These worries seem, rather, to come from mistakes philosophers have made about how judgement must work—e.g. by recourse to statable, non-evaluative, rules which can be applied in uncontroversial, perhaps mechanical, ways, and which when applied correctly give a unique answer. The fact that we judge and choose shows this mistaken—or it shows that our judgements and choices are almost all arbitrary and unreasoned.

So, I agree that if good judgement requires rules which are statable and non-evaluative, which can be applied in uncontroversial, perhaps mechanical, ways, and which when applied correctly give a unique answer, plural values will be a bar to good judgement. But I see this as a strong and indeed an overwhelmingly strong reason to reject that account of sound judgement. For I see it as overwhelmingly clear that almost all our acts and reasoned decisions—whether easily made or made only with difficulty, whether admitting of only one decision or many—involve plural values. For this reason, I will not bother with the question of whether, where there is only one value in play, there can be such rules.

This, then, is why I will not even attempt to give a theory of judgement for plurality—e.g. of how we form and use higher synthesizing categories. Assessments involving plural values, of course, require judgement. And, as always, it would be good to have a theory or at least a general understanding. But before theorizing or attempting to understand matters, it is important to see what the data are. And if I am right, the data—plurality—are found in the most ordinary and unproblematic, as well as the extraordinary and problematic, areas of our lives. Plurality should thus be adequately handled by any adequate general theory of judgement. To offer a special theory of judgement for plurality would lend support to the falsifying misunderstanding of what needs to be explained.

9. SIMPLICITY

In the remainder of this chapter, I want to deal briefly with three issues. The first, taken up in this section, is that I have talked only about very simple and, for that reason, unproblematic cases of plurality. The second, taken up in section 10, is that I do not address other understandings of monism and pluralism. The third, the topic of section 11, concerns a real difficulty in making comparisons between plural values.

The cases used to make my claims about plurality have been very simple ones—e.g. whether to take a bus or a car across town, which meal to have, which gustatory pleasure to enjoy. These are hardly momentous. But it is difficult to see how that bears on the issue of whether plurality, as such, entrains difficulties.

Perhaps it will be said that in the simple cases there are no problems because it does not matter which option is chosen. This could even be to deny that there can be a reasoned choice in these cases. Now, I certainly agree that in at least most of these cases, the agent will not act evilly, or even very irrationally or very stupidly. The issues are too small for that.

But their smallness can be put to good use. We can consider situations where the agent has to choose between one of them and an option that is important because of different evaluative considerations: e.g. choose between staying at dinner to finish the chosen piece of cake or do something of moral moment, e.g. save a child's life.

Some might say that the case is so easy because the choice is between a non-moral value and a moral value, or between a not very important value and a duty. For this to bear on the issue, the claim about plurality must be modified accordingly. So it could be held that there are serious problems only where the plural values are both moral, or are both serious, or where either both are duties or both are not duties. Or, it might be held that where there are importantly different sorts of values, such as agent-centred and impersonal values, or where disparate strands of our moral sensibility come into play, we cannot make sound judgements.

I see no reason to accept any of these emendations. If, as many think, these different sorts of values and strands are so important and so pervasive, then the difficulties they are supposed to entrain should also be pervasive and apparent. I mean this: these differences are presented as differences, not just at the edge of our ethical and evaluative thought and life, but at their very centre. They are found throughout our life and experience and not only in special cases. So, for example, our daily life at its most usual is caught up with both personal and impersonal concerns. But then, if such plurality precludes sound judgement, our daily life at its most usual should be problematic. But, at least often, it does not seem to be.

I do indeed recognize that we can and do have problems in making sound judgements. But often, this sort of difficulty is entirely consistent with—and may well even require—our thinking that even in such cases there is a correct or at least a better judgement.

For the difficulty often seems to be in making a sound judgement, not just in ending thought about what to do.

Further, the difficulties some philosophers think attend comparisons where there are plural considerations may come, not from the plurality, but from the very thinness of the descriptions of those considerations and the choice situation. So, we may find it difficult to declare on whether a life of excitement is better than one of contentment—when, as so often, each of the lives is described no more fully than that. But we may find it possible, even easy, to declare on two lives we know a lot about in which the chief thematic difference is that one is a life of excitement and the other is one of contentment. (This is pursued in section 11.)

Along these lines, too, explicit provision must be made for an adequate discussion of the issues. Strangely, it seems to be assumed that ethical problems should be soluble easily or not at all. Perhaps this is an inheritance of the view that, if they admit of truth or resolution, they are a priori, and of the view that what is a priori should be seen directly and immediately and with no trouble or disagreement.

Finally, it must be shown that there is a different sort of difficulty entrained by plural values than entrained by one. For we also seem to have difficulties even with one value. Suppose that I have a box of my favourite chocolates and that I must decide whether to eat them all this evening or to spread the pleasure out over the next few weeks, having one each night. As so often, it is difficult to see whether it is better to have a large amount of a pleasure at one time or, instead, to parcel it out over a stretch of time.

Some might take this as suggesting that this case involves plural values—that the value of the pleasure of the chocolates eaten at one time is different in kind from that of having them one each day. But if this difference—whether of intensity alone or that and other quantity—is taken as constituting different values, monism is in serious trouble, if not clearly shown untenable, and at best a philosophical ideal or idol. For what is now being said is that more of a given value may indeed give us more, but of a different value.

We might, thus, conclude that it is not plurality that causes problems for judgement. One line to take is that judgement can always have problems. Indeed, if it did not concern what is problematic, it is unclear why we would need judgement at all, rather than, say, mere calculation. Alternatively, we might conclude that it is asking too much of judgement when we judge it by its being able to give clear and decisive judgements in all cases. Judgement and reason may well have done enough, perhaps all we should expect of them, if they help us to find what is good. It need not, that is, be any failure if they do not, or cannot, show us what is best.

What this last means, especially from the agent's own point of view, will be pursued in the chapters on maximization. Part of what it means in regard to political and social pluralism— multi-person situations—is indicated by the fact that even those who have differing ruling conceptions of The Good, and are thus political opponents, may agree about what is good to do in the social and political circumstances—e.g. what sort of compromises to make.

Thus, my response to those who think plural values problematic is this. First, they must make out a case that shows plural values do engender problems. To be fair to the issues, they must give detailed and realistic descriptions of the case and they must also give us time for the serious discussion that serious issues require. Second, they must show that there are not the same problems even where only one value is concerned. And finally, they must show that if there are such problems, then there is something defective about moral or practical reason, or about ethics. Since I find so much difficulty in seeing that the first two requirements have been satisfied, I will rest my case without taking up the third requirement.

Here I think it important to acknowledge the recent arguments holding that pluralism is incompatible with ethical realism[10] and explain why I abstain from them. My reasons are these. First, those arguments seem to depend on having certain answers to those three issues—answers which I, at least, do not think we have. Second, it should be useful, if only to sharpen the terms of the debate, to present issues about pluralism, and to argue for pluralism, in ways that are as neutral as possible on this other contentious issue.

---

[10] For claims connecting pluralism with non-realism, see B. Williams, 'Ethical Consistency', and 'Consistency and Realism', in *Problems of the Self* (Cambridge: Cambridge University Press, 1973); O. Flanagan, 'Admirable Immorality and Admirable Imperfection', *Journal of Philosophy*, 83 (1986), 41–60; and W. Sinnott-Armstrong, 'Moral Dilemmas and Moral Realisms', *Journal of Philosophy*, 84 (1987), 263–76, 'Moral Dilemmas and Incomparability', *American Philosophical Quarterly*, 20 (1985), 321–5, and *Moral Dilemmas* (Oxford: Basil Blackwell, 1988). For a

10. OTHER UNDERSTANDINGS OF MONISM

Let us turn now to other understandings of monism. To an important extent, this work is not concerned with the following three traditional understandings of monism, often associated with Plato and Aristotle. The first of these focuses on relations between a universal and particulars. It holds that Plato is a monist because on his view all goods instantiate The Good and are for that reason good, while Aristotle is a pluralist because he does not think that this is why the various goods are good.

To be sure, the relations between goods and goodness are important, as are Plato's and Aristotle's views. But, at least by the time of the *Symposium*, and even more clearly in the *Republic* and the *Philebus*, even if Plato is a monist about The Good, he is not a monist about goods. In these works, the lesser goods seem good in their own particular ways. A leading metaphor here is that of colour as given in the *Philebus*. Colour is a many, not a one, as shown by the fact that black and white are both colours, but they differ *qua* colour and are not the colours they are in virtue of manifesting colour. Similarly, the various goods are all good, but they differ *qua* good and are not good, nor the good they are simply in virtue of manifesting goodness.

The second understanding of monism which I will not discuss has it that there is only one real good—e.g. contemplation, acquaintance with The Good or with God—and that everything else is irrelevant except as a means, or often an impediment, to that. But for this to support monism, it is necessary that this good, itself, is unitary. It is also necessary that the lesser goods are not simply 'not really good' but are really not good at all, except perhaps as means to that one good.

Thus, it must be that from the standpoint of what is really good, there is literally no ground to a complaint about missing out on a given lesser good. This goes considerably beyond holding that such a lack makes no difference in the long run, or that having attained the real good, we would be so completely satisfied that what was lacked would then be seen as a paltry good and not worth regretting. It holds, rather, that one would then see that it was never a lack at all, but at most the illusion of one.

criticism of Williams, see P. Foot, 'Moral Realism and Moral Dilemmas', *Journal of Philosophy*, 80 (1983), 379–98.

Certainly this view is found in some religious thinkers, and it is at least suggested by certain parts of Plato and Aristotle. But because of its rejection of clear human goods, even if lesser ones— and even more because of what it holds to be The Good—such a monism would be so foreign to the contemporary disputes about pluralism and monism that to discuss it would be not to discuss them. Indeed, to discuss it would come at least close to not discussing ethics.[11]

The third sort of monism which I will not discuss is a monism of sorts of lives—e.g. the life of pleasure versus the life of reason or wisdom versus the mixed life, as this is discussed in the *Philebus* and also the *Nicomachean Ethics*. I have already said why I do not call any of these a monism. As Plato and Aristotle argue, pleasure is not a one, but a many. And further, a life of one of these sorts involves, and gives at least some weight to, elements from, and characteristic of, the other lives. Any monism here is a monism of emphasis or form, not a monism of singleness or exclusivity. What I mean by a monism of emphasis is shown in the claim that pleasure is the only really important value—or more likely, that it is by far the most important value. A monism of form is shown in the claim that a religious life shows the unity informing—perhaps the purpose behind—various and disparate moral duties, practices, and the like.

I I. DIFFICULTIES WITH SORTAL COMPARISONS

I have been concerned to show that plural values are the rule rather than the exception, and that evaluating and choosing are, none the less, often enough unproblematic. There are, however, some comparisons of plural values which are in principle problematic, perhaps even impossible. But as we will see, these involve a special sort of comparison and the difficulties with them do not transfer to the comparisons we have so far been concerned with.

This special sort of comparison is of sorts as sorts, rather than of instances of these sorts. To give a name to these differences, I will call the former sortal comparisons, and the latter simply comparisons. We are concerned with a sortal comparison if we ask

---

[11] My thanks are owed to Kimon Lycos here.

e.g. whether promise-keeping as such is morally more important than gratitude. We are concerned with a comparison of instances when we ask whether a particular act of keeping a given promise is more important than a particular act of repaying a given debt of gratitude.

I have argued that near enough every act and choice involves comparisons of instances of different values, and none the less can be unproblematic. There is a general and simple reason which at least suggests that there are few, if any, unproblematic or usable sortal comparisons. Once we see what the reason is, we will also see why it may not be possible to prove that there are few, if any, unproblematic or usable sortal comparisons. To put the point, let us turn to Ross's account of prima facie duties.

These duties are not lexically ordered. Thus, in some clashes between a promise and debt of gratitude, the former holds sway, in others the latter does, and perhaps in some it is a toss-up. This can be explained by the fact that within each sort of duty, there are instances of differing strengths. Some promises are more stringent than others, and some debts of gratitude are more stringent than others. And even though a strong debt of gratitude may override a weak duty to keep a promise, a somewhat stronger duty to keep a promise may override a weaker debt of gratitude.

To get useful sortal comparisons we have, I think, two main options. The first is to find other ways, e.g. more fine-grained ways, of describing the sorts of consideration so that in terms of these other sorts, instances of one sort are always more important than those of another. The second is to find a weaker, or at least a different, relation between the sorts: e.g. instead of being more important, being presumptively more important. I will take these up in turn.

The problem with sortal comparisons is that at least within the obvious and broad sortals there are instances which overlap in strength: some from one sort are more important than some from the other sort. Thus Ross says, 'For the estimation of the comparative stringency of these prima facie duties no general rules can, so far as I can see, be laid down.'[12]

None the less, as part of his attack on utilitarianism, he immediately gives us a general rule: duties of perfect obligation are

---

[12] *The Right and the Good* (Oxford: Oxford University Press, 1963), 41.

generally more stringent than duties of beneficence. So he says that the former have 'a great deal of stringency' compared with the latter. He does not seem aware of the difficulty in holding these various claims. Perhaps the reason is that he would accept one or the other of the following interpretations of his claim about duties of special obligation—interpretations that will be useful for understanding sortal comparisons.

The first and more restricted interpretation makes use of factoring or Mill's method of difference. This has Ross saying that if you can produce the very same good, e.g. the very same benefit, in fulfilling a duty of ordinary obligation and one of special obligation, you have a stronger obligation to fulfil the latter. So, suppose that you have promised to benefit a given person in a certain way—e.g. by giving that person a specific sum of money—and suppose further that you see that you could instead give someone else just that benefit by giving that person the money. Despite the fact that the benefit in the two cases would be exactly the same, Ross's claim is that you have a stronger obligation to keep your promise and benefit the former person than simply to benefit the latter.

Ross's claim about differential stringency also admits of a more general interpretation. This interpretation makes use of his claim that rightness and goodness provide two different scales on which to measure the value of an act. (The goodness here includes, but is not restricted to, the goodness of the act's consequences and the act itself.) Utilitarianisms and some other views hold that acts maintain the same order on the scales of goodness and rightness: if and only if a given act tops another on one scale, does it do so on the other.

Ross's claim about differential stringency is meant to refute this claim about sameness of ordering by showing how the orderings of acts on these two scales can diverge. His claim, then, is that an act which fulfils a duty of ordinary obligation can be, in terms of goodness, the equal of or even better than another act which fulfils a duty of special obligation, but the latter can none the less come out above the former in terms of rightness. This is to hold quite generally, and not just about the same good, that what has more good need not be more right.

Let us now return to our problems with sortal comparisons. Like Ross, we can factor and use the method of difference. This will be of some use to us. For example, we can usefully ask whether intentionally bringing about a given bad is worse than un-intentionally bringing it about. Or we can ask whether bringing about a given impersonal good would be worse if it were a personal good. But, we can factor values only where the one includes the other.

So let us turn to the broader interpretation—the one in terms of two scales, one of goodness and the other of rightness. As we know, Ross held that rightness is not the same as goodness. Those who disagree with Ross can none the less construct different scales by using different sorts of goods. So, one scale might be concerned only with hedonic values and another with all values which involve consciousness, or one might be concerned with personal goods and the other with impersonal goods. But even though we can find and use different scales, they will not be of use to us.

The reason is easy to state, if not so easy to defend. When we ask our question about sortals—whether one sort is more valuable than another—we are asking in terms of the very same sort of value, perhaps simply value taken in its full generality. We thus have only one scale. And we thus cannot give even trade-off functions. For a trade-off involves a comparison, showing equality, between different values. Nor, therefore, can there be lexical relations. For a lexical relation is the limiting case of a trade-off.

Our problem, then, is whether in terms of value, taken generally, we can rank sortals or whether some instances of the one will be more weighty than some instances of the other. There is a natural reason to think that it must be possible to rank sortals. For it is natural to think that the value of instances is determined by their particular features and circumstances. Thus it might well seem that these particularities can be used to formulate more fine-grained sorts which do allow for useful sortal comparisons.

The problem with my claim against the possibility of sortal comparisons, it could be said, is that it trades on the coarseness of coarsely-formulated sortals: it is because of this that we cannot use them. More fine-grained sortals would allow for rankings.

Here I can only announce my despair at being able to complete, or even make much of a start on, finding the more fine-grained sortals which do allow for rankings of sortals. Rankings and strength seem determined by such a welter of heterogeneous considerations, that failure seems inevitable. This explains, I think, why it is so easy to find counter-examples to suggested sortal claims.[13]

It should be noted that I am not claiming that there can be sound comparisons of instances without there also being sound sortal comparisons. If here and now keeping this promise does take precedence over doing a given duty of beneficence, my claim allows that promises exactly like this one in exactly this sort of circumstance are more important than duties of beneficence exactly like this one in exactly this sort of circumstance. My claim allows this because it allows that there are sound sortal comparisons. It denies only that there are many sound and useful sortal comparisons. And if the debate over universalizability has shown anything, it has shown that the sortals obtained by simply generalizing from instances, as above, are too often not useful.

Indeed, the content of the generalizations figuring in the sortals may even not be restricted to general terms, but may simply be gestured towards, e.g. by 'and in other ways exactly like these particulars and this situation'. Further, even if we can somehow specify the content of the generalization and thus the sortals involved, what we get may not be useful. These sortals may well be so specific that, except by the rarest of chances, we are unable to use them to determine the moral status of a new case.

Some may conclude that if we cannot make sound and useful sortal comparisons, we are therefore unable to make sound and useful comparisons of instances. If my arguments are right, we should rather conclude that our being able to make sound and useful comparisons of instances does not rely on our being able to make sound and useful sortal comparisons. Here we can borrow from other areas of philosophy to argue that the absence of a certain relation between types need not show the absence of that relation between tokens.

For these reasons, then, I do not think that we can get useful categorical—e.g. lexical or trade-off—sortal comparisons by recurring to fine-grained sortals. Rather, I think we will have to take the second option mentioned above: find weaker, or at least different, relations between sortals. I here suggest we consider presumptive or *ceteris paribus* sortal comparisons.

I think it obvious that we do make presumptive comparisons and

[13] See J. Dancy, 'Ethical Particularism and Morally Relevant Properties', *Mind*, 92 (1983), 530–47; and my 'Some Problems With Counter Examples'.

that we do take them to be sound. This is so both in and out of ethics. For example, we may hold that in selecting someone for a university position in philosophy, creativity is more important than perseverance; that in painting, form is more important than colour; that in a house, privacy is more important than the prospect of financial gain; that in a life, self-development is more important than pleasure.

There is no suggestion of categorical relations here—that even the slightest amount of the preferred quality will outweigh even the greatest amount of the other quality or that some statable measure of the one stands in a trade-off relation with a statable measure of the other. Nor is there a suggestion that we are thinking in terms of more fine-grained sortal relations among these considerations.

I cannot here give an account of how these sortals are understood and used. Perhaps of most importance, however, is the way they show and depend on 'moral worlds'—e.g. the world or worlds that are taken to be normal, typical, and expected. This would explain how we understand stereotypical controversies between stereotypical soldiers and artists over the relative importance of social order or personal order, or between stereotypical bankers and social workers over the relative importance of taxation levels. The disagreements here may seem to concern evaluations, and thus suggest relativism. But they may simply reflect differences in the assumed and often unnoticed paradigms and backgrounds that inform the evaluations.[14]

This understanding of presumptive comparisons would also show how and why we can use such comparisons in noting changes in a person or a society: e.g. from the idealism of youth to the conservatism of old age. Similarly, it would give us a way to understand what it is for there to be a wholesale shift from one sort of weighting to another—e.g. for a person to value promise-keeping over gratitude when younger, but later in life to come to value gratitude over promise-keeping, or for a change in laws or social attitudes to give extra weight to welfare rights and less to liberty rights.

Presumptive sortals can sometimes also be understood in terms

---

[14] See e.g. K. Duncker, 'Ethical Relativity', *Mind*, 48 (1939), 39–56.

of extrinsic features—e.g. of the sort often found in policy issues.[15] Consider this analogy. Epidemiologists might be unable to rank the causal importance of various factors that lead to a certain disease. None the less, they can hold that given present knowledge, improvements in sanitation are more cost-effective than work on developing a vaccine. This is so even though a successful vaccine would eliminate the disease, while even the best sanitation would only reduce its incidence.

Similarly, it may be overall better to try to increase one sort of value rather than another. In terms of overall improvement to some societies, it will be better to work for an increase in rights than welfare. This can be so whether or not rights are, as such, more important than welfare. All that is here needed is the far more modest and extrinsic claim that the improvement in the society gained by spending the available time and money on strengthening rights is greater than the improvement gained by spending them on improving welfare.

12. CONCLUSION

This concludes my comments on comparisons of sortals. Let me now review briefly. On the most plausible accounts, plural values do not admit of sound and useful sortal comparisons. This has been taken as showing that plural values, as such, pose serious if not insuperable problems for judgement and action. But as I have argued, to take matters this way is to make two mistakes. First, even if comparisons of sortals are problematic, this in no way shows that comparisons of instances must be. Second, even if there are no sound and useful categorical sortal comparisons, other sorts of sortal comparisons—presumptive or *ceteris paribus* ones—none the less seem unproblematic.

Thus, once again we see that plural values seem not to be an impediment, much less a bar, to sound judgement. At most, they seem to be an impediment or perhaps a bar to sound and useful categorical sortal judgements. We might thus wonder whether those who think that plural values impede or preclude sound judgement also think that sound judgements of particulars require

---

[15] On this extrinsic use of plural considerations, see A. MacKay, *Arrow's Theorem: The Paradox of Social Choice* (New Haven: Yale University Press, 1980).

sound categorical sortal judgements. But then, it is they—as well as others who think comparisons of plural values so problematic—who owe us an explanation of how judging, choosing, and acting seem to go on so unproblematically.

For, as argued throughout, with very rare exceptions our choices are choices among plural values. Thus either plural values, as such, are no impediment to sound judgement and action, or even at its most ordinary, our ordinary life does not admit of sound judgement and action.

PART III

Plurality and Conflict

7

Akrasia: The Unity of the Good, Commensurability, and Comparability

IN this chapter, I will consider whether the conflict found in akrasia, weakness of will, requires plural values. As well as helping us to understand the particular relations between akrasia and plurality, it will serve as an introduction to 'Monism, Pluralism, and Conflict', which considers more general relations between conflict and plurality.

I. THE PROTAGOREAN PREDICAMENT

Some have thought that all akratic acts are internally incoherent in that they are supposed to require that the agent's goal is contradicted by what the agent believes. The paradigmatic example of such internal incoherence is presented in the *Protagoras* where it is said of akratic hedonists that they perform their akratic acts in order to maximize pleasure even though they believe that another act open to them would produce even more pleasure.

The structure of such internal incoherence is that the akratic agent believes both that the akratic act will not secure the goal that the act is supposedly done to secure—e.g. maximize pleasure— and also that another possible act would secure that goal. Many would undoubtedly agree with David Wiggins's claim in 'Weakness of Will, Commensurability, and the Objects of Deliberation and

My thanks are owed to Graeme Marshall for many discussions of the issues in this chapter. My thanks are also owed to Graham Nerlich, Peter Railton, Henry Richardson, Nancy Sherman, and the Philosophy Departments of the University of Melbourne and the Australian National University for their comments. This is a revised version of 'Akrasia and the Object of Desire', which appeared in J. Marks (ed.), *The Ways of Desire* (Chicago: Precedent Books, 1986). The first half of that was a revision of 'Some Structures for Akrasia', *History of Philosophy Quarterly*, I (1984), 267–80.

Desire',[1] that if the akratic act will not secure the goal the act is done to secure, and if another possible act would secure the goal, an akratic agent can have no reason at all, much less any good reason, to do that act. After all, securing that goal is the reason for acting and, as the agent believes, the other act will do that while the akratic act will not. If an agent has no reason at all, much less any good reason, to do an akratic act, it might well seem incoherent. Indeed, it might well seem so incoherent that it does not even qualify as an act. I shall call this set of worries about akrasia the 'Protagorean Predicament'.

Many philosophers, including Wiggins, hold that coherent akrasia—i.e. akrasia which escapes the Protagorean Predicament—requires incommensurable plural values.[2] In this chapter, I argue that this claim is mistaken and that it requires virtually unusable notions of unity, plurality, and commensurability; that it trades on unacceptable understandings of action and reason; and that we can have coherent akrasia in regard to one value.

My argument is directed against only this one argument in Wiggins's paper—not against the separable, even if not separated, argument that the objections of at least many philosophers against the possibility of akrasia fail because they depend on mistakenly simple views of moral psychology. I agree with Wiggins that once the real complexity of moral psychology is recognized, we can see any number of ways a person can act akratically without falling into the Protagorean Predicament.[3]

---

[1] *Proceedings of the Aristotelian Society*, NS 79 (1978–9), 251–77 (see 267), reprinted with some changes in A. O. Rorty (ed.), *Essays on Aristotle's Ethics* (Berkeley: University of California Press, 1980), 255. (In citations below, these works will be referred to by *PAS* and *EAE* respectively.) See too M. Burnyeat, 'Aristotle on Learning to be Good', in *Essays on Aristotle's Ethics*, 87. In showing that there can be reasons for akratic acts, Wiggins and Burnyeat argue against that description of akrasia.

[2] See, among others, Burnyeat; D. Davidson, 'How is Weakness of Will Possible?', J. Feinberg (ed.), *Moral Concepts* (Oxford: Oxford University Press, 1969); and M. C. Nussbaum, 'Plato on Commensurability and Desire', *Proceedings of the Aristotelian Society*, suppl. 58 (1984), 55–80, and *The Fragility of Goodness* (Cambridge: Cambridge University Press, 1986), ch. 4. My argument that coherent akrasia does not require plural values was originally presented in 'Some Structures for Akrasia'. Another argument to this end is given by Frank Jackson in 'Davidson on Moral Conflict', presented to the 1984 conference on Davidson and published in E. LePore and B. McLaughlin (eds.), *Truth and Interpretation* (Oxford: Basil Blackwell, 1986).

[3] Complementary arguments are given in A. O. Rorty, 'Where Does the Akratic Break Take Place?', *Australasian Journal of Philosophy*, 58 (1980), 333–46, and 'Akratic Believers', *American Philosophical Quarterly*, 20 (1983), 175–83; and in my

In the argument under examination, Wiggins claims that the attack on the possibility of akrasia in Book 7 of the *Nicomachean Ethics* is importantly different from the one in the *Protagoras*. The important difference is said to be that in the *Protagoras* there is only one good—pleasure—but that Aristotelian eudaimonia involves plural and incommensurable goods. And, Wiggins holds, Aristotle can thus allow for coherent akrasia. He argues that Aristotle does not exploit this in his account of akrasia, but that he could and should have, and that if he had, his account would have been a better, and perhaps even a more Aristotelian, account of akrasia.

I shall not discuss whether this is the correct interpretation of Aristotle on akrasia. So, too, except for some comments toward the end of this chapter, I simply accept Wiggins's interpretation of the *Protagoras*. For I am here concerned to discuss monism, pluralism, commensurability, and comparability, and their bearing on akrasia, rather than the interpretation of classical texts.

2: THE PROTAGOREAN ARGUMENT

To make out his case that the *Protagoras* treats akrasia differently from the *Nicomachean Ethics*, Wiggins focuses on 354d–355d, especially where Socrates claims it is 'ridiculous nonsense' to suggest that an akratic agent might 'do evil knowing it to be evil because he is overcome by good . . . By being overcome you must mean taking evil in exchange for greater good . . .' (*PAS*, 267; *EAE*, 255). So taken, the akratic hedonist must be understood as knowingly taking a lesser pleasure in exchange for a greater one, which from the hedonist's own point of view, is ridiculous nonsense. Wiggins's gloss on this passage is worth quoting at length:

Let F be the universal or all-purpose predicate of favourable assessment. A man will only be incontinent if he knows or believes the thing he doesn't do is the thing with most F to it. But if that is the alternative that has most F to it, and if nothing else besides F-ness counts positively for anything, there is nothing to commend any other course of action over the one that is most F. He could have had no reason, however bad, for choosing the other. The choice of a smaller amount of pleasure now against a larger amount of pleasure later is explicitly described as a form

'Desiring the Bad', *Journal of Philosophy*, 76 (1979), 738–53, and 'Affectivity and Self-Concern', *Pacific Philosophical Quarterly*, 64 (1983), 211–29.

of ignorance in the supposedly single dimension *F*; . . . If everything with any relevance to choice is comprehended in the question how *F* a given course of action is, and how *F* its competitors are, then no rational sense can be made of weakness of will. This is the *Protagoras* argument (ibid.).

What is of central importance is the understanding of 'everything with any relevance to choice'. According to Wiggins, Socrates took those he attacked in the *Protagoras* to hold that hedonism, indeed maximizing hedonism, gives the proper evaluative and motivational understanding of that everything.[4] On this view, a hedonist in choosing between a piquant pleasure and a languorous one will ask only which is the more pleasurable and will choose the more pleasurable one. Below, I will consider some problems in accepting this account of hedonism. For now, it is sufficient that it is understood as asserting a unitary good and source of motivation and attraction.

3. COMMENSURABILITY AND COMPARABILITY

Aristotle claims that the goods that make up human good—eudaimonia—are not unitary: 'But of honour, wisdom, and pleasure, just in respect of their goodness, the accounts are distinct and diverse.' (*NE* I. 6, 1097a24, tr. Ross.) For these and other reasons, many have taken him to hold that eudaimonia is not one thing. And indeed, the very next sentence reads, 'The good, therefore, is not some common element answering to one Idea.'

We, however, need not enter into the disputes about the nature of eudaimonia and its relations to its elements.[5] For even if eudaimonia admits of the sort of unity Wiggins denies, the various elements of eudaimonia are mutually irreducible. They are also irreducible to eudaimonia at least in the sense guaranteed by the fact that they are good even when they do not help conduce to eudaimonia: '. . . for if nothing resulted from them, we should still choose each of them . . .' (*NE* I. 7, 1097b2 ff., tr. Ross.)

---

[4] Socrates does not attack this view but rather its conjunction with the claim that akrasia is possible. See e.g. G. Santas, 'Plato's *Protagoras* and Explanations of Weakness', *Philosophical Review*, 75 (1966), 3–33.

[5] See e.g. Wiggins, section 6; W. F. R. Hardie, 'The Final Good in Aristotle's *Ethics*', *Philosophy*, 40 (1965), 277–95; and J. L. Ackrill, 'Aristotle on Eudaimonia', *Proceedings of the British Academy*, 60 (1974), 339–59, reprinted in *Essays on Aristotle's Ethics*.

Wiggins concludes that if eudaimonia is not one thing, it cannot play the role of one goal which, on the Protagorean model, the akratic must at once go towards and away from. The Aristotelian agent can, thus, act akratically without falling into the Protagorean Predicament.

Whether or not coherent akrasia requires incommensurable values, akrasia requires that they be comparable. For in acting akratically, agents knowingly choose and do a lesser instead of the better act, what they should not do instead of what they should, and so on. (Henceforth, I use just 'better' and 'lesser'.) To make sense of acts being lesser and better, comparisons of them must make sense. Thus, if coherent akrasia is possible and requires incommensurable values, incommensurable values can be comparable.

How incommensurability can allow for comparability is discussed in Chapters 5, 6, and 10. Here we might recall the use of these notions in ancient Greek mathematics. The side and the diagonal of a square were said to be incommensurable because it is impossible to express these two lengths in rational numbers or ratios of them. Because of the non-rationality of π, we can also show that there are no common units that give the length of a radius and circumference of a circle. (I say 'we' since ancient Greek mathematics held π to be a ratio of rationals.) Despite this incommensurability, certain comparisons of these lengths can be made. So, the diagonal is provably longer than its side and the circumference longer than its radius. And thus incommensurables can be ranked. (In Chapter 10, I show how incommensurables may be evaluated even if they cannot be ranked.)

4. COMPARABILITY, AFFECTIVITY, AND FRAGMENTATION

A single good, then, supposedly precludes coherent akrasia. But, we are told, plural and incommensurable goods allow for it. To follow Wiggins's account of how they do, we must introduce the difficult and important distinction between the cognitive and the affective. Wiggins says that the lesser act may have 'some peculiar or distinctive charm [which the better act lacks] that the incontinent man is susceptible to' (*PAS*, 269; *EAE*, 257). Charmed by the lesser act, the agent akratically does it.

The distinction between the cognitive and the affective turns on how the relevant object is taken up.[6] It might be, so to speak, seen or appreciated through reason, even if this is a thoroughly evaluative reason. Or it might be felt. The difference does not lie in the object of cognition or feeling. The very same thing can be the object of either or both the cognitive and the affective.

Using pleasure as an example, a person can see—cognitively see, we might say redundantly—that a given course of action promises pleasure and for that reason pursue that action. So too, pleasure can function affectively: feeling—affectively feeling—the pleasure, the person acts. Similarly for obligatoriness: a person can see that a given act is obligatory and for that reason do it. And a person can be charmed by the thought of doing what is obligatory and for that reason act.

Wiggins conjoins the distinction between the affective and the cognitive and the distinction between commensurability and comparability to show akrasia coherent.[7] For, he holds, were the acts or their values commensurable, then what the agent found attractive in the lesser act would also be in the greater act. Thus, if the lesser act were attractive, so would be the greater act to at least the same degree as the lesser. But if the values are only comparable, the acts can come apart so far as attraction is concerned. In regard to incommensurable values, the akratic agent is not in the position of at once going towards and away from the same thing. Their being incommensurable guarantees that what is attractive about the akratic act is not found in the better act.

We can put Wiggins's argument as follows: the *Protagoras* holds that 'In weighing pleasures against pleasures, one must always choose the greater and the more . . .' (356b, tr. Guthrie). There is only one value here, pleasure, and the more pleasurable act, by being more pleasurable, must always attract more than the less pleasurable act. Thus, there is no room for akratic attraction. But

[6] This is discussed in 'Affectivity and Self-Concern' and my 'Psychic Feelings', *Australasian Journal of Philosophy*, 61 (1983), 5–26.

[7] In 'Some Structures for Akrasia', I used the distinction between the affective and the cognitive, as well as the distinction between guiding concerns and goals—developed in 'Values and Purposes', *Journal of Philosophy*, 78 (1981), 747–65—to explain how akrasia is possible. In parts of 'Some Structures' not incorporated in this present work, I also used the latter distinction to account for—not only to do the work in regard to akrasia of—the distinction between commensurability and comparability. It now seems to me that these last two distinctions have little, if anything, to do with each other in regard to akrasia.

if there are plural and incommensurable values, we can be akratically attracted to what is not best, by being akratically attracted to a value that then and there should not be sought. Coherent akrasia requires a fragmentation between value and desire, and the fracture lines, allowing for such fragmentation, are found between, and only between, incommensurable values.

As Wiggins says, 'Incommensurability was introduced . . . in order to suggest the heterogeneity of the psychic sources of desire satisfaction and evaluation', for these have 'a certain liability to fragmentation' (*EAE*, 262; not in *PAS*). In short, that there are plural values shows that and how they are liable to fragmentation. Where value is fragmented, there is room for the affective to diverge from the cognitive. This divergence shows how akrasia can be coherent and possible—how akrasia can avoid the Protagorean Predicament.

The mechanism for such divergence does not rely on problems of knowledge or understanding. So, it does not rely on any uncertainty about how the various goods are to be compared, or about how they help constitute happiness. Nor does it rely on akratic agents having so focused on the lesser act or its attractive features that they are no longer even aware of the better act or its values. Nor does it rely on the agents having so focused on the lesser act that they now value it more than the better one. These would all explain how agents can choose the lesser act. But they would do this in a way that precludes akrasia. For the agents here would not be going for what they see to be lesser.

Rather, the mechanism is itself at least partially affective. This is to speak directly of the attractive feature as having a special lustre, of its being more attractive, more compelling, and the like. The better act is still in the agent's cognitive range of attention and is still seen as better. But now the demandingness and the allure of the act which is seen to be better is either not felt at all or not felt with any considerable strength. Either it has entirely left the agent's affective range of attention; or if it is still there, it is there less vividly than the lesser act.

I call this an affective range of attention to emphasize that its conditions of membership are importantly affective, even if they are also in part cognitive. This distinguishing of the affective from the cognitive takes sides in the dispute over the possibility of coherent akrasia. By allowing that the lesser can charm, fascinate, attract us more, we are clearly well on our way to making akratic action coherent. For allowing this is to allow for what is, or comes very close to being, an akrasia of attention and of attraction—being attracted more by the lesser than by the greater.[8]

Those who think akrasia incoherent are thus presented with a severe problem. They must reject the possibility of an affective range of attention, or of its independence from the cognitive range of attention. Rejection of either, however, flies in the face of clear phenomenological facts. I see no plausible way to deny that there is an affective range of attention and that it is importantly independent of other ranges of attention.[9]

There is no need here to investigate the issue of whether reasons that incline to action can be purely affective, or must also be cognitive. Since I take those reasons which are affective to be also cognitive, I see the live and important question as being whether a non-affectively charged cognitive reason can incline to action, perhaps even lead to akrasia. There is no need to investigate this matter now. I have mentioned it to signal the issue, and to issue the warning that although for simplicity I will henceforth talk mainly of features of acts that serve as reasons for, or goals in, acting simply as attractions, I leave it open whether they are all attractive, i.e. affectively charged.

5. HEDONISM ALLOWS FOR AKRASIA

The argument so far has been that (1) the sort of akrasia depicted in Wiggins's account of the *Protagoras* is incoherent, since it involves a single good; (2) the sort of akrasia depicted in the *Nicomachean Ethics* is coherent, since it involves incommensurable goods; (3) akrasia can be coherent if the agent has incommensurable values.

I think (2) and (3) are correct. But for the same reasons that they seem correct, we must re-examine (1). In particular, we must ask whether there is room for the distinctions central to (3) even within a single value, such as that allowed by hedonism, or within a wholly commensurable group of different values. If even in such contexts there is room for these distinctions—if even here there can

---

[8] On this and other varieties of akrasia, see A. O. Rorty, 'Where Does the Akratic Break Take Place?' and 'Akratic Believers'.

[9] See 'Desiring the Bad', 'Values and Purposes', and 'Affectivity and Self-Concern'.

be fragmentation—the distinction between the unity and plurality of values will be seen to be irrelevant to the issue of whether akrasia is possible. To show that even here there is room for fragmentation will be to show that Wiggins is mistaken in thinking that the sort of fragmentation required by coherent akrasia can occur only between different, and indeed incommensurable, values. My goal here will be to show that it can occur even within a single value—at least when the notion of a single value has use.

To ask whether hedonism precludes coherent akrasia, let us consider an akratic agent—Akrat—whose attention is restricted to two possible acts, drinking wine laced with pepper and drinking unadulterated wine. Akrat knows or believes that the latter would be more pleasurable. But the former has a certain feature that fascinates Akrat—its being laced with pepper. It is not that Akrat expects to find drinking the peppered wine more pleasurable than drinking the pure wine. Rather, Akrat is fascinated by pleasure coming from that unusual concoction. The wine *qua* laced with pepper occupies the centre of Akrat's affective range of attention. Thus Akrat drinks it, despite seeing that drinking the pure wine would be more pleasurable.

Here it must be kept in mind that we are taking it that the cognitive and the affective can diverge. So we must guard against taking the above story as showing that a monistic hedonism, so to speak, is inadequate to Akrat's cognitively held or appreciated values. So, for reasons given above, we are not interested in a story in which novelty as such, or novel pleasures *qua* novel, are now seen by Akrat as being, in themselves, good. Rather, our story has it that Akrat is the same sort of hedonist as before. But now there is an important divergence—an akratic divergence—between what Akrat sees as best and what attracts most. Now, what is seen as most pleasurable does not attract most.

If this sort of story is coherent, then, even within hedonism, fascinated action is possible. Thus, even within hedonism, akratic acts can avoid the Protagorean Predicament—if, that is, such affective considerations show that Aristotelian akratic acts can avoid the Predicament. And if hedonism can escape the Predicament, so can at least many of the more complex sets of commensurable values.

It might be objected that while the above story is, itself, coherent, it is not hedonistically coherent. The reason would be that a hedonistic account of value or motivation would not allow that such features of a pleasure as its origin, as such, can be relevant for hedonistic evaluation or motivation. These and all other features can be relevant if, but only if, they affect or are believed to affect the pleasurableness of the pleasure.

Even if we differ about the hedonistic status of an interest in origins and variety, we are faced with the problem of understanding pleasurableness. We need to know what features of pleasure are proper to pleasure. But for two reasons, we need not pursue this difficult issue. It is a problem not only for those espousing hedonism, but also for anyone concerned with the nature of pleasure. Further, we can use features that are clearly within the ambit of hedonism to show that hedonism can allow for akrasia without falling into the Protagorean Predicament.

Time as propinquity is one such feature. Some people are so impatient for pleasure that they will not wait for the larger pleasure and instead take the temporally nearer one even though it is lesser. As discussed in the *Protagoras*, some interpret these people as making calculative errors about time, over-discounting future pleasure. And of course, some impatient people do make these intellectual errors about time.

But other impatient people go wrong in more affective and desiderative ways. Their impatience is to be understood in terms of the over-strong felt pull of what is nearer and the difficulties in waiting for the better. In this, they are the opposite of those who so procrastinate and put things off that they do not take what is better if it is available now, and wind up having to settle for what is lesser later on.

There are, of course, those who will continue to interpret such defects as impatience and procrastination in terms of calculative defects. But at least a large measure of their reason for holding that position is that they resist allowing the affective to have a life of its own, diverging from the intellectual. Those who allow, as Wiggins and I do, that the affective has at least some independence from the cognitive, should have a correlative lack of difficulty in allowing that there are forms of impatience and procrastination which involve affective, rather than calculative, defects. (This will be discussed further in section 11.)

Even apart from this issue, it may be held that time is not internal to the value or pleasurableness of pleasure. At most, time makes a difference to how much we should value or want particular pleasures, rather than to the value or pleasurableness of the pleasure. And thus, it could be said, even if time does allow for akrasia within hedonism, it does this only because the ways we have of measuring and appreciating pleasure allow for this, rather than because pleasure itself allows for akrasia.

We would, thus, do well to consider the intensity of pleasure. Intensity certainly seems to be a feature proper to pleasure. It serves as an individuating feature of pleasures, in the way that time does not. Further, it is central to at least many hedonisms to insist that, other pleasurable features being equal, one pleasure is to be preferred, and that it is better as a pleasure, if it is more intense. Using intensity, we can retell our story to show that hedonism can allow for akrasia without falling into the Protagorean Predicament.

Suppose Akrat is considering which of two pleasurable acts to do. One act is believed more pleasurable—perhaps simply because it has a greater intensity of pleasure. But Akrat has never before come across an act with just the intensity of pleasure that the other act has. Fascinated by just that intensity, Akrat acts akratically and does the less, rather than the more, pleasurable act.

Intensity is clearly not the only dimension of pleasure which is proper to pleasure. There are the dimensions discussed by Bentham—including that most quantitative one, quantity. As well, there are all the more purely phenomenological modalities—e.g. piquancy, sharpness, languorousness.

All of these allow for a distinction between pleasures. They allow for different objects of attraction, charm, fascination. And more importantly, they allow for the degree of such affectively felt attraction, charm, and fascination to diverge from the degree of cognitively seen pleasure. It is possible to be so charmed by the particular piquancy, say, of an act's pleasure that one does that act even though another and even more pleasurable act is seen to be possible.

To preclude such divergences, it would have to be held that people could be attracted only by pleasure and not by any features pleasure might have, not even by any pleasurable features. On this view pleasure would be like a metaphysical point—proof against fragmentation—so far as attractiveness is concerned. While it might well have, and be seen as having, distinct features, it would have no features, other than itself in its entirety, that attract. There

would be no room in any of the aspects of pleasure for attraction
to gain a foothold. Pleasures so understood would attract only in
virtue of their being pleasurable—not also in virtue of being the
distinct sorts of pleasures they are. Further, they would attract
either in proportion to their pleasurableness or simply if they are
maximally pleasurable.

For reasons I will mention below, this may well be the view
Socrates attacks in the *Protagoras*. Perhaps that view does have it
that the only object of attraction is maximum pleasure, where this
means that maximum pleasure and only maximum pleasure can
attract. This would allow a nice contrast between the view of
pleasure in the *Protagoras* and that of the *Philebus*, where pleasure
is said to be 'a many'. Perhaps all pure or true hedonisms are
committed to what may be the *Protagoras* view. If so, the position
I suggested above, and also that of the *Philebus*, are not real
hedonisms, but only quasi-hedonisms.

Thus, I think we have constructed a hedonism or quasi-hedonism
that parallels, with sufficient closeness, Wiggins's understanding of
eudaimonia and its role in akrasia. But then, we now have a
hedonism or quasi-hedonism that can allow for coherent akrasia.
This should make us wonder whether Wiggins's distinction between
commensurability and comparability is relevant for understanding
akrasia—or whether, as I think, his argument depends either on
an implausible account of what it is for value to be one or
commensurable, or an implausible account of hedonism.

6. HEDONISTIC INCOMMENSURABILITY RECONSIDERED

To help sustain these last claims, let us consider a further objection
to the claimed parallel between the hedonism developed above and
eudaimonia. The hedonism used to generate coherent hedonistic
akrasia takes particular sorts of pleasures as objects of attraction.
So, for example, it allows that a languorous pleasure *qua* languorous
pleasure can attract. This is to say something importantly different
from saying that a pleasure which as it happens is languorous can
attract, but that it does this simply *qua* pleasure. It further allows
that a languorous pleasure can attract *qua* languorous even if an
instance of another sort of pleasure then and there available, a
piquant one, say, is seen as even more pleasurable.

The worry, then, is that I have introduced incommensurable pleasures into my hedonism. For a languorous pleasure *qua* languorous pleasure is incommensurable with a piquant pleasure *qua* piquant pleasure. Using Wiggins's terms, the charge is that in my hedonism there is no one feature F such that 'everything with any relevance to choice [between the two pleasurable acts] is comprehended in the question of how F a given course of action is, and how F its competitors are'.

This charge brings us to the crux of the issue. Many of us, including Wiggins, allow that 'everything with any relevance to choice' covers more than justifying reasons. For if only justifying reasons had this relevance, there could be no akratic choice—or at least, there could be nothing relevant to such choice. What is decisive for akratic choice, then, is clearly not given by a justifying reason.

So far as justifying reasons are concerned, monistic evaluative hedonists would hold that only pleasurableness—perhaps only the greatest amount of pleasure—is relevant for choice. A justifying reason for choosing one option over another would concern only pleasurableness in general and not also piquant pleasure. In this sense, our akratic hedonist could find everything with any relevance to choice comprehended in the question of how pleasurable the two acts are. But, since the act is akratic, the answer to that question would not determine which act is done.

There is, however, a wider sense of reasons and of what is relevant for action. This includes justifying reasons but it also includes what the agent finds attractive about the act. If an act is done in order to secure what is attractive, what is attractive is relevant for action in this sense. In our case, since the languorous pleasure as languorous is what is attractive, seeking that act is intentional and, if successful, gets what the agent intended to get— namely what is attractive, the languorous pleasure. This is so even if the agent recognizes the act is not justified, but is, say, akratic.

Before proceeding, we should note the following two points about these two senses of reasons relevant for action. First, to allow that what is relevant for action in the second sense can be an attraction for action need not be to declare on whether attractions have 'desirability conditions'—whether we can be attracted only to what we think good. For it does not require, nor does it even have to allow, that we can be attracted to what we find in no way good.

It requires only that we can be more attracted to what we find less good.

Second, in so far as attractions which are not seen as best can provide reasons, we must be very cautious in how we understand claims that whatever brings one to act akratically must be seen as a cause and not a reason. For even if attractions which are not justifying reasons differ importantly from justifying reasons, they also differ importantly from causes such as excess caffeine, a brain tumour, or a psychological tropism or compulsion.

These points made, we can put the objection against my use of the variegated hedonism this way: my argument claims that even with a field of commensurable values such as pleasure there can be coherent akrasia; but it works, or seems to work, only because it, albeit covertly, relies on incommensurability—e.g. between languorous pleasures as such and piquant pleasures as such. Thus it would be held that my argument sustains, rather than confutes, the claim that the distinction between commensurability and comparability is important for coherent akrasia.

However, this worry is importantly self-refuting. For it holds only to the extent that the notions of unity and commensurability it involves are unimportant for akrasia—and indeed, for much else. My claim remains that the distinction between commensurability and comparability is unimportant for akrasia.[10]

7. SINGLE AND PLURAL VALUES AND OBJECTS OF ATTRACTION

To see why this is so, let us consider cases of choice which involve instances of the very same value. Here we might consider a person who is concerned simply with the monetary return on an investment and thus chooses an investment paying 15 per cent instead of one paying 10.255 per cent. Or we might consider a person concerned simply with a certain sort of pleasure—of this chocolate cake, say— and who thus chooses the somewhat larger piece.

These may well be cases where the differences grounding choice involve only one value. And these cases certainly need not be akratic. If all cases of akrasia, including those I have discussed,

---

[10] My thanks are owed to Richard Sorabji for discussing this, and much else in this work, with me.

involve plurality, these cases of choice with only one value will show a difference between some non-akratic and all akratic acts. If the non-akratic investment case involves only one value, I think we can modify it so that a corresponding akratic act also involves only one value. The modification is this: our akratic agent chooses the lesser return of 10.255 per cent over the greater of 15 per cent.

There are various ways to argue that such a choice of the lesser over the better is possible. One is in terms of the 'spiritual maladies' discussed in my 'Desiring the Bad' and 'Affectivity and Self-Concern'—e.g. timidity, lack of confidence, tiredness, depression, and accidie. People suffering from these conditions all too naturally set their sights lower than they need, and certainly lower than the best. They naturally turn away from what is best, as being too much or too good for them, or simply as not being for them.

A common objection here is that these people really value something else, such as moderation. They do not seek what they think is lesser, but rather what others, who do not value moderation, think is lesser. Precisely because it is moderate, they think it is best. But this is not right. To be sure, some other sorts of people do value moderation and think that it helps make for what is best. However, even if these latter people and those with the spiritual maladies seem to pursue the same goals, they are importantly different. The latter do not seek moderation. They, rather, avoid what they think is best. And they do this because, as we might say, their desires or their spirits are too weak.

These spiritual maladies can, then, explain why a person knowingly seeks what is lesser. And they can do this without positing plural values. But because they invoke a lack or weakness in desire and spirit, they may not help us explain akrasia—at least not paradigmatic Aristotelian akrasia. For that involves a failure to do and feel as one should because of over-strong desire, and more exactly of over-strong epithumetic, bodily desire. And it may be thought that doing what is lesser because of over-strong desire may still require plural values, even if doing what is lesser because of a lack of desire does not.

This, of course, suggests that what requires plurality is not simply choosing what is lesser, but choosing what is lesser because of over-strong desire. There is some point to this. We might well think that lack of desire can lead us astray, not so much by aiming at something other than what is best, but by failing to have any determinate goal and in this inchoate way derivatively aiming at what is not best. There may well be enough substance in this claim to allow us to take seriously the suggestion that if desire, taken as a force rather than as an absence, leads us astray, there must be plural values.

To see whether this is right, let us change the case from one where desire is too weak to one where it is too strong. Here our investor has never had a chance to invest at precisely 10.255 per cent and, charmed by this novel possibility, akratically makes that investment rather than choosing the one at 15 per cent.

This, of course, is still not a case of paradigmatic Aristotelian or Platonic akrasia. For this over-strong desire is not epithumetic. And indeed, Plato and Aristotle argue that epithumetic desire can have only certain sorts of objects—e.g. simply drink and not tasty drink. But we should be satisfied if we find that over-strong non-epithumetic desire does not need plural objects of attraction, even if we are left unsure about over-strong epithumetic desire.

This said, let us consider the akratic act of choosing the lesser investment because of being over-charmed by its rate of return, 10.255 per cent. In this case, the agent is attracted to what is lesser. If it is simply a lesser instance of the one good, akrasia does not require plural values.

Some might object that this case is psychologically too implausible, if not impossible: rates of return are not objects of attraction. In this, they differ from the pleasures that can, and all too easily do, lead to akrasia.

But this objection shows a lack of understanding of psychological reality. Instead of holding that such attraction is impossible, we should instead hold that it is fetishistic. And it must be recognized that some, if not most, people sometimes do 'suffer' such attractions and are, to this extent, fetishists.

So, perhaps the psychological objection is that we do not know of any usual, plausible, and, we might say, healthy sources of akratic attraction in mere differences of quantity. However, I see little reason to take these as exhausting the range of akratic attractions. And indeed, I do not see the concern with only what is maximal—whether it be financial return or pleasure—to be usual, plausible, and healthy.

Let us now turn to two more conceptual objections which are

intended to show that the investment case involves plural values. The crux of this objection has it that instead of there here being only quantitative differences between the options, there are qualitative ones (see e.g. Nussbaum, *Fragility*, 115–16). It would hold that in the case of being charmed by the investment of 10.255 per cent, there is a difference in quality, not simply of quantity, between this act and the better one, and thus this case involves plural qualitative considerations. The reason for holding there to be a qualitative difference here follows from what it is to treat quantities quantitatively—taking them only as a measure of value and not as a constituent of it. Quantity taken quantitatively is, so to speak, transparent. We are not concerned with it, but with what it picks out.

To state this, we might frame the following 'principle of quantitative care': to care for F in a quantitative way is to care more for more F and most for most F. Of course, if it is conceptual of caring for F that one care more for more F and most for most F, then all care will be quantitative. But even if that is not conceptual of all care, the quantitative principle might still describe what it is to care in a quantitative way for F. This principle would give us a way to argue that to be moved by the particularities of that rate of return—e.g. that it is exactly 10.255 per cent—is to take a quantitative feature or measure as making a qualitative difference. And thus, it is held, we here have plural values.

A similar objection—which does not rely on the difficult distinction between quantity and quality—is that in the very telling of the story, I have shown that a different object of attraction is at work in the akratic case than in the non-akratic case and thus that here we do not have a case of monistic akrasia. In our case of akratic investment, this other feature is novelty.

Now, since this is a case of differential choice—choice based on a difference—I agree that it involves plural objects of attraction. Indeed, it seems to me that to show differential attraction is to show different objects of attraction. To say that there are plural objects of attraction in this case seems to say simply that the person chooses the act because its rate of return is 10.255 per cent and thus novel rather than 15 per cent and usual. I see no reason to deny this, nor to deny the more general point that akratic acts must have other objects of attraction than had by their non-akratic alternatives. After all, an akratic act must have at least one object of attraction that the non-akratic act lacks—if it is to be singled out and chosen.

It might seem that I am conceding the point to those holding that akratic choice, unlike non-akratic choice, requires plurality— but am downplaying it as a mere conceptual point. I agree that it is a conceptual point, whether it is merely that or not. However, there are two far more important points. The first is that it is not a conceptual point merely about akratic action, but rather about differential choice quite generally. The second—and here crucial— point is that what is conceptual about differential choice is that there are plural objects of attraction, not that there are plural values. I will take these up in turn.

Since differential choice is made on the basis of differences, we may say that the akratic investor chooses on the basis of novelty. And we may go beyond this and hold that for that agent at that time, novelty is a separate source of attraction—separate, that is, from the return on the investment.

But we cannot stop with this, thinking that we have thus shown a difference between akratic and non-akratic differential choice. For the same argument would have us conclude that in the non-akratic choice of choosing the best return, being best is also a separate source of attraction—again, separate from the return. For its being best is the feature of that return which singles it out from the lesser return and which serves as the basis of its being differentially chosen. This is little more than carrying over into the realm of attraction the logical point that if b differs from c by having feature F, then c differs from b by not having F.

So, I agree that differential choice—whether akratic or non-akratic—involves plural objects of attraction. What must also be shown, however, is that these plural objects of attraction involve plural values.

One might think that it is entirely in the spirit of the argument of Wiggins and others, that coherent akrasia requires plural values, to hold that plural objects of attraction require plural values. But, on the contrary, it seems to show that argument, at best, misleading. For as we have seen, non-degenerate differential choice requires plural objects of attraction. More than one option must be attractive. In particular, the lesser option must be a real option: to some extent, it must be attractive.

But then, if plural objects of attraction require plural values, non-degenerate choice requires plural values. This would be shown by the very same argument used to show that coherent akrasia, because it involves plural objects of attraction, also involves plural values. (This of course assumes what seems unobjectionable: that the sort or degree of attraction needed for a lesser option to help constitute a non-degenerate choice is similar enough to that needed for coherent akrasia.) Now, this does not show that coherent akrasia does not require plural values. But it does show that the argument of Wiggins and others is, at best, highly misleading. For that argument suggests that there is something special about akrasia in virtue of which there must be plural values. But now, it seems that akrasia is held to require plural values simply because akrasia involves non-degenerate differential choice, and such choice, quite generally, requires plural values.

The argument is thus misleading in two important and related ways. First, it is offered as an argument about the object of akratic choice. But it is really about something far more general: the object of non-degenerate differential choice. Second, it is offered as an argument that an evaluative monism is inadequate for akrasia. But, if right, it would show something far more general: that an evaluative monism is inadequate for non-degenerate differential choice.

Some might be glad to accept these charges—gladly switching their attack from the limited claim that monism cannot allow for coherent akrasia to the far more extended one that monism cannot allow for non-degenerate choice. Perhaps because they are such natural contraries, I find the claim that non-degenerate choice requires plural values strangely reminiscent of the claim, discussed in the chapters on conflict, that conflict can be understood in terms of mere incompossibility. In any case, they are both mistaken. Other chapters show this about that other claim. The present chapter shows that there can be plural objects of attraction—for akrasia and other sorts of non-degenerate choice—without there also being plural values.

To conclude this section, let us consider two additional reasons why it might be thought that coherent akrasia requires plural values, not just plural objects of attraction. First, some would draw this from the claim that we can be attracted only to what has value—or, more strongly, only in virtue of its having value—or as it is sometimes put, that there are desirability conditions for desire.

However, even if that claim is well-taken, and even if there are such conditions, this is insufficient for our purposes. It must also be shown that different instances of one and the same value, and in virtue of being instances of that one value, cannot provide plural objects of attraction. So for example, it must be shown that we cannot be pulled between two instances of the very same pleasure or, more exactly, that we cannot be pulled akratically to the lesser.

Put in terms of our example, it must be shown that monistic hedonism cannot allow for someone being pulled in two directions by two instances of pleasure—e.g. a languorous lesser pleasure and a piquant better pleasure. And I do not see how this can be shown. To be sure, it could be shown if only maximal pleasure attracts or if what is pleasurable attracts only in proportion as it is pleasurable. But this simply precludes akrasia, as well as allowing only for degenerate differential choice. Perhaps it could be shown if pleasure had no attractive features other than being simply pleasure. But this allows for only degenerate differential choice. For these reasons, and others given above, I do not think that recourse to the nature— the quantity or quality—of what attracts can show that plural objects of attraction allowing for coherent akrasia must also be, or involve, plural values.

Let us now turn to the second, and different sort of, reason that it might be thought that plurality of objects of attraction requires plural values. This reason has to do with the different explanatory requirements of akratic and non-akratic choice. Put briefly, the claim is that caring more for what is better is in a markedly different explanatory position than is caring more for what is lesser. The underlying reason for this is that concepts are given their content by their normal and healthy applications. Thus, we cannot explain instances of normal and healthy relations between valuing and caring in terms of valuing and caring, since our very understanding of those notions is given by their normal and healthy relations. The corresponding claim would be that we can explain defective relations between valuing and caring in terms of these relations— by explaining how they fail and by doing this in terms of other, interfering features. And, it would here be suggested, other values provide those other, interfering features explanatory of the akratic, defective relations between valuing and caring.

Whether or not the general claim about explanation is right, I do not think the particular claim about valuing and caring is. So, it is argued in my 'Desiring the Bad' and 'Affectivity and Self-Concern' that caring more for what is better is not characteristic of a normal and healthy person, but rather of a particular sort of self-concerned person.

But we need not go into those arguments here. We can, instead, consider the relevance of this issue for the present discussion. Wiggins and others claim they are making a conceptual point about relations between desire and value, where these are taken quite generally—not simply about the normal and healthy sorts of relations between these. So, even if they succeed in presenting us with conceptual truths about those sorts of relations between desire and value, they will not have succeeded in what they set out to do.

At most, they will have shown that to explain an act of coherent akrasia, we must use considerations other than those used in explanations of non-akratic actions. They will still not have shown that plural values must figure among these other considerations. Those other considerations may be given by other objects of attraction which are not other values. Or they may be given by desire being stronger than value warrants. Or they may be given by various spiritual maladies, such as timidity, lack of confidence, tiredness, depression, and accidie. None of these need involve other values.

My conclusion, then, is that coherent akrasia is possible with a single, unitary value. Indeed, it is possible if and in just the way non-degenerate differential choice is also possible with such a value. To be sure, there is a notion of unitariness of value or object of attraction which precludes coherent akrasia and also non-degenerate differential choice—given terms of a featureless point or whole. But this only aids my claim that it is the notion of a single value that precludes coherent akrasia, not the possibility of coherent akrasia, that needs severe questioning.

8. ARE THERE ANY UNITARY VALUES OR ATTRACTIONS?

Some further points about unitariness are worth making. Consider the following question that we might take the *Protagoras* to be asking: what can a person who is committed to maximal pleasure find attractive in an act seen not to be—or not seen to be—

maximally pleasurable? On the understanding of plurality that
figures in the worry about my argument, that question can be
appropriately answered by citing some feature of the akratic act,
such as its being pleasurable, albeit non-maximally so. But this is
not an answer to what I take the question to be asking: how could
a maximizing hedonist, a person committed to maximal pleasure,
be sufficiently attracted by what is seen to be non-maximally
pleasurable so as to go for that instead of what is seen as maximally
pleasurable?

To be sure, these questions can come very close to each other.
If one goes for something other than maximum pleasure, one is
not then and there a maximizing hedonist. And if, contrary to what
was thought, one is not such a hedonist and does not have
maximum pleasure as one's goal, it is important to ask what the
goal of one's action then is. This is even more important if we start
with the presumption that such hedonism is the only viable account
of motivation.

In the concluding section, I will offer some comments about
Socrates' claim about hedonism in the *Protagoras*. For the moment,
however, there is no need to discuss whether Socrates did have
that view of hedonism—nor whether he held a similar view about
seeking other values or valuable things. For I am here concerned
with this view, whether or not it is Socrates' in the *Protagoras* or
elsewhere.

On this, it seems sufficient to say that if Socrates did hold that
maximum pleasure and only maximum pleasure can attract, then
what I suggested was implausible as an answer to the question
about akrasia—telling what was sought rather than how it could
be sought—comes at least close to answering his question. But
equally, the considerations which I took to show that that was an
implausible answer now show that such a theory of motivation is
implausible. And it is shown to be implausible precisely because it
holds that goals are featureless points or wholes, and not subject
to fragmentation.

This is implausible because the good, or eudaimonia, or pleasure,
or the wanted, and so on—including these maximized—can be,
and really must be, understood as having distinct features. When
they serve as goals, they present an array—often a disturbing
array—of different features. It is in regard to goals so understood
that at least many problems of akrasia arise, including the

Protagorean Predicament and similar worries about coherence. Indeed, to the extent that goals are not like metaphysical points and featureless wholes, the present notions of unity and plurality are of little, if any, importance in the discussions of akrasia. And this is so for quite general reasons, not simply reasons having to do with akrasia: these notions are of little, if any, importance in the understanding of goals, taken either as objects of attraction and desire or as reasons.

9. VALUE FINALITY

If I am right that the present distinctions between unity and plurality are unimportant for understanding akrasia—and even more so if I am right that few significant choices involve single values rather than plural ones—we need an account of what was going on in the *Protagoras* argument. Did Socrates think— mistakenly, as we now see—that these issues settled the matter? Or was something else in play?

The dialogue does not provide an answer to this. Whether other dialogues do is not a question I will consider here. Rather, what I will do to conclude this chapter is draw attention to two features of the *Protagoras* argument which could lead someone to take the argument to turn on these issues. These features are what I will call value finality and value maximization. As I think will be clear, many take Socrates to argue for both features. Whether or not they are right is not of concern now. What is, are these two doctrines about value, which I will present in this and the next two sections.

Value finality is—roughly, but adequately for our purposes—the view that only what are taken as good reasons can motivate. Put briefly, only the good can attract. So, I can be attracted to this pleasure only if I believe that it will conduce to what I take to be good. Value finality is, thus, a claim about what people find to be reasons for acting. It is a claim about acting and about good reasons.

For value finality to show coherent akrasia impossible, it must go beyond the claim that only the good can motivate. For even if they should not be done, akratic acts can still have some value.

The obvious response is that the reasons for doing the akratic act may be good reasons but they are simply not good enough.

These reasons do not tell us which act should be done. But then, for value finality to show coherent akrasia impossible, it must go beyond the claim that only the good attracts and hold that only those reasons which in the circumstances show that an act should be done can attract. The former claim, though widely held, is implausible enough. The latter is totally implausible.[11]

There is, however, a less objectionable use of value finality—a regulative or hortatory use. The divergence between values and sources of attraction can, and often enough does, point to a moral defect or problem.[12] Here we might note the probative force of asking someone 'How could you not live up to your values?' This sort of question functions as a reproof and as an invitation to reconsider and to choose differently.

This points to one reason for its being important to allow for akrasia which is not cast explicitly in terms of value, and which may well not involve value. Understanding how a maximizing hedonist might choose what is less than maximally pleasant involves at least many of the same problems as does understanding how a good person might choose what is not best.

10. VALUE MAXIMIZATION

In the previous section, I gave the outline of two views of value finality: only good reasons motivate and only reasons which show that an act should be done motivate. Some people argue—and some claim that Socrates argued—that to hold the first commits one to holding the second. The argument for this depends on, or is, an argument for maximization.

Maximization comes in different varieties. Psychological maximization holds that one desires only, or desires most, what one takes to be best. On the assumption that one does what one desires most—or restricting attention to those acts one does because one desires them most—psychological maximization has it that one does only what one takes to be best. Moral maximization holds that

---

[11] See 'Psychic Feelings', 'Desiring the Bad', 'Affectivity and Self-Concern', and 'Emotional Thoughts', *American Philosophical Quarterly*, 24 (1987), 59–69.

[12] This is discussed in my 'The Schizophrenia of Modern Ethical Theories', *Journal of Philosophy*, 73 (1976), 453–66 and also 'Desiring the Bad', 'Values and Purposes', 'Affectivity and Self-Concern', and 'Psychic Feelings'.

one acts morally only if one does what is, or one takes to be, best. Rational maximization makes parallel claims about acting rationally. Interpretive maximization is the view that in order to be able to interpret an act as an act, we must interpret the agent as trying to do what is, or is taken as, best. I will discuss these claims in Part IV of the book.

Here, however, two points should be made about psychological maximization. First, there are special problems with the claim that we desire only what we take to be best. On this view, 'the best' is an indissoluble object of attraction. It holds that there is nothing attractive, and perhaps nothing good, about what is less than the best, denying that there are plural objects of attraction. The choice it allows between what is best and what is not best now turns out to be a choice between what has all the attraction then in play and what has none at all. It, thus, allows for only degenerate differential choice.

Such maximization, further, takes what is supposedly a quantitative measure—being maximal—as qualitative. For it holds that, say, maximal pleasure, taken as an indissoluble complex, is the only object of attraction. So, what seems to attract in this case is the comparative, relational feature—that this object is the best available, thus better than any other—rather than the object itself.

To want maximal pleasure in this way is quite different from most wanting this pleasure because it is maximal. The difference is this: taken quantitatively, the maximality is in the attraction. Taken qualitatively, however, maximality is in the object and it is what makes the object attractive. We may think of the person who wants the 10.255 per cent return as a number fetishist. So too, we may think of the person whose object of attraction is maximality—or more plausibly, maximal pleasure or maximal gain—as another sort of fetishist, of reified quantity.[13]

Second, psychological maximization can, of course, be taken as holding that desire is proportional to value, and thus that the lesser can be desired—albeit less desired than what is taken as better. The bearing of this on the argument that coherent akrasia requires plural and incommensurable values might seem clear. For, the akratic investor case will now be interpreted so that the agent

[13] My thanks are owed to Terry Winant here.

values novelty as well as a return on the investment, and values and wants a mix of those two most—and thus values and wants that mix more than the greatest return on its own. Some think that we can none the less allow for coherent akrasia here because of the incommensurable values: we can allow that the values served by the akratic act differ from those served by the non-akratic act and against which the akratic act is akratic.

But this does not work. The incommensurable values are either incomparable or comparable. If they are incomparable, their acts are not within the ambit of maximization: neither can be said to be better than the other, nor can either be taken as the better or best act. But since neither is lesser than the other, it is not akratic to do one instead of the other.

Suppose now that the incommensurable values are comparable. Now one of the acts can be taken as better and one as lesser. But given psychological maximization, we are faced with exactly the same problems in seeing how coherent akrasia is possible as we did when there was only one value. For according to psychological maximization, the better act, even though its values are incommensurable with those of the lesser act, must be desired more than the lesser act. And on the assumption that we do what we most want to do—or that, especially because we are concerned with akratic acts, we are now concerned with acts done from the greater desire—the lesser act cannot be done. At the least, it cannot be done from a greater desire.

To summarize: if because of incomparability, acts with incommensurable values cannot be ranked, no act can be taken as lesser nor can any be akratic. But if they can be ranked, then on the assumption of psychological maximization, the lesser cannot be done, nor therefore is akrasia possible. Or rather, the lesser cannot be done, nor can an akratic act be done, from a greater desire.

We should here note how this tells against Wiggins's claim that because Aristotle's values are only comparable, whereas those of the *Protagoras* are commensurable, he can allow for coherent akrasia. But Aristotelian agents are committed to seeking and being most attracted to eudaimonia. What this involves is discussed at the end of 'Maximization: Some Evaluative Problems'. But in no way does it require that eudaimonia is seen or felt as one value, or that eudaimonic elements are seen or felt as commensurable.

Rather, all that is required is that these elements be comparable in regard to their contribution to eudaimonia.

If Aristotelian agents are committed to seeking eudaimonia, it is difficult to see how they can seek what tells against eudaimonia. It is as difficult to see this as it is to see how a lesser pleasure can be sought by a Protagorean maximizing hedonist. In each case, the difficulty is due to what is sought. It is not due to the monism of what is sought, nor is it avoided by the pluralism of what is sought.

II. HEDONISM AS A PURE INTELLECTUAL IDEA

In this concluding section, I want to turn again to the distinction between the cognitive and the affective. I argued that it is this distinction, and not the one between comparable and commensurable values, that allows for coherent akrasia. In particular, it allows for coherent akrasia in regard to either comparable or commensurable values, where these are understood in useful ways. It allows for coherent akrasia in regard to plausible hedonisms. Without this distinction, akrasia all too easily, and perhaps necessarily, confronts the problem of the Protagorean Predicament even if the values in question are comparable though incommensurable.

Kimon Lycos has argued that the cognitive–affective distinction is also central to the argument about akrasia in the *Protagoras*.[14] Whether or not we endorse his interpretation, we can use it to help put various claims made earlier in this chapter. In the next several paragraphs, then, I merely present that part of Lycos's interpretation which is of importance for us.

Socrates deploys the argument about akrasia and hedonism immediately after Protagoras tries to distinguish between boldness and courage in terms of the different reasons informing bold acts and courageous acts. He there understands reasons in terms of their content—what answers to 'What are the agent's reasons?' They are thus not understood in terms of how they are held, e.g. with strength and commitment. Nor are they understood in terms of the character of the person having the reason. Nor are they understood in terms of how—or even whether—the agent acts on

---

[14] 'Socrates and Akrasia', unpublished.

them. Rather, as said, they are understood simply in terms of their content. Reasons are here understood intellectualistically.

If a reason is the content, then to understand people's reasons for acting, we look only at how they see the act. If they think the act is maximally hedonic where it is not, then they are not overcome by pleasure. They are simply making a mistake. In this way maximizing hedonists can go for what is not maximally hedonic. But if they see that the act is not maximally hedonic—or if they do not see it to be maximally hedonic—then there will be absolutely no room for an account of why they did the act. Or at least, there will be no account in terms of reasons. For a reason simply is its content and the only content of relevance for a maximizing hedonist is the presence or absence of maximum pleasure.

Lycos takes Socrates as pointing out that this conclusion flies in the face of the views of The Many. They hold that maximizing hedonists can be overcome by pleasure, e.g. by their impatience for pleasure. In this, they can have reasons—albeit, by their own lights, bad reasons—for doing what is not maximally pleasurable. But if reasons are understood intellectualistically, as contents, they do not have a reason to do the akratic act, for it is not maximally pleasing. This is to use The Many's view on hedonism and akrasia to present a problem for Protagoras's intellectualistic account of reasons. For if he cannot show how reasons can be understood intellectualistically—e.g. in regard to akrasia—he cannot sustain his distinction between boldness and courage. (Nor, as Lycos also argues, can virtue be identified with knowledge if knowledge is understood intellectualistically, in terms of holding to be true on good grounds what is true, as opposed to understanding it in terms of wisdom and thus character.)

I now want to use Lycos's interpretation to summarize various points of this chapter. We can start by noting that if value finality holds—and more clearly if value maximization holds—it would be incorrect to hold, as I did, starting in section 4, that the cognitive and the affective can diverge in regard to reasons. For example, the impatience that leads one to take the lesser because it is nearer, rather than wait for the better, would have to be understood in terms of intellectual errors, such as those involved in over-discounting the future. So too it would be incorrect to hold, as I did in section 6, that there are two senses of 'reasons for acting' relevant for akrasia—one limited to good reasons, and the other which includes attractions. The latter is concerned with whatever can make the act done for a reason in the sense of being intentional and intended in the sense of getting what one is attracted to and aims at.

We can now see once again that unless we do allow for reasons considered as attractions, where these may not be the best reasons, we will lack one of the most important ways of allowing and accounting for coherent akrasia and also for non-degenerate differential choice. These and other considerations show the content of reasons is not limited to value considerations. They also show that there is more to reasons than their content.

It might be said that everyone of course recognizes that there is more to reasons than this: reasons must be held and acted on. This might seem at once completely obvious and also completely acceptable to all philosophers, even those who deny the possibility of akrasia. But taking stock of that point is dangerous for the view that denies akrasia.

For, as I have been concerned to argue in this and other chapters, once we look seriously at holding and acting on reasons, we see that reasons go far beyond what value finality and value maximization allow. We see that the notions of holding and of acting on reasons go well beyond some neutral implementation of those favoured contents. We also see that other contents can be held and enacted in ways sufficient for acting—and sufficient for acting on reasons. We see that what is found attractive, not simply what is found good or best, can ground reasons that are held and acted on. We thus see how—for we have always seen that—akrasia is possible.

What, then, is to be said about value finality and value maximization? The first thing to say in answer here is that they are not conceptual truths about value, valuing, and attraction. It is simply, even if unfortunately, true that we are not attracted only to what is good or what we take to be good, much less only in proportion to how good it is or seems.

In the chapters on maximization, I will argue that value maximization is not an ideal of a good or ideal person—both that one can be good even though one is not a maximizer and also that to be a maximizer may involve not being good. It may be, however, a conceptual truth that value finality holds for a good or an ideal person. After all, it does seem an ideal of goodness and of moral perfection that only the good attracts—or that only goods attract.

Similarly, it seems an ideal of goodness or moral perfection to have such an internal harmony that one is attracted only to what one values. These are high human ideals, as wonderful as they are difficult.

To achieve them we need knowledge, but we also need understanding and wisdom. These require not only holding the right reasons, but holding and acting on them in the right way. They require having the right sort of character. As I understand him, this is Aristotle's teaching. If Lycos is right, it is also that of the *Protagoras*.

8

Monism, Pluralism, and Conflict

THIS chapter examines the following line of thought meant to show that value conflict requires plural values:

> I can be conflicted over whether to betray my friend or my country, and I can be conflicted over whether to keep a death-bed promise to hold an expensive wake or whether to do something more useful with the money. The ground of the conflict is that whichever option is chosen, even if it is the better one, it will lack something valuable had by the other option. And I can be conflicted by having to endure that lack. If, however, both options are valuable in the very same way, the better one will lack nothing of value that could be made good by the other. Here there is no lack to endure, nor therefore to be conflicted by. Thus, conflict requires plural values.[1]

I will argue that this is right, but only about a certain sort of conflict—rational conflict restricted to practicable options. This has to do with the fact that, when so restricted, conflicts are over lacks which only a pluralism can handle.

It is clear that not all conflicts require plural values. Epistemic conflicts about value do not. These latter can involve a conflict

My thanks are owed to the philosophy departments of La Trobe University and Syracuse University for discussion of this chapter. My special thanks are owed to John Campbell, Charles Larmore, and my seminar at Syracuse University.

[1] The claim that conflict requires plurality is found, for example, in various discussions of akrasia: e.g. D. Davidson, 'How is Weakness of Will Possible?', *Moral Concepts*, J. Feinberg (ed.), (Oxford: Oxford University Press, 1969); D. Wiggins, 'Weakness of Will, Commensurability, and the Objects of Deliberation and Desire', *Proceedings of the Aristotelian Society*, NS 79 (1978–9), 251–77, reprinted in A. O. Rorty (ed.), *Essays on Aristotle's Ethics* (Berkeley: University of California Press, 1980); M. Burnyeat, 'Aristotle on Learning to be Good', in *Essays on Aristotle's Ethics*; and M. C. Nussbaum, 'Plato on Commensurability and Desire', *Proceedings of the Aristotelian Society*, suppl. 58 (1984), 55–80, and *The Fragility of Goodness* (Cambridge: Cambridge University Press, 1986). The particular issue about plurality and akrasia is discussed in the previous chapter, 'Akrasia'.

over which means, considered simply as a means, to use to achieve the very same value. So, I may be concerned to have the nicest tasting dish and have an epistemic conflict between two offerings since I cannot tell in advance which will be nicer. Or, to borrow from Kant in the *Foundations* (Akademie edn., 415), parents can be conflicted over what skills their children should be taught, since they do not know which will be most useful.

In epistemic conflicts about value, the only evaluative risk is that the forgone option would have secured the sought-after value better than does the chosen option. This is an important sort of risk. But evaluatively, what one risks by doing one option can be exactly what is risked by doing the other. There need be only one value in all the options. Thus, if conflicts are to show that there must be plural values, the conflicts cannot be simply epistemic conflicts about value. (Since a value conflict may also involve an epistemic conflict about value, we may be concerned with the latter, but not because they involve epistemic conflict.)

So too, at least some non-rational conflicts do not require plural values. Instead of showing something about the nature or number of value, they may show only something about us and our rationally improper relations to value. If the argument of 'Akrasia' is right, the irrational conflict of akrasia does not require plural values, but only plural objects of attraction. And as we will see below, the irrational conflicts of dithering and ambivalence do not need plural values, nor even plural objects of attraction. For it is possible to dither or be ambivalent over almost any choice even where there is absolutely no evaluative or desiderative difference between the options, and thus even where there may be only one value and one object of attraction.

Thus, one of the tasks of this chapter will be to show what sorts of conflict—what sorts of rational conflict—require plural values.

I. INSTANCES AND SORTS OF VALUES AND CONFLICTS

If a value conflict does involve loss, it might be thought that a monistic theory of value—i.e. a theory of value which acknowledges only one value—cannot allow for conflicts. But the monism of evaluative monisms concerns universals, not instances. So for example, a monistic hedonism claims only that there is exactly one sort of good, pleasure. It can allow that we may have to choose between this pleasurable act and that pleasurable act.

This suggests an easy answer to how a monism can allow for conflict: since each of these acts is good and since we can do either of them but not both, the conflict can arise in the choice of which act to do and which not to do. Put schematically: (1) act *b* has value, (2) act *c* has value, (3) *b* and *c* are severally but not jointly possible to do. This is the incompossibility account of value conflict.[2] The incompossibility account of conflict of desires holds that there is a conflict of desire where: (1) act *b* is desired, (2) act *c* is desired, (3) *b* and *c* are severally but not jointly possible to do. In what follows I will be mainly concerned with value conflicts, but much of what I say also applies to conflicts of desire. So, too, I will often talk of good acts. But what I say applies equally to bringing about what is good.

Because of (3), the incompossibility account requires that the elements of the conflict—*b* and *c*—are severally possible. But as discussed in the earlier chapters on conflicts, there are also conflicts where the elements are not severally possible. Suppose that I have wasted my money and now can repay only one of two creditors. I may be indifferent about which to repay but be conflicted over not being able to repay both. Or suppose that when I was a child I brought some plums to school for lunch, and the school bully took all of them from me, telling me that he would keep the plums in one of his hands, giving me back those in the other, and that I was to choose which handful I got and which he got. I may have been indifferent about which handful I had, but none the less conflicted over having to choose between them rather than have all my plums.

As also discussed in earlier chapters, monisms can easily allow for such conflicts. This, however, may not address the serious issue of whether monism can allow for conflict—i.e. conflicts between acts which are severally possible. To do that, we must focus on conflicts as given in the incompossibility account.

To examine this account, we should make use of three views about the relations between universals and particulars: that of

---

[2] See e.g. B. Williams, 'Ethical Consistency' and 'Consistency and Realism', *Problems of the Self* (Cambridge: Cambridge University Press, 1973); and F. Jackson, 'Internal Conflicts in Desires and Morals', *American Philosophical Quarterly*, 22 (1985), 105–14.

property instances, transcendence, and immanence. It will here be useful to follow philosophy primers. So let us consider a case where we have several tins of white paint, and let us ask the usual sorts of question: does each tin, or even each smallest amount of paint, have its own whiteness? Is there a whiteness which they all instantiate? Is whiteness wholly in each of them? Let us now turn to value.

Property instances. Here it is held that each instance of a value— e.g. each happy experience—has value or is a value. This no more and no less requires many different values, many different happinesses, than are needed by the different whitenesses of each tin or each drop of paint. Since it seems that there can be a conflict between different instances of happiness—e.g. I can make only you or, alternatively, only someone else happy—it would seem that a monism which allows for property instances can account for conflict. The conflict will not, of course, be between what is valuable in one way and what is valuable in another way. Rather, it will be between different, distinct instances of the one value.

Transcendence. If a value stands to its instances transcendentally, it might seem that there can be no value conflict between the instances. For, as it might be said, all that is important about any of those instances is that they instantiate the universal. What is important is not what instantiates it, but only that it is instantiated. Thus, it might be thought better to say that this is simply what is important, rather than that this is what is important about those instances.

Immanence. If a value stands to its instances immanently, then it is wholly in each of its instances. On this view, it is difficult to see how the non-existence of one instance could constitute a loss of that value if another instance with that value is actualized. But if the values are somehow different, we might wish to reverse this claim.

This argument might suggest that an evaluative monism can allow for value conflicts if conjoined with a property instance account of instantiation, that it cannot allow for conflicts if conjoined with a transcendent account, and that it is unclear what holds if conjoined with an immanence account. But matters are not so simple as this. To be sure, on a property instance account, we can hold that each instance has its own value. But it is unclear that we can do so in a way that allows for conflict.

Consider the parallel with whiteness again. On a property instance account, we can say that this lot of paint has its own whiteness and that it differs from the whiteness of that lot of paint. Perhaps we can say something similar on an immanence account. We cannot say it on a transcendent account.

This, however, is to speak only of plurality. Let us turn to conflict and ask what sort of conflict there can be—e.g. for someone interested in painting the wall. It is easy enough to see how there can be a conflict in choosing between one lot of paint and another if they differ in colour, price, manufacturer, or the like. But suppose that the two lots of paint do not differ in any of these or other universal respects. The question, now, concerns the sense or nonsense of a conflict over two such identical lots where they are different only in that they are different instances of the exactly resembling whitenesses. Some might suggest that we simply take the incompossibility account as giving conditions for conflict: that simply is what conflict is.

But as just seen—and as will be discussed further—doing this runs the very real risk of robbing the question of whether conflict requires plurality of any importance. It also runs the severe risk of divorcing two related notions of conflict and forgetting the one that, as will be seen, is more important. The first notion is that of conflict between value instances or between values, as given by the incompossibility account. The second is that of conflict within an agent. I will call this being conflicted. Being conflicted is importantly a moral psychological notion, involving caring about, perhaps being bothered by, and perhaps being brought to vacillate or be uncertain about, the resolution of the conflict.

Let us continue with the distinction between value conflict and being conflicted. Even if choosing between these lots of paint does involve a value conflict, it is extremely difficult to see how anyone could be conflicted by such a choice. For it is difficult to see how anyone could care about, be bothered by, or be brought to vacillate or be uncertain about, which lot of paint is used. Indeed, it is unclear how these could even be individuated in a way allowing for differential caring, much less conflict.

Some might think that the case of the different instances of happiness is just the same: if they do not differ *qua* happiness, if they are instances of the same infima species of happiness, no one could care about, much less be conflicted by, which instance is actualized. But this is clearly wrong. Just suppose that the choice is between oneself or, alternatively, someone else being made happy. No metaphysical theory about universals and particulars should have trouble with the way this answer presupposes individuating the instances.

This answer does, however, raise serious evaluative issues. I do not mean the seeming egoism in the answer. For this is only an artefact of the example. There are equally no metaphysical problems in allowing for the individuation required by caring differentially about the happiness of a friend and that of a stranger.

The argument so far might seem to have shown that whether an evaluative theory can allow for value conflicts can be primarily a metaphysical question. At the least, it might seem to have shown that a monism holding a transcendent theory of value instantiation cannot allow for conflicts. But I think it a mistake to hold that whether an evaluative theory can allow for conflicts is, in this way, a metaphysical issue. To see why, let us consider some relations between rightness and goodness.

Rightness is not the same as goodness. That the one may depend on the other is here not denied. Indeed, it can be used to make the point. To the extent that the one does depend on the other, it would be useful to know the function that describes the dependence and takes us from considerations of goodness to those of rightness or vice versa.[3] Maximization is one such function—or one sort of theory embracing a function—holding that the right act is the best act. Different functions give us different ethical theories. These differ in how they see the relations between rightness and goodness.

Some functions and theories are such that if two options are equally good, there can be no reason to do one option rather than the other. But others allow, or even require, us to give extra weight to an option and, on that account, choose it over an equally good one. This can be so whether the equally good options involve the same or different goods.

---

[3] See e.g. my 'Consequentialism and its Complexities', *American Philosophical Quarterly*, 6 (1969), 276–89, and 'Rightness and Goodness: Is There a Difference?', *American Philosophical Quarterly*, 10 (1973), 87–98. As explained there, to assume a simple distinction between rightness and goodness is doubly misleading. First, there may not be evaluative, but only metaphysical, distinctions between rightness and goodness—rightness may be of acts and goodness of situations. Second, rightness

So for example, a theory could hold that *qua* sort of good there is no difference between a friend's happiness and a stranger's happiness, even though it also holds that in deciding what to do we may be entitled, and perhaps even required, to give extra weight to the one over the other. According to such a theory, an agent may be entitled, or even required, to deliberate as follows: 'What I may do is benefit my friend and not the stranger, but a friend of the stranger may help that person and not my friend.'

Now, I do think that ownership and other indexical and relational properties are evaluatively important. For example, acts can be different enough to present seriously conflicting options simply because one will benefit a friend while another will benefit a stranger.[4] Sometimes this will tell in favour of the friend, sometimes in favour of the stranger, and, of course, sometimes it will make no difference at all.

To the extent that it does make a difference, indexically differentiated goods are shown important for plausible ethical theories. This is obviously important for understanding relations between rightness and goodness. It is also important for understanding relations between conflict and plurality. For, if such indexicals are relevant in these ways, there now seems room for conflict between options even where they involve the very same good. So, for example, there can be a conflict between making a friend happy and making a stranger happy.

Thus, whether a monistic theory can allow for conflicts is independent of the metaphysics of value instantiation—at least as so far stated. So, even a monistic theory espousing a transcendent account of value instantiation can allow for conflicts—by allowing for indexically individuated values.

Moreover, all monisms, whether transcendent, immanentist, or property instance, may use, and perhaps need, indexicals to allow for conflicts. To be sure, a property instance monism will not need indexicals to account for conflicts as understood in terms of mere incompossibility. But it is difficult to see how, without recourse to indexicals, a property instance monism can even allow, much less

is not the only important evaluation of acts. But to make the present point, we can go along with the usual assumptions.

  [4] See e.g. my 'Act and Agent Evaluations', *Review of Metaphysics*, 27 (1973), 42–61; 'The Schizophrenia of Modern Ethical Theories', *Journal of Philosophy*, 73 (1976), 453–66; and 'Values and Purposes', *Journal of Philosophy*, 78 (1981), 747–65.

account for, being conflicted. For without such recourse, it is difficult to see how there will be differences over which one can be conflicted.

Indexical individuation of a good may well allow for conflict. But at least with happiness, this seems of no use to monisms. For, as it seems to me, this-person's-happiness and that-person's-happiness involve plural values: the differently-owned happinesses. This holds even if they are instances of the same infima species of happiness.

Monists might deny my claim of plurality, holding that the instances are commensurable, since they can be compared in terms of how much of that infima species each has. Perhaps comparisons can be made on that basis. None the less, the instances are incommensurable: the incommensurability we are concerned with does not require comparisons of different values, but rather a failure of substitutivity (see p. 176). And most importantly, the instances involve plural values: each lacks something of value had by the other (see pp. 170–1).

Monists might still argue that different ownership does not make for different values, but is only a way of taking the value into account, e.g. in determining what should be done. They can also remind us that any theory will need some function or other to move from what is good to what is right. They might conclude that, since monisms are possible, functions are not among the elements of a theory that are to be counted in determining whether it is monistic or pluralistic.

If this is right, we have a simple way to show that moral conflict does not require value plurality. It is obvious that there can be conflicts between theories which agree on a single value but differ over functions. For example, there can be conflicts between a monistic hedonism which holds that the right act maximizes total pleasure and one which holds that the right act maximizes average pleasure. So too, there can be conflicts within one monistic theory which allows evaluations in terms of both the maximizing and the averaging function.

Some might welcome such a simple answer to the question about whether conflict requires plurality. But I think that the question is more serious than that and that we must take note of functions and not just values. There is also an independent reason to do this.

Let us start with an analogy from logic. An axiom in one system of logic can be a leading principle in another. If these systems differ only in this, they need not be counted as different systems. Turning now to ethics, some ethical systems take fairness to be a principle of distributing goods, while others take a fair distribution itself to be one good among others. Yet, apart from the terminological difference of whether fairness is said to be a good or a principle, these systems may not differ in their act evaluations, whether action-guiding or not, or in other evaluations.

So, of course, an ethical theory which takes happiness to be a good is pluralistic if it also takes fairness to be good. But then, it is difficult to see how an ethical theory which takes happiness to be the only good could be monistic if, despite denying that fairness is a distinct good, it includes fairness in its function. Similarly, if a theory is pluralistic because it holds that differently owned goods are different values, it is difficult to see how a theory which takes ownership into account, but only in its function, could be monistic.

Some functions, I think it clear, have to be counted as an element in determining whether a theory is monistic or pluralistic. The clearest of these are functions that within themselves involve a good, perhaps by taking one as an argument or by being a stand-in for it: e.g. the function of distributing goods fairly, which at least comes close to being a stand-in for fairness. Many other functions also seem to involve goods. So for example, various functions have us count each person equally. This involves equality, and perhaps even the values Kant expressed by holding that each person has worth rather than price.

Of course, there may well be other functions which do not have to be counted as one of the elements which shows a theory monistic or pluralistic. Let us call these neutral functions. If there can be a monistic theory of ethics, there must be neutral functions. At the least, this is so if, as it seems, we always need some function or other to go from goodness to rightness.

Many think that metaphysical notions—such as time, location and duration, persons, and quantity—are, in the presently relevant sense, neutral. In this and the following chapters, I argue that so far from being neutral, they often generate plural values. This will show, once again, that plurality is the rule, not the exception. It will also help us understand whether conflict requires plurality.

To conclude this section, it should be noted that we have so far been unable to answer the question of whether conflict requires pluralism. Perhaps all that we are now in a position to say is, first, that this question, which at the outset seemed so straightforward, is complex and obscure. And second, it now begins to appear that what is complex and obscure is what it is for value to be one or many and thus what it is for a theory to be monistic or pluralistic.

2. TIME AND CONFLICT

Let us now turn to time and its relevance for conflict. Suppose that I am in the middle of dinner with just one sip of wine left and I am thinking about whether to have it now, with the main course, or whether to save it for dessert. If being conflicted requires plural values, either this wine case involves plural values or there can be no conflict.

The latter seems implausible. For I can be conflicted. I can vacillate and be uncertain about when to have the wine. I can have the regret that characterizes conflict. Similar cases are easily found: e.g. I can be conflicted over whether to have a cavity filled today or to put it off till next week.

Yet it would seem that in these cases, the only source of conflict is time—now or later. And thus, if conflict requires plurality, and if there is conflict here, it would seem that mere differences in time make for different values. But where time does make for different values, we will not have a conflict or even a choice between achieving a given value at one time or another. For in these cases, the different instances of value, simply because they are at different times, are instances of different values rather than different instances of the same value. And this, too, seems implausible.

We might, thus, wish to reject the claim that conflict requires plurality. The argument for this has, however, been too quick. Before declaring on that claim, we should pursue our examination of the relations among time, plurality, and conflict.

Of course, there can be evaluative differences associated with the time differences: the case of the wine could have it that my host has asked me to try some wine now, and the dental case could have it that I have an important engagement this afternoon and the effects of the dental treatment would not have worn off by then. In these cases, what happens at different times is evaluatively different, not because they simply happen at different times but because different things happen at the different times.

The question remains whether time, itself, makes a difference. In *Reasons and Persons*,[5] Derek Parfit gives an argument that pure time preference is irrational: that time as such makes no evaluative difference. The argument can be summarized thus:

> If pure time differences do make a rational difference, it would be rational to accord moral relevance to, say, Tuesdayness. It would then be rational to care whether something does or does not occur on Tuesdays. But of course Tuesdayness does not have moral relevance. Nor therefore, do pure time differences.

I agree that Tuesdayness does not make an evaluative difference and that it would be irrational to use it as a reason for choice. But this may well show only that some purely temporal features do not make a rational difference. It remains to be seen whether Tuesdayness and the like are representative of all purely temporal features. If they are not, we still need to know whether other temporal features can make a rational difference.

We are, however, faced with a prior difficulty in knowing what it is to be purely temporal and whether any significant features or elements of our lives are purely temporal. Here we could start by noting that much of our life is through and through temporalized. I do not mean only that it occurs in time. Far more important are its internal and external temporal relations. The internal temporal relations are those had by various elements or parts of a life to other elements or parts of that life or to the whole life. The external temporal relations are those had by those elements or parts, or the whole life, to other people, events and structures outside the person, and so on. These various temporal relations are essential to these elements being what they are and to their having the value and importance they have. And, as we will see, they are essential to its being a matter of rational concern, and even conflict, which of these values we get.

To see this, we might begin with the fact that our most basic categories for moral understanding and evaluation are temporalized. I am thinking here of acts, experiences, and lives—to name only three. Our acts are temporalized: they are in time, and more

---

[5] Oxford: Oxford University Press, 1984.

importantly they involve time. They take time and they are concerned with getting things done at the right time and in the right temporal order.[6]

So too, our experiences are importantly temporalized. They take time and they also have a temporal order. Without both, but especially without the latter, they might simply be the sensations the *Philebus* suggests are available to sea creatures without reason: mere present sensations. To mention one point, some of our important experiences are about developments in our life, such as past failure and presently growing success. If these and other important experiences—e.g. of oneself or of love—are to have the undoubted importance they do have, they must reflect and be part of how things are in the world and for us. Otherwise, they would be false in many of the ways that, again, the *Philebus* discusses.

These issues could be pursued through Kant and his discussions of time and experience. Or they could be pursued in still more modern terms by showing how our important experiences are broadly psychological, rather than narrowly so—i.e. they make essential reference to facts 'outside' of the experiencer, rather than only to internal ones. To make the point, it would further have to be shown how the value of experiences turns not only on how they present themselves to us at a moment or at a series of moments, but also by being part of and true to our lives. They are experiences of a self which is in time and for which temporality is of the essence. And these experiences help give this essence to that self.[7]

Other aspects of our lives are also temporalized. Consider, for example, the centrality of different periods of a life, such as childhood, adulthood, and old age, for understanding ourselves and others.[8] Or consider such facts as these: what counts as a success

---

[6] See C. M. Korsgaard, 'Personal Identity and the Unity of Agency: A Kantian Response to Parfit', *Philosophy and Public Affairs*, 18 (1989), 101–32; and R. de Sousa, *The Rationality of Emotion* (Cambridge, Mass.: MIT Press, 1987).

[7] On the distinction between the broadly and the narrowly psychological see e.g. T. Burge, 'Individualism and Psychology', *Philosophical Review*, 95 (1986), 3–45, and J. A. Fodor, *Psychosemantics* (Cambridge, Mass.: MIT Press, 1987). For recent discussions of the importance of experiences being accurate, see e.g. R. Kraut, 'Two Conceptions of Happiness', *Philosophical Review*, 88 (1979), 167–97, and L. McFall, *Happiness* (New York: Peter Lang, 1988).

[8] See Aristotle, the *Nicomachean Ethics passim* and the *Rhetoric* 2. 12–14. See also A. MacIntyre, *After Virtue* (Notre Dame, Ind.: University of Notre Dame Press, 1981); M. Slote, *Goods and Virtues* (Oxford: Clarendon Press, 1983); and A. Baier, 'Familiar Passions', unpublished, read to the University of Cincinnati Philosophy Colloquium, 'The Concept of Emotion', March 1985.

for a child may not do so for an adult, and the importance of success at different times of a life may be significantly different.

Further, the elements or parts of our lives, such as personal relations, projects, and emotions are also temporalized. So for example, there are important differences between an intimate relationship that starts poorly and ends well and one that starts well and ends poorly. To be sure, on many accounts, these relationships can have the same overall and total value. And thus, according to some systems of evaluative accounting, there would be no reason to choose either over the other. Whatever we say about those accounting systems, and about the question of which relationship is to be chosen, a relationship that starts poorly and ends well is, simply in virtue of its direction, importantly different from one that starts well and ends poorly. Further, lives can be importantly different sorts of lives simply in virtue of the fact that they have one or the other of these different sorts of relationships.

As with relationships, so with many activities and projects. Their temporal direction is important, and at times essential to their being what they are and having the value they do. So too, their temporal location in a life is important and at times essential. Consider again, the question of when one enjoys success. Or consider the question of when one comes to accept one's own mortality.

So too, the care and concern found in emotions are also importantly temporalized. It is unexceptionable and hardly significant if I am annoyed by even a minor insult just delivered. But if after more than forty years, I am still smarting from a minor slight by a friend when we were both five years old—or if now seeing for the first time that I was slighted by my childhood friend, I am hurt—that may well indicate something of some significance about me.

Attitudes to time, further, are among the important determinants of different character sorts. We might here consider the differences between preferring to get pain over with and preferring to postpone the evil day. So too, we might here consider the differences between those who want their pleasures here and now and those who like to store them up for special occasions—those who are impatient and those who procrastinate.

Many sensibilities, abilities, and virtues also seem importantly temporalized. So for example, the courage and love of the young are, almost necessarily, different from those of the mature or elderly.

Even such seemingly simple goods as pleasure are temporalized. Here we would do well to remember the claim made by Aristotle and Mill that children's pleasures are not really for adults. Of course, some philosophers take this as saying only that what pleases children does not please adults. But it also says something far more important: the very pleasures are different.

I will conclude this list by noting that throughout our lives, proper timing is of great evaluative importance and that it can involve the most difficult sort of evaluative judgement.[9] The difficulty and fineness of judgement needed to get the timing right shows, almost by itself, the evaluative importance of temporality.

Temporality, then, is absolutely central to our lives—both for living them and also for understanding and evaluating them. Differences in time are often enough not simply differences in time but also differences in what occurs and in the value of what occurs. Given these latter differences, it is no wonder that there can be conflicts over when to have a particular good or bad.

This, however, may not show that considerations of pure temporality are evaluatively relevant, much less important. For the arguments used to show the importance of time do not really show that pure temporality makes a difference. Rather, they show that what might look like differences of pure temporality are really other sorts of difference.

What I mean can be brought out through a discussion of two cases, which will also show why it is rational to have time preferences, even if not pure time preferences. The first case is concerned to show that simply by being in the past, values or valuable things are different from those in the present or future. The second argues similarly about values which are in the present or future.

The first case: some time ago, I had to have a series of six unpleasant dental treatments.[10] Towards the end of the series, I forgot whether I had already been four or five times. Upon checking my diary, I found—and with pleasure—that I had been five times. My pleasure was over the fact that the pain involved in the fifth

[9] My thanks are owed to Graeme Marshall here.

[10] For use of this sort of example, see R. Kraut, 'The Rationality of Prudence', *Philosophical Review*, 81 (1972), 351–9, a discussion of T. Nagel's *The Possibility of Altruism* (Oxford: Oxford University Press, 1970); Nagel, ibid., 71 (acknowledging B. Williams); and A. N. Prior, 'Thank Goodness That's Over', *Philosophy*, 34 (1959), 12–17. My thanks are owed to John Campbell and Jonathan Bennett for help here.

treatment had already been experienced and was not still to come. Of course, I recognized that the total pain from all the dental treatment would be the same, whether I had then already made five visits and had only one to go or I had so far made only four visits and had two to go. None the less I was pleased that I had already been through the pain of the fifth visit.

Some might here claim that this shows irrationality—e.g. that I did not consider my past self fairly, as being on a moral par with my present and future self. I find this claim implausible. We are of course clearly concerned with the past and, indeed, with our past. But we are not concerned with it in all the ways we are concerned with the present and future.

One central reason for this is that we have a special concern for what is in our power and control. This, after all, is the proper object of deliberation and action. And even that part of the past that was in our power to change, now, simply by being past, no longer is. This helps explain why we quite naturally and reasonably have a different sort of care for at least those parts of the present and future we take to be in our power and control than we do for the past.

That the past is different from the present and future is, I think, obvious. What is not obvious is just how it does make a difference or how it should make a difference. Nor is it obvious how concern for other times—e.g. the present, the near future, the distant future—does or should make a difference. This raises serious issues in ethics and moral psychology.

So for example, some people live much more for and in the future and some live much more for and in the past. Those who go too far in the former way seem deficient in commitments, loyalties, and responsibilities. They might be thought to be too pragmatic, too given to holding that 'what is past is past' and to urging everyone to let 'bygones be bygones'. Those who go too far in the latter way seem unable to get on with things and start anything afresh. They might seem to have too much difficulty in letting go.[11] We need to strike the, or simply a, correct balance.

Let us now turn to a case where all the values or valuable things are in the present or future—our original case concerning wine. Even here, it is false that the only differences are temporal. We can

---

[11] For a profound treatment of various attitudes to the past, see N. S. Care, 'Living with One's Past', unpublished.

start by noting that the case is not even described in purely temporal terms, e.g. having the wine simply now or later. The choice was described as having the wine now with the main course or alternatively later with dessert.

These are of course temporally related—dessert comes after the main course. But that is hardly the only or even the most important thing that can be said about them. Even restricting ourselves to a concern with gustatory taste and pleasure, to think that here there are only temporal differences would require thinking that the taste and pleasure of the wine are the same whether had with the main course or the dessert. But there is no reason to think this.

This is not because it is unclear whether the quantity of the pleasure will be different. Even where we suppose that it will be the same, there can well be important differences. It shows a poor understanding of taste and pleasure not to recognize this. These tastes and pleasures are different in at least two importantly related ways. First, they are importantly organic wholes—e.g. of the wine tastes and food tastes—where the elements form and inform each other, making up a complex and often multi-faceted whole.

Second, there are intrinsic differences in the order of tastes and pleasures. So for example, the whole constituted by tasting something sweet before something sour is not the same as the whole constituted by tasting those in reverse order. This is not due simply to how the order of tastes affects our short-term discriminative abilities—e.g. that sweetness makes differentiation more difficult. Nor is it simply a way of suggesting that what might be called a proper meal will follow a certain order. The order I am concerned with, rather, has to do with—and indeed is what helps ground— the possibility of a gustatory aesthetic and the reality and importance of gustatory excellences such as those of development, surprise, contrast, enhancement, and the like.

My claim, then, is that many gustatory pleasures are found in wholes which are temporalized. In these wholes, the order of the elements is itself important. Our wine example involves such temporalized wholes. Thus, the options of having the wine with the main course or dessert differ not only temporally, but also in other and far more important ways.

Taken one way, then, the wine example does not even bear on the claim that pure temporality is irrelevant to rational care and choice. For it is not a case of pure temporality. The conflict is not between having the self-same good, the self-same pleasure, now or later. It is between having one good now or another one later.

But taken another way, the wine example bears heavily against the claim that pure temporality is irrelevant to rational care and choice. It does this, not by showing the claim mistaken, but by forcing us to ask what import the claim could have, whether or not it is correct. For it forces us to ask which temporal differences are only temporal differences. And it at least suggests that very few are.

That question and that answer have already been invited by earlier examples. But many of those involve so many other and more important differences that we are not likely to think that they involve only temporal differences. Thus, we are put under a far stronger requirement to answer that question if the temporal differences in the wine example involve other differences. For here, we are concerned with relatively insignificant tastes and pleasures. If even here, temporal differences are not only temporal differences, where are they only temporal differences?

Of course, we are able to give a schema to answer this question: make the temporal difference large enough to be noticed but small enough not to make any other difference. So, the time must be short enough not to help constitute a different sort of life, or a different sort of activity, relationship, manner of eating a meal, and so on. Our question now would be whether there can be a conflict between my having the wine right now or waiting one minute— or if that is too long, waiting one second—and then having it. I think we can agree that notwithstanding the importance of time and timing in the gustatory aesthetic, perhaps one minute, and certainly one second, need not help constitute other differences.

Thus, here we may at last have a case where the values differ only in when they will be actualized. I agree—as I did in regard to Tuesdayness—that if this is right, there may well be no rational basis for preference here. Of course, there are people who are conflicted by having to wait at all for their wine: they want to have it exactly when they want it. But it may well seem irrational, or at least childish, to be bothered by having to wait a second or perhaps even a minute for one's wine.

It might thus seem that I agree that purely temporal considerations are morally and desideratively irrelevant or at least irrational. Perhaps my arguments do point in this direction. But what I think is far more important is that in order to find a case where no value differences seem occasioned by temporal differences, I had to resort to trivial and basically very silly examples. I think this, and the arguments leading to it, show that it is at best highly misleading to ask whether the temporal features of a value—e.g. when it is actualized—can make an evaluative difference. Of course, we can answer this. To the extent that the arguments given so far can be generalized, the answer seems 'No' if the question is taken as asking about purely temporal differences, and 'Yes' if it is taken as asking about temporal differences which are not purely temporal.

What is misleading about that question and those answers is the way they are part and parcel of the view that time is of no real importance in or to our lives. (Of course, the limit imposed by death is sometimes taken into account. This seems about the only temporal matter that many philosophers do take into account.) As noted earlier, this fits naturally, even if not necessarily, as cause or effect or both, with the view that only those experiences which can be had at a moment or at a series of externally related moments have value. At an extreme—but one occupied by many philosophers—this is the view that only simple sensations have value.

The better answer, which shows why both that question and those answers are misleading, is that often enough differences of temporality make for different values. Often enough, we do not have the same value which can be actualized at one time or another. By being actualized at the different times, they are different values. Of course, the time here in question is not clock time, but rather time in a life or of a life—lived, human time. Our life is not only in time. It is also temporalized. And so are at least many of our values.

This is important for a general understanding of value and, of course, for the issue of whether value is plural. But it poses a difficulty for our present concern with the question of whether value conflict requires pluralism. As shown by our examples, the difficulty need not be in seeing whether there can be a conflict between actualizing a value at one time or another. Our examples show such conflict. Nor need the difficulty be in seeing whether the conflict involves plural values. Our examples also show such plurality.

The source of the difficulty is that—if my general claims about the temporalization of values are correct—the way these values are actualized at different times makes them different values. And indeed, we are shown, or at least given strong evidence, that they are different values by the fact that there can be conflict over when to actualize them. It thus remains to be seen whether conflict requires plurality. In particular, it remains to be seen whether what allows for conflict in these cases is connected in the right ways with plurality or whether all we can say about them is that as it happens they are plural and they also allow for conflict.

At the end of the chapter, I will return to an examination of this connection. I want now to conclude this section by explaining in a somewhat different way, why time is a special problem for monists. In particular, this will show why they are confronted by the issue of the rationality of pure time preference.

In reply to the worry that many of my examples show that we do and should have pure time preferences—i.e. care simply when various goods or bads occur—I argued that because of the ways these goods and bads are temporalized, they are different goods and bads. It was for this reason that I urged that it can be rational to care when various sorts of happenings take place in a relationship or in a life.

This, I claim, is rational because of the differences between these happenings. So for example, pain now or tomorrow is not the same as pain yesterday. Nor is courage the same when young as when old. And so on. Thus, contrary to the way it might seem, my argument does not commit me to pure time preference. For I can allow that different times make for different values.

I think that monists must deny this. They can, of course, hold that where something will have different evaluatively relevant interrelations if it occurs at one time rather than another, to that extent it will be evaluatively different at different times. But, monists must account for all these differences in terms of their one value. One way monists typically do this is in terms of quantitative differences of that value. So, they can hold that drinking the wine later will be more pleasurable than drinking it now, even if they must also hold that whichever time it is drunk, it will be pleasurable in exactly the same way.

I find accounts of such differences in terms of mere quantitative differences totally implausible. It is difficult to judge how this implausibility compares with the implausibility of appealing to pure time preferences to account for evaluative differences. It is also difficult to compare these implausibilities with the implausibility of thinking that the only, or even the main, differences made by time are quantitative differences—as if quantity is the only or main difference between a relationship that starts well and ends poorly and one that starts poorly and ends well.

3. PEOPLE, CONTEMPORANEOUS CONFLICT, AND PLURALITY

Showing that conflict between temporally distinct values at least seems to involve plural values is important. But it leaves unanswered what has some title to being the central question about plurality and conflict: is plurality required for conflict between contemporaneous value instances—i.e. between values or value instances that are to be actualized at the same time?

Let us, now, turn to contemporaneous conflict. (Of course, if doing one act precludes doing another, then not to do the former is not to preclude the latter; and if the latter has value, then so should not precluding it. Thus, non-contemporaneous conflict may also involve a sort of contemporaneous conflict. But it is not the sort we are concerned with.) Suppose that I have the option of attending a lecture on Aristotle or staying at lunch and having dessert. We can easily understand how these can conflict if circumstances require me to choose only one. For we can easily understand how each has something of value that the other lacks. We can understand, further, how I might choose each for that feature. This, indeed, seems the basis of our understanding how there can be conflict here.

Now suppose that I choose to attend the lecture and that upon reaching the lecture hall, I am faced with the option of sitting in the one remaining seat or standing up. Each has its attractions. The seat is more comfortable, but standing up will allow me to leave more easily if the lecture is boring. Again, we can understand how there could be a conflict here.

But now suppose that my options are only to choose between two seats and that so far as I can see there is no advantage or disadvantage had or lacked by the one not also had or lacked by the other. Here, some may find it difficult to see how there might be a conflict. I would have no reason to be upset or sad or regret whichever choice I make. For whichever seat I take, I would get and miss exactly the same things.

Here some care is needed. For this case to show no ground for conflict, it cannot simply be that I will get and miss the same sorts of things whichever seat I take. It cannot be, for example, that if I take one seat I will sit next to one friend and that if I take the other, I will sit next to another friend. For this is true of both acts. None the less, I can be conflicted about which seat to take, because I can be conflicted about which friend to sit with.

The problem is how to describe the difference between this case and the earlier one, where I am indifferent about which seat to take. In both cases, each option, simply by being a different option, is a different instance of the relevant value or values. In both cases, each option instantiates the same sort or sorts of values.

The issue here is important enough to be reinforced by some other examples. Consider an army commander who experiences no conflict in sending one battalion rather than another to the front. Some conclude that he does not care for the soldiers involved, or at least that he does not care for them as individuals. But this does not follow from his lack of conflict. As we might put it in terms of care: that he does not care who is sent does not show that he does not care for those sent. None the less, we need to contrast his care with the care parents may have for their children where they are conflicted by disadvantaging one in benefiting another.

In all of these cases—those of where to sit, the army commander, the parents—the agent can see and respect each person who is involved as a locus of separate and ultimate value. None the less, in some of the cases there is no conflict—and indeed, there may well be no ground for conflict.

The difference may of course lie in the different ways one cares for friends as opposed to strangers. I care for a friend in a way constituted by the fact that I like being with that person. But moreover, my care is also constituted by my feeling that I am missing out on something and suffering a loss when I am not with that person. Similarly, the parents feel the loss to the disadvantaged child.

However, characterizing the care—and thus the values important for conflict—this way runs a risk of circularity. For conflict was originally characterized in terms of the feelings of loss and of missing out. But now we are characterizing the sort of care and values we are concerned with, in terms of loss and thus the possibility of conflict. For, it must be emphasized, I can accord value to both strangers and friends and the army commander can value each and every one of his soldiers.

My point here in noting the possibility of circularity is not to fault the line of argument connecting conflict, care, and plurality. For all I have argued, there may well be other ways of characterizing these forms of care which do not make reference to conflict. And even if there are none, circularity here might not be a defect but instead might help to show the intimate connections between conflict and plurality.

4. DIFFERENTIAL CARE AND RATIONAL CONFLICT

There is a worry, however, with using care in our investigation of whether conflict requires plurality. The worry is this. It has been argued that conflict requires different reasons for doing each of the incompossible acts. Plural values may be able to provide these different reasons and thus be able to ground a conflict. However, a monism can clearly allow for different reasons for doing each of the incompossible acts. That is, monism can allow for non-degenerate differential choice. For example, I can have a reason to choose each of two dishes of ice-cream because each will be pleasurable.

The question for us, however, is whether any difference allowed by monism—such as a difference in amount of pleasurableness— can ground a conflict. Some would say that it cannot, since it is clear and obvious that what is more pleasurable should be chosen over what is less pleasurable. Most monists who take pleasure to be the good hold this. And many other philosophers also hold this, given the proviso that other things are equal. Quite generally, many philosophers hold that it is clear and obvious that one should choose the better over the lesser and thus that when confronted by such options there is an obvious ground for choice and thus no ground for conflict.

Several separable claims have just been made. The first is that it is clear and obvious that one should choose the more pleasurable over the less pleasurable, or the better over the lesser. I will examine these claims in the chapters on maximization. The second is that where it is clear and obvious which option should be chosen, there is no ground for conflict. Some, indeed, hold that the conflict simply is the uncertainty. But, as argued in the earlier chapters on moral conflicts, this is mistaken. Dirty hands cases and other moral conflicts are possible even where it is clear what should be done and one resolutely does what should be done. Further, if, as I have argued, it is possible to be conflicted over not being able to do something that is impossible, then conflict is possible over what one knows one cannot and will not do.

Some brief additional comments will be useful. If uncertainty is necessary for conflict, then plural values are often not sufficient for conflict. For it is often clear and obvious which option to choose, even if they have different values. So, it can be clear and obvious, and I can be certain, that I should save my life by running from my burning house even if this will prevent me from hearing the last part of a radio lecture on Aristotle.

Further, if uncertainty is necessary for conflict, at least sometimes it is not uncertainty about what to do. After all, akrasia involves a form of conflict. And akratics may be uncertain about what they will do—their internal battle may not be decided. But they need in no way be uncertain about what they should do. Akratic hedonists can experience conflict between the greater and the lesser pleasure and can indeed fail to do what they are certain they should do— pursue the greater pleasure. They can be caught up in a fight against, and be overcome by, what they know to be the lesser pleasure. By their own lights, they are irrational. But their conflict in no way depends on their uncertainty about what to do.

Akrasia thus shows that there can be conflict even where one is certain about what to do. But the bearing of this on our concerns is unclear. To see this, it will be useful to set out how we reached this point in the discussion. Against the claim that conflict requires uncertainty about what should be done, I replied that akratic conflict allows for certainty about what is to be done. Indeed, this is one of the reasons akrasia seems irrational. But if akrasia is, in this way, irrational, there is a natural riposte to my claim that akrasia shows that conflict does not require uncertainty: the irrationality of akrasia is precisely the irrationality of being conflicted where there is no conflict.

This riposte is very important. It forces us to confront, once again, the distinction between conflict and being conflicted. And it does this in a way that forces us to confront the distinction between rational and irrational conflict. We need to do this in any case, if we are to use conflicts to show plurality. For it is possible to be irrationally conflicted over just about anything, even where there is no conflict—e.g. because the conflicting options have exactly the same evaluative and desiderative features. Thus, irrational conflict may show little, if anything, about the plurality of values—even if it shows a great deal about us. Some brief comments on dithering and on ambivalence should make this clear.

Dithering. I can be conflicted over the choice of which of two portions of ice-cream to choose, where I can detect absolutely no evaluative or desiderative differences between them. In the case of Buridan's ass, absolutely equal alternatives resulted in the paralysis of stasis. I am now suggesting that it can also result in the paralysis of conflict: I vacillate, reaching now for one and then for the other dish and then back again; I dither; and whether or not I finally pick one, I am conflicted. But, of course, such conflict is not rational and it shows little, if anything, about the plurality of values, even if it shows much about us.

Ambivalence.[12] Most of the conflicts dealt with in this work have been, and will continue to be, conflicts of value—between the value of one option and of another, such as between that of lying on the beach and of studying philosophy or between that of betraying a friend and of betraying one's country. Differences in the 'existential valence', i.e. the existence or non-existence of these values or what has them, can make for differences in 'evaluative valence', i.e. whether and how they are valued—valued, disvalued, or neither. So, if I value studying philosophy there is an obvious, even if not always applicable, explanation of why I disvalue, or at least do not value, what prevents me from doing that.

There can also be cases of evaluative ambivalence—having various evaluative valences—in regard to the 'same object'. Turning first to a non-evaluative area: I can sometimes like, be in the mood for, a certain sort of food which at other times leaves me cold, or even repels me. Moving now to what is partially evaluative, I can sometimes love a person I sometimes hate or am indifferent to. And now, turning to the out-and-out evaluative, I can be ambivalently

[12] On ambivalence, see P. S. Greenspan, 'A Case of Mixed Feelings: Ambivalence and the Logic of Emotion', in A. O. Rorty (ed.), *Explaining Emotions* (Berkeley: University of California Press, 1980). My thanks are owed to Graeme Marshall for discussion.

conflicted over my beloved's gentleness. Not only can I sometimes love it and sometimes hate it, sometimes be attracted to it and sometimes be repelled by it, but I can sometimes value it and sometimes disvalue it. This, I think it clear, is a form of conflict— a conflict of valuings, but not of value.

As presented, this is a case of diachronic ambivalence—a valuing of one valence now, and another at another time. But, quite importantly, it seems that there are also cases of synchronic ambivalence: at the very same time valuing and disvaluing the same thing.

Some find diachronic ambivalence theoretically bad enough. But at the least, it allows for an intimate and coherent connection between valuings and values. Valuings can still be intentional—i.e. be of objects, or of the values of those objects. 'All' that is required is that the valences of the valuings are not given by the valences of the values. And, of course, some do hold that the latter can be given by the former. Indeed, some hold that whether something is a value at all is given by whether it is valued. On such a view, diachronic ambivalence involves diachronic inconstancy, which may be importantly different from inconsistency.

Synchronic ambivalence, however, violates even very weak demands of consistency. If any relations between valuings, objects, and values of objects are to qualify as non-rational or irrational, those found in such ambivalence rank among the most highly placed contenders for that evaluation.

My point so far about ambivalence is not that there are monistic synchronic conflicts of ambivalence of valuings. It is, first, that if there are, they are not rational. And second, for the reasons and in the ways they are not rational, they would not give an interesting answer to the question of whether monistic conflict is possible. For, to the extent that monistic conflicts of valuings seem possible, they seem to show something only about us, not about values.

Even though not necessary to make those points, it will be useful for other claims about plurality and conflict at least to raise a question about the real unity of the object of a synchronic conflict of valuing. Just because that object can be given by one term, e.g. 'my beloved's gentleness', we cannot conclude that it is one object as required by monism. That object may have different aspects, each with different values. It may be these differences that ground, or serve as objects of, the different evaluations.

So, I may value my beloved's gentleness as allowing me a peaceful life, but disvalue it as expressive of a weak spirit. It might thus be suggested that I value gentleness-as-peaceful and disvalue gentleness-as-weak. In this case, then, the conflicting valuings are grounded by, are about, what at least seem to be different values.

As should be clear, the question of whether the objects of synchronic, or even diachronic, ambivalence can be unitary is very complex—and this for both monism and pluralism. Its answer depends on the nature and extent to which changes in valuings involve psychic structures such as taste, mood, and energy, and the nature and extent to which those structures help divide up, perhaps even create, our world and its different objects of value. For as Heidegger, Wittgenstein, and others argue, it is mistaken to see us as simply taking up the same world in different moods. In important ways, a world given by one mood is a different world from that given by another mood. And the difference includes different values. If this is right, ambivalence may create, not simply show, plural values.

The import of these difficulties for my general and overall concerns is to show just how intimate are the relations between plurality and conflict—now a conflict of valuings. Their import for the more particular concern of this chapter is that, as with dithering, the ambivalence of a conflict of valuings does not give us a case of monistic conflict which can be taken as showing something about values, rather than about us. (In what follows, I revert to a near-exclusive concern with conflict over value, rather than conflict of valuings. The latter, at least when rational, seems to depend on the former, or alternatively is too complex to be dealt with simply in passing.)

My conclusion so far, then, is that the simple question of whether conflicts require plural values will not tell us what we really want to know: whether rational conflicts require plural values. As argued in the chapters on dirty hands and moral conflicts, for a conflict to be rational, it is not necessary that it be rational to choose each of the conflicting options. Rather, something along the following lines is sufficient: even if it is properly forgone, the forgone value is a source of rational regret. It is not simply an overridden value. It still has weight. It is a remainder.

The question, thus, is whether the remainders necessary for rational conflict require plural values. One of our real difficulties here is that almost all cases of conflict do involve plural values. I do not offer this as a conclusion of an argument, but as an observation—the backing for which, if needed, comes from what grounds the correlative observation that almost all choices involve plural values. As seen earlier in this chapter, and as seen in 'Akrasia', we have to work hard, going to some lengths, to find cases of choice and conflict that have any chance of being monistic. My suggestion is that we now turn to the monistic akratic cases from that chapter—e.g. choosing a lesser pleasure because it is piquant, or the lesser return of 10.255 per cent because it is novel—to see if they can be modified to give us cases of rational monistic conflict.

Modification is necessary, since these cases were presented as akratic and in that way not rational. Indeed, it seems that it is precisely because of the way they are akratic and not rational that they show akratic conflict not to require plural values. For the object of akratic attraction—the piquancy or the novelty—was simply an object of attraction, and not also a separate good. The akratic hedonist was attracted to the piquant pleasure even though its piquancy was not seen as making it good or pleasurable in any way that the better and non-piquant pleasure was not also seen as being good or pleasurable. Similarly, the akratic investor was attracted by the novel return of 10.255 per cent despite seeing that the novelty did not make it a good investment in any way that the better investment at 15 per cent was not also good. The better act had all the good—the very same good—as the lesser, and some additional goodness as well.

This suggests an easy answer to the question of what is needed to transform these monistic cases of conflict into ones where there is rational conflict. The agent must see something good in the lesser option not also seen in the greater, which gives an evaluative reason to do the lesser rather than the better. If, as seems un-exceptionable, there is is also a reason to do the better rather than the lesser, this is to hold that in a rational conflict there is a reason to do each option rather than the other. So, even if it is clear which option is to be done, there is still, if only as a remainder, a reason to do the other.

We can easily transform the akratic hedonist case to meet this requirement. The pleasure as piquant is seen as itself being good—good, that is, over and above its simply being a pleasure. On this view, what is good about a piquant pleasure is that it is a pleasure and also that it is a piquant pleasure. Correlatively, what is good about a languorous pleasure is that it is a pleasure and also that it is a languorous pleasure. Some may not see such differences as allowing for rational conflict, since they do not see it as rational to be concerned about what sort of gustatory pleasure one gets. But even if there can be rational conflict between such pleasures, what allows for the rationality of the conflict—the difference in these pleasures as pleasures—also gives an evaluative pluralism of pleasures. Thus, if this is a case of rational conflict, it is not one of monistic conflict.

So let us turn to, and modify, the akratic case involving mere quantity—that of the akratic investor. The modification here involves having it that the investor thinks there is something good about the lesser investment not also had by the better one. Now, some see what is lesser to be good precisely because it is lesser. Those who think there is something unseemly, perhaps grasping, about what is best, might hold this. They might, none the less, pursue what is better—either because it is not all that much better than what is lesser, or because it is so very much better that it cannot be resisted. These people might, thus, be conflicted by a choice between a lesser and a greater good.

But if the lesser good is seen as a good because it is lesser, its being lesser is treated qualitatively, and indeed evaluatively so. Its being lesser constitutes a separate value. It is good by being a lesser good, rather than by being a less good instance of the value also had by what is better. Thus here too we have plural values.

I do not think there is much point continuing with this exercise of modifying monistic akratic cases. For what is obviously in question—and what is obviously giving us plural values—is my requirement that each of the conflicting options has something good about it not also had by the other. If this good is of the proper sort to remain as a good, even if properly forgone, we may have rational conflict. But we also have plural values.

There is something clearly right about the claim that where options have no differences it is rational to care about, rational conflict is impossible. We often do argue that conflict is irrational precisely by arguing that the conflicting options have exactly the same features, or that they differ in ways which either in fact, or from the agent's point of view, are not matters of any concern.

And if the agent sees everything good about one option in the other, it is difficult to see how the agent could be conflicted by doing the latter rather than the former. And if the agent is, none the less, conflicted, it is difficult to see how this could be rational.

So, in the discussion of temporality, it was shown that time makes for different values, and that this is shown by the fact that temporal relations are essential both to elements of our lives being what they are, and by its being a matter of rational concern, and even conflict, which of these temporalized values we get. The possibility of rational concern and conflict, then, was used to show plurality. Correlatively, the fact of plurality was used to show the rationality of concern and conflict.

In the discussion of differential care about people, it was shown that we hold that each person—e.g. oneself, a friend, a child—can constitute, or at least serve as a locus of, different values. Again, the obvious concern and conflict we have over whom to benefit or harm, or whom to be with, was used to show plurality. Correlatively, the value of individuals as individuals was used to show the rationality of this concern and conflict.

It is important to emphasize that what we have here is a correlativity. The fact that conflict between sitting either with one friend or with another is rational helps us see that different people, as such, constitute different values. So too, the fact that we think it rational to be conflicted by having to choose between items which seem to differ only temporally helps us see that they really involve different values. This might be taken to show that the notion of rational conflict is prior to and explanatory of plurality. However, unless we have reason to think that a conflict involves plurality, it is difficult to see it as rational.

To see what is at issue, and to help advance the general issue about conflict and plurality, it will be useful to reconsider conflict over what is impossible—e.g. the school bully plum case. Some anti-monists might argue that monism cannot handle such conflicts. The argument is in two parts. The first, drawn from 'Moral Conflicts', is that what is impossible does not always help constitute a rational conflict. Otherwise, we could always be rationally conflicted. After all, whatever we do, we never achieve absolute perfection on earth. But of course, even though we always do not achieve this, it would be at best misleading to hold that we fail to achieve it. It is not a relevant option.

The point, of course, is that only some impossibilities can serve as terms of a conflict. As argued in the chapters on dirty hands and moral conflicts, among these we find what has been made impossible in certain special ways—e.g. through violations and betrayals or by being immorally coerced into helping implement another's evil plans. The second part of the argument is an attempt to show that monisms cannot account for the weight and role, perhaps cannot even single out, these special ways.

I am not sure this is right. If it is, monists will be unable to recognize some conflicts where the conflict is over what is, itself, impossible. But, they may be able to recognize other conflicts over what is impossible—e.g. where a natural occurrence creates the impossibility. Here we might consider a case where a flock of birds is about to eat the plums on two trees distant enough from each other that I can save the fruit on either tree but not both. I may be indifferent over which lot of plums I save, but none the less be conflicted over not being able to save both. I see no reason monists cannot acknowledge this sort of conflict and acknowledge it as rational.

To make it clear that this is not an epistemic conflict about value—not knowing which lot of plums is more worth saving—we can change the case so that one tree has far more and far better plums. In this case, it may be clear to me that I should save its plums rather than the fewer and less desirable ones on the other tree. Here I care which of the practicable options I choose. I resolutely choose the better one. None the less I am conflicted: not over which of the practicable options to choose and do, but over having to choose at all and not save all of my plums.

What is conflicting in these cases is that one is forced to choose the lesser rather than the better. That this can be conflicting is hardly news. But it may be useful for us, showing a simple way to construct cases of monistic rational conflict. We need only look from the standpoint of not choosing the better. In the last plum example, the better is impossible. And in cases of akrasia, the agent is tending to choose, or has chosen, the lesser.

Now, I take it that in both sorts of case, the conflict can be rational. It can be rational to regret having to choose one option rather than both, even if it is impossible to choose both. And it can be rational to regret not doing the better when it can be done. (In the discussions of maximization, it will be shown that not choosing the best need not be a matter of rational regret.) Further, I think it clear, monisms can allow for both of these sorts of rational conflict.

Let us first consider the latter sort of conflict—conflict over not choosing the better. We might be told that this is not the sort of conflict we are concerned with when we ask whether monism allows for rational conflict. For we want to investigate only those sorts of conflict which show something about the nature or number of value—perhaps because the conflict is unavoidable—and not conflict showing something about us, perhaps even a defect in us. But in this case, conflict shows only something about the agent. After all, the agent need only choose, or have chosen, the better to avoid the conflict.

The question for us, now, is why there is not also conflict over not choosing the lesser option when the agent chooses the better option. We are not asking about being conflicted by not being able to do what is impossible—e.g. not being able to do incompossible acts—but only by what is possible. The question, then, is: restricting attention just to practicable options, why can it not be conflicting to choose and do the better rather than the lesser?

Of course, choosing the better and forgoing the lesser can be conflicting for an akratic or enkratic person. And quite generally, it can be conflicting on the assumption of non-rationality. But again, this may not show us anything about the nature or number of value. So, the question should be: restricting attention just to practicable options, why can it not be rationally conflicting to choose and do the better rather than the lesser?

Now, such a choice might be rationally conflicting where we have plural values. Even if I see it is better to sit with this friend than with that one, I can be rationally conflicted over not sitting with that one. But it seems that if I see that it is better to choose this lot of plums rather than that one, I cannot be rationally conflicted over not choosing that one. I can be rationally conflicted over something else—over having to choose at all, and not being able to have both lots of plums—just as I can be rationally conflicted over not being able to sit with both friends. But we are concerned only with practicable options. And we are concerned with the possibility of rational conflict on the assumption of monism, as in the plum example, rather than on the assumption of pluralism, as in the case of the friends. The question thus is: on the assumption of monism and restricting attention to practicable options, why can it not be rationally conflicting to choose and do the better rather than the lesser?

If there were no reason at all to do the lesser—if it were in no way good—we would have an answer to this question. For unless something is in some way good—even if only by being the lesser of evils—it is difficult to see how its absence could be a ground of regret, much less of rational regret or rational conflict. However, this answer is not available to us. For there is a reason to choose the lesser option. Even though it would preclude something better, it is none the less good. It is simply less good than the better option, with which it is incompossible.

The question for us is why, on the assumption of monism and practicability, its being less good does not ground a rational conflict. The answer is, I think, as simple and obvious as it may be unhelpful: in this special case of conflict—made special by the assumptions of monism and practicability—there is no ground of rational conflict because the better option lacks nothing that would be made good by the lesser. Correlatively, the lesser is not good in any way that the better is not also at least as good. There is no way, then, that the lesser option is better than the better one. And thus, there is no rational reason to regret doing the better—i.e. to regret doing it rather than the lesser.

Monism thus cannot allow for the lack and loss involved in rational conflict over practicable options. Even though it can allow for a reason to do the lesser rather than the better, it cannot allow for this in a way that gives a rational conflict. To do that, the reason must be a remainder. It must involve a lack that could be made good by the lesser. But on the assumption of monism, the lesser would not make good any lack in the better. In this comparative way then, what is monistically better has no lack—i.e. it has no lack that any practicable, and similarly monistic, option could make good. It was for this reason and in this sense that it was claimed in 'Plurality and Choice' that pluralism can, but monism cannot, allow for a lack in what is best.

The reason this may be unhelpful is that we still have not seen what it is that allows for a lack in the choice between friends but not between plums. The answer here may seem simple: our concern with plums is satisfied just by having plums, no matter which they are, provided that they are enough in quantity and quality. But our concern with friends is satisfied by being with particular friends. Concern with plums is directed at a general feature—plumness, say. But concern with friends is directed at each friend.

This, however, is mistaken on both counts. Not every rational concern with friends is directed at each friend. If I want simply not to spend the afternoon friendless, any friend might do. And it is possible that my concern for plums is not directed at plumness, but at particular plums or at different sorts of plumness. So I might want the plums raised by you and those by another friend, or those of one variety and those of another.

Of course, some of these concerns with particular plums may not be rational. They may, instead, be on the order of a concern for the numerological features of the rate of return on an investment. If so, they will not ground a rational regret or rational conflict. But, such particular forms of concern about plums—correlatively such regret and conflict—can be rational. A plum connoisseur might properly be concerned to taste different varieties of plums, and a plum orchardist might be properly concerned to taste plums from different trees, even if all of the same variety, to check for consistency and quality.

My point in going through this—all over again—is to reinforce my claim that our views about lacks and about rational conflict sustain and depend on each other. To the extent that, and because, we think it not rational to care about the numerological properties of a rate of return, or whether the plum is from this basket or that one, we think there is no room for rational regret or rational conflict over not getting that rate of return or a plum from a given basket. But also, to the extent that, and because, we think that such regret and conflict are not rational, we do not think that there are lacks in these cases. Alternatively, if we think the agent some-how finds lacks in them, we do not find that rational. The same holds for conflict over which friend to sit with.

The correlativity of finding lacks and finding room for rational conflict is also usefully shown by examining views we reject as mistaken. We might start with those who, as we think, go too far in seeing items in the universe the way we see people: with each of these items having its own value as an individual. Here we might consider someone who identifies, and identifies with, each plum or each animal—even to the point of giving it a name—as some people do when they have worked hard and intimately in raising the fruit or animals. In such a case, if eating a plum or animal remains thinkable, it will make an evaluative difference whether it is this one or that one—just as it makes an evaluative difference for us which friend we sit with. So, it may matter to the person who has raised the turkeys whether we eat this one or that one.

We may well think that these people have exposed themselves to an over-abundance of regret and conflict. (Thus we counsel children not to become too attached to animals being raised to be sold or eaten.) Moreover, we reject as mistaken, indeed not rational, both their individuating values in that way and also their finding lacks, and perhaps regrets and conflicts, in the relevant choices. In rejecting either one, we reject the other.

On the other side, those concerned just with 'total value' or just with questions of which option is overall better will see no room for rational concern, regret, or conflict if the chosen option is at least as good as the unchosen one. We—or at least some of us— reject both their monism and their denial of the possibility of lacks, regrets, and conflicts. Again, in rejecting either one, we reject the other.

My point then is this: our thoughts about lacks and about rational regret and conflict sustain and depend on each other. It is important to see what I am and am not saying. I am, of course, not saying that wherever we have options with different values, we have conflict. Indeed, I have argued against that view. So, the correlativity I have been arguing for is not between plurality and conflict. It is between lacks, which only plurality allows for, and conflict.

More exactly, it may be between only some lacks and conflict. For there may well be some lacks which a lesser option could make good which, none the less, do not help constitute a conflict. To recur to the characterizing features of lacks given in 'Plurality and Choice', not every falling away from an ideal and not every disappointment is conflicting—at least not rationally conflicting. Some should be simply endured or, more lightly and easily, simply accepted with equanimity.

If this is right, some lacks should not be taken up in regret. But then, lacks and regrets do not stand to each other as ground and what is grounded. Even if all rational regrets are grounded by lacks, some lacks will not ground rational regrets. But then, even if, as I have generally taken it, regrets and conflicts are continuous with each other, lacks and conflicts are not.

Once again, we are faced with the difficulty of saying which conflicts are conflicting. The difficulty here is saying which lacks ground rational regret. But even without having solved that issue, I think we have seen that, with certain important restrictions, questions about rational conflict over practicable options and the lacks allowed by plurality are not so much different questions, as different ways of asking the same question.

Monism, then, cannot allow for certain sorts of conflict—precisely because it is monistic and thus does not allow for certain sorts of lacks—lacks in what is best among practicable options.

This shows an important defect in monisms. But it is important to see what it does not show. It does not show that monisms are unable to account for all conflicts. It shows only that they are unable to account for conflicts over practicable options. Monisms cannot allow for a rational conflict over not doing the lesser act. They can allow only for an irrational, e.g. an akratic, conflict over not doing the lesser act. Once again, they can acknowledge a good reason to do the lesser act—on its own, so to speak. But they cannot acknowledge a good reason to do the lesser act rather than the better act.

The conflict monisms are unable to accommodate is, we might say, internal to the choice: over doing one option rather than another. (This is a central locus of akratic conflict.) But monisms may be able to accommodate conflict over having to make the choice at all. They may, that is, be able to accommodate conflict over not being able to do what is impossible—e.g. all the incompossible options.

I do not mention this to offer consolation to monists, but to remind both monists and pluralists of the importance of such conflicts. As argued in the opening chapters on dirty hands and other moral conflicts, conflicts involving what is impossible are among the most important conflicts. It would be ludicrous, were it not so morally stupid, to hold that the incompossibility of remaining faithful to one's friend and also to one's country precludes conflict over having to choose between them—especially if one has to make this choice because of one's own or someone else's immorality or stupidity. We might also remember that even sensible ideals are often unrealizable. None the less even when unrealizable, not living up to them can be conflicting. Putting the point briefly, the failure to give important moral weight to what is impossible is one of the central characterizing features of the moral insensitivity or blindness of hard-headed, if not also hard-hearted, practical-mindedness.

There is, then, a nice irony in the fact that monisms may be able to allow for conflicts over what is impossible. For what so many philosophers find attractive in monism is just what also leads them to reject the rationality, and perhaps also the possibility, of conflicts over what is impossible. What I mean is this. Monism often seems to attract because it seems to allow that ethics might, to some extent anyway, be hard-headed, scientific, and provable. Ethics might, that is, be open to those who are practically-minded. But practical-mindedness easily leads to restricting the proper ambit of ethics to questions about what is to be done, and thus to a particular sort of evaluation of only practicable options. And this, of course, is to reject the moral importance of what is impossible, e.g. what is ideal or what has been made impossible by immoral action.

Thus, it is by recurring to what many monists want precisely to reject that monisms can allow for at least some sorts of rational conflicts. That at least many monists will reject this way of accounting for conflicts is no reason for us not to offer it to them. But, of course, that and why they reject it is one of the central reasons we should take them to task.

So, it does seem that monisms can—even if few monists do—allow for at least some important sorts of conflict. Whether they can in fact do this, or whether it only seems that they can, remains to be seen. For it remains to be seen whether they can give an account of which impossibilities are properly taken up with regret or with conflict, and which should be simply endured or even accepted. Of course, it also remains to be seen whether pluralists can give an account of this. But there is a greater difficulty for monists—their monism. For even if my account is tentative and incomplete, it is pluralistic.

We are still left with several issues. We still have to see what makes a conflict conflicting—either the conflict of choosing one option rather than another or the conflict of having to choose—and when conflict is rational conflict. And we also still have to see whether monism can accommodate conflict over having to choose—i.e. conflict over what is impossible. I earlier declared my inability to make much headway on what makes a conflict conflicting and what makes a conflict rational. I now declare that I will not proceed with the question about monism and conflict. I think it sufficient to have found out how rational conflict and monism stand to each other in regard to what is possible—i.e. to conflict over doing one practicable option rather than another. Understanding the possible has been difficult enough, I think, to justify leaving the impossible for another time.

PART IV

Maximization

9

Maximization: Some Conceptual Problems

As we have seen, to understand plurality and conflict, we must assess maximization. This chapter considers arguments that maximization holds for strictly conceptual reasons; the next, that it holds for moral or more broadly evaluative and rational reasons. It will be argued that maximization fails, and that this is all to the good. For as well as the general troubles maximization has with many other issues in morality, it has particular problems in accommodating conflict and plurality.

It should be stated at the outset that the maximizing claims I am concerned with have their home in accounts of value and motivation, especially those deployed in regard to akrasia. They are similar to those found in economics, decision theory, and game theory. But I shall not be concerned to argue how similar they are, nor whether my objections also tell against these other maximizing claims.

I. THAT MAXIMIZATION IS NOT CONCEPTUALLY TRUE

Different reasons have been advanced to show that maximization holds for conceptual reasons. To some, it seems a necessary consequence of value and evaluation. So, David Wiggins writes that 'if nothing else besides *F*-ness counts positively for anything, there is nothing to commend any other course of action over the

I am grateful to the philosophy department at the University of Melbourne and to the ethics discussion group at La Trobe University for help with this chapter. My special thanks to John Bigelow, Graeme Marshall, John McCloskey, and Robert Pargetter; and to Adrian Piper for discussion and for showing me her 'Consistency Constraints on Maximizing Expected Utility', unpublished.

one that is most *F*'.[1] Care, thus, is proportional to value: where only *F*-ness counts positively, one must care more for more *F* than less, and most for most *F*. Thus, to be a hedonist, one must be a maximizing hedonist: to care only for pleasure is to care most for most pleasure.

Some restrictions, of course, are placed on *F*, the object of care. First, what one cares for must be cared for in itself. I can care for sugar in my tea without caring more for three teaspoons than for one. For I do not care for sugar itself. I care for sweet tea. Here there is a relation of means to ends.

Even with sweetness, the issue arises about caring more for more of what I care for. Despite caring for sweet tea, I need not care more for very sweet tea than for moderately sweet tea. Maximizers reply that I do not care for sweetness as such, but for pleasant-tasting tea. Here there is a constitutive relation between sweet tea and pleasure.

However, even if I care for pleasant-tasting tea in itself, I need not care more for tea that is more pleasant tasting. I might want to maintain a balance between the tastes and pleasures in a meal and not want the tea to be as pleasant as possible, lest it over-balance the other tastes and pleasures. Maximizers reply, giving the second restriction, that I thus show myself to care not only for the pleasure of sweet tea but also for a balance of pleasures. Taken generally, the claim is that one can care for something in itself but not care more for more of it if the more would tell against other objects of care.

These are restrictions, not exceptions, to the maximizing claim that one must care more for what is better. More accurately, they are part of that claim. They specify what it applies to: what is cared for in itself and to the totality of what is cared for in itself. Where *F* stands for this, the maximizing claim is that to care for *F* is to care more for more *F* and most for most *F*. Such maximization, it is said, adds nothing to the claims about the caring. It is already implicit in them.

Another closely related set of claims in favour of maximization is based on conceptual claims about decision and action or about

[1] 'Weakness of Will, Commensurability, and the Objects of Deliberation and Desire', *Proceedings of the Aristotelian Society*, NS 79 (1978–9), 267, reprinted in A. O. Rorty (ed.), *Essays on Aristotle's Ethics* (Berkeley: University of California Press, 1980), 255.

the requirements for interpreting someone as deciding and acting. The basic claim is that a denial of maximization precludes explaining and interpreting in terms of reasons. To act for or on reasons is to do what, as one thinks, the weight of reason points to. Thus, there can be no reason, but only causes, for choosing what is non-maximal—e.g. for acting akratically. So, it is held that if agent *B* does *c* to get *F*, *B* must believe *c* to conduce to the most *F* available (perhaps discounted in the light of probabilities). Similarly, it is held that in order to interpret *B* as doing *c* to get *F*, we must ascribe to *B* the view that doing *c* will conduce to the most *F* available.[2]

If some such maximization principle is correct, then whenever I do an act which I take to conduce to less *F* than another act I could then do, *F* cannot constitute my total reason for acting. So for example, if I choose an option which I believe less pleasurable than another option, I cannot be acting simply for pleasure. There must be some other feature—perhaps a complex that contains pleasure as one of its elements—that is my total reason for acting. And it will be concluded from its being the total reason I act on that this other feature is what I care for most.

We thus have four plausible, interrelated claims:

If having *F* makes things good, then having more *F* makes them better.

If *F* is why they are desired, more *F* makes them more desired.

If *B* cares for something because it has *F*, *B* should care more for what has more *F*.

In order to interpret *B* as doing *c* in order to get *F*, *B* must be taken as holding that *c* has the most *F* then and there available.

However, we are not concerned with whether these claims are plausible, but with whether they hold for conceptual reasons. One central problem I have in accepting that they hold at all, much less that they hold for conceptual reasons, is that I see nothing incoherent, nor even problematic, about non-maximizing care. In

---

[2] These principles of interpretation are drawn from Donald Davidson, e.g. from his 'How is Weakness of Will Possible?', in J. Feinberg (ed.), *Moral Concepts* (Oxford: Oxford University Press, 1969). I put the claims in terms of value. Some put them in terms of the product of value and the probability of its being realized—i.e. utility as understood by decision and game theorists. This in no way would affect my argument.

the remainder of this section, I will present various non-maximizing forms of care that also seem reasonable. I will also argue, primarily in the next chapter, that we can and often should understand care in those non-maximizing ways.

As it seems to me, and as will be argued later, someone who chooses holidays on the basis of pleasure might want a pleasurable holiday, but not care whether it is more pleasurable than simply 'very pleasurable indeed'. If this is right, it seems possible that a person caring only for F might care only that there be some F and that once that amount has been attained, not care more for still more F, nor therefore most for most F.

Further, it seems possible to want a pleasurable holiday provided that it does not involve too much pleasure: one might want pleasure but be repelled by more than a certain amount. If this is possible, it seems that one can care only for F but care that there should not be more than a certain amount of F, and above that amount care less for more F.

Just as there seem to be different forms of non-maximization, there may be different forms of maximization. If maximization focuses on what is maximally F and requires caring most for it, it leaves open how one cares about what is non-maximally F. One maximizing theory might tell us to care non-maximally for what is non-maximally F, e.g. proportionally to how F it is. But another might tell us to care for only maximal F and to not care at all for what is less than maximally F. Put in terms of wants, this latter way wants everything in the strong, and often strange, sense that less than everything is no better than nothing—as found in 'If I can't have all your love, I want none of it.' As discussed in 'Akrasia' this latter maximization seems to take maximality as a qualitative feature—a feature of the object in virtue of which it attracts at all. The former takes maximization quantitatively, and to reside in the attraction.

Hedonists who maximize in the first way care most for what is most pleasurable but also care—albeit less—for what is less pleasurable. Hedonists maximizing in the second way care only for what is maximally pleasurable. They care for pleasure, but only on the condition that it is maximal.

If it is conceptually possible for there to be these different ways about caring only for F, it is simply not true, much less conceptually true, that to care only for F is to care more for more F and most for most *F*. There are at least two ways of caring only for *F* where one cares most for some *F*. And there are at least two ways of caring only for *F* where one does care most for most *F*.

Maximizers have replied to me in two ways. The first is to argue that I have failed to see that for there to be the possibility of coherent non-maximal care for *F*, *F* cannot be the only value in play, and that since maximization is about all the values in play, these possibilities are thus no problem for maximization. The second is to argue that what is to be maximized is precisely what I put forward as a problem for maximization: namely some *F*. I will take these in turn.

There seem to be several metaphysical thoughts underlying arguments for the first alternative. The first is put in terms of the metaphysics of judgement. It is held that a judgement that more *F* is not better than less *F* requires a standpoint external to *F* from which to do the judging, and that this standpoint must be given by a value other than *F*. If *F* is the only thing that is valued, it is asked how we could even judge a lesser amount of *F* better than a greater amount except by using some other value which the lesser amount of *F* has more of than that had by the greater. We clearly cannot be using just *F* for this comparison. For here what has more *F* is not better than what has less *F*. What has less *F*, but is none the less better, must have more of some other feature and it must be in virtue of having more of this other feature that it is better. But if what has more *F* is better than what has less *F*, there may well be no other feature in virtue of which these items are valued.

An analogy may be useful here. Within the middle, human range of weights and weighing, weighing an item can be understood in terms of counting the number of standard weights of a gram, kilogram, and so on that it takes to balance a beam-scale with that item in one of its pans and the weights in the other. Suppose now we are told that in a particular region of space, after we pile together ten kilograms of standard weights, adding still more of them does not increase the total weight. To make sense of this claim, or at least to test it, weighing cannot be understood simply in terms of quantity of weights. Thus, it seems that judging that more weights do not give more total weight requires a special understanding of weighing, whereas judging that more weights do give more weight has no such requirement.

The claim in question is that more *F* can fail to be better than less *F* only if there is some other value in play, and thus that maximization is not shown false by that failure. For in that case *F* is not the only value in play. This, if right, is a very powerful argument. If it is correct, we cannot show that maximization fails, except by recourse to an infinity of values: just as, on the basis of that claim, if more *F* is not better than less *F*, there must be some other value *G*; so too if more of the complex of *F* and *G* is not better than less *F* and *G*, there must be some other value *H*; and so on until there is some value *Y* such that more of the complex of *F*, *G*, . . . *Y* is better than less. Or alternatively there is an infinity of values.

This argument has it that there is a need for another value *G* to understand the claim that more *F* is not better than less, but that there is no such need for another value to understand the claim that more *F* is better than less. This was the point of the weighing analogy. But, in fact, that analogy does not show, or even suggest, what is needed. For both in the case where more weights weigh more and also in the case where more weights do not weigh more, we need to know how weights behave. In neither case is it a conceptual truth that more weights weigh more than less.

The issues here may be obscured by—or the obscurity caused by—the double use of 'weight'.[3] When we ask about the weight of weights, it seems natural to think that all we have to do is count them, and it thus seems natural to think that if counting them does not give us the right answer, something special is happening. But once it is seen that we want to know how weights stand to weight, our view should change. It might help to put this schematically. Using *W* for weight, *w* for a standard weight, and *n* and *m* for numbers, where *n* is greater than *m*, consider (1) $W(nw) = W(mw)$, and (2) $W(nw) > W(mw)$. In both cases we need to know the relations between the number of weights, the *w*s, and weight, *W*. We may determine that it is given by quantity, so that just where *n* is greater than *m*, the weight of *n* weights is greater than that of *m* weights. But this is to be determined—even if only by stipulation.

The issue is, thus, whether the addition of value signalled by 'more of *F*' is or is not like what is signalled by 'more weight' or

---

[3] My thanks are owed to John Robertson for suggesting this way of putting the matter and to Mark Brown for discussion.

'greater number' as these apply to our standard experience—i.e. where within standard regions there is continuous increase. We can schematize the question of whether the value of more of what is valued is or is not greater than the value of less of what is valued as follows: using V to stand for value, the question is whether $V(nF)$ is greater than $V(mF)$ just where n is greater than m. This must be determined. Simply to assume that it is is to beg the question in favour of maximization.

As we are helped to see by this schematism, even though we need to evaluate what is valued, that evaluation is not in terms of another value taken into account in the valuing. Indeed, if it were, monism could not allow for comparisons of instances of its one value. Every judgement of the form that $V(nF)$ is greater than $V(mF)$ because n is greater than m would be pluralistic—by involving both F and V.

For these reasons, I do not think that this argument cast in terms of the metaphysics of judgement can be used in support of maximization. (This argument will be discussed further.) And thus, I think we need other reasons to hold that where more F is not better than less, F cannot be the only value in question.

A second reason can be put this way. What is less than maximally F is only impurely F, where the impurity is given by the presence of something else G. So, an instance of a colour will be as purely that colour as possible unless it is also an instance of another colour.

Now, it is clear that in many cases, non-maximal care does involve limitation given by some other object of care which also provides an independent evaluative standpoint which justifies the care being non-maximal. So, Aristotle writes that 'even good fortune itself when in excess is an impediment, and perhaps should then be no longer called good fortune; for its limit is fixed by reference to happiness' (*NE* 7. 13, 1153b22 ff., tr. Ross and Urmson).

Good fortune ceases to be good by telling against another good— here happiness—where, further, this other good imposes a limit on the goodness of good fortune. We see that excess good fortune is not good by evaluating it in terms of happiness—another good, and indeed a higher order good. And because of the way it tells against happiness, excess good fortune is not better than a lesser, and more moderate, amount of good fortune.

Other examples where non-maximal care is justified by con-siderations of impurity are also found in the *Nicomachean Ethics* and of course the *Philebus*. So, it is argued that less than maximal care for bodily pleasures—or care for less than maximal bodily pleasures—is justified by the fact that great and intense bodily pleasures involve great and intense bodily pains.

Correlatively, an unwillingness to carry out a plan to its 'logical conclusion' is often taken as showing a less than total commitment to that plan. Here we might think of an unwillingness to use violence or ruthlessness to achieve political or business goals. Critics of such unwillingness often use it as a sign of commitment to an alien goal. Defenders, on the other hand, often argue that an unlimited commitment would tell against the real goal of the plan.

Thus, at least some examples of non-maximal care involve, and indeed are explained by, plural objects of care. But we lack a general argument that non-maximal care requires such limitation. Until we have the argument, I do not see why we should hold that if it is rational not to care for the maximal amount of F, then there must be another object of care in play.

The arguments that I have just rejected were meant to show that only where there is another value in play can non-maximal care for a value be rational. I now want to pause to show how similar considerations are used in the claim that non-maximization is possible or even rational—but only on the assumption of a pluralism of values. The claim is that a monism must be maximizing, but that perhaps a pluralism need not be.

The basic claim here is that it is possible, perhaps even rational, to value less than maximal F if maximal F tells against some other value G. Even though this seems right, it does not show what is required. For it does not show that pluralism allows for non-maximization where there is a higher-level synthesizing category H which encompasses both F and G. For if there is, then the question of the rationality or possibility of non-maximization arises all over again, now about H. So, even if one can rationally not care for maximal pleasure where that would tell against a good of the same level, such as wisdom, and also against a higher-level good, such as a good life, which includes both pleasure and wisdom, we must ask about the rationality of non-maximal care for a good life.

The thought that pluralism somehow tells against maximization, or allows for non-maximization, depends, I think, on there being no highest-level synthesizing category. This, of course, is to hold that values are incomparable and that we cannot assess the comparative goodness of the various goods. Rather than take up the issue of comparability, I will say only that if we want to reject maximization, we should do this directly, not via questionable assumptions about plurality and incomparability.

Let us now turn to the second objection to my argument that non-maximal care is possible. This objection allows that we can care for some F, e.g. a moderate amount of F, in a way consistent with caring only for some F. And it agrees that there need be no other object of care then in play. But, it claims that this is no objection to maximization, because in these cases a moderate amount of F is precisely what this person—or this person's preference schedule—maximizes. Similarly, it claims that to care for maximal F but not at all for what is non-maximally F is not really to care for F, but to care only for maximal F.

As I think this shows, however, it requires only cleverness to describe what purports to be an object of care which a given preference schedule maximizes. In the most degenerate and least clever form, the object of care is simply 'satisfying that preference schedule'. (The moves here are similar, if not identical, to those leading to the conclusion that we always do what we most want to do.) At best this shows an ability at redescription. The arguments for and against maximization should not rely on such possibilities of redescription.

What we must be concerned with is not the mere possibility of making out a maximizing or non-maximizing claim, but with the plausibility of the claim. We must, that is, be concerned with plausible descriptions of goals, values, and attractions. As I will argue below, our moral concerns and theories provide us with these and they also show that maximization need not be accepted as a requirement for good choice and action.

The suggestion that we can take 'some F' as the object of care to be maximized is misleading, if not mistaken, in a still more important way. As noted above, we may always be able to find something that might make it look as though the agent is concerned to maximize it. But if such an object is taken as what is to be maximized, then the theory may be maximizing in name only. In particular, it may lack the theoretical attractions claimed for maximization, especially those concerning discriminations and rankings among options.

What I mean is this. A proportioned maximization can be as fine grained in its rankings of things with F as F itself allows. So, a proportioned hedonistic maximization can rank items in terms of goodness with all the fine-grainedness it can rank them in terms of pleasure. Sometimes, I suggest, this will allow the fineness of rankings to outstrip that of care. Be that as it may, this fine grain is lacking from schemes which, in the presently relevant way, care for some F. They will be able to divide things only into two categories: those with and those without enough F to qualify as having some F. Within each group, there will be complete indifference.

But of course, it is not only schemes which care for some F which divide all things into just two groups. There is also a way of caring for maximal F which does this: caring only whether something is or is not maximally F. Further, some ways of caring for some F involve caring more for more F up to a point, and only then caring neither more nor less for still more F. And some other ways of caring for some F are as fine grained as any maximizing scheme: they involve caring more for more F up to a point and then caring less for what has still more F.

These last points may well not convince a maximizer, since they turn on the real possibility that maximizing may not hold. So let us turn to another point against maximization—or at least against the usefulness of redescribing a person's care for some F in such a way that it can be said to be what is maximized.

To bring out this point, let us consider the sort of caring for some F which involves caring more for more F up to a point and then being indifferent about more F. This, we might say, is to care for enough F. We can take enough F to be the value that is to be maximized. But if we do, the resulting maximizing theory will be no more fine grained in its rankings of options than a non-maximizing theory which cares for that same enough F. Both can be equally fine grained about acts up to that cut-off point. But, neither can be fine grained about options that have more than that amount.

Both the maximizing and the non-maximizing theories justify not differentiating among options beyond this point, but they do this in different ways. The maximizing theory holds that even though one of them does have more F than the other, neither has more of what is here relevant—enough F. The non-maximizing theory holds that even though one option has more F than the other, this makes no difference, since each has enough F.

If this is right, maximizing theories will allow more fine-grained distinctions than non-maximizing ones only when they are restricted to certain sorts of objects of care. But which objects are of these sorts is exactly what is in question. If I am right, this is not simply a conceptual question. It involves substantive questions about the objects and the care they elicit. This, of course, is to say that it is not simply a conceptual matter whether caring for F involves caring more for more F.

I have so far not addressed the argument for maximization given in terms of requirements for interpretation. But, similar considerations to those discussed above show that this argument, too, fails. Further reasons to reject the argument from interpretation are given below.

2. BETTERNESS IS THE MORENESS OF THE GOOD: SOME CONCEPTUAL PROBLEMS OF EVALUATIVE MAXIMIZATION

So far, the arguments both for and against maximization have been very schematic. And what seems possible or even plausible when put so schematically may, when filled out, be seen to be impossible or implausible. To further the argument, it would thus be useful to examine maximization taken as part of a moral theory.

One problem here is that there are many different theories of moral maximization. They may all agree that we should or must maximize value. But they give different answers to the following questions: what is valuable, e.g. pleasure or well-being? Whose value is in question, e.g. only people, or all rational beings, or sentient beings, or still some other group? Are the beings in question all potentially existing beings—i.e. all beings who could be brought into existence—or only actual or reasonably expectable beings? Is the value to be maximized e.g. the total overall value, or the average value, or the value enjoyed by the representative person, or, inspired by Rawls, the value enjoyed by representatives of all strata, starting with the least well off, then moving in steps upwards? Is value to be maximized or disvalue minimized or is some mixture of these required? Are we concerned with objective or subjective value, and is it actual value or that discounted by the objective or subjective probability of its being actual? If there are agent-relative values, or otherwise indexically individuated values, is the maximization only from the agent's point of view or from some more general point of view?

Undoubtedly they disagree over other matters too. Sorting out and arguing for particular maximizing theories poses difficult problems for those espousing maximization. But, if the fact that they work on them is any guide, many theorists think they can be solved.

For reasons I will now suggest, I do not think they can be solved. For I do not think any theory of moral maximization is plausible. The problems I am concerned with—conceptual ones in this section and evaluative ones in the following sections—are quite general, and thus there will be no need to detail which maximizations I am criticizing.

To start on the conceptual problems, let us consider the following well-known worry about maximization: at least some maximizing distributions of goods are unfair. There are standard replies in defence of maximization. Some hold that fairness which conflicts with maximization has no moral weight. Others who agree that fairness is itself important argue that the unfairness of maximizing distributions is only an apparent problem. They remind us that maximization requires maximizing all values in play, not just some, and they point out that the unfair maximization is not a maximization of all goods but only of such goods as pleasure or well-being. They hold that fairness, or a fair distribution, is also a value, and thus they hold that what needs to be maximized is the combination—or as is said, the mix—of fairness and the other goods.

There is, of course, a serious question of why we should think that this will give the right relations between fairness and maximization. But there is also the serious conceptual question of how to understand the claim that we should maximize the mix of these plural goods.[4]

The maximizing theory we are here concerned with tells us to maximize all relevant goods. It holds that if pleasure is the only

---

[4] On this and other problems with maximization discussed below, see also J. Griffin, *Well-Being* (Oxford: Oxford University Press, 1986) and R. Hardin, 'Rational Choice Theories', in T. Ball (ed.), *Idioms of Inquiry* (Albany, NY: State University of New York Press, 1987).

value in question, then we should do what maximizes pleasure. If fairness is the only value in question, we must pursue the fairest course of action. Correlatively, it holds that if choosing between options both of which involve pleasure and fairness, the correct course of action is the one that has most of these plural goods— i.e. that maximizes the mix of those goods.

This last suggestion is highly problematic. We are often enough able to tell whether one course of action will produce more pleasure than another. So too, we are often enough able to tell whether one course of action is fairer than another. Further, in special cases, where one option has at least as much of one of the values as the other option and more of the other value than the other option, we may be able to tell that one mix of these different values has more of them than another mix: e.g. one course of action is productive of more pleasure than the other and is at least as fair as the other.

Below, I will show that there are problems for maximization even in these special cases. But let us look first at the more usual cases. These are cases where one mix has more of one good and less of another than does the other mix—e.g. one mix is more productive of pleasure but is also less fair than another. In these cases, I find close to unintelligible the claim that the better option has the greater mix of these goods.

To bring out my reasons for this, consider this parallel. Suppose that we want to compare the size of the contents of different barrels, each of which contains apples in water. Someone might propose the following scheme: add the apples and the volume of water by adding the number of individual whole apples and the number of cubic centimetres of water. Although this can be taught and used, it seems ridiculous.

One reason it seems ridiculous is that it depends on a wholly artificial and groundless convention. We could as well have counted apples by the pair and water by the cubic metre. And of course, a barrel with more apples but less water than another can come out as having the larger content according to the first counting method and as having the smaller content according to the second. This is what we should expect, given the arbitrariness of the counting procedure.

But now consider this variation of the counting method: count the apples however one likes—by tenths, halves, quadruples or whatever of apples; and measure the volume of water however one likes—by cubic centimetres, cubic metres, cubic inches, or whatever. So that these variants are not merely notationally different, one is not allowed to indicate the units of the counting, e.g. quadruples of apples or tenths of apples, or cubic inches of water or cubic metres of water. All one can do is present the two numbers and add them.

This last begins to approximate the problems faced in asking which mix of pleasure and fairness has more of both those goods. We—or at least I—have no idea of how the comparisons within pleasure stand to those within fairness. We may see that one mix has much more pleasure than the other mix and that the other is moderately fairer than the first. But I have no idea of how to compare the much moreness of pleasure with the moderateness of fairness.

Even a ridiculous scheme, like the first barrel measuring scheme, would be a vast improvement. At least with such a scheme, we can attach some determinate meaning to the claim that this barrel has much more water than the other and that the other has moderately more apples. Unless we can fix on some ways, even purely conventional ones, of measuring these different values, I do not see how we can have a workable, even if ridiculous, scheme for values. (In 'Plurality and Choice' I suggested some ways we have of understanding 'much more'—e.g. in terms of what is typical. But, as I think clear, these will not suffice here.)

Thus, to ask which of these mixes of these goods has more of these goods places us in, at best, the situation of those using that entirely unconstrained scheme for measuring the contents of barrels. This is the reason why I find unintelligible those maximizations which tell us to maximize the mix of goods. The problem here is not specific to maximization, of course, but to comparisons. We do not have a way to understand what it is for one mix to be greater than another.

It might be concluded that comparisons involving plural considerations are unintelligible. I think this would be a serious mistake. It had better be a mistake. First, as discussed below, it is unclear that we are better placed in regard to instances of a single value. Second, as discussed in earlier chapters, almost every decision and action involves plural considerations.

My conclusion is more limited. What is unintelligible is a particular form of comparison—the one that talks about a greater mix of the plural considerations.

But we can often compare mixes directly, not via their constituents. So, we can find one distribution, or meal or party, better than another—without having first found that the first has more and greater constituent goods than the other. When asked to make a direct comparison of mixes, I understand what is being asked. I know what to look for. At the least, I can often find it.

Some might agree with me that claims that one mix has more goods than another are different from claims that one mix is better than another. And some might reply that to rank mixes in terms of which is better is simply what its having a greater amount of its constituent goods amounts to. I want now to show how these issues—whether these claims are distinct, and also whether the one amounts to the other—are problematic for maximization.

Indeed, sorting out these issues shows that if maximization is intelligible, it is not useful, and is, in addition, parasitic on other, competing views. To show this, I will argue that we cannot find out which course of action is best by finding out which mix has the most and the greatest goods; and that, instead, we have to find out which mix is best—and perhaps also which has the most and greatest goods—by finding out directly which mix is best.

To put the issues, let us, first, turn to maximizing hedonisms. On such a view, we should choose what has the most pleasure, i.e., is most pleasing. If faced with a choice between mixes of different pleasures, we should choose that mix with most pleasures— i.e., with the most, or the most and greatest, pleasures. From among the many different sorts of mixes we might be confronted with, let us restrict attention to just three sorts: a mix of a smallish pleasure and next to no pain, a mix with a far more intense pleasure but an intense pain, and a mix with an exceptionally strong pleasure and an extremely painful pain. If pleasures and pains are comparable, then instances of such mixes could have the same overall amount of hedonic value. And of course, the possibility of such mixes being comparable and having the same hedonic value is central to at least many hedonisms.

Maximizers tell us to choose the best mix and gloss this as the mix with the most, or the most and greatest, goods. In a parallel fashion, hedonistic maximizers tell us to choose the most pleasing mix and gloss that as the mix with the most, or the most and greatest, pleasures. My problem with this maximizing claim about mixes is that determining that those mixes are of equal hedonic value does not show that it is indifferent which is chosen. At the least, it leaves that an open question.

To be sure, reasoning from the overall hedonic value of these mixes, there will be no maximizing hedonistic reason to choose any one over the others. But, as I think is clear, we often do not reason to the pleasingness of a mix this way. Even if considerations of overall hedonic value are relevant, they are not decisive. We can understand and accept how one of these mixes can be preferred to the others and that this is so because it is found more pleasing than the others.

To say that we can understand and accept this is to put it too weakly. For I take it as obvious that one mix can be preferred to the others and this because it is found more pleasing. This is shown in everyday practice and judgement. If a view—perhaps our maximizing hedonism—cannot allow for this, that would, in itself, be sufficient reason to reject that view.

My claim, then, is that it is possible for there to be a difference in pleasingness among mixes of equal hedonic value. Put more weakly, there can be an open question for a maximizing hedonist of which to choose. From either of these it follows that the extent of the pleasures of a mix fails to determine what is most pleasing— or alternatively, it fails to determine the overall hedonic value of the mix. And the failure of either of these tells decisively against the present maximizing hedonism, which tells us to choose that mix with the most, or the most and greatest, pleasures.

It might be replied that my argument really shows only the well-known problem of comparing pleasures and pains, rather than a problem with comparing mixes of pleasures. This, however, is a dangerous reply for the maximizer. For, as is also well known, many pleasures—and, as argued in the *Philebus*, many strong pleasures and almost all bodily pleasures—are mixtures of pleasure and pain.

But even apart from this, there is a problem with the present maximizing hedonistic claim. For the following seems possible and indeed plausible: a given mix of several intense pure pleasures has more, or more and greater, pleasures than a mix of fewer of these pure pleasures. But that may well not determine which mix maximizing hedonists would choose. Some might want as many intense pure pleasures as possible, and thus find the former more pleasing. But other maximizing hedonists might find that too much—too intense—and find the latter, smaller mix more pleasing.

It might be objected that no sense can be made of the hedonic size of a mix of pleasures—how great its pleasures are—apart from how pleasing it is. But this is no objection to my claim. It agrees with me that how pleasing a mix is, is not settled by the extent of its pleasures. It does, however, go beyond my claim. For where I find an independence between the extent of pleasures and the extent of pleasingness, it claims that the first depends on the second. (In section 3, it will be shown that this objection is, in fact, an objection against hedonism.)

Let me now put my claims about comparing mixes in another way. Suppose that 'If *F* is an object of care, one must care more for more *F*' gives a conceptual condition for something's being an object of care. As seen, neither the sugar in one's tea nor the sweetness of tea is an object of care since caring for either does not commit one to caring more for more of it. A natural question is which—and indeed whether any—object of care satisfies that conceptual condition.

If *F* is not the only object of care in question, not even maximizers hold that to care for *F* must involve caring more for more *F*. After all, the increase in *F* might be bought only at a greater decrease in the overall value, e.g. because it requires such a decrease in another particular value. And, of course, it will not follow from this that *F*, or *F* beyond the point where it increases the value of wholes to which it is added, is not good. It would follow if what is good can never tell against what is better. For then we would never have a choice between what is good and what is better: by telling against what is better, that 'good' would be shown to be only an apparent, and not a real, good. But, as said, this claim of the unity of values is implausible.

So, maximizers hold that only the totality of objects of care, taken as a totality, obeys those strictures. The particular and differing objects of care must be somehow gathered up into, and considered only as parts of, such a totality—e.g. as given by the higher-level synthesizing categories discussed in 'Plurality and Choice'.

Because of their abstract and evaluative nature, these totalities and categories offend against the philosophical sensibilities of many prominent maximizers, who are maximizers because they think it hard-headed and scientific—in part at least because they think it can be formulated and used without recourse to evaluative considerations. This explains, I think, why many maximizers are tempted into thinking that pleasure is the only good and that the only evaluatively relevant features of pleasure are quantity, intensity, and the like.

But even if a maximizer is willing to countenance abstract and evaluative categories, these totalities still pose a problem for maximization. The problem is how to understand what it is for one mix to have more of two or more different objects of care than another. The answer now being canvassed is that of maximizers who make recourse to a higher synthesizing category and talk about the mix which stands higher in regard to that category.

My contention is that this has really evaded the original question of which mix has more of those objects of care and has instead told us what has more of something else. So for example, faced with the problem of understanding what it is for one salad to have a greater mix of the sweet pleasure of carrots and the sharp pleasure of mustard than another, they answer in terms of which tastes better. And to the question of which of two courses of action has a greater mix of pleasure and fairness, they answer in terms of which is morally better.

I now want to show two problems maximizers have with these categories. First, maximizers may well not be able to advise choosing this salad because it is the tastiest one. For what is tastiest may, for other reasons, not be best—e.g. the carrots are unhealthful or were grown by underpaid workers. This is simply an instance of the argument that maximization is concerned to maximize all values in play, not just some of them.

It is no reply to hold that maximizers can tell us to evaluate salads simply in regard to their tastiness on the assumption that they differ evaluatively only in regard to tastiness. For this does not disregard other values. It, rather, assumes that no others play a role here.

To avoid this first problem, then, maximizers may have to be understood as always advocating that we do what is overall best, where the values relevant to this good include all values or at least all the values there in question. This brings us to the second, and I think far more serious problem for maximizers.

The problem flows from there being two different understandings of the moreness of value. The first understanding is a mathematical or quasi-mathematical one, given in terms of adding more of what is said to be good. (In the language of 'Monism, Pluralism, and Conflict', this moreness may be a neutral function.) The second takes the 'more' evaluatively and internally to the notion in question. So 'more value' is understood in terms of being better. Put in terms of pleasure, we have the mathematical notion of having more pleasure and the internal evaluative notion of being more pleasing. We have, of course, already encountered these two understandings when we asked whether more of a good is better than less of it. Using our schematism, in the claim that $V(nF)$ is greater than $V(mF)$, the mathematical notion is given by the relations between n and m, and the internal evaluative understanding by the relations between the Vs.

These two understandings can come apart. Sometimes more pleasure is no more pleasing, and sometimes even less pleasing, than less pleasure. And sometimes more of a good is no better than, and sometimes even worse than, less of it. This gives us one possible understanding of the claim that the better can be the enemy of the good.

We can now put the problem for maximization: if maximization is to be telling us something worth listening to when it tells us to determine what is better in terms of what is good, it had better be using the first understanding. But then it can be mistaken. For more of the good need not be better. And similarly for pleasure, since more pleasure need not be more pleasing.

If maximization is concerned with the second understanding of 'more', it may well be correct about what is better. But then, we cannot promote maximization as telling us how to move from what is good to what is better by means of moreness. For instead of telling us how to do this, it simply uses that notion of goodness where the more is better.

It might seem that the most that could be charged against maximizers making this move is that they have trivialized max-imization by making it conceptually true. Many maximizers would, I think, take this as an encomium, not a charge.

But I think they would be mistaken in seeing matters this way.

For maximizers are now open to the charge of shirking the needed honest toil, and perhaps even of engaging in theft. After all, one important task in ethics and moral psychology is finding which objects of care are such that more of them is better. It is insufficient simply to announce the conceptual requirement that the good is such that more of it is better. As shown by Plato's and Aristotle's arguments about the unity of the virtues, finding out which, if any, goods are like this involves serious evaluative inquiries into the exact nature of the parts and the whole of goodness and, perhaps ultimately, the whole of a good life. (But we may also need to go further, at least to the level of a good polity. For what seems good for one person may tell against what is good for others in such a way that we may hold that increases in that good do not make things better.)

Thus, if a theory restricts itself to those goods and limits where the more is better, it may be right about what is better. But as just suggested, the explanation for this may simply be that it is right because it is parasitic on other ethical views that have done the required hard work.

This point is important in the contemporary polemics about maximization. For as noted, maximization is put forward as a scientific and hard-headed way to understand and settle ethical issues in ethically neutral and non-question-begging ways. It is thus offered as a contrast to those theories which rely on such morally loaded notions as eudaimonia and other moral categories. Of course, it is acknowledged that there are some problems with maximization—e.g. choosing among different maximizations and then applying the particular maximization. But, maximizations are supposed at least to start from firm and non-question-begging— and, above all, ethically uncontroversial—foundations.

However, if my arguments are right, they do not have such a foundation. To conclude my case for this, let us remember the arguments Aristotle and at least the later Plato give that a good life involves both plural goods and their proper balance. To assess the effect of adding a good to a life, we cannot argue that since a good will be added, the life will be better. To see whether adding it is good—and whether its more is better—we must evaluate the life that includes it. The goodness of adding the part thus depends on the goodness of the resultant whole. Goodness here depends on betterness. The point for us is that the understanding and determination of the proper balance of goods is a thoroughly moral enterprise.

Of course, some might wonder whether an archaic notion like balance is relevant to the concerns of modern ethicists. To answer this, it should here be sufficient to see that the issue of balance is at least very similar to the issue of organic wholes, which clearly is of concern to modern ethicists in general and to maximizers in particular. For as noted earlier, maximization does not hold that just one of the values in play is to be maximized. It recognizes that an increase in one value can involve a still greater decrease in overall value. One of the ways this can happen is if the added good forms an organic whole with the other goods, resulting in a whole of overall lesser value.

As should be clear, this problem of organic wholes attends both adding different sorts of values and also adding different instances of the very same infima species of value. Whether pluralists or monists, maximizers need a way to guarantee that more of a good is better. So, pluralists will need to ensure e.g. that the course of action that produces more pleasure is not worse because of too great a diminution of fairness. Monistic maximizers also need a way to exclude cases where more of their good does not make things better or even makes matters worse—e.g. because the added pleasure is false, demeaning, or immoral. Correlatively, hedonistic maximizers need a way to exclude cases where more pleasure is no more pleasing or is even less pleasing—e.g. where an increase in the intensity of a pleasure does not make for a more pleasing pleasure, and may even make for a less pleasing one.

One way of putting my point is to acknowledge two debts to G. E. Moore: organic wholes and the open question argument. For in raising the question of whether more of a good is better, I use organic wholes to show an open question. His question was whether we can define goodness in terms of a good or goods. Mine is whether more of a good need be better.

My claim, then, is that betterness may well be—and often is— prior to goodness. That is, for the evaluative decisions maximization is concerned with, we are often guided in our understanding of what is good by what is better. Thus, here at least, we construct the good from the better, rather than the better from the good. To the extent that the better is prior to the good, maximizations that tell us to do what is best are parasitic on other evaluations.

Indeed, they are parasitic in a particularly debilitating way: they may not even be able to use in a maximizing way what those other evaluations recognize as good. They may be able to analyse what those other theories identify as best into their constituent goods. But, to the extent that there are organic wholes, maximizing the goods found that way may well not give us what is best in other circumstances that also consist of those goods. For what helps make one organic whole best may well not help make another best. At an extreme, then, each combination of goods must be judged on its own—to see whether it satisfies or violates demands of balance and measure.

In conclusion, then, more of a good need not be better than less of that good. Put schematically, even if n is greater than m it need not be that $V(nF)$ is greater than $V(mF)$. This last, of course, allows that more goodness is better than less. That is, it allows that nV is greater than mV, where n is greater than m. For that speaks, not about the amount of F, but about the amount of V, which is the standard for measuring or valuing F.

So, it may be a conceptual truth about goodness that more of it is better than less—that the better is better than the lesser. But even if it is, that does not show that adding what has goodness will, by being added to a complex, make that complex better. There is the possibility of an organic whole. And this possibility is simply the possibility that by adding what has goodness to the whole we will not add that goodness to the whole—i.e. it will not be made better. But, that item 'on its own' is good. So, even where the good is not secondary to the better, and even where we are concerned with goodness and betterness, we need an independent way of assessing the better.

This concludes my argument that betterness is the moreness of the good we are interested in. It also concludes my argument that maximization, where it is intelligible, may well not give us such moreness, but instead depend on it. To the extent this is right, to do ethics, we must do ethics, not mathematics. And ethics, as Aristotle argues, requires judgement, not mere measurement.

3. A SUGGESTION ABOUT FALSE PLEASURES

It will here be useful, and I think fitting, to acknowledge the many substantial debts the previous section owes to Plato's *Philebus*. We could note its claim about difficulties with units of different items found at 56d; and its conclusion that a good life is a mixture. But rather than footnote my borrowings or explain more remote relations between my views and Plato's, I want to try to repay part of my debt. I will do this by suggesting one reason for us to think that the *Philebus* is right in holding that mixed pleasures—i.e. those which essentially involve pains—are false or unreal pleasures.

I say this is one reason, but not that it is the only reason. I also say this is a reason for us, rather than that it is a reason offered by Plato, even though I think it is. For I am concerned to show that it is a reason for that view, rather than a reason presented in the *Philebus*.

The hedonist, as portrayed in the *Philebus*, holds that pleasure is The Good, that the greater the pleasure the better the pleasure, that the greater the pleasure the better the life that contains it, and that the best life contains the greatest pleasures. Part of the argument against such a hedonism involves showing that the greatest pleasures are mixed and false.

We can here focus on two points made to show that those pleasures are false. First, these pleasures are internally, not merely causally, intermixed with pains. For they are pleasures taken in eliminating pains and in satisfying painful desires. Second, the pains remain as pains even in the mixture, rather than simply reducing the overall pleasure of the mixture. They thus contrast with costs in a financial transaction, which can be seen as simply reducing its bottom line, overall profit. The pains of mixed pleasures do not merely reduce the overall pleasurableness of the pleasure—even if to some extent they also do this. They remain as ineliminable and painful parts of the mixtures in which we also find the pleasures and from which the pleasures cannot be extricated.

It may be possible to care for pleasure to such an extent and in such a way that one is either totally indifferent to pain, or at least is willing to suffer any pain, no matter how great, so long as it helps get a pleasure, no matter how small. The former accords pain no value or disvalue whatsoever. The latter ranks its absence lexically below pleasure.

Whether or not a hedonism can accept either of these, neither one can be included in a plausible account of what is good in a good life. Some pains make some pleasures not worth having, either on their own or where there is a less pleasurable, but also less painful, option. They do this as pains, and not simply by reducing overall pleasure. Once again, we are concerned with a mixture of pain and pleasure, not simply a complex that has less overall hedonic value because of pain.

A plausible hedonism cannot, therefore, advocate only pleasure. Nor can it advocate always choosing a greater pleasure over a lesser one. It must also take account of pain. And it must ensure that the pleasures and pains are in the correct balance and proportion. Plausible hedonisms, then, are concerned with mixtures of pleasures and pains. They will, presumably, hold that a good mix of pleasure and pain is what is good and that what is best is the best mix of pleasure and pain.

There seems hedonistic terminology to put this point. Instead of talking simply about pleasure and more pleasure, we can also talk about what is pleasing and what is more pleasing. Perhaps, then, hedonists can hold that The Good is what is pleasing, that a life is good in proportion as it is pleasing, and that the most pleasing life is the best life.

The *Philebus* argues against this more plausible hedonism—not so much by arguing that it is false as by arguing that it is not a hedonism. It does this by questioning whether pleasingness is even a hedonistic notion, or whether, instead, it depends on non-hedonistic value. Since pleasingness may seem so obviously a notion from within hedonism, some explanation is needed.

Let us start by noting that at least part of our understanding of hedonism is given by contrast with other evaluative views, such as those giving independent value to reason or honour. Hedonism is the view that holds, unlike other views, that all value notions and evaluations depend simply on pleasure and pain. The reason pleasingness may pose a problem for hedonists is that pleasingness may not depend simply on pleasure and pain.

There is, of course, considerable obscurity in the notion of judging simply on the basis of pleasure and pain. So, it might be held that even such judgements as 'this experience has more pleasure than that one because it involves a more intense pleasure or because its pleasure lasts longer' are not made simply on the basis of pleasure. For in invoking intensity or duration we are obviously not judging simply on the basis of pleasure but also intensity and duration. And they are not pleasures, but rather measures and modalities of pleasure.

One conclusion that might be drawn here is that few evaluations can be made simply on the basis of pleasure. About all that could be judged simply on this basis is whether something has some pleasure, so understood that if it has just any amount of pleasure, it will have some pleasure. So understood, we could not judge simply on the basis of pleasure whether one option has more pleasure than another. Further, if we keep to this understanding of 'simply' and move to evaluating simply on the basis of both pleasure and pain, what we come up with is whether something is hedonically interesting—i.e. whether it has some pleasure or some pain, or is instead bereft of both. We would not have a basis for thinking better of a pleasure than of a pain. Thus, we could hold that not even hedonism judges simply on the basis of pleasure and pain.

A better conclusion, therefore, is that we need another understanding of what it is to judge simply on that basis. Here we should remember the polemical context of the claim that hedonism judges simply on the basis of pleasure and pain. It is meant to distinguish hedonism from other evaluative theories, not to set out a complete list of the elements of the hedonistic theory. The 'simply' in 'simply on the basis of pleasure and pain' excludes the sorts of considerations proper only to those other theories, but does not exclude simply every consideration other than pleasure and pain.

Among the acceptable additional features of a hedonistic theory will be such general metaphysical notions as duration and quantity. So too, they include features internal to pleasure and pain, e.g. intensity. They also include such phenomenological modalities of pleasure and pain as sharpness, languorousness, and the like.

These features cannot, however, include the non-hedonic, e.g. straightforwardly moral, value of the pleasure or pain. Nor can they include a restriction that we consider only those pleasures which are judged good on non-hedonic grounds. Nor can they be restricted to what Plato's and Aristotle's good people find pleasing. To use any of these last features would be to evaluate, not simply on the basis of pleasure and pain, but on the basis of non-hedonic evaluations and straightforwardly moral value.

The question of whether pleasingness is a hedonic notion can now be put this way: it seems that when we judge simply on the basis of pleasingness, we do not judge simply on the basis of pleasure and pain. Rather, we also judge on the basis of the balance and proportion of pleasure and pain. The question, then, is whether such balance and proportion, and thus pleasingness, is within the spirit of hedonism.

One traditional answer here is that the balance and proportion needed for pleasingness are understood in terms of mathematical or quasi-mathematical functions of pleasure and pain. So, some hold that we are to subtract the pain from the pleasure to see how pleasing the complex is. If balance and proportion could be understood in terms of some such function of pleasure and pain, hedonism might well be complex, but at least it would be straightforwardly hedonistic.

However, even if in some cases pleasingness can be understood in this way, often it cannot. Here we must remember that pleasures and pains often do not cancel each other out, but can remain as intermixed pains and pleasures. In much the same way, they do not cancel each other to generate pleasingness. To repeat a point made earlier, I agree with hedonists that pleasures and pains are comparable in a way allowing that a given small pleasure can be the hedonic equal of a great pleasure less its attendant pains. Even so, there is no reason to think that the small pleasure and the complex of great pleasure and great pain must be equally pleasing. There could still be a reason in terms of pleasingness to choose one over the other. We can still understand, and often accept, a hedonist's claim to find one more pleasing than the other.

Further, in some cases, pleasingness seems to depend directly on non-hedonic, perhaps straightforwardly moral, value. Here we can think of Plato's and Aristotle's good people who find things pleasing because and in proportion as they find them good. The reason we should think of these people is that to some extent, we too find things pleasing because we find them morally good.

The question, then, about whether pleasingness is a hedonic notion asks two questions. First, is there a way of finding things good simply on the basis of pleasure and pain? I mean a way that gives plausible evaluations. Second, if there is such a way, must it involve considerations that are proper only to other evaluative theories or that are, for other reasons, contrary to the spirit of hedonism?

To be a hedonist is, of course, to answer 'Yes' to the first and 'No' to the second question. There is controversy over whether Plato answers 'Yes' to the first question. But it should be clear that he answers 'Yes' to the second. So, for example, one of the main claims of the *Philebus* is that we cannot understand in hedonic terms the balance and proportion that mixtures of pleasure and pain must have if they are to be pleasing. And indeed, the necessary understandings are contrary to the spirit of hedonism. For, they are understood in terms of knowledge, mind, or intelligence—and the goals and values inherent in them.

To announce various philosophers' views about pleasingness is not, of course, to settle whether pleasingness admits of an understanding that is part of, or at least not contrary to the spirit of, hedonism. But for our purposes, it is sufficient to have seen that this is an important question and that there are at least two different and at times divergent sorts of assessments we can make of pleasure: one that speaks of greater pleasures, and the other that speaks of what is more pleasing. Even if it is clear enough how hedonism can—or its adherents take it that it can—evaluate things on the basis of the moreness of pleasure, it is unclear how, while remaining true to its own spirit, it can evaluate them on the basis of greater pleasingness. This is to say that it is unclear whether pleasingness can be properly understood hedonistically.

To return now to an earlier concern, we now see why it is fatal to hedonism to hold that what is more pleasing must have more hedonic value—more overall pleasure, or a greater balance of pleasure over pain. For as we now see, this gives primacy to the evaluative, non-hedonistic notion of pleasingness over the hedonistic notion of hedonic value. So, for example, it will hold that increasing the intensity or duration of a pleasure sometimes does not lead to more pleasure. For, what is more intense may not be more pleasing, and thus on the present supposition, it cannot have more hedonic value.

Now, of course, it may be said that if what is more intense is not more pleasing, then it is not the pleasure that is more intense but only e.g. the feeling that is more intense. Hedonists can easily agree, and indeed will insist, that from the fact that the feeling of having one's back rubbed is pleasurable, it does not follow that an intensification (or a prolongation) of that feeling need have more hedonic value. On their view, only if it is the pleasure that is intensified, need there be more hedonic value. So, it will be held, some pleasant feelings do and some do not afford more pleasure when more intense, but all pleasures afford more pleasure when more intense.

But instead of saving hedonism, this makes pleasure or intensity non-hedonistic. For on the present claim, nothing can count as a more intense pleasure unless it is more pleasing. And thus, the central and supposedly naturalistic, scientific, and hard-headed notions of hedonism turn out to be, at bottom, evaluative. Thus, either hedonism is formulated hedonistically in terms of pleasure and neutral functions such as intensity—in which case it is implausible, because of the way its greater pleasures need not be more pleasing. Or alternatively, hedonism is non-hedonistic, with pleasure depending on an evaluative and non-hedonistic pleasing-ness.

The reasons for holding that there are these two sorts of assessment of pleasure and that they can diverge show how my arguments from earlier sections are at least in the spirit of, if they do not simply derive from, the *Philebus*. They also help resolve those issues from 'Plurality and Choice' and from 'Monism, Pluralism, and Conflict' about whether, because we need a function to move from goodness to rightness—and thus because we have at least two elements: one good and the function—there can be no monisms. The answer lies in whether the function is true to the spirit of the good.

They further hold out the possibility that monists might not be restricted to ordering comparisons based on quantitative differences of their one good. But they also suggest that monists who remain true to the spirit of their monism will not be able to invoke the sorts of consideration that allow for a theory which is at once plausible and monistic. They will need standards of judgement which are not available to their monisms. Borrowing from Charles Taylor, these standards involve deep, not only shallow, evaluations.[5] And it is difficult to see how the functions of a monistic value can, while remaining true to that value, accommodate deep evaluations.

The reasons for holding that there are different assessments of pleasure—in terms of what has more pleasure and what is more pleasing—also make it easy to present my suggestion about why mixed pleasures are false pleasures. They are false precisely because

---

[5] 'The Diversity of Goods', in A. Sen and B. Williams (eds.), *Utilitarianism and Beyond* (Cambridge: Cambridge University Press, 1982).

their more is not always better and indeed may even be worse. The falsity—now seen along the lines of a contaminant—is what prevents the more from being better. The correlative claim is that in the case of pure pleasures, and thus true or real pleasures, what is more is better.

I will not discuss whether, as I think, these correlative claims are found in the *Philebus*. (See *NE* 7. 14, 1154a11 ff. and 1154b15 ff.) So too, I will not take up the general issue, also raised in the *Philebus*, of what it is about sortals such that in some cases the more is better but in others it is not. Here I will simply make two claims. If I am right about the *Philebus*, Plato held—and correctly so, I think—that this shows a serious, perhaps insuperable, problem for hedonism. If I am right on other matters raised in the previous section, then, for much the same reasons, it is also a serious problem for maximization.

Maximization: Some Evaluative Problems

THE conceptual problems for maximization presented in the previous chapter centre on difficulties in ranking mixes of values, on problems with organic wholes, and on the fact that mathematical moreness can come apart from internal, evaluative moreness. These problems tell against maximizations which put forward a compositional theory of betterness in terms of goods and goodness, holding that the better can be constructed from the good and that more goods make for what is better. But, maximizations need not be compositional.

After all, maximization is integral to various economic theories and game theories which acknowledge changes in marginal utility. These changes are often put in terms of positive value: adding a good to a complex increases the value of the new complex, but not always by the same amount. For example, even where getting a given amount of money will increase the usefulness of one's wealth, the increase can be different depending on whether one is poor or rich. Further, there is no need for changes in marginal utility to be positive. Economists and game theorists allow that at least within certain regions, adding a good to a whole may make absolutely no evaluative difference or may even make it worse.

They can, that is, allow for organic wholes.[1] And of course, they

I am grateful to the philosophy department at the University of Melbourne and to the ethics discussion group at La Trobe University for help with this chapter. My special thanks to John Bigelow, Graeme Marshall, John McCloskey, and Robert Pargetter.

[1] So Kenneth Arrow talks about evaluations of social states, which are wholes of all values: see his *Social Choice and Individual Values* (New Haven: Yale University Press, 1963), 17. I owe this reference to R. Hardin, 'Rational Choice Theories', in T. Ball (ed.), *Idioms of Inquiry* (Albany, NY: State University of New York Press, 1987). Hardin, espousing maximization, uses the problems about organic wholes ('complementarities') and mixes to argue for reforms in the understanding of maximization. My thanks are owed to Hardin for discussion of these issues.

can agree with Leibniz that adding some goods to some complexes will result in new complexes of lesser value.

The central claim of maximization, then, when stripped of a compositional claim, is that we must do what is best. And indeed, whether or not maximization is compositional, it must tell us to do what is best. If it is mistaken here, it is simply mistaken.

I. THAT THE BEST IS NOT MORALLY REQUIRED

I think maximization is mistaken here whether it is understood as giving moral or rational requirements. There need be no moral or rational defect in doing—in knowingly and intentionally doing— what is less than best. To show this, I will first argue against maximization taken morally and then both morally and rationally. In this section, I will summarize arguments given elsewhere about supererogation, self-regard, akrasia, and friendship.[2]

What is best may be supererogatory. But then, it cannot follow from the fact that an act is best that it must be done. Further, there is often nothing wrong in refusing a good for oneself. This is so even where what is best involves a self-regarding good. We thus have a second reason why it cannot follow from the fact that an act is best that it must be done. Nor, therefore, can it follow simply from the fact that one knowingly and intentionally does not do what is best that one acts akratically. For even where it violates

---

[2] On supererogation see e.g. my *Supererogation* (doctoral dissertation, Harvard University, 1966), 'Agent and Other', *Australasian Journal of Philosophy*, 54 (1976), 206–20, and F. M. Kamm, 'Supererogation and Obligation', *Journal of Philosophy*, 82 (1985), 118–38. On the differences between self- and other-regarding values, see e.g. 'Agent and Other', and M. Slote, 'Morality and Self–Other Asymmetry', *Journal of Philosophy*, 81 (1984), 179–92. On akrasia see 'Dirty Hands and Conflicts of Values and of Desires in Aristotle's Ethics', 'Affectivity and Self-Concern: The Assumed Psychology in Aristotle's Ethics', *Pacific Philosophical Quarterly*, 64 (1983), 211–29, and N. O. Dahl, *Practical Reason, Aristotle, and Weakness of the Will* (Minneapolis: University of Minnesota Press, 1984). On friendship see my 'The Schizophrenia of Modern Ethical Theories', *Journal of Philosophy*, 73 (1976), 453–66; 'Values and Purposes: The Limits of Teleology and the Ends of Friendship', *Journal of Philosophy*, 78 (1981), 747–65; 'Friendship and Duty: Toward a Synthesis of Gilligan's Contrastive Ethical Concepts', in E. Kittay and D. Meyers (eds.), *Women and Moral Theory*, (Totowa, NJ: Rowman and Allanheld, 1986). See also Susan Wolf, 'Moral Saints', *Journal of Philosophy*, 79 (1982), 410–39, and 'Above and Below the Line of Duty', *Philosophical Topics*, 14 (1986), 131–48.

the demands of maximization, turning down a self-regarding good or not acting supererogatorily need not be akratic.

My claim so far is only that in these cases not doing what is best may, none the less, not be wrong. I have not made the stronger claim that in these cases it would be wrong to do what is best. Out-and-out deontological considerations would show such wrongness—unless, of course, the good and the best are secondary to the right. But to invoke such considerations here might attract the charge of question-begging. So I will not invoke them, but rather take up features which at least seem more in keeping with the spirit of maximization, and perhaps even internal to it.

If one focuses, as I have done, on the agent and the options the agent has—e.g. to seek or not to seek what is self-benefiting, or to do or not to do what is supererogatory—it would seem that doing what is best could hardly be wrong. But this is too narrow a focus. It forgets the relations between one person's options and other people's obligations.[3]

To put this, we must distinguish between two senses of having an option. There are self-involving moral options. For me to have such an option between two acts requires only that it would be morally all right for me to choose either. There are also other-involving moral options. For me to have such an option to choose between two acts involves others being under a moral constraint not to force me to choose a particular one of these. Others—some or all others, absolutely or defeasibly—must allow me to make the choice.

The relations between these sorts of options are complex, as seen in the disputes over the enforcement of morals. None the less, it should be uncontroversial that at least some of the moral options we have in regard to self-benefit and supererogation are at once self-involving and also other-involving. If there are such other-involving moral options, then it may be wrong to act in a maximizing way—not in regard to oneself, but rather in regard to others. For suppose that despite the fact that my doing an act would be maximizing, I have a self-involving moral option not to do it be- cause of the way it would benefit me or would be super- erogatory. What are we to say about my other-involving option not to do it—i.e. of the morality of others forcing me to do it? (The

---

[3] I am here indebted to David Schmidtz for bringing out clearly how for one person to have an option, others must have obligations.

parallel between this question and whether traditional utilitarian-isms can recognize justice should be clear.)

Now, as I see matters, maximizers will have to argue that because of what such forcing involves, even if the forcing does get me to do the act, my doing it would no longer be maximizing. That is, even if my freely choosing and doing an act would be maximizing and thus better than not doing it, my doing it, having been forced to, would be worse than my freely not doing it. Perhaps they could make this out. But I am dubious. At the least, it would require giving a far greater value simply to acting freely, or a far greater disvalue simply to being forced to act, than typically given by maximizers.

It thus remains to be seen whether in fact, or as thought by maximizers, values will fall out in a way that allows others to dictate to us where we have moral options: that is, whether our moral options are simply self-involving rather than both self- and other-involving. Thus, it remains to be seen whether such options show that acting in a maximizing way can be wrong. In any case, if we do have even the self-involving moral option of doing or not doing what is best, maximization is wrong.

Other sorts of goods pose problems for maximization for reasons having to do with their nature or internal structure. We can start by considering goods which, according to some philosophers, are not very important for moral concerns: amusement and friendship.

Amusements can be good and worth enjoying without being maximizing—and this in two ways. A given amusement can be good and worth having even if it is not the most amusing amuse-ment or in other ways the best amusement then and there avail-able. And it can be good and worth having even if having it does not maximize value, e.g. by making one's life as good as is pos-sible. Indeed, about the only way one could think an amusement maximizing in the second way is by thinking of it as therapy—as something that helps refresh us for more serious enterprises. This suggests that one is thinking of the relaxation of amusements as necessary for the good health of our moral fibre—as if to be as strong as possible for as long as possible, it cannot always be tensed. But I think this is a mistakenly pernicious, far too pragmatic, view of amusements and their value. The free play of amusement is, in itself, good—even if it is also good for other reasons.

Friendship is also in opposition to maximization. One can, of course, recognize that certain friends and friendships are better than others and that one could have more or better friends and friendships than one does. In certain cases, once such possibilities are seen, they should lead to action.

However, if in general one will give up a friend and friendship for another because the other would be better—or if in general, one is even prepared to do this—then whatever the first relationship is, it is not a good or a true friendship. True and good friends and friendship involve a sort and strength of commitment that is importantly proof against the claims of betterment. Of course the required commitment is not absolute, taking precedence over everything. That one will not murder for a friend does not show that one is not a good and true friend. None the less, the required commitment strongly violates the canons of maximization.

Some complain that at most I have shown only that it may not be best to seek what is best when considered on its own. They note that we must also take into account the value, largely the costs, of determining and achieving ends. So, even though it is better to have a better than a lesser friendship, it may well not be better to give up the lesser for the better friendship or even to seek the better friendship. After all, giving up one friendship, or seeking another, involves risks of ending the day with no friendship at all or only the lesser one made still lesser because of the lack of commitment and trust. Success also has costs—again, such as the damage to the trust and loyalty needed for friendship.

Much the same holds for amusement. Often enough, the difference between a good amusement and a better one is not great enough to cover the costs of finding the better one. Further, being on the alert for a better amusement may so detract from the enjoyment of an amusement, that on out-and-out maximizing grounds, it is better to remain content with what may well be a lesser one.

This, of course, is an attempt to understand my claim about friendship and amusement as showing only that maximizers should be, broadly speaking, satisficers.[4] This understanding would be used to reject my anti-maximizing claims by arguing that I have a truncated view of the field of action—that I take it that when we have to choose what to do, all our possibilities and their values are already fully present to us and that we only have to choose one of

---

[4] On related issues, see P. Pettit and G. Brennan, 'Restrictive Consequentialism', *Australasian Journal of Philosophy*, 64 (1986), 438–55.

them e.g. according to maximizing principles. But choice and action also involve discovering and evaluating one's possibilities. And the values and disvalues involved in such discovery and evaluation—when these are seen as activities—must also be taken into account in deciding what to do.

Put briefly, then, the question for an agent will often enough not be, which of the various acts now seen to be open should I do? It will also be whether to look for still other possibilities. So too, we will often enough question whether we should reconsider the values we think our options have. And we should remember that maximizers tell us that when they recommend maximization, what is to be maximized is all the value then in play. In the present case, this can go beyond the value of actualizing those options we now see with the values we now attribute to them. It can also include the value of looking for still other options and of reassessing the value of the various options.

While I do see it as important to take these other values into account, I do not think that doing so tells against my claims. For my arguments against maximization in regard to friendships and amusements are not based on satisficing. Rather, they have to do with internal, structural features of friendship and amusement—e.g. that simply to be a friend requires a direct commitment to the friend, which is to some large extent independent of how even the most complex and sophisticated maximizing evaluations turn out.

Some might be inclined to dismiss this argument because they think, even if it is right, it is unimportant. Amusements are not of central moral or rational value and maximizers might thus be unconcerned if they are wrong about them. So too, friendship might be seen as ethically peculiar, perhaps even ethically anomalous. Maximizers might not mind being wrong about this, either.

I would make three replies to their claims. The first is to ask just how many so-called unimportant details can maximization be mistaken about and still deserve to be taken seriously? For now we have four such details: self-regard, supererogation, amusement, and friendship.

Second, I find it very difficult to see how a serious ethics can take amusements and friendship to be unimportant. I, of course, see how a serious ethics can hold that in certain circumstances—e.g. of great danger or pressing social needs—amusements and friendships will have to be put to the side. But our ethical theories are not simply about such difficult situations. They should also be guides for a good life in good circumstances. And it is difficult to see how amusements and friendships will not play important roles in those more fortunate times.

Third, the internal structure of commitment found in friendship is importantly similar to that found in other commitments—e.g. to a profession or a country. It is difficult to see how a maximizer could even take on such commitments, much less do well at, or by, them. I will return to this point below.

2. MAXIMIZATION, MORAL PSYCHOLOGY, AND LEVELS OF GOODS

I want now to show in another way that maximization fails both morally and rationally. I will do this by showing that at least some of the essential touchstones of moral and rational choice do not involve maximization. They are, as might be said, concerned with goods and not with bestness. What I will be concerned to show is that at least often we judge the morality and rationality of a course of action by its role in a larger whole—e.g. a life or a project—and that for the course of action to be counted as good, the whole it serves need not be the best one open to the agent, nor need that course of action be what, in terms of the whole, would be best. In both cases, all that is needed is that it—the whole or the part—be good enough.

Let us start with the claim that we often decide what we should do in terms of our projects. So, the fact that I am in the midst of completing a book can be sufficient reason for me to decide to continue working on it. And it can be sufficient for me, even though I see that there are better things I could do.

Such claims about projects and their personal and moral import-ance must, of course, be heavily qualified. Not just any project is worth pursuing, either in itself or in the circumstances. Some are in themselves worthless or close to being so—e.g. counting and recounting the number of bricks in a wall. And some that are in themselves worthwhile are not important enough to continue in some circumstances—e.g. continuing writing my book when that involves not going to the aid of a child I see drowning in the river outside my window, or when it involves not taking part in the defence of my country against a vicious enemy.

So, we must take care not to understand claims in favour of projects as claims in favour of self-indulgence or self-centredness. The claim must be that in some cases—that is, in only some cases—one can be justified in continuing with a project despite the fact that there are better things one could do.

Of course, many maximizing theories and claims are not concerned with what is best for the agent, but rather with what is best in a wider sense—perhaps in as wide a sense as possible, as given by the notion of what is best overall. None the less, it will be useful to continue with an examination of maximization applied simply to one person. For to the extent that an act affects the agent, maximization which looks to what is best overall will have little chance of being right unless a maximization which looks to what is best for the agent is also right.

We can see this last by seeing what would have to be true for my continuing to write the book not to be maximizing for me, but to be maximizing in regard to all value. Of course, we know how to make this true—e.g. my work will affect many people. But how often will maximizers be able to find such facts, where the agent is justified in doing what, so far as it affects the agent, is non-maximizing?

Some maximizers might say that my continuing with the book when I see that I could be doing something better shows me to be immoral. But this charge can be made to stick only if the better things are better in certain ways. The fact that another activity would be much more financially profitable for me might show that it would be better for me to stop writing the book. It might also show that my continuing with it is silly. But it would be unlikely to show my sticking with it immoral. Even if the better activity is much better morally—in the narrow sense of morality, having to do with duty—it might be supererogatory for me to engage in it and thus it would, now for a different reason, not be immoral for me to continue with my writing.

Let us now turn to concerns that have more to do with principles of interpretation and understanding. From this area of concerns, there is a different sort of objection to the claim that I can continue with a project despite seeing it not to be best. This objection is that there has been an important equivocation or misdescription of the case. So, it is claimed that if I knowingly and freely choose to continue with my project, then it is only in certain special ways that I can possibly not think it best. So, I might not think it morally best—e.g. because I think it largely outside the ambit of duty and morality narrowly understood. Or I might not think it best in the sense that it is not what I really want to do in the sense that it is not most pleasing, or that I feel under pressure, even if entirely justified pressure, to do it, and so on.

But, it is said, there is also a sense—and especially from the point of view of interpretation, it is the sense—of thinking something best such that if I knowingly and freely choose to do something, I show that I do think it best. This claim starts us on a well-known train of argument. So for examples I point to the nature and the outcome of my project and of other options and I try to show that I really do think another option, such as the financially more rewarding one, better. The reply immediately comes back that we must also look at how I value completing this project. And it may be said that, like many people, I place a very high value on completing projects and that when this is added to the other reasons I have for completing the book, it is seen that I do value completing it more than not completing it.

To be sure, I do place a high value on completing projects. A life would hardly be a life without a commitment to them. More generally, it is hard to imagine how without such commitments there could be a human life and society. But whether I value completing projects in general or in cases like this one is not in question. What is, is whether by sticking to my project, I show that I think that the complex of my project and sticking to it is better than other possible activities and projects. My answer to this question is 'No'.

To help defend that answer, let us consider a related sort of case. Suppose that as I see and feel things, I have achieved a good life, which has been one of my long-term and guiding concerns. Suppose further that I am now offered an opportunity to make my life even better by changing jobs. I think that it need not indicate any moral or rational failing to decline the offer. So, I can hold that although the change would make my life better, the improvement will not be worth the effort.[5]

---

[5] On such cases and on the general issue of moderation, see M. Slote, 'Moderation, Rationality, and Virtue', *Tanner Lectures on Human Values*, vii (Salt Lake City: University of Utah Press, 1986). My thanks are owed to Slote for our discussion of these matters. See also R. Routley, *Maximizing, Satisficing, Satisizing: The Difference in Real and Rational Behaviour under Rival Paradigms, Discussion Papers in Environmental*

Those who defend maximization by appeals to interpretation claim that by turning down a chance to better my life by changing jobs, I show that I do not think that the complex of my having the new job and the bother and disruption in getting it—the former discounted by the latter—would be better than what I now have. Two different, and not entirely consistent, reasons are often given for their claim. First, because of the complexity of the issues, I cannot have sound and rational reasons for believing of either life that it will be better than the other. Second, my choice and the justification I gave for it show that I do not really believe that the life with the new job would be better.

My reply to the first claim about complexity is a variant of the argument about the similar claim that plural values preclude sound judgement. (It may be more than similar, since many maximizers see plurality of values as an important source of the complexity.) Complexity is typical of comparisons needed for many of our choices. Thus, either we can make sound comparisons, even in regard to such changes in life, or alternatively, large parts of our lives cannot be assessed rationally. And if they cannot be assessed, how can the claims of maximization apply?

Let us now turn to the maximizers' second reason. This has it that my choice and the justification I gave for it in terms of what is worthwhile shows that I do not believe that the change in jobs would make for a better life. I disagree. I think that we are often justified in not making an effort that is rationally justified. Putting the point one way, we can say that even where making the effort gains us far more than it costs, we can be justified in not making the effort.

Another way to put it is that neither rationality nor morality requires us to be as hard on ourselves in the pursuit of value as maximization requires. Supererogation shows this in regard to that part of morality which focuses on duty. For what is characteristic of many supererogatory acts is that, even though the other-regarding value of the act more than outweighs the harm or difficulty the agent will suffer by doing the act, the way it would affect the agent justifies not doing that act. My present claim is that much the same holds in regard to pursuing a good life for oneself. The difference is that in this case both the benefit and the harm are self-regarding: the benefit to oneself is not worth the cost, even though the value of the benefit more than outweighs the disvalue of the cost.

To sustain my claim that I really do think the life with the better job would be a better life, I could give detailed descriptions of my cares and concerns to show that I do see a life containing the complex of my undergoing that bother and having the new job to be better than my present life. These descriptions would also show that I am not irrational in sticking with the latter. So, I might say something along these lines:

> Making the effort would pay off—and indeed would be maximizing. I would carry it off and would wind up in an overall better situation. But making the effort would be hard on me. In the past, I have been hard on myself and have made all such efforts— provided of course that I thought that I would succeed and that, taking the costs into account, it would be worth it. But now, I want to take life somewhat easier. I recognize that all things considered, my life would be better were I to make the effort. None the less, I have decided to let this opportunity pass.

However, I have found that such accounts rarely satisfy maximizers. They typically insist that if I choose one option because it is easier, I thus show that I give enough value to the ease so that it makes the complex which includes it better than the other. I find this mistaken, and objectionably so. For in making that claim they are, in effect, trying to saddle those who hold that they knowingly choose the lesser over the better with evaluative arrogance or stupidity. In this particular case, they are claiming that I somehow must see my ease as having greater importance and value than what I could achieve. Yet, except in special circumstances, I would have to be arrogant or stupid to think this. The better understanding is that I see that my ease lacks this importance, but that I none the less believe that I am justified in taking it.

The general point, which I think tells decisively against maximization, is that we need not pursue, or even welcome, what is for the best, if it is too hard on us. It must be kept in mind that 'too hard' is not understood as it would be by maximizers—as lowering the total value of the complex below other possible complexes. It is, rather, to be understood in terms of the nature of what is too hard and what is gained and lost by undergoing or not undergoing what is too hard.

For example, one might now have profound self-understanding, even wisdom, that came from overcoming severe and prolonged personal suffering, such as a very painful ending of a love relationship. One might see that this understanding more than makes up for the suffering and also that this understanding is of far greater depth and value than the sort of understanding that one could have attained had one led a luckier, or at any rate a more uneventful and smoother, life. On maximizing grounds, then, the suffering was worth it—and indeed, had one been able to predict its outcome, maximizing principles would have required one to undergo it. None the less, because of the nature and extent of the suffering, one might reasonably wish that one had had a less instructive life. Precisely because of what one had to go through to attain the better state, one might gladly and rationally settle for the lesser.

This, of course, is not the end of the matter. Maximizers typically claim that there are still other details of a life, or ways those details are appreciated, that show that the agent really does think it would be better not to make the effort or undergo the suffering, or does not have any reason to think that one option is better than the other. One way to reply to their claims would be by supplying still further details and interpretations of the life. But that would require far more detail than is possible or tolerable, except in a long novel by a good novelist.

I think a more frontal attack is needed. Maximizers hold that the absence of any attainable good is, as such, bad, and that a life that lacks such a good is therefore lacking. I disagree. One central reason for my disagreement stems from the moral psychological import of regretting the absence or lack of any and every attainable good. This regret is a central characterizing feature of narcissistic, grandiose, and other defective selves. It is also characteristic of those who are too hard on themselves, who are too driven and too perfectionistic. These last can never relax and enjoy innocent amusements, or really simply enjoy themselves.

To be sure, there are also character defects which involve being too easily satisfied, too complacent, too ambitionless, too easy on oneself, too soft, too lacking in drive, and so on. But that there are defects on this side in no way shows that the maximizing personality is not also defective. There seem, rather, to be defects on both sides. The difficult task is in striking the proper balance—e.g. seeing how and when to strive for perfection and be hard on oneself and how and when to be satisfied with less than the best.

It may be replied that my arguments could not prove maximization wrong, but at best only that being a maximizer—having max- imization as a leading principle in one's character—is, itself, not maximizing. This leads some to hold that maximization is not a view that is to be embraced and made part of one's character, but is to some extent anyway an esoteric doctrine. However, the fact that being a maximizer may not be maximizing was not my reason for saying that maximization all too easily can be part of a defective character. The defect is shown, and indeed is constituted, by the sort of self that this involves—e.g. one that is narcissistic or too driven.

Further, I see it as a severe problem for a theory if, by its own lights, it cannot be embraced and followed. Of course, I do understand how it might be claimed that an ethical theory is, in this way, esoteric. What I have trouble in understanding is why we should be expected to think that a theory which is so esoteric as the one now in question is worth serious consideration as our ethical theory.

My objection to esotericism might be thought to provide grounds against my anti-maximizing arguments based on those psychological and moral psychological claims. For one of the main objections to esotericism is that it requires us to conceal the truth from ourselves and others, rather than facing it and being guided by it. But, it can now be said against me, if truth is to be our guide, we must see whether maximization is correct before we can see whether adopting it as one's leading principle shows a defect. After all, if adopting it shows or helps constitute a defect, whether or not it is correct, that would be a powerful argument in favour of esotericism.

This may be right about the order of conceptual priority. But if we want to start our inquiry with what is better known, we would do well to start with these moral psychological claims—or as I would say, facts—and use them to help us find their underpinnings.

One of their central underpinnings is a feature of values which has already been exploited, without having been made explicit: relations between the goodness of wholes and the goodness of parts. It is now time to make it explicit.

Let us start by noting that the goodness of parts and their wholes may not be continuous. So for example, increases in the goodness of the constituent goods of a life need not make the life a better life. People who hold that their lives have been good need not forget that they did not achieve various attainable good things. More importantly for us, they can also see that having those good things would not have made their lives better. They can see that a vacation would have been better had they taken enough warm clothing but that, none the less, had the vacation been better in that way, their lives would not have been better.

This is a point about the discontinuity of the goodness of parts and of wholes in general and not simply about optional and somewhat luxurious goods. So, people can see that they have had a good life overall—or in more limited compass, a good professional life, a good personal life, a good life with friends, and so on—even though they have had fights, disappointments, and other bad incidents and times. Thus, they can see that various parts of their lives would have been made better by the absence of those bads but see that none the less their lives would not have been made better by the absence of those bads.

My claim allows that if the problems, disappointments, and the like, had been severe, their lives would have been better had they been spared these bads. It also allows that if some parts had been markedly better, the lives would have been better. It holds only that the change in the value of a life need not vary with variations in the value of its parts.

But then, maximization fails. For an act can be justified because it helps achieve a good life, even if it is not the best life. And acts which are justified because they help achieve such a life need hardly be aimed at, or help achieve, what is best.

Further, as I now want to argue—or really, argue once again— in order to be morally and rationally justified because of the way it serves a larger whole, an act need not serve that whole as well as it could be served. It need only serve it well enough. If this is right, maximization is mistaken about both acts and the wholes they serve.

To bring out these points, let us change the details of the story about my wanting to take life somewhat easier now, rather than pushing as hard as possible. Suppose that my university career is one of the central large-scale goods and projects of my life. Suppose further that I see that learning classical Greek would be very good for my career, but that learning logic would be even better. My present suggestion is that if learning Greek would be good enough, I can be justified in studying it rather than logic.

If it be asked why I choose the lesser, I might point to its greater interest for me. Maximizers may take my reply as showing that I think that the complex of knowing Greek and satisfying those interests is better than the corresponding complex involving logic.

But I see no reason to accept this. Again, I need not be caught up in the evaluative arrogance or stupidity of thinking that satisfying my interest is so valuable that it makes the complex containing it better than the one lacking it but including studying logic. I still think that studying logic, despite my lesser interest in it, would be better than studying Greek. I think it better for me and I also think it better more broadly, e.g. for my university department. So, I recognize that I would act rationally were I to study logic. None the less, the complex of my greater interest in Greek plus the knowledge of Greek can be good enough to warrant being chosen.

So too, the parts of my studying Greek may be good enough to justify choosing them over better ones. I might be justified in taking a less intensive course, or studying with a less thorough and penetrating teacher, and so on—provided that the course, teacher, and so on are good enough. Here again, there will be an attempt by maximizers to understand the choice as either maximizing or unjustified. It will be said that choosing the less intensive course is justified only if, e.g. because of the greater time it leaves open for other activities, the complex it helps constitute is better than the one involving the more intensive course. Once again, my reply is that this is mistaken. The complex need be only good enough.

My claim, then, is that as with wholes, so with parts: they need only be good enough. It, of course, remains to be seen how good something must be to be good enough. But if what is less than best can be good enough, two points of utmost importance follow. First, maximization is mistaken: acts can be justified even if not best.

Second, to return to Chapter 6: ranking, and the comparability it allows, are not needed for sound judgment. For even where we cannot rank acts or lives, we may be able to judge soundly whether in a good enough way an act helps achieve a good enough life.

3. GOODS ARE NOT SIMPLY GOOD ENOUGH

My claim so far is partly categorical and partly conditional. The categorical claims are these. First, a good life or a good project need not be a maximizing life or project—the agent need not be a maximizer, nor need the life or project be the best one available or believed available. Second, a better part of a whole—e.g. of a life or project—may well not make the whole better. The conditional claim is that if an act can be shown justifiable and rational by its being shown to be part of, or conducive to, a good life or project, an act can be justifiable and rational even if, as the agent sees, there is a better alternative act and thus even if it is not maximizing. To defend my claims, and to help convert the conditional claim to a categorical one that also tells against maximization, it will be useful to consider several objections.

The first is that even if a better part would not make the whole better, it would none the less and for other reasons be better to pursue the better part and indeed it would be irrational not to pursue it. So, even if having a better vacation would not make one's life better, pursuing the lesser vacation when the better was available would be irrational (costs and other things being equal, of course). My reply to this worry is contained in my reply to the second objection.

The second objection is that I have undercut the possibility of a whole way—and some think, the only way—of giving sound moral or rational advice. When giving advice about what is to be done, maximizers have a principled answer to the question of what is to be done: do the best. The best, we will be told, is a natural and final stopping point. We will also be told that interpretation in terms of reasons is possible and that practical reason determines what is to be done only if maximization holds.

In contrast, it is claimed, non-maximizers are on a slippery slope or in yet other ways are caught up in arbitrariness. They advise doing something which has less than a maximal amount of goodness. But, we are told, there is no reason why that particular less-than-maximal amount is fixed on rather than a somewhat larger or even a somewhat smaller amount. Do non-maximizers, perhaps, expect us to pursue only a certain proportion of the available good? And if so, why that particular proportion? Further, how can non-maximizing acts be interpreted as rational? For there is no reason for choosing the non-maximizing over the maximizing act. This, of course, is to say that a non-maximizing act cannot be the conclusion of practical reason.

To show that the source of the arbitrariness is the failure to maximize, and not certain particularities of the cases, we are asked to consider choosing between options where the only distinction is in how valuable the options are—i.e. in quantity of value.[6] To focus our attention on this, we are asked to imagine a philosopher's case: that by the merest means, e.g. simply by crooking one's finger this way or that, we can have either something that is good in a certain way or something else which is good in just the same way but better. We are told that here there could be no reason for choosing the lesser. (Those telling us this are at least similar to those ethicists Kant said look upon all motives as homogeneous and thus consider only their relative strength or weakness (*Foundations*, Akademie edn., 391).)

We are expected to agree that where the only difference between options is amount of value, one would have to be silly and perhaps irrational to forgo the better and choose the lesser. We are also expected to agree that since reasons for acting are given just by considerations of value, this argument can properly be generalized to show that it is always silly and perhaps irrational to choose the lesser over the better.

Another way to put the argument is that since reason is concerned just with value, all other differences between options are irrelevant differences—i.e. irrelevant so far as reason and rationality are concerned. A difference is rationally relevant only because of its bearing on value. Thus, once all evaluatively relevant considerations have been taken into account and it has thus been determined which option is better, it is a rational requirement to choose the better rather than the lesser. Only this is justified by what is relevant.

Indeed, many think that we can reject this claim about rational relevance only by severing the connection between reason and value in a way that would be to endorse arbitrariness or irrationalism. Although I disagree with them, I do agree that the argument is persuasive. But, I now want to suggest, this persuasiveness has to do with a specific and non-general feature of

---

[6] This seems the gravamen of Philip Pettit's criticism of Michael Slote's argument against maximization. See their 'Satisficing Consequentialism' Parts II and I

the argument—the elimination of all but quantitative evaluative differences. So, we were asked to consider two cases which differed only in that one is better than the other.

This feature, of course, was required to ensure that the options differed only in regard to value and thus to ensure that the argument could be generalized to value and reason taken generally. But what it rather does is have us focus not on value and reason taken generally, but only on abstract value and reason.

This abstractness is found in the fact that the argument looks only at value taken generally and indifferently, and not at the particular value or values concerned. It asks simply which option is better, and not what is good about the options and why one is better than the other. Similarly, it talks about reason and what reason singles out, and not about the content of the reasons. Quite naturally then, the argument sees non-maximizers as advocating— almost in so many words—doing what is less than the best or what is good enough, perhaps even what is second best, if not second rate.

But, non-maximizers can instead be understood as advocating concrete sorts of lives, projects, courses of action, friendships, and so on. These are advocated because of what they concretely are— that is, the sorts of lives, projects, and so on that they are.[7]

So for example, it is because of the concrete care for a person as a friend that friendship is the good it is. Friendship involves caring directly and ultimately for the friend, and not simply for some abstract value, such as goodness or friendship, nor for the friend as exemplar or bearer of that abstract value. Indeed, if we care only for value as such, or for the friend for that value, we will ᴜᴌere necessarily lack friendship.

So too, I do not choose to study Greek because of its abstract value. My reason is not that it is less than maximally good, nor that it achieves some proportion of available value. Rather, I choose it because of the concrete ways it is good—e.g. how it will fit into my life, what I will then be able to do, and so on.

Lives, projects, friendships, concerns, pleasures, and other elements of lives are good (or bad) and can be seen to be such in

respectively, *Proceedings of the Aristotelian Society*, suppl. 58 (1984), 165–76 and 139–64. See also *Principia Ethica*, sect. 60.

[7] On an importantly related point, see C. Korsgaard, 'The Right to Lie: Kant on Dealing with Evil', *Philosophy and Public Affairs*, 15 (1986), 325–49, especially 345–6.

terms of the concrete way they are. They are not the concrete and important sorts of good they are because they are good—because, as might be said, they have some general and abstract goodness. (This, I think, is part of Aristotle's criticism of Plato on The Form of the Good in *Nicomachean Ethics* 1. 6.) So too, they are worthy of choice and are justifiably chosen because of the goods they are. Here too, simply and abstractly being better than other options is not necessary.

My claim is only that in some cases a good which is then and there not the best good available can, none the less, be good enough to make choosing it both rational and moral. Obviously, this is not always the case. So, for example, financial managers of a retirement fund may have an obligation to invest deposits at the best return. So too, it is reasonable to impose an obligation on those in charge of lifeboats to rescue as many passengers as possible.

But these may be special sorts of cases. After all, fund managers may plausibly be thought to have the job of maximizing return. Since the case is special, I could concede it to maximizers. But we should at least note two points. First, there are 'side-constraints', such as legality, which must be met before questions of maximization come up. Thus if this case does support maximization, it supports only a sort of maximization—maximization after various other considerations are met. Further, since the safety of an investment is a consideration, what must be maximized is a mix of safety and return. Some risks will be worth taking and some not. So, it is not return that must be maximized but some expectable return. And thus we must contend with the problems of maximizing mixes, discussed in the previous chapter.

Second, there is the theoretically more difficult problem of the balance between the professional concerns of fund managers and their more private ones—e.g. how they are entitled to take their own welfare into account. A simple and straightforward suggestion is that they are entitled to seek their own welfare only when doing the good they will get for themselves will not be bought at a greater loss for their company. This would certainly accord with maximization.

But suppose, as seems plausible, that managers will do best by their clients, and thus be most successful as managers, by staying at their desks an extra two to four hours a day, working through most week-ends, never taking a vacation of more than a day or so at a time, and the like. Whatever their duties during a financial crisis, in normal times, shorter days and holidays seem justified. But not according to maximization. Maximization is also too hard on moral saints and heroes. Volunteer workers in refugee camps would not be entitled to a vacation or even leisure, no matter how long and hard they have worked, if they could do more good by continuing.

To turn now to the lifeboat case. This, too, is special. For many of us, anyway, most of our lives are, fortunately, poorly modelled in terms of a lifeboat situation. Thus, although many discussions of ethics are conducted in such life-and-death terms, what should first be discussed is whether lessons for a more ordinary and less fraught life can be properly drawn from those cases.

But even in this lifeboat case, it is unclear whether the immorality of needlessly leaving some to die is to be explained in terms of the better good simply being so much better than the lesser. Perhaps, instead, it is to be explained in terms of the lesser good being so bad. Or perhaps it is to be explained in terms of the particular concrete natures of what is better and what is lesser and how they are better and lesser. So for example, it might be put in terms of the worth, instead of the price, of each human life, or in terms of the rights each has not to be abandoned.

These points should also be put in terms of interpretation and explanation. To the extent that choice is seen as based simply on value taken abstractly, it is natural to think that forgoing the better for the lesser is arbitrary and not in conformity with reason, perhaps even in conflict with it. And it is natural to think that here practical reason could play no real role.

The basis of those natural thoughts is that since reason is concerned with value, reason can tell us only to do what is best. To recur to the opening concerns of 'Maximization: Some Conceptual Problems', it is thus easy to think that to care for something on the basis of value is to care for it in proportion to how valuable it is. And thus, it is easy to think that the choice of the lesser can be explained only in terms of causes and not in terms of reasons, or in terms of desire which is different from reason, even if it is not exactly a mere cause.

But if we base our choices on the concrete evaluative nature of the options, then even if an option is not so good as another, choosing it need not be arbitrary (or surd, as Davidson puts it). It can, instead, be reasoned and reasonable. This is to say that it can be chosen on the basis of reason. The reason is given by the value of the option. But here, value is understood concretely in terms of what is valuable about the option, rather than abstractly in terms of how valuable it is.

This is shown, once again, by my choice of Greek over logic on the basis of my greater interest in Greek. My claim is that this choice is reasoned and subject to rational interpretation, not merely causal explanation. This does not require the arrogance or stupidity of holding that my interest gives my studying Greek enough extra value to make it better than logic. Rather, the greater interest and its justifying power has to do with what studying Greek involves and how it fits into my life. It involves understanding and evaluating studying Greek and why I choose it—not in terms of abstract value, but in terms of concrete value, e.g. how it fits into and enhances my life.

To be sure, maximization is neither necessary nor sufficient for evaluating in terms of abstract value. It is not necessary, since even some non-maximizers may think that we should do our ethics and live our lives in terms of such abstractions. It is not sufficient since it is possible for those who understand value abstractly to see how what is non-maximizing could be justified. But, it is natural for them not to see this. It is also natural for them to be unable to see that much of what is worth valuing cannot be adequately described or even evaluated in terms of such abstractions.

And, if my earlier arguments are right, there are important and natural connections between non-maximization and evaluating in terms of concrete value. Once we start thinking in terms of concrete value, we will see ways, different from those which endorse maximization, to follow the dictates of reason and morality. For we will see that whether we act reasonably and well can, instead, depend on the concrete nature and value of what we do.

To conclude this section, I will make three claims about understanding value concretely. First, one of the signal advantages of understanding value this way is that it helps us see how we can be reasonable in rejecting maximization. For it helps us see that even if reason does have to do simply with value, it need not be proportioned according to value. Rational valuing need not vary according to how valuable what is valued is.

Second, we are helped to see and appreciate an important role played by reason and desire. Reason is needed to choose which good to pursue, not merely to determine which good is best. Similarly, we now see a way to hold that desire can stand to reason co-operatively, rather than antagonistically, without holding that desire creates or even reveals value: we can desire what is valuable and reasonable, even where our desire is not aimed at value nor proportioned to value. Such uses of reason and desire show our dignity as reasoners and desirers—and show us as, in this sense, legislators, if only for ourselves.

Third, understanding value concretely helps us see that value is plural. We can easily lose sight of the plurality of value if we are concerned only with abstract value: e.g. general goodness and betterness. But once we are concerned with the concrete nature of value—the various goods and what is good about the various goods—the fact of plurality becomes obvious. For there simply are many different concrete ways goods are good.

4. A FAMILIAR EXAMPLE WHICH SEEMS MAXIMIZING BUT IS NOT

It will be useful to put various of the claims made so far in a somewhat different way: showing that even when we seem to be maximizers—even when we claim that we are concerned to do what is best—we are not. Or better, showing that to be concerned with the best need not involve concern with the best as understood by maximizers, but can instead involve concern with what is especially good and is thus of the best or the highest quality.

This can be put in terms of the grammatical distinction between relative and absolute superlatives.[8] As used in maximizing claims, 'best' is a relative superlative: there is nothing better in the relevant comparison class, e.g. available options, than what is best in this sense. 'Best' can also function as an absolute superlative, as in 'You're the best' or 'This is of the best quality', or 'The best of friends'. Something can be best in this sense, even if within the relevant comparison class there is something better. My claim is that, at least often, when we hold that we should do what is best, we are not holding that we should do what has no better—what is best relatively. Rather, we are holding that we should do what

---

[8] See e.g. H. W. Smyth, *Greek Grammar* (Cambridge, Mass.: Harvard University Press, 1980), sect. 1085.

is really and especially good, of the highest quality—what is best absolutely.

To bring this out, let us start with the following objection to various of the anti-maximizing claims made so far.[9]

> We should not be surprised if maximization fails in regard to amusements. For they are not morally serious. Nor should we philosophers be surprised if we do not think fund managers are bound by maximizing strictures. Many of us have deep suspicions about the real moral legitimacy or importance of such work. So too, we think of a choice between studying Greek or logic as optional and thus not really important. And moral saints and heroes are always anomalous. But when dealing with what we understand and take to be important, we are maximizers. As serious and committed philosophers doing serious work—e.g. writing for publication—we do not settle for what is simply good enough. We think we should work as hard as possible and we want the work to be the best, or at least the best we can do. Here we reject what is second rate and second best and demand what is best.

There are various 'internal' problems with this objection. We might well wonder what sort of defence of maximization it is that allows that maximization need not hold in many cases. So too, there is the worry of at least coming close to begging the question in the way options are treated—that they are said not to be serious because maximization is not required.

But even if maximization does hold only in cases we take very seriously, that would be important. And indeed, it might secure for partisans of maximization all that they really want—or at least, all that those who are satisfied by what is non-maximal would think could reasonably be wanted: correctness about what is, or is taken as, most important. So, in what follows, I will not focus on these internal problems, but on showing that maximization does not hold even about what is most important. I will show that it is a serious mistake to think that what is less than the best is, at best, second rate.

Let us start by noting that to be serious about one's philosophy, or about a piece of philosophical writing, it is simply not required

9 My thanks are owed to Mary Mothersill for suggesting this and for discussion.

that one do whatever is necessary to make it as good as possible. First, we may see that we are not able to make it as good as possible—i.e. as good as the best philosopher might do. But we can count ourselves as serious and good philosophers and our work as serious and good philosophy even if we think Aristotle or Kant, say, would have handled the issue better. This, however, is not to say that philosophical ideals of perfection, as given by such exemplars, play no role here. If we fall too short of these standards, even if we can somehow still be taken as serious about philosophy, our quest may be seen as so misguided and quixotic that evaluation may be pointless, if not impossible.

Second, we may see that we are not able to make the work as good as we ourselves could make it. For that might require abandoning all other activities and responsibilities of a life in fa-vour of writing this paper. Even if these other activities do take away from the work, we may be unwilling to live like monastic scholars—spending no time with our loved ones, taking no part in political activity, and so on.

Of course, as the list of non-philosophical activities a person is unwilling to abandon grows larger, our doubts may strengthen about the seriousness of the commitment to philosophy or to doing the best work in philosophy. And it can grow large enough to settle that issue decisively. I do not want to dispute this claim. It does give at least partial expression to our understanding of serious commitment—as differentiated from something on the order of a wish or even a conditional commitment, i.e. what one would do if circumstances were different. But I do think it important to see that if we do accept that claim, we are rejecting the account in terms of maximization of what it is to take philosophy seriously.

We can bring these points together by holding that such total commitment is heroic or saintly commitment. Where philosophy gives the relevant evaluative standpoint, this is supererogatory commitment. We might naturally extend this by holding that such philosophical supererogatory commitment is an ideal, which, if not achieved, need not show a failure.

The objection, then, might be modified so that the philosophy is done within the context of a more ordinary scholarly and academic life. It is philosophy as a part of life, or at least as allowing for a life, that is serious—at least for most of us. To be sure, the rest of the life cannot obtrude too much and for too long. If it does, then there is a real question as to whether one is committed to doing the best in philosophy—or at least whether one is there and then expressing and acting from that commitment. So the maximizing claim might be something like this: we want to do the best philosophy we can do, while living some form of good life.

But even this is not enough. For we all recognize that were we to take unusual and heroic academic measures—which we could do and still live a good life—a given piece of work would almost certainly be better than it is. I am thinking of such measures as rereading and rethinking the philosophical corpus that sustains and gives rise to the issue, attending courses given by those we acknowledge as masters in the field, organizing seminars on the subject with a group of smart and irreverent students, and studying the matter with a reading group.

But of course, we may not have time to do this. The deadline for submitting the work may be too close, if not already past. As well, there may be other constraints of publication: e.g. the work must be no more than twenty pages long. But we may think that we could handle the subject far better in a work five times as long. None the less, to delay the work or to 'allow' it to be one hundred pages long could so inconvenience the editor, other authors, and so on, that we keep to the schedule and length.

Further, even though we want to do the best we can do with this piece of work given those and similar constraints, we may have other work we also want to do. And to give this piece of work all the time and effort needed to make it the very best we could— even on the assumption that we submit it on time and in the proper length—would require slighting other philosophical needs and commitments. As well, we have other professional commitments that have to be met. Even if it will take time away from this piece of work, we have to teach classes, meet with students, read work sent to us for evaluation and help, and so on and on.

This is not to point to the truisms that we must make choices and that we must be concerned with mixes of goods. Rather, I am concerned to indicate how these other goods tell against doing what is best. Or perhaps it would be better to say that these other goods give a shape to the notion of doing what is best that shows that in this case at least, what is best is not correctly understood in a maximizing way.

One way, then, to take my suggestion is that we do not count as defects in a piece of philosophy what could be avoided only by sacrificing 'too much' of the rest of one's life. We might say that these are poorly understood as defects, since they are the very factors which give shape to the activity of philosophy as a human activity. It is as if one were taking the resistance of marble to being sculpted as a constraint, which as a constraint is understood as engendering a defect, rather than as helping inform the very possibility, and contributing to the evaluative conditions, for such sculptures. Or it is as if one were taking our having bodies with certain possibilities and impossibilities of movement, and constrained by gravity, as a constraint engendering defects in ballet, rather than as helping inform its possibilities and excellences. Those who feel uncomfortable with these Sartrean claims may feel more at ease in agreeing that there is, in any case, difficulty in seeing something to be a defect if its absence can be secured only by magical means, or even only heroic or saintly means.

It must be emphasized that it would be mere hopefulness for a maximizer to claim that what the philosopher must be aiming at is the very best life, with philosophy as a part of that. To the extent that values, or the possibilities of realizing them, are interconnected, we may, of course, have to moderate the pursuit of one to achieve another in order to achieve what is overall best or better. But there is enough lack of close-knittedness, enough looseness, among the values in a good life that includes good work in philosophy to make it too implausible to hold that every justified lack of perfection in one's philosophy will be justified by an increase in overall value of the life. Neither the philosophy nor the life need be best to be justified.

Let us now turn from the life that includes work in philosophy to the work itself. Here again, we find constraints. And now they do seem to tell against the work being the very best we could do. So we may well think that the work would be better if we could, first, reread the corpus of philosophy, undertake courses on the issue, not have to keep to a publication schedule or prescribed length, have time off from classes, meetings, and so on. This is clearly not to speak of what is merely ideal. Our professional practice shows that we do see these as telling against, perhaps even compromising, the quality of our work. After all, one of the chief justifications of seeking grants, taking time off from teaching, writing a book rather than an article, and so on, is precisely to do better work—to do better with that work.

Now, my point is not to suggest that we can do only poor work if we teach, adhere to publication requirements, and so on. Obviously, good work—some marvellously wonderful work—is done under these conditions. My point, rather, is to suggest that by 'the best work' we often enough can at most mean the best work in given circumstances—circumstances which we know tell generally and systematically against the work being as good as we could make it.

So it will not serve the claims of maximization to hold what may be right: that we want to do what is best in the circumstances. For the circumstances not only give shape to what is to be counted as the best, as in the case of life constraints; they may also prevent the work from being as good as it could be.

This is not at all to suggest that a good and dedicated philosopher can be satisfied with what is second rate. Indeed, to some large extent, to be a good and dedicated philosopher is to be unable to let problems in one's work go unnoted and errors go uncorrected. After all, errors and problems are among the central and besetting defects of philosophy.

But, as said, this is so only to some large extent. We must acknowledge the seriousness of the paradox of the preface—'I believe of each claim made in this book that it is correct, but I am certain that some of the claims are mistaken.' We do know that our work will include some errors. And we also know that we could find and eliminate at least some of them. But we might also think that this would require too much effort—take too much away from other work or other parts of our life. If this is right, then even in regard to errors and problems, we do not demand the very best.

Once again, this is not to accept, much less hallow, the second rate. Rather, it is to help us see just what we mean when we require the highest standards and require doing what is best. Or better, it is to help us see what we do not mean. We do not require a work that in fact avoids all errors, nor even all those we could have avoided. The relevant standards are standards given by what it is possible and reasonable to expect of good and hard-working philosophers. If ranking makes any sense, they may not even be second best. But they are hardly second rate.

My point, then, is that the circumstances referred to by 'the best in the circumstances' can generally and systematically prevent the work from really being the very best it could be. It at least comes close to the truth to hold that we can count the work as the best in the circumstances if it is what would be done by good and hard-working—or very good and very hard-working—philosophers in those circumstances.

This is not exactly right. There are some circumstances so hostile to doing good philosophy that the best work even the best philosophers could do in them would be unlikely to be good philosophy—e.g. some forms of oppression, illness, civic troubles, and the like. So it might be better to say that our standards are given by what good and hard-working people can do if circumstances are good enough. Further, if the circumstances of a particular philosopher are very good—e.g. very good working conditions, lots of time off, peace and plenty—we may require better work than simply what could be done in circumstances which are simply good enough.

Now, again, I am not concerned to argue that what is done by serious and committed philosophers in circumstances that are good or good enough, trying as hard as reasonable, and so on must be accepted as what is the best in the sense that none could be better—i.e. 'best' used as a relative superlative. After all, better work may well be possible. In this last, I do not mean merely possible, or possible for someone in some conditions. Rather, it may well be possible for us at that time in regard to that work.

Indeed, my argument against maximization is better served if we hold that the work is not the best. For then it will be even easier to see that doing what is best is not a requirement of being a serious and committed philosopher. For it is easy enough to see that we do not require of serious and committed philosophers that their work be better than the work of very good and very hard-working philosophers in good circumstances.

But in any case, my anti-maximization point is, I think, easily enough seen. Serious and committed philosophers need not do what is best, but at most only what is best in the circumstances. Another way to put this is that what is best in the circumstances simply is not best in a maximizing sense. Rather, it is what is really and especially good. It is in the group of really and especially good pieces of work—a group the members of which are not all of the same value. They are all of them really and especially good and in this sense best, but some are better than others.

Perhaps the failure to see this is motivated—and perhaps is well motivated—by something like the Aristotelian desire to fight against the stronger danger (*NE* 2. 9). We think, perhaps we know, that we are too inclined to take things easily—that if we are allowed an inch, we will try to take a mile. So, we suspect those who deny that we must seek the best as really saying that the second rate is good enough. They will not stop at studying Greek instead of logic, but will instead go on to spend their time lounging about and merely giving the occasional fond thought to philosophy. For a parallel, we might look at politicians who tell us what we all know: that they sometimes lie to us. Our uncertainty with the conversational implicature of this is what is disturbing. Our question is, if politicians who simply lie to us tell us that they do not, what are those who tell us that they lie really doing? We have difficulty in accepting the answer that they are simply lying to us, since we know that when they do that, they tell us that they are not lying.

So, it may well be a good, even the best, policy to say that the best, in the sense of none better, is to be aimed at. Human frailties and lack of interest in what is really good will ensure that most of us do not go overboard. But, as mentioned earlier, in this work I am concerned with what is true, not with what is useful to say or believe. And even if it is useful to say or believe that only the best is to be aimed at, this is not true. And that it is not true can be seen by examining just what is required when we require that serious and committed philosophers do, or try to do, the best philosophy and not be satisfied with anything less.

5. ARISTOTLE ON MAXIMIZATION

Many of the moral and evaluative arguments of the last sections against maximization are drawn from, or at least are inspired by, Aristotle's discussion of eudaimonia and its parts. It will be useful to show this, both to help reinforce those arguments and also to help correct some views about Aristotle.

It might be thought that in arguing against maximization, I should take care not to mention Aristotle's view of eudaimonia. For he is often taken as a paradigmatic maximizer. After all, he does say that a life of eudaimonia is a life lacking in nothing and that eudaimonia is the most desirable good (*NE* I. 7, 1097b17 ff.). And it might seem obvious that to the extent that a life does not maximize goodness, e.g. to the extent that it has missed out on some goods, it is lacking in something, namely those missed goods, and thus that it cannot be the most desirable good.

Some find this argument given explicitly by Aristotle several lines after he says that a life of eudaimonia is lacking in nothing. This is where he says both that 'of two goods the greater is always the more desirable' (19 ff. tr. Rackham) and also that the addition of even the smallest good to another makes the whole greater than the other (18 ff.—cf. also 10. 2, 1172b32 ff. and the *Philebus* 60b ff.). Many draw the obvious conclusion—so obvious that Aristotle did not even bother to state it—that therefore, eudaimonia must include all goods.

Now I do think that eudaimonia is an—indeed, the—inclusive good, and not simply a very important, perhaps dominant, good. But I do not join those who take this as requiring that it, literally, includes all goods. I do not think that if a life lacks even the smallest good, it must also lack eudaimonia.

Nor, I want to suggest, does Aristotle hold this. Indeed, he uses those claims as part of a *reductio* of that view. They are not concerned to show that eudaimonia includes all goods—that a life of eudaimonia has all goods—but rather that eudaimonia is not a good like other goods: 'Moreover, we think eudaimonia the most desirable of all good things without being itself reckoned as one among the rest . . .' (17 ff.). The *reductio* runs as follows: A life lacking some goods can none the less have eudaimonia. (This is shown below.) If eudaimonia were one good among others, so that the addition of even the smallest good would make it better, adding a good to such a life would make it better. But then, eudaimonia would not be perfect and most desirable.

Allowing that a life with eudaimonia might lack some goods does not entail that it is not the best of all ends. It can be the best of all ends without each life having it being the best of all lives. A parallel would be: Blue whales are the largest mammals, but to be a blue whale a given animal need not be the largest mammal. After all, some blue whales are larger than others. (To be sure, some particular animals that are not blue whales are larger than some that are, but no life lacking eudaimonia is as good as any having it. None the less, the parallel serves us well enough.)

Of course, this view can be ascribed to Aristotle only if he takes it that eudaimonia does not include each and every good. He does not make that claim here. But, I suggest, it is this and not its contrary that he took to be obvious—so obvious that he did not bother to state it here. However, elsewhere he does make it clear that he accepts it, as I shall now suggest. Since our main concern is not Aristotle but maximization, I will do this by making four brief points intended as much to show what is wrong about maximization as to sustain my interpretation of Aristotle.

First, Aristotle clearly holds that to achieve at least some of our goals we must use means which are only means. These are costs we have to pay to achieve our goals. But a cost is a sacrifice of a good—even if it is an entirely justified sacrifice. Thus, if eudaimonia includes all possible goods, it is not open to humans. Yet he holds that eudaimonia 'is a good within human reach' (1. 6, 1097a34, tr. Rackham).

Second, if Aristotle does require that eudaimonia include even the smallest good, it is very difficult to understand his claims that eudaimonia is open to at least many people. For he would then have to hold the totally unrealistic view that it is open to many people never to miss out on any of even the smallest goods. Further, he holds that a person 'will not be dislodged from his eudaimonia easily, nor by ordinary misfortunes but only by severe and frequent disasters . . .' (1. 10, 1101a10 ff., tr. Rackham). If misfortune does not preclude eudaimonia, it is difficult to see how it would be precluded by lacking some of the smallest goods. Finally, he allows that people who have lost eudaimonia through severe misfortune may be able to recover it. But the recovery is not achieved through the impossible task of somehow retrieving those lost goods. It is rather through other 'high distinctions and achievements' (1101a12 ff.).

Third, Aristotle holds that the contemplative life is better than the practical life, but also that the latter allows for eudaimonia.[10] And he says that the life of magnificent or great-souled people is better than that of ordinary good people, but also that the latter can have eudaimonia. So, lesser lives can have eudaimonia.

[10] See on this J. M. Cooper, 'Contemplation and Happiness: A Reconsideration', *Synthese*, 72 (1987), 187–216.

My conclusion, so far, is that eudaimonia need not include all goods. But the issue for us is not exactly whether a good life must include even the smallest goods. It is whether rational and good people must be maximizers. This, of course, asks whether people who aim at what it is rational and good to aim at—eudaimonia, a good life—must be maximizers. Aristotle's claim does not say that they need not be maximizers, but only that they need not succeed in getting all goods. The quote just given is consistent with his holding that even if people lack some goods, it can none the less be a condition for their having eudaimonia that they have all the goods available to them in their particular and concrete circumstances. He could be saying that although it is possible to have eudaimonia having suffered misfortunes and thus lacking some goods, it is impossible to have eudaimonia unless one consistently strove to avoid these misfortunes and indeed to get all goods one could.

To take up these possibilities would lead too far afield. So I will turn to my fourth and last consideration. We are told in the *Nicomachean Ethics* (9. 4) that good people, and thus people with eudaimonia, can look back on their lives and have 'nothing to regret'.[11] If Aristotle requires maximization for eudaimonia, we should expect him to hold that these people will have a lot to regret—namely the various goods they did not achieve.

These considerations are not conclusive. Even if everything I have said is accepted, it would be possible to take Aristotle as holding that indeed these people can and should regret those non-achieved goods, especially if they were achievable. I think that it runs completely against the tenor of Aristotle's views on the nature of a good character to saddle him with the view that the loss of any and every good is regrettable.

These points do not prove that Aristotle is not a maximizer. If he is, we should disagree with him. What is important for us— what justifies at least many of our acts, both morally and rationally—is a good life, and not a perfect or the most desirable life. At least some clear goods need not be maximized in order for us to have a good life. To the extent that we can look to a good life to show what is rationally or morally incumbent on us, we see that maximization fails at least for these goods. At the very most,

[11] 1166a29, tr. Ross. Rackham, strangely, translates this—i.e. *'ametameletos'*— as 'not apt to change his mind'.

what is required is that our life be especially good—a really good life. And it can be this even if it could be better—even if, in a maximizing sense, it is not best.

6. CONCLUSION

Maximization, then, is mistaken, irrelevant, and parasitic. Mistaken, because what is less than best may be good enough. Irrelevant, because we often evaluate items in terms of their concrete value and not in terms of whether they are best, or how close to being best, or even how good, they are. Parasitic, because even such seemingly maximizing evaluations as 'best' or 'good enough' can depend on the concrete value of what is evaluated, and not on how good they are.

So, you may be justified in doing an act, not because it is best or ranks high enough among incompossible acts, but because, in a good enough way, it helps achieve a good enough life. Your life may be good enough, not because it is the best life or ranks high enough among lives, but because of the concrete ways it is good. And you may be leading the best of lives even if your life could be better.

It remains to be shown what it is to understand value concretely, rather than abstractly or comparatively. It also remains to be shown how we use higher synthesizing categories. Thus, it remains to be seen where, because rankings of acts or lives are needed, incomparability would be problematic. And it also remains to be seen exactly how we deal with the myriad of plural and conflicting values we commonly and unproblematically confront. But if we are now better able to see that plurality and conflict are, in themselves, not problematic, and also how and why we should reject maximization, those other tasks should be more easily undertaken, and perhaps even accomplished.

BIBLIOGRAPHY

ACKRILL, J. L., 'Aristotle on *Eudaimonia*', *Proceedings of the British Academy*, 60 (1974), 339–59, reprinted in *Essays on Aristotle's Ethics*, A. O. Rorty (ed.) (Berkeley: University of California Press, 1980), 15–33.

ADAMS, ROBERT M., 'Involuntary Sins', *Philosophical Review*, 94 (1985), 3–31.

ARISTOTLE, *Eudemian Ethics*.

—— *Nicomachean Ethics*.

—— *Politics*.

—— *Rhetoric*.

ARROW, KENNETH J., *Social Choice and Individual Values* (New Haven: Yale University Press, 1963).

BADHWAR, NEERA K., 'Friendship, Justice, and Supererogation', *American Philosophical Quarterly*, 22 (1985), 123–31.

BAIER, ANNETTE, 'Familiar Passions', unpublished, read to the University of Cincinnati Philosophy Colloquium, 'The Concept of Emotion', March 1985.

BARRY, BRIAN, 'Tragic Choices', *Ethics*, 94 (1984), 303–18.

BENN, S. I., 'Private and Public Morality: Clean Living and Dirty Hands', in S. I. Benn and G. F. Gaus (eds.), *Public and Private in Social Life* (London: Croom Helm, 1983).

BISHOP, SHARON, 'Connections and Guilt', *Hypatia*, 2 (1987), 7–23.

BRANDT, RICHARD, 'Toward a Credible Form of Rule Utilitarianism', in Hector-Neri Casteneda and George Nakhnikian (eds.), *Morality and the Language of Conduct* (Detroit: Wayne State University Press, 1963).

—— 'Utilitarianism and the Rules of War', *Philosophy and Public Affairs*, 1 (1972), 145–65.

BRENNAN, GEOFFREY, and PETTIT, PHILIP, 'Restrictive Consequentialism', *Australasian Journal of Philosophy*, 64 (1986), 438–55.

BURGE, TYLER, 'Individualism and Psychology', *Philosophical Review*, 95 (1986), 3–45.

BURNYEAT, MYLES, 'Aristotle on Learning to be Good', in Amelie O. Rorty (ed.), *Essays on Aristotle's Ethics* (Berkeley: University of California Press, 1980).

CARE, NORMAN, 'Living with One's Past', unpublished.

CHARLES, DAVID, *Aristotle's Philosophy of Action* (London: Duckworth, 1984).

CHARLES, DAVID, 'Aristotle: Ontology and Moral Reasoning', in *Oxford Studies in Ancient Philosophy*, *A Festschrift for J. L. Ackrill* (Oxford: Oxford University Press, 1986).

CLARK, S. R. L., *Aristotle's Man* (Oxford: Oxford University Press, 1975).

COOPER, JOHN M., 'Aristotle on the Goods of Fortune', *Philosophical Review*, 94 (1985), 173–96.

—— 'CONTEMPLATION AND HAPPINESS: A RECONSIDERATION', *Synthese*, 72 (1987), 187–216.

DAHL, NORMAN O., ' "Ought" and Blameworthiness', *Journal of Philosophy*, 64 (1967), 418–28.

—— *Practical Reason, Aristotle, and Weakness of the Will* (Minneapolis: University of Minnesota Press, 1984).

—— 'Obligation and Moral Worth: Reflections on Prichard and Kant', *Philosophical Studies*, 50 (1986), 369–99.

DANCY, JONATHAN, 'Ethical Particularism and Morally Relevant Properties', *Mind*, 92 (1983), 530–47.

DAVIDSON, DONALD, 'How is Weakness of Will Possible?', in Joel Feinberg (ed.), *Moral Concepts* (Oxford: Oxford University Press, 1969).

DE SOUSA, RONALD, *The Rationality of Emotion* (Cambridge, Mass.: MIT Press, 1987).

DONAGAN, ALAN, 'Consistency in Rationalist Moral Systems', *Journal of Philosophy*, 81 (1984), 291–309.

DUNCKER, KARL, 'Ethical Relativity', *Mind*, 48 (1939), 39–56.

FLANAGAN, OWEN, 'Admirable Immorality and Admirable Imperfection', *Journal of Philosophy*, 83 (1986), 41–60.

FODOR, JERRY A., *Psychosemantics* (Cambridge, Mass.: MIT Press, 1987).

FOOT, PHILIPPA, 'Moral Realism and Moral Dilemmas', *Journal of Philosophy*, 80 (1983), 379–98.

FREELAND, CYNTHIA, 'Aristotelian Actions', *Nous*, 19 (1985), 397–414.

GAITA, RAIMOND, ' "Better One than Ten" ', *Philosophical Investigations*, 5 (1982), 87–105.

—— 'The Personal in Ethics', to appear in the Festschrift for Rush Rhees, Peter Winch (ed.).

GARCIA, J. L. A., 'The *Tunsollen*, the *Seinsollen*, and the *Soseinsollen*', *American Philosophical Quarterly*, 23 (1986), 267–76.

GORDON, ROBERT M., 'The Passivity of Emotions', *Philosophical Review*, 95 (1986), 371–92.

GOWANS, CHRISTOPHER (ed.), *Moral Dilemmas* (Oxford: Oxford University Press, 1987).

GRANT, ALEXANDER, *The Ethics of Aristotle* (London: Longmans, Green and Co., 1874).

GREENSPAN, PATRICIA S., 'A Case of Mixed Feelings: Ambivalence and the Logic of Emotion', in Amelie O. Rorty (ed.), *Explaining Emotions*, (Berkeley: University of California Press, 1980).

—— 'Moral Dilemmas and Guilt', *Philosophical Studies*, 43 (1983), 117–25.

GRIFFIN, JAMES, *Well-Being* (Oxford: Oxford University Press, 1986).

HARDIE, W. F. R., 'The Final Good in Aristotle's *Ethics*', *Philosophy*, 40 (1965), 277–95.

HARDIN, RUSSELL, 'Rational Choice Theories', in T. Ball (ed.), *Idioms of Inquiry* (Albany, NY: State University of New York Press, 1987).

HARE, R. M., 'Rules of War and Moral Reasoning', *Philosophy and Public Affairs*, 1 (1972), 166–81.

HILL, THOMAS, jun., 'Kant on Imperfect Duty and Supererogation', *Kant Studien*, 62 (1971), 55–77.

—— 'Moral Purity and the Lesser Evil', *The Monist*, 66 (1983), 213–32.

HUDSON, STEPHEN D., *Human Character and Morality* (Boston: Routledge & Kegan Paul, 1986).

HUMBERSTONE, I. L., 'The Background of Circumstances', *Pacific Philosophical Quarterly*, 64 (1983), 19–34.

IRWIN, T. H., 'Reason and Responsibility in Aristotle', in Amelie O. Rorty (ed.), *Essays on Aristotle's Ethics* (Berkeley: University of California Press, 1980).

JACKSON, FRANK, 'Internal Conflicts in Desires and Morals', *American Philosophical Quarterly*, 22 (1985), 105–14.

—— 'Davidson on Moral Conflict', in Ernest LePore and Brian McLaughlin (eds.), *Truth and Interpretation* (Oxford: Basil Blackwell, 1986).

—— AND PARGETTER, ROBERT, 'Oughts, Options, and Actualism', *Philosophical Review*, 95 (1986), 233–55.

KAMM, FRANCES MYRNA, 'Supererogation and Obligation', *Journal of Philosophy*, 82 (1985), 118–38.

KANT, IMMANUEL, *Foundations of the Metaphysics of Morals*.

—— *The Doctrine of Virtue*, tr. Mary J. Gregor (New York: Harper and Row, 1964).

—— *On a Supposed Right to Lie from Altruistic Motives*.

KOLNAI, AUREL, 'Deliberation is of Ends', in *Ethics, Value and Reality* (Indianapolis: Hackett Publishing Company, 1978). An earlier version appeared in the *Proceedings of the Aristotelian Society*, 62 (1961–2).

KORSGAARD, CHRISTINE M., 'Aristotle and Kant on the Source of Value', *Ethics*, 96 (1986), 486–505.

—— 'The Right to Lie: Kant on Dealing with Evil', *Philosophy and Public Affairs*, 15 (1986), 325–49.

—— 'Personal Identity and the Unity of Agency: A Kantian Response to Parfit', *Philosophy and Public Affairs*, 18 (1989), 101–32.

KOSMAN, L. A., 'Aristotle's Definition of Motion', *Phronesis*, 14 (1969), 40–62.

—— 'Substance, Being, and *Energeia*', *Oxford Studies in Ancient Philosophy*, 2 (1984), 121–49.

KRAUT, RICHARD, 'The Rationality of Prudence', *Philosophical Review*, 81 (1972), 351–9.

—— 'Two Conceptions of Happiness', *Philosophical Review*, 88 (1979), 167–97.

LEVI, ISAAC, *Hard Choices* (Cambridge: Cambridge University Press, 1986).

LYCOS, KIMON, 'Socrates and Akrasia', unpublished.

McCONNELL, TERRANCE, 'Moral Dilemmas and Consistency in Ethics', *Canadian Journal of Philosophy*, 8 (1978), 269–87.

McFALL, LYNNE, *Happiness* (New York: Peter Lang, 1988).

MACINTYRE, ALASDAIR, *After Virtue* (Notre Dame, Ind.: University of Notre Dame Press, 1981).

MACKAY, ALFRED, *Arrow's Theorem: The Paradox of Social Choice* (New Haven: Yale University Press, 1980).

MARCUS, RUTH BARCAN, 'Moral Dilemmas and Ethical Consistency', *Journal of Philosophy*, 77 (1980), 121–36.

MERLEAU-PONTY, MAURICE, *Humanism and Terror* (Boston: Beacon Press, 1971).

MILL, JOHN STUART, *On Liberty*.

—— *Utilitarianism*.

MOORE, G. E., *Principia Ethica* (Cambridge: Cambridge University Press, 1960).

MORGENBESSER, SIDNEY, and ULLMANN-MARGALIT, EDNA, 'Picking and Choosing', *Social Research*, 44 (1977), 757–85.

MORRIS, HERBERT, *On Guilt and Innocence* (Berkeley: University of California Press, 1976).

NAGEL, THOMAS, *The Possibility of Altruism* (Oxford: Oxford University Press, 1970).

—— 'War and Massacre', *Philosophy and Public Affairs*, 1 (1972), 123–44.

—— 'The Fragmentation of Value', in *Mortal Questions* (Cambridge: Cambridge University Press, 1979).

—— *The View from Nowhere* (New York: Oxford University Press, 1986).

NUSSBAUM, MARTHA C., 'Plato on Commensurability and Desire', *Proceedings of the Aristotelian Society*, suppl. 58 (1984), 55–80.

—— *The Fragility of Goodness* (Cambridge: Cambridge University Press, 1986).

O'NEILL, ONORA, 'Consistency in Action', in Nelson T. Potter and Mark Timmons (eds.), *Morality and Universality*, (Dordrecht: Reidel, 1985).

PARFIT, DEREK, *Reasons and Persons* (Oxford: Oxford University Press, 1984).

PARGETTER, ROBERT, and JACKSON, FRANK, 'Oughts, Options, and Actualism', *Philosophical Review*, 95 (1986), 233–55.

PEARS, DAVID, 'Aristotle's Analysis of Courage', in P. A. French, T. E. Uehling, jun., and H. K. Wettstein (eds.), *Midwest Studies in Philosophy*, iii, Studies in Ethical Theory, (Morris, Minn.: University of Minnesota Press, 1978).

—— 'Courage as a Mean', in Amelie O. Rorty (ed.), *Essays on Aristotle's Ethics* (Berkeley: University of California Press, 1980).

PENCE, GREGORY E., 'Recent Work on Virtues', *American Philosophical Quarterly*, 21 (1984), 281–97.

PENNER, TERRY, 'Verbs and the Identity of Actions: A Philosophical Exercise in the Interpretation of Aristotle', in Oscar P. Wood and George Pitcher (eds.), *Ryle: A Collection of Critical Essays* (London: Macmillan, 1970).

PETTIT, PHILIP, 'Satisficing Consequentialism', Part II, *Proceedings of the Aristotelian Society*, suppl. 58 (1984), 165–76.

—— and BRENNAN, GEOFFREY, 'Restrictive Consequentialism', *Australasian Journal of Philosophy*, 64 (1986), 438–55.

PIPER, ADRIAN, 'Consistency Constraints on Maximizing Expected Utility', unpublished.

PLATO, *Philebus*.

—— *Symposium*.

—— *The Republic*.

PRIOR, A. N., 'Thank Goodness That's Over', *Philosophy*, 34 (1959), 12–17.

RAWLS, JOHN, *A Theory of Justice* (Cambridge, Mass.: Harvard University Press, 1971).

RICHARDSON, HENRY S., 'Commensurability as a Prerequisite of Rational Choice: An Examination of Sidgwick's Position', *History of Philosophy Quarterly*, 8 (1991), 181–97.

RORTY, AMELIE O., 'Explaining Emotions', *Journal of Philosophy*, 75 (1978), reprinted in Amelie O. Rorty (ed.), *Explaining Emotions*, (Berkeley: University of California Press, 1980).

—— 'Where Does the Akratic Break Take Place?', *Australasian Journal of Philosophy*, 58 (1980), 333–46.

—— 'Akratic Believers', *American Philosophical Quarterly*, 20 (1983), 175–83.

—— (ed.), *Essays on Aristotle's Ethics* (Berkeley: University of California Press, 1980).

ROSS, W. D., *Foundations of Ethics* (Oxford: Oxford University Press, 1963).

—— *The Right and the Good* (Oxford: Oxford University Press, 1963).

ROUTLEY, RICHARD, *Maximizing, Satisficing, Satisizing: The Difference in Real and Rational Behaviour under Rival Paradigms*, Discussion Papers in Environmental Philosophy, 10 (Canberra: Philosophy Department, Australian National University, 1984).

SANTAS, GERASIMOS, 'Plato's *Protagoras* and Explanations of Weakness', *Philosophical Review*, 75 (1966), 3–33.

SARTRE, JEAN-PAUL, *Being and Nothingness* (New York: Philosophical Library, 1956).

SARTRE, JEAN-PAUL, *Anti-Semite and Jew* (New York: Schoken Books, 1965).

SCHNEEWIND, JEROME B., *Sidgwick's Ethics and Victorian Moral Philosophy* (Oxford: Oxford University Press, 1977).

—— 'Natural Law, Skepticism, and Methods of Ethics', *Journal of the History of Ideas*, 52 (1991), 289–308.

SEN, AMARTYA, 'Plural Utility', *Proceedings of the Aristotelian Society*, NS 81 (1980–1), 193–215.

SINNOTT-ARMSTRONG, WALTER, 'Moral Dilemmas and Incomparability', *American Philosophical Quarterly*, 20 (1985), 321–9.

—— 'Moral Dilemmas and Moral Realisms', *Journal of Philosophy*, 84 (1987), 263–76.

—— *Moral Dilemmas* (Oxford: Basil Blackwell, 1988).

SLOTE, MICHAEL, *Goods and Virtues* (Oxford: Clarendon Press, 1983).

—— 'Morality and Self–Other Asymmetry', *Journal of Philosophy*, 81 (1984), 179–92.

—— 'Satisficing Consequentialism', Part I, *Proceedings of the Aristotelian Society*, suppl. 58 (1984), 139–64.

—— 'Utilitarianism, Moral Dilemmas, and Moral Cost', *American Philosophical Quarterly*, 22 (1985), 161–8.

—— 'Moderation, Rationality, and Virtue', in *Tanner Lectures on Human Values*, vii (Salt Lake City: University of Utah Press, 1986).

SMART, J. J. C., and WILLIAMS, BERNARD, *Utilitarianism, For and Against* (Cambridge: Cambridge University Press, 1973).

SMYTH, HERBERT WEIR, *Greek Grammar* (Cambridge, Mass.: Harvard University Press, 1980).

SORABJI, RICHARD, *Necessity, Cause, and Blame* (Ithaca: Cornell University Press, 1980).

STOCKER, MICHAEL, *Supererogation*, doctoral dissertation, Harvard University, 1966.

—— 'Professor Chisholm on Supererogation and Offence', *Philosophical Studies*, 21 (1967), 87–94.

—— 'Consequentialism and its Complexities', *American Philosophical Quarterly*, 6 (1969), 276–89.

—— ' "Ought" and "Can" ', *Australasian Journal of Philosophy*, 49 (1971), 303–16.

—— 'Rightness and Goodness—Is There a Difference?', *American Philosophical Quarterly*, 10 (1973), 87–98.

—— 'Act and Agent Evaluations', *The Review of Metaphysics*, 27 (1973), 42–61.

—— 'The Schizophrenia of Modern Ethical Theories', *Journal of Philosophy*, 73 (1976), 453–66.

—— 'Agent and Other: Against Ethical Universalism', *Australasian Journal of Philosophy*, 54 (1976), 206–20.

—— 'Good Intentions in Greek and Modern Moral Philosophy', *Australasian Journal of Philosophy*, 57 (1979), 220–4.

—— 'Desiring the Bad: An Essay in Moral Psychology', *Journal of Philosophy*, 76 (1979), 738–53.

—— 'Values and Purposes: The Limits of Teleology and the Ends of Friendship', *Journal of Philosophy*, 78 (1981), 747–65.

—— 'Psychic Feelings: Their Importance and Irreducibility', *Australasian Journal of Philosophy*, 61 (1983), 5–26.

—— 'Affectivity and Self-Concern: The Assumed Psychology in Aristotle's Ethics', *Pacific Philosophical Quarterly*, 64 (1983), 211–29.

—— 'Some Structures for Akrasia', *History of Philosophy Quarterly*, 1 (1984), 267–80.

—— 'Akrasia and the Object of Desire', in Joel Marks (ed.), *The Ways of Desire* (Chicago: Precedent Books, 1986).

—— 'Friendship and Duty: Toward a Synthesis of Gilligan's Contrastive Ethical Concepts', in Eva Kittay and Diana Meyers (eds.), *Women and Moral Theory* (Totowa, NJ: Rowman and Allanheld, 1986).

—— 'Dirty Hands and Conflicts of Values and of Desires in Aristotle's Ethics', *Pacific Philosophical Quarterly*, 67 (1986), 36–61.

—— 'Emotional Thoughts', *American Philosophical Quarterly*, 24 (1987), 59–69.

—— 'Some Problems with Counter Examples in Ethics', *Synthese*, 72 (1987), 277–89.

—— 'Moral Conflicts: What They Are and What They Show', *Pacific Philosophical Quarterly*, 68 (1987), 104–23.

TAYLOR, CHARLES, 'The Diversity of Goods', in Amartya Sen and Bernard Williams (eds.), *Utilitarianism and Beyond* (Cambridge: Cambridge University Press, 1982).

ULLMANN-MARGALIT, EDNA, and MORGENBESSER, SIDNEY, 'Picking and Choosing', *Social Research*, 44 (1977), 757–85.

URMSON, J. O., 'A Defence of Intuitionism', *Proceedings of the Aristotelian Society*, NS 75 (1974–5), 111–19.

WALZER, MICHAEL, 'Political Action: The Problem of Dirty Hands', *Philosophy and Public Affairs*, 2 (1973), 160–80.

WIGGINS, DAVID, 'Weakness of Will, Commensurability, and the Objects of Deliberation and Desire', *Proceedings of the Aristotelian Society*, NS 79 (1978–9), 251–77, reprinted in Amelie O. Rorty (ed.), *Essays on Aristotle's Ethics* (Berkeley: University of California Press, 1980).

—— 'Truth, Invention and the Meaning of Life', *Proceedings of the British Academy*, 42 (1976), 331–78.

WILLIAMS, BERNARD, 'Consistency and Realism', *Problems of the Self* (Cambridge: Cambridge University Press, 1973).

—— 'Ethical Consistency', *Problems of the Self* (Cambridge: Cambridge University Press, 1973).

WILLIAMS, BERNARD, 'Conflicts of Values', *Moral Luck* (Cambridge: Cambridge University Press, 1981).

—— *Ethics and the Limits of Philosophy* (Cambridge, Mass.: Harvard University Press, 1985).

—— and SMART, J. J. C., *Utilitarianism, For and Against* (Cambridge: Cambridge University Press, 1973).

WOLF, SUSAN, 'Moral Saints', *Journal of Philosophy*, 79 (1982), 410–39.

—— 'Above and Below the Line of Duty', *Philosophical Topics*, 14 (1986), 131–48 (originally circulated as 'The Superficiality of Duty').

YOUNG, CHARLES M., 'Aristotle on Courage', in Q. Howe (ed.), *Humanitas: Essays in Honor of Ralph Ross* (Claremont, Calif.: Scripps College Press, 1977).

—— 'Virtue and Flourishing in Aristotle's Ethics', in David J. Depew (ed.), *The Greeks and the Good Life*, (Fullerton, Calif.: California State University, 1980).

—— 'Aristotle on Temperance', *Philosophical Review*, 97 (1988), 521–42.

INDEX LOCORUM

INDEX OF NAMES

GENERAL INDEX

abstract value 2, 26, 71, 139, 182–3, 235, 298, 327–31
  see also comparative value, concrete value
acceptance and regret 119–20
accidie (spiritual tiredness, sloth) 225, 231
achievement and eudaimonia 64–5
action-guiding act evaluations
  and conflict 10–17, 35–6, 90–7, 101–5, 109–25, 182–4
  and monism 182–4
actualism and possibilism 96–109
actualization (*energeia*) 76–9, 82
admirability and dirty hands 31
admirable immorality Ch. 2 *passim*
  and agent evaluations 39
aesthetic pleasure/s and judgement 38–42, 134–5, 184–8, 256–7
affectivity 213–21
  and akrasia Ch. 7 *passim*, 215–18, 231, 237–8
affectlessness, the moral defect of 113–17; *see also* intellectualism
agent evaluations and conflict 11–13, 31, 35, 93, 111–21
akolastos/ia (profligate/cy), 136, 189
akrasia (weakness of will) Ch. 7 *passim*, 81–2, 88, 225–6, 263–71, 281, 284, 311–12
algorithms and mechanical judgements 149, 177, 194
ambivalence 74, 75, 81, 82, 87, 120, 143, 144, 242, 264–6; *see also* dithering
ametameletos (regretless) 341
amount, *see* Mean, maximization, good enough
amusement/s 313–16, 321–2
anti-maximization Chs. 9–10 *passim*
anti-utilitarians 28
attention and conflict 16, 113–17
arbitrariness and maximization 179, 325–31

arrogance and maximization 320, 324, 330
art and value 38–42
atonement and conflict 29–31, 111–12

baion (forced) 55
balance
  and maximization, Ch. 9 *passim*, 322, 328
  and The Mean, Ch. 5 *passim*
  of plural considerations, Ch. 6 *passim*
baseness (*aischron*) and eudaimonia 55–9, 65–6
best/better
  absolute and relative best 331
  and akrasia 81, 311–12
  concern with, bad for ethics 182–3, Chs. 9–10 *passim*
  not good enough or bad 27–8, 35, 43, 46, 48, 50, 65, 82, 108, 110, 169, 171, 272, 312–13
  prior to good 291–302
  see also comparative value, concrete value, abstract value, and maximization
blame and dirty hands 29–31, 55–6, 112
bodily (*epithumetic*) pleasures 75–6, 81–3, 135–6, 225–6
boldness (*tharsos*) Ch. 5 *passim*, esp. 156–64

care
  and maximization Chs. 9–10 *passim*
  and monism 174, 182–4, 245–6
  quantitative care 227, 282
  see also emotions
categorical comparisons of sortals 200–6
character 58, 73, 93–5, 113, 321
choice 10, 73, 153, 227, 334
  see also differential, degenerate
  and plurality 178–80